Byline of Hope

Collected Newspaper and Magazine Writing of Helen Keller

Byline of Hope

Collected Newspaper and Magazine Writing of

edited by

Beth A. Haller, Ph.D.

The Advocado Press

Louisville, KY

Byline of Hope: Collected Newspaper and Magazine Writing of Helen Keller

Published by The Advocado Press, Inc., P. O. Box 406781, Louisville, KY 40204
www.advocadopress.org

Thanks to Helen Selsdon, archivist with the American Foundation for the Blind, and Page Miller of the Library of Congress Copyright Office for the determination on those articles from the American Foundation for the Blind Helen Keller Archives now in the public domain.

Photographs facing page 1 and on pages 92 and 308 reproduced from pages of *The Home Magazine* in the AFB archives.

Cover photograph courtesy of the Perkins School for the Blind Archives.

Library of Congress Cataloging-in-Publication Data

Keller, Helen, 1880-1968.
[Essays. Selections]
Byline of hope : collected newspaper and magazine writing of Helen
Keller / edited by Beth A. Haller, Ph.D.
    pages cm
Includes bibliographical references.
ISBN 978-0-9627064-1-7 (alk. paper)
I. Haller, Beth A., editor. II. Title.
PS3521.E39A6 2015
814'.52--dc23

                                                            2015024144

Dedicated to Helen Keller,
whose progressive words of optimism still shine today.

Contents

Foreword

I n our day, celebrities are the bread and circuses of the masses. Social and corporate media inundate us with every detail of their lives. It might be hard for us to imagine how huge a celebrity Helen Keller became in an age before television, fast international travel, the internet, or Twitter. But for much of her life she was one of the best-known people in the world.

The word traveled much more slowly then. Still, it was anticipated and shared in magazines and newspapers. Keller began her presence in the written media at the start of the 20th century when she entered Radcliffe College in 1900. Two years later her first book, *The Story of My Life,* was published and the world was soon enthralled that a person with her disabilities had accomplished so much in such a short time.

Over the years, more books followed, as well as numerous articles in magazines aimed at a wide range of readerships, from *Ladies' Home Journal* to *The Atlantic Monthly* to *Zoological Society Bulletin*. Some of these articles have been studied and remain fairly well-known. Others have faded into obscurity as their sources succumbed to changing tastes. In this book, Beth A. Haller has collected most of them.* Together they serve as a wonderful introduction to the mind and the passions of this remarkable woman.

Keller is remarkable not just for the way she transcended the limitations to her senses but for the brilliance of the intellect revealed when language

---

* Three articles from *The Home Magazine* are lost, and Keller produced several very similar versions of an article on infant blindness caused by gonorrhea for different publications, so only one of them was included here.

belatedly burst onto her inner vision like fireworks. It is hard to comprehend the pace at which she absorbed and organized the information that poured into her ravenous mind, transforming her from a near-feral little animal to a best-selling author in not much over a decade.

Although Keller's experience was so singular as to be almost unique, it gave her the empathy and compassion to understand the difficulties others faced. She became a passionate suffragist and socialist, believing in the right of all to a life of decency and dignity. The fact that she had been able to accomplish so much suffused her with an unthwartable optimism that she shared with the world through her writing.

This collection ranges from short inspirational pieces to lengthy explorations of the issues of her time. Most (such as the unequal distribution of wealth) are just as relevant in the present day. The articles are organized not chronologically but thematically. The reader builds of a picture of Keller in a pointillistic way, moving back and forth in time between maturity and youth.

The tone of her writing is both elevated and elevating. Some of it shows the importance of religion to her, and the Bible is an obvious influence on her style in those instances. Sometimes her prose is literally flowery; her passion for nature is one of her persistent themes. Using the three senses she had, plus the words she received from others through her fingers and memories from her pre-illness infancy, she created vivid scenes that are extraordinary in their immediacy and liveliness.

Other articles show the realism of her understanding of the problems of society: the unequal rights of unenfranchised women; the poverty and unemployment of the Depression years of the 1930s; the depredations of disease and disability. But Keller's realism was always brightened by her optimism, her hope that positive change could occur. And sometimes she shows an impishly sharp sense of humor. The overall feeling that grows as acquaintance with her develops through the course of the book is a kind of exhilaration. She really does inspire her readers with her positive outlook.

If, while proceeding through the book, the reader experiences a sudden, intense sensation of *deja vu*, not to worry: since her audience was so varied, and she wrote over the span of more than a half a century, Keller had no qualms about borrowing from herself, both from her books and from earlier articles. So you will come across a few passages where she has picked up sentences and even whole paragraphs.

As these articles were collected from such a wide range of sources, we decided to reproduce them just as they originally appeared, without any attempt to impose a uniform style. Some publications used terminal commas before "and" in a series, some didn't. At least one has English spelling ("neighbour" instead of "neighbor"). And Keller herself has a very subjective way of Capitalizing Words. But even when the style seems of a past era, the ideas and feelings it conveys are timeless.

Barrett Shaw
President
The Advocado Press

Introduction

T hroughout the years there have been many analyses of Helen Keller's activities. The life of this world-famous deaf-blind woman offers much for study: she was an author, a socialist,[i] the star of an early silent film,[ii] a vaudevillian,[iii] a suffragist, an international advocate and fundraiser for blind people,[iv] and even a controversial proponent of eugenics.[v] This book collects and analyzes most of the articles she wrote for publications like *Good Housekeeping, Ladies' Home Journal, The Atlantic Monthly,* and *The New York Times,* as well as a regular column in a little-known magazine that carried her byline in the early 1930s.

Her writings for these publications were valued for the inspirational impact of the byline—a byline of hope—as much as their content, especially during the Great Depression. The pieces were primarily commentary on her own life or on numerous social issues, but they also give us insight into American culture during the early 20th century and show how her iconic status as an inspirational disabled person blended with her own agenda to write about her social and moral beliefs. Introducing her magazine columns, *The Home Magazine* explicitly stated—with incorrect facts—that her role is to provide a positive outlook: "A series of messages to women by a woman who, born blind, deaf, and dumb, is today an undaunted exponent of optimism."[vi] Keller, of course, was not born deaf and blind.

English professor Paula Cohen has written that Helen Keller as an icon was a metaphor for the potential America held. "Unlike the Old World model that allied civilization and sin, America and Helen Keller allied civilization with a greater share of innocence and optimism," Cohen says.[vii]

This book is organized around the themes in her writing. Keller was a woman of diverse interests, but most of all she wanted the world to be a better place for people less fortunate than herself. In contrast, the general public just wanted to hear about her life and how she navigated in the world. A large category of her magazine topics was the "world I live in" theme, in which she recounts sensory experiences. Her other writings dealt more specifically with moral uplift, blindness or deafness issues, women's rights issues, education/children's issues, and socialist programs.

Optimism had long been a theme for Keller. In fact, she wrote a short book called *Optimism (An Essay)* in 1903, and her well-known positive outlook combined with her iconic status as an inspirational disabled person imbued any writing with her byline with an aura of hopefulness.

Still, early in her life some were skeptical about Keller's cheery outlook, believing that her family and teacher sheltered her. These skeptics also illustrate how ableism was embedded in many interpretations of Keller's persona—refusal to believe that someone deaf and blind could be happy and optimistic. Friend and interpreter Nella Braddy made an effort to contradict those beliefs in the foreword of *Midstream*: "There are people who think of Miss Keller as cut off from all that is unpleasant, living in a happy realm of ideality where everything is as it should be. This has never been true."[vii] Her teacher Anne Sullivan reported that from her earliest days of teaching Keller she had always tried to answer any of Helen Keller's questions truthfully—Keller was a voracious reader, and anything that couldn't be obtained in braille was read to her. Her theme of optimism actually came from many years of education that developed her core belief that positive social change could occur. In essence, hers was the perfect message for the 20th century, especially the Great Depression.

Keller's optimism is not syrupy or sentimental, but is tied to her socialist beliefs and her own accomplishments. She believed members of society working together could make changes. Her own personal successes bolstered her optimism. Sullivan saw early on that Keller could be "a symbol of human potential and creativity"[ix] and gave her student a belief in herself that she carried into her writing.

Helen Keller relied heavily on others for the information presented in all her writings. She was a prolific writer, publishing nine books and numerous articles. She easily had the material and the drive to write the many newspaper and magazine pieces bylined with her name. In fact, in 1938 she published a 308-page book, her journal covering six months of her travels in Europe and time at home.[x] Her style is unmistakable—a merging of philosophy, religion, socialism, optimism, and her life experiences. However, because the columns rarely touch upon specific news events, it seems likely that she prepared most of them far in advance of publication. As was her style, the columns merged current and past events. For example, in a June 1931 column she wrote about meeting Bengali poet Sir Rabindranath Tagore as if it were a recent occurrence. She begins: "I had the good fortune to meet and talk to Sir Rabindranath Tagore during his visit to New York."[xi] Keller mentions that Tagore, who was the 1913 Nobel Prize winner in literature, is 69; however, Tagore would have been 70 in June 1931. So Keller met with Tagore probably a year before when he visited New York that fall.[xii] Most of her columns, however, did not contain this type of time-specific information.

For the most part, Keller's writings were valued for their dual inspirational message—from both the optimistic content and her byline. Her columns in *The Home Magazine* provided powerful symbols of hope, for women especially, during the devastating early years of the Great Depression. When the columns began, *Home* said that her contributions were to be optimistic messages to women from a woman "undaunted" by blindness and deafness. The first year and a half of the columns included Keller's actual signature, as if to reinforce that Keller was speaking to the women directly.

Keller's columns were a type of public performance of fortitude and optimism in trying times. *The Home Magazine* displayed marketing genius by having the world's most famous disabled person appear in the publication monthly. What could be more uplifting and in turn inspire people to purchase the magazine in a time when money was scarce?

During the worst years of the Great Depression, 1930 to 1933, the economic statistics were shocking. "From the top of prosperity in 1929 to the bottom of the Depression in 1933, GNP dropped by a total of 29 percent, consumption expenditures by 18 percent, construction by 78 percent, and investment by an incredible 98 percent. Unemployment rose from 3.2 percent to 24.9 percent. By almost any standard, the United States was in its worst crisis since the Civil War."[xiii] If *Home* readers were going to spend a precious dime, they would want the magazine to provide hope. Helen Keller's column did so in generous portion, through her words, her image, and her iconic status. Keller's power to inspire has been confirmed numerous times. Many of her books remain in print. When she became the first woman to receive an honorary degree from Harvard University in 1955, it was said, "From a still, dark world she has brought us light and sound; our lives are richer for her faith and her example."[xiv]

Although Keller died in 1968, she made *Time's* list of the 100 most influential people of the century in 2000.[xv] And the 1959 play about her life that went on to win an Academy Award has been called "foolproof" as a hit revival for any American theater.[xvi] Teachers use "The Miracle Worker" to educate children about Helen Keller and Anne Sullivan as symbols. "Their story shows the strength and power of human will and its ability to triumph over the most devastating handicaps. Helen Keller is one of the most remarkable people ever to have lived."[xvii] ("The Miracle Worker" created many of the myths surrounding Keller such as that she learned to speak in the famous water pump scene. In fact, she had learned to finger spell w-a-t-e-r days before and did not speak verbally at the water pump. Philosopher Justin Leiber says the play's "mythic 'wah-wah' [scene] panders to the prejudice that insists that 'real language' has to be spoken and heard language."[xviii])

Keller's writings have proven extremely quotable over the years. Hallmark cards began using quotes from her books, poems, and *The Home Magazine* columns in the early 1960s.[xix] In 2000, the American Foundation for the Blind Press issued a new book of Keller's quotes, some of which come from *The Home Magazine* columns.[xx]

Keller allowed the writings of others to feed her own imagination. She often acknowledged her debt to other writers for their descriptions and their inspiration to her. In her 1929 autobiography she lists many of her favorite authors, calling Walt Whitman her favorite American poet. She said Joseph Conrad was her best-loved author because of his writings about the sea, which represents a happy place for her because there is much to smell and touch.[xxi] And following Conrad's lead, she wrote her own sea tale in a 1934 *Home* column about a rowboat ride off the Scottish coast.[xxii] The column has many visual descriptions that either were relayed to her via sign language or sprang from her imagination.

It is doubtful that reading audiences cared that Keller never saw or heard what she described. The very presence of her byline was all that was needed to invoke the inspirational symbolism of Helen Keller. As Cohen said, "she affected her audience more through her physical presence than through anything she wrote."[xxiii] In the case of her newspaper and magazine writings, her byline was her physical presence, and that's all the audience needed to "read" the iconic status of the world's most famous disabled person and draw optimism from her existence.

Notes:

i. Philip S. Foner, (Ed.), *Helen Keller, Her Socialist Years* (New York: International Publishers, 1967).

ii. Joseph P. Lash, "Helen Keller: Movie Star," *American Heritage*, 1980, 31(3), pp. 76-85.

iii. Kathi Wolfe, "Helen Keller," *Mainstream*, August 1996, pp. 33-35.

iv. Kathi Wolfe, "Helen Keller," *Utne Reader*, July/August 1996, pp. 16-20.

v. Martin S. Pernick, *The Black Stork: Eugenics and the Death of 'Defective' Babies in American Medicine and Motion Pictures Since 1915*, (Oxford: Oxford University Press, 1996).

vi. Helen Keller, "Women and Peace," *The Home Magazine*, February 1930, p. 6.

vii. Paula Marantz Cohen, "Helen Keller and the American Myth," *The Yale Review*, Vol. 85, No. 1, January 1997, p. 8.

viii. Nella Braddy, "Forward," *Midstream, My Later Life* (NY: Greenwood Press, 1929), p. xvi.

ix. Cohen, *op. cit.*, p. 5.

x. Helen Keller, *Helen Keller's Journal* (NY: Doubleday, Doran & Co., 1938).

xi. Helen Keller, "The Voice of Humanity," *The Home Magazine*, June 1931, p. 8.

xii. *The New York Times*, "Tagore Arrives in U.S.," October 10, 1930, p. 12.

xiii. Robert S. McElvaine, *The Great Depression* (NY: Times Books, 1984), p. 75.

xiv. Roger Shattuck, "Helen Keller. Brief life of a woman who found her own way: 1880-1968," *Harvard Magazine*, July-August 2004, http://harvardmagazine.com/2004/07/helen-keller.html.

xv. Diane Schwur, "Helen Keller," *Time*, 14 June 1999, pp. 163-164.

xvi. Lawrence Devine, "'Miracle Worker' proves to be a foolproof drama," *Detroit Free Press*, October 26, 1998.

xvii. Teach with movies website. Learning guide to "The Miracle Worker," 2010. http://www.teachwithmovies.org/guides/miracle-worker.html

xviii. Justin Leiber, "Helen Keller as Cognitive Scientist," *Philosophical Psychology*, Vol. 9, Issue 4, 1996, pp. 419-441.

xix. Letter from Nella Henney to Janson Noyes Jr., April 22, 1960, and Letter from M. Robert Barnett to Arnold Shapiro, Managing Editor, Hallmark Cards, Inc., March 15, 1966.

xx. Helen Keller, *To Love this Life, Quotations by Helen Keller* (NY: AFB Press, 2000).

xxi. Keller, *op. cit.*, *Midstream*, p. 322.

xxii. Helen Keller, "Summer Day in Scotland," *The Home Magazine*, August 1934, p. 50.

xxiii. Cohen, *op. cit.*, p. 20.

1

Helen Keller's Writing Life

Helen Keller is probably the most well-known person with a disability in the world. She was on *Time* magazine's list of the 100 most influential people of the 20th century.[1] Her life is part of both the elementary school curriculum and theatrical history because of "The Miracle Worker," the movie of which won Oscars for Anne Bancroft and Patty Duke. A documentary on Keller's life, "The Unconquered," won an Academy Award in 1956. Keller's fame even inspired her own joke category.[2] She is the subject of numerous books and articles because her life as a deaf-blind person is an ongoing fascination for people worldwide. However, few scholars have looked at her work in journalism.

Keller began her life as a non-fiction writer right after she entered Radcliffe in 1900. Her internationally successful and enduring autobiography, *The Story of My Life,* actually began as a five-part serial for the *Ladies' Home Journal.*[3] To turn the series into a book, she was paired with a young Harvard instructor and the editor of *The Youth's Companion,* John Macy, who later married her teacher, Anne Sullivan. Macy took charge of Keller's early writing career and even acted as agent, negotiating her book's contract.[4] The book was a phenomenal success and stays in print more than 100 years later. Edward Everett Hale, an author, social reformer, and friend of Keller's, said, "Kipling's *Kim* and Helen's book are the two most important contributions to literature which 1902 [has] given us."[5] And a reviewer for *The Century* magazine called the book "unique in the world's literature."[6] With the universal acclaim of her first book, Helen Keller became a success as a writer.

However, her life as a writer would continue to be plagued by one major concern about a deaf-blind woman as author: plagiarism. An incident in 1891, when Keller was 11, was always to give critics ammunition. She sent a story called "The Frost King" as a birthday present to Michael Anagnos, director of the Perkins Institution for the Blind in Boston (and the person who sent Anne Sullivan to teach Keller). He and Keller's family were very impressed by the story of fairies and the jewels they melted to create the rich hues of autumn. Anagnos gave the story, which he felt was wonderfully original and showed student excellence, to the school's alumni magazine, where it was picked up and reprinted by *The Goodson Gazette*, a publication of the Virginia School for the Deaf and Blind. However, within days of publication, a teacher brought to attention Margaret Canby's *Birdie and his Fairy Friends*, which had a story almost identical to Keller's. Keller and Anne Sullivan said they had no memory of reading the book, but after Sullivan made some inquiries, it was discovered a friend might have read the story to Keller during a summer stay in Massachusetts.[7]

This incident was to haunt Keller for many years, and Anagnos later severed his connection to Keller and Sullivan, believing Sullivan had taught Keller to deceive. He even admitted to calling Helen Keller "a living lie."[8] Sullivan/Keller biographer Joseph Lash believed that Sullivan did not consider Keller's "Frost King" story plagiarism and that is why she let the child send it to Anagnos; however, he surmised that Sullivan knew Keller had read the original Canby story.[9] Helen Keller, a child at the time, probably had little memory of having been told the Canby story and was writing something she thought was original. Later, Keller said her greatest shame from the incident was the suspicion she brought upon the teacher she loved.[10]

But many of Keller's friends and supporters felt that *The Story of My Life* put to rest any question of her abilities as an original writer. Mark Twain, a Keller friend, wrote that he especially liked her recounting of "The Frost King" incident in her autobiography because as a fiction writer, he said "substantially all ideas are secondhand, consciously or unconsciously drawn from a million outside sources."[11] However, another plagiarism suspicion arose in her adult writing when she lifted a verbatim passage from Dr. James Martineau's essay "God in Nature" for her own essay in *The Century*.[12]

As an adult, Keller admitted her weaknesses as a writer, calling her style "crazy patchwork . . . a promiscuous borrowing and stitching together of the works of others."[13] Keller said that when she was being read to, many times she did not know the name of the book or author. She explained that she knew she should cite others' work, but sometimes did not know whose work she was quoting.[14] Paula Marantz Cohen in her article "Helen Keller and the American Myth" argues that Keller's writing problems came from her secondhand experience with language. Other people described the world they saw and heard to Keller. "She describes how she was taught to write about her experience, first by drawing on her limited sensory perception and then, with her teacher's help, filling in conventional adjectives and adverbs to lend color and music to the description"[15] Cohen suspects that the descriptions that Anne Sullivan gave to Keller came primarily from the words of others because Sullivan had an uneven education due to her impoverished beginnings. Therefore, Sullivan would describe an object in basic words and then quote a poem or read to Keller directly from a book on the topic. In that way, Keller acquired the words of others to recognize the world.

It seems clear that Keller knew many of the words she wrote were not her own. In her book *Midstream* she wrote, "I know that I am not original in either content or form. I have not opened new paths to thought or new vistas to truth but I hope that my books have paid tribute in some small measure to the authors who have enriched my life."[16] Unlike a sighted writer, Keller fashioned her narratives completely from memory, and any visual memories were constructed by others' words. In his book on becoming blind, John Hull described the shifting way his memories were constructed after his blindness.[17] This difference in the "mind's eye" made Keller a unique writer. English professor Jim Swan explored this relationship Keller had to writing and the subsequent charges of plagiarism against her: "It is in the space between 'proper' and 'promiscuous' reading, then, that Helen Keller finds herself accused of plagiarism, the space where she cannot tell for sure whether something is hers or someone else's, and where she feels at times that she ought to stop writing altogether."[18]

Whatever she lacked in originality did not seem to matter to readers: they seemed interested in her unique perspective on the world. Her 1908 book, *The World I Live In,* confirmed the appeal of letting people view the world through her fingers and nose. "*The World I Live In* explained how Helen made the senses of touch, smell, and taste compensate for her two missing senses. One reviewer called the essays 'psychological classics,' the work of 'a genius,' which no one else could have written."[19] Her next two books were to be more topical than autobiographical: *Out of the Dark* about her socialist beliefs, and *My Religion* about her Swedenborgianism. Her last autobiographical book-length work was *Midstream, My Later Life*, published in 1929. Little did she know that she would live another 39 years until the age of 88. (In 1955 she also wrote *Teacher* about Anne Sullivan.)

But Keller was happy to put aside book-length works, she said.[20] For *Midstream*, she had to write and revise primarily in braille; she rewrote the book four times. It was difficult for her to have a good sense of the book until it was printed in braille. Cohen called Keller's writing process "painful and arduous" and she needed much editing help from friends.[21] When it was finally complete, the 49-year-old Keller reportedly announced: "There will be no more books. I put the best years of childhood and youth into *The Story of My Life*. I have put the best years of my womanhood into *Midstream*. There will be no more books."[22] From then on, Keller wrote mostly shorter pieces for magazines or newspapers. She was to devote her life to this type of writing, speaking engagements, and her international travel as spokesperson for the American Foundation for the Blind.

HELEN KELLER'S WORK IN JOURNALISM

Keller wrote her first magazine article as a teenager when she composed an autobiographical sketch for *The Youth's Companion* in 1894. But it was her work after *The Story of My Life* in 1902 that can be considered her magazine writing career. As mentioned, her autobiography began as a *Ladies' Home Journal* series. It appears that some of her other magazine works were either directly from or retooled versions of her books. Her 1908 book, *The World I Live In,* provided the most sensational subject of interest to the general reading public—how Keller experienced the world around her without sight or hearing. Because some of the same kind of awe of a disabled person's activities continues today, it can be surmised that readers of the early 20th century would also be mesmerized and titillated by Keller's unique insight. She wrote a two-part series in *The Century* that mirrors *The World I Live In*: it covers in the same way the topic of how she experiences the world as a deaf-blind woman. The editor's note on the article makes no mention of her book. But her articles, like her book, seem to be a response to some critics who questioned her use of visual images and sounds in her writing. "They assert we (blind people) have no moral right to talk about beauty, the skies, mountains, the song of birds, and colors. They declare that the very sensations we have from the sense of touch are 'vicarious,' as though our friends have felt the sun for us! They deny *a priori* what they have not seen and I have felt," Keller said.[23]

The theme about her unique way of experiencing the world was to be

4

prevalent in many of her writings, whether by her choice or a publication's choice. The public has never tired of using her disabilities to draw inspiration. As Cohen explains, Keller wasn't just a deaf-blind woman, she was one of America's first all-purpose celebrities. People were interested in all aspects of her life. Just being Helen Keller was in itself a public performance.

Another "world I live in"-type article in *The Century* in 1910 delved into her psyche by revealing how a deaf-blind person dreams. Once again she appeared to be answering critics who believe "that everything outside of myself is a hazy blur." She explained the sensation of smell, touch, and taste in her dreams, and also that she had some sight and hearing in her dreams, which she suspected came from her "babyhood" before illness took her vision and hearing. Most enjoyable to her was that in her dreams she needed no guide: "Even in a crowded street, I am self-sufficient, and I enjoy an independence quite foreign to my physical life," she explained.[24]

This type of article was to serve her well for many years, and in 1951 the *Ladies' Home Journal* published an updated version of her "world I live in"-themed piece called "The World Through Three Senses." It was beautifully illustrated with photographs of Keller smelling a flower, sitting in the sun in her study, and touching a child's face. It contained her usual information about how she uses her three senses, touch, smell, and taste, and her childhood learning. But she also added new experiences from her travels. "Never have I had a group of smell memories more delectable than those of Portofino, Italy, where Polly Thomson and I found rest on a mountaintop overlooking the Mediterranean last May. I reveled in the Italian sunshine and fragrances," she writes.[25] The article is an excellent example of how her writing about her three senses had developed. At age 71, she had mastered lush descriptions of smells, tastes, and feelings. She had traveled through much of Europe, the Pacific Rim, Australia, and South Africa by this point in her life, and the many new sensations of these trips seem to have made a lasting impression.

Although Keller said she disliked the public's obsession with her life story, she was able to use it as a way to discuss a variety of topics of interest to her, from social programs to blindness issues to women's rights to education issues. Cohen says, "She used her life as a metaphor, drawing on references to sight, hearing, and touch to launch a broader social critique."[26] Clearly, in addition to describing her own life, Keller's writings focused on many of her causes. Her plea to prevent blindness made the front page of *The Kansas City*

Star in 1914. If written by anyone else, her article might have been controversial because she discusses newborn blindness resulting from venereal disease. She spends the first section of the article arguing for open discussion of the topic, which she says some find "indecent and shocking." Her status as famous "blind girl," which is what the *Star* called the 34-year-old Keller in its headline, allows her to state the facts about the disease directly: "It is a specific germ contracted in cohabiting with prostitutes which the mother has received from contact with her husband previous to the birth of her child."[27] She reported estimates that 75% of men carry the infection. Keller's article is surprisingly nonjudgmental of American men; her main criticism is of "false modesty," which she says has silenced the needed "publicity, education, and knowledge." She explains the need to get silver nitrate solution into hospitals so it can be put into the eyes of newborns to save them from blindness. This article illustrates that Keller's iconic status allowed her take on even a taboo subject such as sexually transmitted diseases, and the usually puritanical American public seemingly took no offense. When an editor of the *Star*, W. R. Nelson, sent Keller a letter and the clipping of the article, its sentimentality illustrates that her writing topics were not of as much interest as her awe-inspiring presence on earth. Nelson addressed his letter to "My dear little Angel," and went on to invoke a "God moves in mysterious ways" argument. The letter had a religious tone in which Nelson discusses the inspiration he draws from her existence. He added that her article was one of the most interesting for several days, calling it "the expression of the sweetest, finest, noblest spirit in the world." He ended by explaining that the *Star* couldn't pay her for the article.[28]

Even before she was officially a spokesperson on blindness issues, Keller's fame gave her byline power on the topic. As early as 1901, when she was 21, she boldly wrote in the *Ladies' Home Journal* about preventing blindness in newborns just as she would in *The Kansas City Star*.[29] Her status as spokesperson allowed her to be the logical choice to write a tribute to Louis Braille in *The New York Times* on the 100th anniversary of his development of an alphabet for blind people. "If we should look for the greatest benefactor of the sightless—the individual who has given them a perpetual source of delight and profit—the choice would certainly fall upon Louis Braille," Keller began the article.[30] The topic and her byline merge to give the article more power than if it had been written by a sighted person.

In 1924 Keller began her work for the American Foundation for the Blind (AFB), which led to another genre of her writings—travel. She began to go abroad extensively after that. Her first trip was in 1930 to Scotland, England, and Ireland. She was a goodwill ambassador on the topic of blindness during most of her trips, but she and Anne Sullivan traveled for rest and vacation as well. Sullivan was elderly and fighting illness, so in 1934 they rented a farmhouse and spent a restful summer in Scotland.[31] Sullivan died in 1936. Keller went on to visit 40 countries during her lifetime.[32] These travels led to her frequent articles in *The New Outlook for the Blind*, an AFB publication. She wrote "My Latest Visit to Europe" in 1948 and "My Work in the Near East" in 1953. The articles are detailed travelogues of her visits to blind and deaf organizations and schools around the world.[33] Keller's celebrity status also made her travel and opinions on international events the subject of media attention. After her summer in Scotland, she was quoted in *The New York Times* chastising Germany for burning her books and Premier Mussolini of Italy for pressing eight-year-olds into military service.[34]

Although Keller's freelance work addressed her sensory experiences, her travels, and blindness issues, her most prolific writing stint was a column in a long-forgotten women's publication, *The Home Magazine*.

KELLER'S COLUMNS IN *THE HOME MAGAZINE*

Keller's monthly column for *The Home Magazine* ran from 1930 to 1935, and in 1933 and 1934 Keller and Sullivan spent much of each year in Europe, especially England and Ireland, where they looked for Sullivan's ancestors.[35] Whether the columns contained much new writing from Keller or were recycled from her previous books and articles is sometimes hard to tell.

A number of the *Home Magazine* columns contained new material from Keller's life and travels, such as two mentions of Scotland in 1934. Keller took her first trip abroad in 1930 to Scotland, and she began writing *The Home Magazine* column in 1930. In her February 1934 column, she uses the Scottish heather as a metaphor for encouraging people "to make the most of the faculties God has given us." She explained that the heather is coarse to the touch, but viewed under a microscope it is exquisitely delicate. She then transitioned to her own story of how Anne Sullivan spurred her as a deaf-blind child to her accomplishments.[36] At this time Keller was 54, and the messages within many of the columns were pointedly uplifting and linked to the wisdom she had gained through her life experiences. During the dark days of the economic depression, Keller seemed to be trying to provide a message of hope about the resourcefulness of the human spirit. Due to her status as the most famous openly disabled person in the world at the time, her message was probably particularly powerful to the readers of *Home*. (Franklin D. Roosevelt was the other famous disabled person of the time, but he worked to keep his disability hidden.[37])

Keller's *Home Magazine* columns contain information about her blindness and deafness, her socialism, her feminism, her spirituality, her moral beliefs. As her biographer Dorothy Herrmann says, "she was an impassioned person," especially about her beliefs in socialism and women's rights.[38] Although Keller once said she would never write more books, she was able to continue to spread her messages in these short, monthly columns.

The Home Magazine was published by Tower Magazines, Inc., which was a unique enterprise: a publishing company that produced magazines that were distributed exclusively in Woolworth's stores. Woolworth's had 1,825 stores in the U. S. in 1929, and the magazine carried advertising of the products available in their stores. Woolworth's claimed to be a booming company with $300 million in sales in 1929 and $400 million in 1942.[39]

The Home Magazine and its Woolworth distribution seemed to be an excellent idea. Magazine historian Theodore Peterson calls Catherine McNelis, the advertising woman who was to become the head of Tower Magazines, Inc., and who brokered the deal with Woolworth's, a pioneer.[40] Tower Magazines published a number of periodicals besides *Home*—*New Movie, Illustrated Love, Illustrated Detective*, and *Mystery*—all of which were distributed exclusively in Woolworth's stores.[41] It seemed to be the perfect marriage of a "five and ten" variety store and Tower's 10-cent magazines directed at women. Tower Magazines claimed one million circulation of its first *Home* issue in 1930 and a year later said the circulation was 1.4 million. Catherine McNelis was lauded as a great woman publisher.

But by 1935 the magazines were no longer appearing and the company fell into bankruptcy.[42]

In 1939, a federal court found McNelis and two other company officers guilty of seven counts of mail fraud, charged with exaggerating the circulation figures of the magazines. These false circulation figures allowed the magazine company to keep $1 million that should have been rebated to advertisers due to a rate structure that varied with circulation. The company's controller testified that Tower Magazines kept two sets of books, one that reflected reality and the other with the inflated circulation figures, which was shown to the Audit Bureau of Circulation.[43] Catherine McNelis was sentenced to a year and a day in prison.[44] Possibly because of these fraudulent circulation activities, Woolworth's own published history makes no mention of its connection to *The Home Magazine*,[45] and the publication faded into obscurity.

Biographies of Helen Keller do not mention her *Home Magazine* columns.[46] Dorothy Herrmann says she was unaware of them during her five years of research for her 1998 biography of Keller.[47]

Based on British disability studies scholar Liz Crow's argument that Keller had to struggle to negotiate her place between disabled icon and her own sometimes radical beliefs, the analysis of the *Home* columns suggests that they gave Keller a platform for her opinions. "To most people, her disability rights work appeared to be in keeping with the saintly public image, so that they were open to her ideas without realising how radical they could be," Crow explains.[48] Kim Nielsen's 2004 biography of Keller argues that Helen Keller tempered her radical views because she knew if she offended the wealthy, she could jeopardize her efforts on behalf of the American Foundation for the Blind and her ability to earn a living.[49]

Much of what swirled around Keller was myth that propelled her to icon status as the sweet and pure blind girl; in reality she was a radical socialist, supported civil rights, was a vocal pacifist, and helped co-found the American Civil Liberties Union. "The saint was in actuality a spitfire, and her rhetoric was forceful and furious," says communications scholar Susan Fillippeli, who wrote a thesis on Keller's rhetoric.[50] The *Home* columns gave Keller a way to speak out on her beliefs while maintaining her saintly image. According to a 1999 British documentary called "The Real Helen Keller," Keller understood the influence her persona had and was savvy about using it. She "recognised the power of her image. Conforming to it maximised her access to an inhospitable world and monitoring and censoring her own behaviour was a constant part of her life."[51]

Notes:

1. Diane Schwur, "Helen Keller," *Time*, 14 June 1999, pp. 163-164.

2. Mac E. Barrick, "The Helen Keller Joke Cycle," *Journal of American Folklore*, 1980, 93(370), pp. 441-449.

3. Joseph Lash, *Helen and Teacher* (NY: Delacourte, 1980), p. 280.

4. Lash, *op. cit.*, p. 283.

5. Lash, *op. cit.*, p. 285.

6. Lash, *op. cit.*, p. 287.

7. Lash, *op. cit.*, pp. 132-136.

8. Lash, *op. cit.*, p. 168.

9. Lash, *op. cit.*, p. 150.

10. Helen Keller, *The Story of My Life* (NY: Doubleday, 1902).

11. Albert Bigelow Paine, (ed.), "Letter to Helen Keller, March 17, 1903," *Mark Twain's Letters* (NY: Harper & Brothers, 1917).

12. Lash, *op. cit.*, p. 342.

13. Paula Marantz Cohen, "Helen Keller and the American Myth," *The Yale Review*, Vol. 85, No. 1, January 1997, p. 9.

14. Lash, *op. cit.*, p. 343.

15. Cohen, *op. cit.*, p. 9.

16. Helen Keller, *Midstream, My Later Life* (NY: Greenwood Press, 1929), p. 328.

17. John Hull, *Touching the Rock: An Experience of Blindness* (NY: Vintage Books, 1992).

18. Jim Swan, "Touching Words: Helen Keller, Plagiarism, and Authorship," in *The Construction of Authorship: textual appropriation in law and literature*, Martha Woodmansee and Peter Jaszi (eds.) (Durham, NC: Duke University Press, 1994): pp. 59-60.

19. Lash, *op. cit.*, p. 343.

20. Dorothy Herrmann, *Helen Keller, A Life* (Chicago: University of Chicago Press, 1998), p. 241.

21. Cohen, *op. cit.*, p. 9.

22. Herrmann, *op. cit.*, p. 241.

23. Helen Keller, "Sense and Sensibility," *The Century Magazine*, 1908, 75(4), p. 566.

24. Helen Keller, "My Dreams," *The Century Magazine*, 1910, 77(1).

25. Helen Keller, "The World Through Three Senses," *Ladies' Home Journal*, March 1951, pp. 53-54, 223, 225.

26. Cohen, *op. cit.*, p. 17.

27. Helen Keller, "A Plea from Helen Keller," *The Kansas City Star*, April 28, 1914, 34(223), pp. 1-2.

28. W. R. Nelson, Letter to Helen Keller, April 29, 1914.

29. Helen Keller, "I Must Speak," *Ladies' Home Journal*, January 1901.

30. Helen Keller, "Miss Keller Celebrates a Sight-giver," *The New York Times Magazine*, Nov. 17, 1929.

31. *Matilda Ziegler Magazine*, "Helen Keller in Scotland," June 1934.

32. "Alphabetical list of countries visited by Helen Keller," Helen Keller Archival Collection, American Foundation for the Blind, NY, NY.

33. Helen Keller, "My Most Recent Trip to Europe," *The New Outlook for the Blind*, March 1948, 42(1), pp. 1-19; Helen Keller, "My Work in the Near East," *The New Outlook for the Blind*, June 1953, 47(6), pp. 151-171.

34. "Helen Keller, Back, Is 'Dismayed by Events in Italy and Germany," *The New York Times*, Sept. 29, 1934.

35. Van Wyck Brooks, *Helen Keller, Sketch for a Portrait* (NY: E.P. Dutton & Co., 1956), p. 106.

36. Helen Keller, "We Can Do More," *The Home Magazine*, February 1934, p. 12.

37. Hugh Gregory Gallagher, *FDR's Splendid Deception* (NY: Dodd, Mead, & Co, 1985).

38. Telephone interview with Dorothy Herrmann, March 7, 2002.

39. *Woolworth's First 75 Years, The Story of Everybody's Store* (NY: F.W. Woolworth Co., 1954), p. 35.

40. Theodore Peterson, *Magazines in the Twentieth Century* (Urbana, Ill.: University of Illinois Press, 1964), p. 105.

41. "They Stand Out from the Crowd," *The Literary Digest*, 4 August 1934, p. 12.

42. "Faces of the Month," *Fortune*, December 1935, Vol. 12, p. 200.

43. "3 Found Guilty in Magazine Fraud," *The New York Times*, 31 December 1939, p. 22.

44. "Miss McNelis Gets Year in Tower Fraud, *The New York Times*, 16 January 1940, p. 44.

45. This was probably because of the fraudulent activities of Tower and the store's sole distribution of their magazines. In fact, Woolworth's didn't carry magazines at all for several years after Tower's demise, although the stores were not implicated in the magazine company's scandal. (See Peterson, *op. cit.*, p. 104). Other independent histories of Woolworth's also make no mention of its connection to Tower Magazines. It is possible that the company may have made an effort to wipe away the event from its past. See: James Brough, *The Woolworths* (NY: McGraw-Hill, 1982); John P. Nichols, *Skyline Queen and the Merchant Prince* (NY: Trident Press, 1973); John K. Winkler, *Five and Ten, The Fabulous Life of F.W. Woolworth* (Freeport, NY: Books for Libraries Press, 1940).)

46. Neither Lash's nor Hermann's nor Nielsen's biographies discuss her *Home Magazine* columns.

47. Telephone interview with Dorothy Herrmann, March 7, 2002. When told about their topics and format, Herrmann said she believes those magazine columns to be some of Keller's most natural and unaffected writings because she needed little help to create them. "This is probably the most genuine of her writings," Herrmann said. "She didn't have Sullivan, and Polly Thomson was not a writer." And, Herrmann said, there was no one else who could have written them for her. Not only was Anne Sullivan weak and nearing death at this point, Sullivan disagreed with some of Keller's more radical beliefs and would not have written them because of the topics. John Macy, who helped Keller fashion *The Story of My Life* and was known to be a radical socialist, was long out of the picture. Herrmann says that Polly Thomson, who took over Sullivan's role as Keller's interpreter in the 1930s, did not have the writing skills to create the columns. "This is probably Helen Keller who Helen Keller was. It's Helen Keller unadorned by helpers."

48. Liz Crow, "Helen Keller: Rethinking the Problematic Icon," *Disability & Society*, Vol. 15, No. 6, 2000, p. 850.

49. Kim E. Nielsen, *The Radical Lives of Helen Keller* (NY: NYU Press, 2004).

50. Susan Fillippeli, *The Revolutionary Rhetoric of Helen Keller* (M.A. Thesis, University of Georgia, 1985).

51. Crow, *op. cit.*, pp. 851-852.

2

"The World I Live In"

Helen Keller frequently addressed her disabilities in her writings. It was clear that she knew her audience would question how she could write so poetically about things people thought she couldn't "experience," so she often made her lack of hearing and sight her subject. "The people who imagine I am shut out from nature do not dream of the world of loveliness that touch and the sense of smell reveal to me," Keller wrote in *The American Magazine* in 1929.[1] She went on to explain how she interprets colors as feelings and how through touching an outdoor railing she experienced the vibrations of a whippoorwill.

Many of her writings on the sense of touch and smell emphasized to sighted and hearing people how much they were missing by not using these two senses to their fullest abilities. In a 1934 *Home* column, she explained that "the nose is as complex as the eye or the ear, and as well equipped for the acquisition of knowledge, but to speak of educating the nose provokes only a smile. . . . I know when certain friends approach me by the cosmetics they use or the cigarettes they smoke. The dear odors of those I love I would not part with for all the perfumes of Arabia."[2]

Her writings about touch were profound in predating what scientists now know about the skin as a sensory organ. The modern-day Scottish percussionist Dame Evelyn Glennie, who is deaf, is a world-renowned musician who uses her sense of touch to hear: "She believes that 'the body is an instrument' and has taught herself to 'hear' the vibration of sound with her whole body."[3] Keller wrote a *Home* magazine column in 1932[4] on the sense of touch, and in the earlier *American Magazine* article, she said:

> I think people do not usually realize what an extensive apparatus the sense of touch is. They are so likely to think it is confined to the finger tips. In reality, it reigns throughout the body, and the skin of every part, under the urge of necessity, becomes extraordinarily discriminating. It is approximately true to say that every particle of the skin is a feeler which touches and is touched, and gives contact which enable the mind to draw conclusions. All through my body I am keenly alive to changes and movements of the atmosphere, and I think the days vary for me as much as they do for anyone.[5]

She also used her senses to explore topics such as the changing of the seasons[6] or her love of animals,[7] from which she created several columns.

Although she rarely stated it explicitly in her sensory columns, her implication appeared to be that those with sight and hearing should be thankful for whatever they are able to experience. Keller's optimistic writings about her own physical limitations probably resonated with non-disabled readers, especially when they may have been struggling not with disabilities, but with financial problems, unemployment or even hunger during the Great Depression. Her articles about making the most of three senses gave readers hope.

Notes:

1. Helen Keller, "I am blind—yet I see, I am deaf—yet I hear," *The American Magazine*, June 1929, pp. 44, 152-156.

2. Helen Keller, "A Neglected Treasure," *The Home Magazine*, June 1934, p 6.

3. Joanne Peters, review of 'The science of the senses," *CM Magazine*, Vol. 18, No. 36, May 18, 2012, http://www.umanitoba.ca/cm/vol18/no36/scienceofthesenses.html.

4. Helen Keller, "Magic in Your Fngers!" *The Home Magazine*, May 1932, pp. 8, 90.

5. Keller, *op. cit.*, *The American Magazine*, p. 152.

6. Helen Keller, "Rejoice with Spring," *The Home Magazine*, April 1933, p. 8.

7. Helen Keller, "My Animal Friends," *Zoological Society Bulletin*, Sept. 1923, pp. 111-118.

June Skies

The Home Magazine, June 1932, pp. 6, 77

What is so rare as a day in June?" Of all the twelve beautiful months of the year—for I love them all because of different delights—I love June best. "Then, if ever, come perfect days"—days of deepest blue, days of sparkle, song and laughter, when the fields are white with daisies, and roses climb over garden walls, and the voice of the bobolink down in the well tells the world, "Life is good!"

If June days are glorious, what about June nights? Since the day of the Psalmist they have been a golden theme for the poets. No, I cannot see the stars you see shining up there in the velvety darkness of the heavens, but other stars just as bright are ever shining in my soul. My mind searches other heavens for their marvels.

Because the sightless cannot look into the heavens for stars, they look into themselves. The inward gaze demands an image—something for the spirit-eyes to feast upon. Imagination puts forth quivering antennae which explore the fields of night and find them a-bloom with star-flowers of light. Seeing the manifold glories of the mind, the blind forget their blindness, as the astronomer of the Greek story, who, gazing enraptured into the starry sky, forgot his science, and in transport of spirit touched earth no longer.

So do we travel out into the immensities of space when we visit a planetarium. This marvel was invented and developed in Germany. Now there are planetariums in fifteen German cities, in Vienna, Rome and Moscow, also one in Chicago and one being built in London. Every night crowds of people, old and young, stand waiting for the performance to begin, and the magnificent spectacle never loses its hold upon them.

You enter a dome which is like a hemisphere, and represents the vault of heaven. As the lights are dimmed, and the stars come suddenly into view, you forget you are in a building, so potent is the illusion that you are out under the open sky! On the clearest night out of doors you see less than three thousand stars with the naked eye, and in the planetarium in Berlin the firmament is radiant with five thousand and four hundred stars! All these stars are projected from an odd-looking apparatus in the center of the floor.

This mechanism, with 119 projectors, looks like a vast dumbbell. On either end of it there is a sort of hemisphere which somewhat resembles a diver's helmet. There must be two "helmets," so that the apparatus may project the stars of both the northern and southern hemispheres. Within each of these "helmets" is

15

a powerful incandescent lamp. Set into the sides in various positions are sixteen lenses. Behind each lens is a kind of diaphragm bearing the right stars in the proper places. These project slender pencils of light, corresponding to each star, to the inner walls of the planetarium dome and "lo! Creation widens in man's view!"

Beside the myriads of the stars the Milky Way is shown, and different parts of the apparatus are worked so that you see the motions of the heavenly bodies. Thus the stars rise in the east before your eyes and set behind the "distant" western horizon. The planets are there, too, moving through the fixed stars at different rates of speed! Other marvels are performed which enable you to picture to yourself how the heavens look, not only from New York or Philadelphia, but also from the Equator, from Buenos Aires, from the Arctic or the Antarctic Pole, and at the Poles you behold the midnight sun!

You also seem to travel, not in space only but also in time. Under the magic of that spectacle you are carried back into the past, so that you see how the skies looked fourteen thousand years ago, or you are swept forward, so that you gain an image of how the heavens will appear ages hence. In a few minutes you get a better conception of the splendors and activities of the heavens than you could in a lifetime of patient outdoor study and observation.

Now the planetarium, so crammed full of interest for the crowds who have the good fortune to visit it, is a splendid example of imagination—the faculty on which the blind depend largely for their enjoyment of life. Parents and teachers should avail themselves of this unique opportunity to acquaint children with wonders of the universe and cultivate their inner vision. For most people think they must suppress as practical men and women the imagination which God gave us all. Very few have any after childhood, and what a pity! The things we perceive with our natural senses cannot compare with the wonders we might create if we would look into our own minds and see the suns and stars shining there.

The divine attribute of the imagination is, it is irrepressible and unconfinable—if we do not clip its wings—and where the real world is shut out, it can create a world for itself; it conjures up glorious shapes and forms and brilliant visions to make solitude populous and irradiate the gloom of a dungeon.

Yes, "God gave man an upright countenance to survey the heavens and to look upward to the stars."

A Neglected Treasure

The Home Magazine, June 1934, p. 6

There is no more inviting time than June, the month of roses, to give thought to the contribution the sense of smell may be to our knowledge and happiness.

For some inexplicable reason smell does not hold the high position it deserves among its sister senses. It has been taboo since the Dark Ages. Some ascetic saint must have discovered that the use of the human nose was dangerous to the soul, and put it under a ban.

However that may be, to me smell is a precious contact with the outside world. It tells me of a multitude of objects beyond the reach of my finger-tips. Everything has its own odor, which is its soul—tree, flower, soil, rain, burning wood. I have just been wading through a sea of clover-blossoms in the field opposite the farmhouse where I am writing, and little rills of joy are still running though me as I recall their indescribable sweetness.

It is also my experience that smell kindles the flame of memory. For there is in odors a power to excite emotions of pain or pleasure. A breath of lilac or trailing arbutus or a whiff of new-mown hay awakens happy memories of long ago. I never smell daisies without living over again the joyous morning when my teacher and I wandered in the fields, and I learned new words and the names of things. All of us know how often the fragrance of a flower suggests not so much its own beauty as a loved one.

Oh the blessedness of smell that thus delicately draws us into the Gardens of the Spirit!

When I consider all the delights the sense of smell brings me, I am amazed that this most intimate sense should be so generally neglected.

The nose is as complex as the eye or the ear, and as well equipped for the acquisition of knowledge, but to speak of educating the nose provokes only a smile. We scorn it and indignantly deny that there is such a thing as an individual odor to ourselves or our friends. Yet Laura Bridgman, the deaf, blind and mute woman whom Dr. Howe taught to read and communicate with others by means of the hand alphabet, could sort by smell the gloves of the visitors who came to see her, and give the right pair to each person. Even I myself can distinguish the garments of the family when they come back from the laundry.

From exhalations I learn much of people—the work they are engaged in and the places they have been in, for instance, the kitchen, the garden or the sick-room. I know when certain friends approach me by the cosmetics they use or the

17

cigarettes they smoke. The dear odors of those I love I would not part with for all the perfumes of Arabia.

Animals are wiser than human beings in the art of smell. The dog knows that everything has a distinct odor. When his master returns from a journey, his dog makes a long nose investigation of him and his belongings, evidently for the purpose of finding out more than the eye can tell him.

Other animals depend on their noses quite as confidently as the dog. The deer with lifted head sniffs danger from afar. The eagle smells prey from on high and swoops down upon it with unerring aim.

Furthermore, smell plays a vital part in the life of insects. In the bee-hive the progeny of each queen has a family odor, and the queens themselves have a distinct queen odor, and the hive has its particular odor. This hive-odor is a kind of card of identification which admits only the right bees to the hive. If a bee with a foreign scent attempts to enter the hive, it is fallen upon by the sister guards and slain. If bees stay out in the fields three days without returning to the hive, they lose their hive-odor, and the guards are likely to kill them when they do return.

If smell is so important in the animal and insect world, why should we not cultivate it? Why should we be more ignorant in our noses than savages or animals? It is astonishing how soon the nomenclature of smells is exhausted among those who possess their full quota of faculties.

Like the other faculties, in order to get the greatest benefit from smell, it must be studied and exercised.

If we maintain a simple curiosity about smell such as animates dogs, children and great men, there will come out of the laboratories one set of facts after another—facts that have never been known before. Then someday a man with a vision—an Einstein in the realm of odors—will arise and arrange the facts in an illuminating order, and smell will be given its rightful place in human experience. With an intelligent use of it we shall extend our knowledge and take another long step in advance toward the Infinite.

Magic in Your Fingers!

The Home Magazine, May 1932, pp. 8, 90

Few people who see realize how many and how great are the marvels of touch. Blinded by their eyes, they never stop to think how vital the sense of touch is in all the processes of their physical development, what a potent ally it is in all the activities of life. They attach far less importance to it than to sight, hearing or even smell. I have to smile when someone pities me, saying, "She has only the sense of touch." "Only," indeed, when touch is the key that opens to me the world of nature—leaf, bud and flower, fluttering wings, singing, cool streams, the sun's warmth, the voice of the violin, fields of wheat swept like Aeolian harps by light breeze-fingers! All the time I pity those who look at things with their hands in their pockets and do not take the trouble to explore the delights of touch or understand how it ministers to their growth, strength and mental balance.

Yet it was with this sense that the earliest forms of life began upon earth and developed into higher organisms. To make this clearer, it is necessary to define touch. It is that peculiar sensibility which causes us to feel the resistance of external matter and perceive the qualities of objects—hard or soft, big or small, rough or smooth, liquid or solid, hot or cold. The baby learns all this through touch in the cradle. He has also a muscular sense which gives touch its amazing power.

The sense of touch resides in every part of the body, but it is most sensitive and efficacious in the palm of the hand and the finger-tips. Perhaps the chief marvel of the hand is the long, mobile thumb with its easy lateral movement which gives man a vast physical superiority over the monkey. It is pretty clear that without the long thumb and its power of opposing each and all the fingers few inventions would be possible, and human arts would probably not be far above the monkey stage. It invents wonderful machines with which it spins and weaves, ploughs and reaps, converts clay into walls and builds the roof over our heads. At its command huge titans of steel lift and carry incredible burdens and never grow weary.

Look upon your hand, reader, and consider the incalculable power folded up in it! Think how the hand of man sends forth the waters to irrigate the desert, builds canals between the seas, captures the winds, the sun, the lightnings and dispatches them upon errands of commerce. Before its blows great mountains disappear, derricks—the hand's power embodied in digits of steel—rear factories, palaces, monuments and raise cathedral spires.

The hand of the blind man goes with him as an eye to his work and by its silent reading with finger on the raised page shortens his long hours of ennui. It ministers as willingly to the deaf, educates them, and if they cannot speak, its fingers speak words of cheer to their eye, which thus becomes an ear.

The Buddhist monks have a symbolism built up on the hand. Each finger signifies a quality essential to human well-being. The first finger stands for benevolence and filial obedience, the second for seemly behavior and wedded happiness, the third for the righteousness and loyalty. The little finger means wisdom and family affection, the thumb sincerity and faithfulness to friends.

We may smile at this elaborate symbolism, but it is a poet's perception of the power of the hand for good and evil. With all our five fingers strong and swift in noble action we can grasp what we will. Opportunity and the precious treasures of the world are ours, but if we are selfish, disloyal or lacking in the community spirit, we break off the fingers one by one. The hand becomes helpless, "it is only a club," as the Japanese put it.

I have experienced marvelously the qualities of the spirit in the hand during my dark, silent life. *For it is my hand that binds me to humanity.* The hand is my feeler with which I seize the beauty and the activity of the world. The hands of others have touched the shadows in my life with the divine light of love and upheld me with steadfast faith. Truly, as seers say, the hand of a good man is beneficence made visible and tangible.

Blessed be the hand! Blessed thrice be the hands that work.

The Earth is Still in the Making

The Home Magazine, September 1932, p. 6

W ho is not grateful to the Creator for Autumn's rich display of tints of gold, crimson, purple and the softer glints of the myriad ecstasies of ripe fruits and grains? . . . The glossy brown chestnut beloved of children . . . the tingling odor of burned leaves scenting the sharpness of the afternoon air?

Who does not love the hue and shape of the peach and pear, of pomegranate and grape and rosy apple?

To many people Autumn brings a sad mood. They think of the stripped tree, the stubble in the field, all the summer charms gone, empty nests clinging to the boughs, brown leaves swinging their last hour in the sharp breeze or rustling crisply underfoot—all the out-of-doors a naked world.

To me the harvest season means not death but promise of life—barrelled apples—wheat at the mill—pumpkin-pie for Thanksgiving—the seed in the bosom of the luscious apple and the tasseled grain in the golden kernel of the corn.

And why look askance when the fateful breezes and greying skies arrive? The fateful breezes push off the ripened seed to its destiny of fruitfulness. They are the Fingers of the Lord scattering the beginnings of another Spring where the snow may lie and the rain fall and the sun shine upon them. Even so death ministers to the beauty of new leaves and blossoms that are to be.

As one beauty of the leaves fades, another beauty comes over them. Their colors turn the hillsides into walls like the New Jerusalem, the city of clear gold whose wall is garnished with all precious stones. The crisp rustle of the falling leaf says, "I have fulfilled my use. I have fed my tree with light and rain-drops, and it has blossomed and borne fruit, and the fruit is the culmination of the plant and the germ of its continued life. I am a perpetual miracle of Cana, I change water into a subtle life-wine and light into the color of the rose. I have fulfilled my use, and I am content."

The seed is the outcome of the tree's whole past, the germ of its future. It is all the old and all the new in one. For this the root absorbed, the sap ran, the twigs budded, the leaves uncurled and veined, spread and filled the tree, breathed the sunshine in, and stood up to greet the showers. And for this the flowers, which are, as we know, the first families of leafdom, arrayed themselves in wedding attire and then chambered their very hearts, that the seed-children might grow and cluster there. All was for them. The seed is the fruit in every tree and violet and grass, in every lichen on its rock, in every cloud-like pulp that stains the

21

soil green, in every weed that swings at anchor in the seas. This seed-making has been carried on through the days and nights since earliest Spring. These potentialities are there to be developed, and harvest time brings us the result.

To look upon the fading beauty of the early blossom is to be reminded not only of something that is, but of the vastly more that may be. There is a potentiality in things and their challenge that is one of the most impressive sights of nature.

The earth is still in the making, and we may have a share in the process. The earth is yet to take on its finest beauty. Its future will eclipse the present as the present eclipses the distant past, provided that man will cooperate intelligently with the Divine Purpose.

Rejoice With Spring

The Home Magazine, April 1933, p. 8

Precious as are all the seasons of the year, none so rejoices the heart as Spring. There is about Spring a gladness that thrills the soul and lifts it up into regions of spiritual sunshine.

The natural world is suddenly transformed into an orchestra of silver trumpets, singing birds, laughing streams and a fairyland of bursting buds. Snowdrops, crocuses, violets, primroses, buttercups and daisies tint the earth with purple, yellow and blue. Each tree and bush puts out tiny leaves of tender green loveliness. It is the festival of Eastertide, and Easter bells of joy ring softly in every heart.

The listening ear of faith hears again the Voice of Jesus proclaiming the victory of Life over Death. "Go and tell the Brethren I am risen," He said to Mary, and with every return of Easter the human soul is renewed by His Message.

If we open our minds fully to that message our lives, like the earth, undergo a transformation of beauty. A wish to renew our feelings and thoughts inundates us like the sap in the trees; we long to take hold of life's problems with new emotions and fresh faculties. But the trouble is, we seldom go further than wishing.

We fear to take a new step and face the consequences. If we had the secret that opens the buds, we could not help being new men and women any more than the flowers can help being new and lovely.

It is unpardonable to know the Vision Beautiful and to live falsely and selfishly. Renewal implies courage to take the initiative, to speak out the truth when others are silent, to foster love instead of hate, to put away small interests and prejudices for large sympathies, to serve others no matter what they think or do.

Columbus saw a new continent beyond uncharted seas. If he had only believed in its existence, and had spread no sail for the unknown shores, he would not have discovered this land we call America.

Let us look steadfastly across the waste of grime and fraud, blood and tears, to a new continent of manhood and womanhood. Let us dare to best the waves of hardship which beetle down upon out soul's prow. Let us trust the Christ who stilled the tempest and steered the ship safely to port.

You hear the inward call to newness of life in the resurrection time—let us heed it and rise to higher planes of being.

Immortality

The Home Magazine, October 1933, p. 8

Have you ever taken a walk underneath the Palisades on a bright October day, or looked up to them, draped in gorgeous tapestry, from a little boat in the Hudson River?

I love to feel the naked, jutting edge of the wall that curves endlessly above the river, and to plunge my feet in crisping drifts of leaves. I also like to cuddle down in a lovely ledge and smell the camp-fires in the distance and feel little scurrying creatures seeking a habitation for the Winter.

For soon the trees will be bare, and the nests of last year will be empty. I imagine the trees are glad to have a space of quiet and rest from sunlight, growth and blossoming. I like to think they are resting with rugged joy and wind-beaten branches for another Spring. Like their buried roots I would be dark and still, drinking deep draughts of the peace of earth, while in my soul I kept a record of sun and tempest, rain and snowfall.

I wonder why so few people enjoy the natural beauty which is so abundant in and around New York. If it were as rare as a comet we would all be out upon the hill-tops to capture what we could of it, yet on an autumn morning those Palisades are as gorgeously colorful as the magnolia gardens in Charleston, S.C., which attract thousands of visitors every Spring.

How much there is to learn, for instance, about Palisades! Fascinated I dwell upon the majesty of these walls which the elements, not man, have fashioned for our delight. Each chink and cranny houses some bright-eyed creature whose ways and habits are full of absorbing interest. Everywhere roots poke inquisitive little fingers into nooks from which they may draw nourishment. Delicate, tactile ferns and mosses seek water, that may again trace their patterns of beauty and grace.

Is there not a sort of parable in the mission of roots? They are God's heralds of immortality. Those who learn to look deeply into this mystery of roots will see in them the perfection of the tree, the dream that is the blossom. Here are laboratories where vital processes are carried on silently, unnoticed, so that no form shall vanish, no beauty perish from earth.

Of all the manifestations of nature the roots are perhaps the most wonderful and instructive. Like people they live under different conditions. Some of them enjoy great advantages and easily send forth a bright harvest, while others, having many drawbacks, finally overcome their harsh environment. But, unlike people, all roots that have the slightest chance work greatly and joyously to keep the earth alive and beautiful and fragrant.

One of these rare days in Autumn go out to the Palisades, or to your own sectional spot of beauty, and you will be surprised to find how refreshed you are. Your spirit will sing, and the song will get into your hands and your work; the whole day will abide in your memory as the roots storing up life-sap and joy for another beautiful, bright Spring.

All Weather Is Good Weather

The Home Magazine, March 1934, p. 12

I believe that we talk more about the weather in March than in any other month. We take for granted April with showers, Summer with its heat and drought, Winter with its frost and snow, but with March it is different.

March is the beginning of Spring. We know of course, that the meteorologist says Spring begins the 21st, but we prefer to disregard that fact and believe that we already sense Spring riding upon the wings of the March wind. We have a premonition of little creatures stirring in the stone walls, and we pretend not to see Winter just peeping round the hedge with a gray cloud in his hair and frosty malice in his eye. We give all our attention to the brave little crocuses pushing out from under his icy feet.

There are many other evidences that Spring has come with March. The rooks have already courted their mates, and are building nests in ash, elm and sycamore—a sign that never fails. Then there are March hares whirling and hissing at each other in the rivalry of love-making. If any creature knows that Spring is here, it should be the March hare.

What of it if Winter has another snowstorm or two up his sleeve? I take my staff and fare forth to greet Spring with three dogs at my heels. They are not very old but they know just as well as I do that Spring is come. What adorable companions dogs are when one goes to trail the footsteps of Spring? They are the first to smell the sweet new grasses and the willow catkins. Every little bud and curled-up leaf causes my heart to jump with gladness; for I know Spring is sure and certain.

True, the north winds and the east winds come howling down from the hills, spin me round and nearly throw me off my feet. I go back to the fire a little crestfallen, only to be called out again by the first warm sunbeam that touches the book outspread on my knee. The big, white-headed mountains laugh at me and bid me go back to the fireside; for Spring in March is a delusion, a fairy dream of poets. Still my heart sings persistently; for the keen winds drop fragrant whiffs upon pasture and moor. I may go to sleep in what seems midwinter, but I am sure I shall wake to catch new scents from the woods blown by a kindly west wind.

This experience of waiting, believing and anticipating each day of March as a possible messenger of Spring teaches me this: All weather is good weather. Really there is no bad weather. Bad weather is a superstition created by people who do not like variety in their weather.

We shall be happier if we learn to like more than one kind of weather. We shall then find all weathers of the year good weather. If we get up in the morning and, looking out of the window, find the day pale gray, cold and rainy, we shall think of lovely new flowers for which it is preparing the way; and the thought should make us more charitable, more kindly not only to that day, but to all that the day brings forth.

Wings

The Home Magazine, July 1935, p. 16

I live in a world that has no visible wings, yet readers of my books find in them the flutter of wings and the song of birds. People who are conscious only of the material world often ask why I write about things I cannot see.

It is true that I cannot see the flash of wings or hear the bird chorus at dawn or eventide, but I was not always blind and deaf. For nineteen months I dwelt in a radiant world astir with wings—golden wings, blue wings, red wings, lovely brown wings and soft dove-wings, and those birds of long ago still nest and sing in my heart.

My catechist persists however: "But how can you be happy in a word without any visible object? It must be all blank—no sky, no mountains, no sea, no flowers!"

These negatives conjure up a world that is indeed without form and void. But fortunately, no such world exists. There is a spiritual counterpart of everything perceived by our physical senses. The birds I see in the heavens are as real to me as those others see with their eyes.

The important thing is to cultivate our minds so that we can create a world out of what we have. Yes, we can make any kind of world out of what we have. Yes, we can make any kind of world we choose, though Destiny may have chained us to a Promethean rock.

The trouble with many of us is that we waste our energies complaining about what we have not got. "Oh!" one often hears, "I am tired of my environment. I am rooted in it and can never get away. I might as well be dead."

I want to answer: My friend, if you were stricken blind for one hour, you would appreciate the light, the color, the freedom of movement that are yours. But, even supposing that our sunlit, sound-filled world is blotted out, how is it that any of us should find time to grumble if we have a home to create, a family to be interested in and work we can do? If all these blessings are ours, and we heed them not, we are like moles burrowing in the dark, when we might open windows and cross new thresholds into Wonderland.

June is the month of wings. We do not have far to seek them even in a crowded city. A few crumbs thrown out daily will bring birds to a dingy alley. The busiest of us can find a moment to watch their graceful motions.

All literature and legend and sculpture are full of wings. Every child loves to hear the story of the messenger of the gods, Hermes, who had wings on his cap and on his sandals—how, when there was news of moment to send anyone on earth, he flew down the steepest mountains, over the widest rivers and across oceans that seemed like the sky in their immensity.

Throughout the Bible there is the sweep of wings. Ezekiel sees in vision mighty wings from which goes forth a sound like the noise of many waters. In Psalm 63 we have this beautiful image: "Because Thou hast been my help, therefore in the shadow of Thy wings will I rejoice." Also we have the promise to be faithful: "Though ye have lain among the pots, yet shall ye be as the wings of a dove covered with silver, and her feathers with yellow gold."

Since my childhood I have derived the greatest inspiration from the might which the artist has wrought into the wings of Victory. Their spread is full of majesty, as when the angel descended from heavens, and lo! the earth lightened with his glory.

Does this delight in wings spring from our love of liberty—the desire to be free of the limitations that circumscribe us? Perhaps flight, not rest, is our natural state. To most of us, certainly, the idea of taking wings and speeding to the ends of the earth is enchanting.

I Am Blind–Yet I See, I Am Deaf–Yet I Hear

The American Magazine, June 1929, pp. 44, 152-56

People often express surprise that I, a deaf and blind woman, can find my greatest enjoyment in the out-of-doors. It seems to them that most of the wonders of nature are completely beyond the reach of my sealed senses. But God had put much of his work in raised print, and the sweet voices of the earth reach me through other avenues than hearing and sight. W. H. Hudson says, "What we see, we feel." With me, it is the other way around; what I feel, I see.

The people who imagine I am shut out from nature do not dream of the world of loveliness that touch and the sense of smell reveal to me. I have the sun and the cool shade, the morning dew upon bush and grass, the stillness of eve—all sweet things—the graceful ferns and a wealth of flowers. For me, too, there is delicious drink in the rill, there are plumes of goldenrod to gather, and the delicate spray of pines quivers in my hand as the wind sweeps over them. For me, too, there is exquisite color. I have a color scheme that is my own. I will try to explain what I mean:

Pink makes me think of a baby's cheek, or a gentle southern breeze. Lilac, which is my teacher's favorite color, makes me think of faces I have loved and kissed.

There are two kinds of red for me. One is the red of warm blood in a healthy body; the other is the red of hell and hate. I like the first red because of its vitality. In the same way, there are two kinds of brown. One is alive—the rich, friendly brown of earth mold; the other's is a deep brown, like the trunks of old trees with wormholes in them, or like withered hands.

Orange gives me a happy, cheerful feeling, partly because it is bright and partly because it is friendly to so many other colors. Yellow signifies abundance to me. I think of the yellow sun streaming down. It means life and is rich in promise. Green means exuberance. The warm sun brings out odors that make me think me think of red; coolness brings out odors that make me think of green.

Black means hopelessness and despair, but gray is like a shawl around the shoulders. White means exaltation.

Light blue means hope, dark blue determination. Violet is tender and deep and half sad. Purple is mysterious. It seems fitting that purple should be seen everywhere in heaven because it symbolizes the deep joy of being alive and moving from one glorious experience to another. It also signifies the depths of love unknown.

I think I have an idea of what sparkling means, for I have felt soap bubbles breaking against my fingers.

I have had many amazing experiences with these fingers which are to me both eye and ear. One of them was "listening" to the song of a whippoorwill. It was soon after I left college, when we were living in an old farmhouse in Wrentham, Massachusetts. My teacher, Miss Sullivan (who later became Mrs. John A. Macy), had had a balcony built for me which opened out of my bedroom so that I could walk there whenever I wanted to. The evergreens came so close to the railing that I could lean over and feel their rustling music. At the south end, I could reach out and touch a wisteria vine which clung to the rail with long, tenacious fingers. At the opposite end, I faced the garden and the apple trees, which were in full bloom, and, oh, so heavenly sweet!

I was standing under the wisteria vine with my thoughts far way when suddenly the rail began to vibrate unfamiliarly under my hands. The pulsations were rhythmical, and repeated over and over, exactly as I have felt a note repeated when I have placed my fingers on a singer's throat. All at once they ceased, and I felt the wisteria blossom ticking against my cheek like the pendulum of a fairy clock. I guessed that a breeze or a bird was rocking the vine. Then the rail began vibrating again. A queer beat came always before the rhythmical beats, like nothing I have ever felt before. I did not dare move or call, but Mrs. Macy had heard the sound and put out her hand through the window and touched me very quietly. I knew I must not speak.

She spelled, "That's a whippoorwill. He is standing on the corner post so close to you I believe you could touch him; but you must not—he would fly away and never come back."

Now that I knew he was saying "Whip-poor-will! Whip-poor-will!" over and over I could follow the rhythmical notes. The singing seemed joyous to my touch, and I could feel the notes grow louder and louder, faster and faster.

Mrs. Macy touched me again and spelled, "His ladylove is answering him from the apple trees. Apparently, she had been there all the time, hiding. Now they are singing a duet."

When the rail stopped vibrating she spelled, "They are both in the apple tree now, singing under billows of pink and white blossoms."

> My ears are dead, the birds are mute,
> And still they sing;
> It is within my heart they sing
> As I pass by.

I think people do not usually realize what an extensive apparatus the sense of touch is. They are so likely to think it is confined to the finger tips. In reality, it reigns throughout the body, and the skin of every part, under the urge of necessity, becomes extraordinarily discriminating. It is approximately true to say that every particle of the skin is a feeler which touches and is touched, and gives contact which enables the mind to draw conclusions. All through my body I am keenly alive to changes and movements of the atmosphere, and I think the days vary for me as much as they do for anyone.

I am conscious of days when the air feels like a veil of gossamer softly dropped in a shower of silver mist. I am conscious of glad days when the sun brings a message of spring. I know great, shouting days that goad me into activity—days when the winds beat against me, challenging me to leap up and wrestle with them.

One of the liveliest of all nature's appeals to me is its infinite movement. Motion lights up the titan features of nature as stirrings of the spirit animate a face, and the wind is the soul of the earth. To me, it gives charm to the most glowing landscape and brightens up the most somber one. To me, motion is the beauty of the trees, the cornfields, and the sea. My fingers thrill as I feel the wind toss nature's "soft hair of grass" or shake its great rustling wings through a world of leaves. Viewless, changeful, unconfined, it is both an emblem of growth and of eternity, roving far over land and sea; it is to my touch what I imagine the horizon is to the eye. It brings me a sense of infinite space, of mystery, of sublimity. The wind symbolizes gladness, the urge and the aspiration with which the spirit of God keeps my inner life aglow.

The most satisfying sense of personal liberty I have ever had came when I felt myself to be a part of the wind. It was when I was in California working on the picture, "Deliverance," and flew in an airplane. The main difference I noticed in the atmosphere was the loss of odor as we climbed the aerial mountains higher and higher, past the flying dust, the ripening vineyards, and the pungent eucalyptus. As we raced with wind, I seemed to feel organ music and the sweep of ocean waves, winds from off mountains and illimitable plains. As the machine rose and fell, my brain throbbed with ecstatic thoughts that whirled on tiptoe, and I seemed to sense the Dance of the Gods.

Do not the dullest of us love water? Is it not to us what a friendly voice is to the ear? The sun beams upon us morning after morning, year after year, and we never tire of it. It is a delight to say, "The sun shines." It is quite as sweet to exclaim, as I have done a thousand times, "Here's the water!" This is one of the most good-natured things I know about the sun and water—they never cease to charm and soothe us.

Blindness makes me no exception. Perhaps it intensifies my affection for an element that seems wondrously akin to my spirit. Changeful, alive, unconfined, resolutely holding its way towards the freedom of the sea, water gives my aching sense its rest because it harmonizes with the aspiring soul within.

The waters everywhere afford rich, thrilling sensations to my touch. Walking along the margin of a lake, or climbing a steep hill, I have captured these touch images from a tiny trickle down a mossy boulder, a rill quivering like violin strings with tense music, a brawling creek, a tumbling cataract, from which I can just lift the spray veil, as it were, and a calm river, flowing, flowing forever.

The ocean does not, however, impart quite the same friendly emotions to me. Its vastness is sometimes oppressive with a cruel power. It is not the vastness of the sun's generous warmth, or the illimitable yet intimate touch of the atmosphere that surrounds me with glad sense of nearness—as if I were a tree with its own home in the bosom of these elements. Perhaps, too, my continual experience with a sea of darkness and silence gives a peculiar tinge to my actual impressions of the ocean. Just as I breathe in the rippling beauty or the sunny quiet of a pond, so I want to fill my soul's lungs with the radiance of light in human eyes, not with the solemn atmosphere of blindness. I become weary of contemplating too long the stern power of the Atlantic, and on calm days I cannot help being conscious of how that ruthless Neptune keeps a placid face above unnumbered wrecks of ships and men—and this suggests a silence too suffocating for thought.

Still, I have my times of playful, defiant encounter with the ocean, when I sail on it or plunge into its billows. It is a keen satisfaction to me to step off the immovable land and feel the liquid world yield and sway under me. If there is a surf, my heart leaps up. The blood sings all over my body as I feel the waves fret and foam. It is a piquant sensation to have the seaweed lift and swing, the shells and pebbles tumble and rattle about my feet, and fancy that the next billow will carry me away from night, even as of old the flood bore Undine away from her faithless lover.

I first visited Niagara when I was a little girl. I stood breathless beside Dr. Alexander Graham Bell on the Chasm's edge, its earth-shaking thunder vibrating through every atom of my body. A thousand lovely coquetries were drawing our souls within the great curve of peril whence billowy clouds of spray arose, wrapping us in a glittering spell. Niagara is nature displaying all her magnificence and cruel power. She is everything at once—awful, treacherous, lovely, gentle as a caress, wild as a tiger devouring its prey, hiding the abyss with rainbow wings. We spent hours exploring the rocks and watching the tumbling waters from different spots. We rode in the little Maid of the Mist, and I felt drowned in an ocean of sound—a million horses galloping round the world spouting spume from their

33

nostrils! I had felt water in many wondrous forms—soft-descending masses of snow, ice imprisoning the streams, spring showers, and the ocean surge; but never had I dreamed that there could be such a commotion of waters!

When I think of what nature has meant to me, I cannot be grateful enough to my teacher, Mrs. Macy, who fostered in me an abiding affection for the glories of earth and sea and air. It was she who led me through the school of the earth and the university of the skies to the only true education, which is understanding the law of life. My mother, too was passionately devoted to the out-of-doors. She loved nothing more than her flowers, and her love of birds was equal to her love of flowers. She would spend hours in the little wood near our house in Wrentham watching their pretty antics when they made love, or built their nests, or fed the young birds and taught them to fly.

I have traveled about the country a great deal but I have never been able to accustom myself to the strangeness of life in cities. At home I have always been where I could breathe the woodland air. Winter and spring have always brought me wind-blown messages across marsh, brook, or stone-walled field. I have felt

> God's great freedom all around
> And free life's song the only sound.

All such peaceful, expansive sensations cannot be enjoyed in the throbbing whirl of a train, the rattle of lurching taxis, or the confinement of hotels and lecture halls. I have never been able to accustom myself to hotel life. The conventional atmosphere wearies me, and there is no garden where I can run out alone and sense the wings of glorious days passing by. At such times, I am painfully aware of the lack of personal liberty, which, next to idleness, is the hardest part of being blind. Nearly all the blind people I know—and I have known many—enjoy walking. It is my favorite relaxation, but there is one kind of walking I never enjoy, and that is in the heart of a great city, where I am played upon like a harp discordantly by the tramp of vast multitudes on the pavement and the rattle of trucks, street cars, and the elevated railroad trains crashing overhead—confusion worse confounded. This avalanche of vibrations seems always to leap at me with a fury of malice, as if it would destroy my body. A loaded cannon pointed at me would not have a more poignant and terrifying effect.

It is in the country that I am at home. Everything my foot touches is alive with interest. It matters not at what hour I enter my garden—whether in the cool, pure dawn, when the golden gates of the sun open, and the first rustle of leaves stirs to consciousness the bird in its nest; or in the noonday when all the banners of life are unfurled, and the sun's rays turn everything to splendor; or in the magical stillness of evening, when shadows steal across my path with soundless feet, and I sense "a folding of a world of wings," and down in the dusk of the grass, fireflies light their glow-lamps—I am filled with infinite gladness, and my heart sings the praise of the Creator, Who, out of space and eternity, made this little place for me, and sent the flowers to be my comforters in the dark hours.

I enjoy my garden in all weathers. Even wintertime has its own sport and charm for me. As I walk briskly along, the wind shakes the snow down upon me from the hedge. Every few minutes, I pull off my gloves to revel in the touch of congealed loveliness on the trees and bushes—wondrous forms which God has

> Insculped and embossed
> With His hammer of wind,
> And His graver of frost.

Usually, by going from the steps along a cement path that turns off abruptly at the right, I find, without the slightest difficulty, the green circle of trees which surrounds my walk. But when the snow is deep, all paths are obliterated, so that there is no unevenness of the ground to guide my feet, and I get completely lost; but the adventure of blundering into every place but the right one gives me a good laugh or two before I successfully orientate myself beside the hedge. Indeed, Mark Twain's felicitous words form a sprightly accompaniment to my steps. For I feel like Sandy when the Connecticut Yankee asked her, "Whereabouts does the castle lie? What's the direction from here?" You remember she replied, "Ah, please you, sir, it hath no direction from here; by reason that the road lieth not straight, but turneth evermore; wherefore the direction of its place abideth not, but is sometime under the one sky and anon under another, whereso if you be minded that it is in the east, and wend thitherward, ye shall observe that the way of the road doth yet again turn upon itself by the space of half a circle . . . it were woundily hard to tell [the leagues distant it is], they are so many, and do so lap the one upon the other, and being made all in the same image and tincted with the same color, one may not know the one league from its fellow, nor how to count them except they be taken apart."

It is when the book of the year opens at the page of June that I want to drop my work, whatever it may be, and enter the Kingdom of delight. It is then that nature receives the spring flowers at her court, and each perfect day brings new beauties to grace the fete.

June-time within the green circle of evergreens that shields my garden is a wondrous woof of odors—evergreens and marsh-grass threaded with the scent of lilac and laurel. Bright-hued flowers march beside me and hold up lovely faces to me. Where the grass grows softest, the violets open their blue eyes and look at me wonderingly. I call them dream flowers, because I always see them grow-ing in the Garden of Sleep—violets and lilies of the valley. The honeysuckle trails over the privet wall, blessing every breeze with its fragrance. The wygelias reach out wraithlike arms to embrace me. When I push them aside to pass, how winged plunderers of their sweets scatter in the sunshine! Tall irises from Japan and Germany display their exquisite gowns across the ribbonlike trails which the gardener has made around the summerhouse. In June the boughs are weighted with loveliness and heart-penetrating odor—oh, nobody has ever put it into words!

If spirits wear garments, I hope mine will smell of lilac.

All through May and early June, a flaming tide of tulips spreads over the lawn, with here and there an island of daffodils and hyacinths. If I touch one of them, lo, a lily is born in my hands! As far as my arms can reach, the same miracle has been wrought. Love, which fulfills itself in giving life, has taken pos-session of my Eden.

A while ago two visitors came and sat themselves upon the dogwood tree, which was all tremulous with white blossoms. It is one of the trees which border my green circle. Morning and evening, as I pass it again and again, I reach up to touch the branches. The two visitors, two robins, had decided to live in that dogwood tree. They went about the business of life with singleness of purpose. They did not seem to mind me.

At first, when I put up my hand to touch the branches, they would fly off to a nearby tree and I could feel them watch me attentively. But they soon became ac-customed to me. I brought them food and in my awkward, human way tried to tell them I was a friend. They seemed to understand; anyway, they came and were quite indifferent to my doings. I would stand perfectly still for a long time with my hand on the branch, and often I was rewarded by feeling the leaves quiver and the twigs bend over so slightly. Once I sensed a commotion very close to my hand and a few days later I felt a tiny claw pinch my finger. It was not many days before the male bird lit squarely upon my hand, and after that there was perfect understanding between us. A bird doesn't stay long on one's hand without saying something. My new bird-friend began to twitter; he hopped back and forth on the branch, telling his mate about me, I suppose. She must have concluded that I was harmless, for she flew away on a foraging expedition, leaving her little ones at my mercy.

Toward the end of the summer, a blind friend of mine came to see me. We were chatting in my study. A thunderstorm came up suddenly, and the rain began to beat in. Elizabeth went to close the windows. As she did so, she heard a plaintive bird-cry, and, catching my hand she drew me to the window. "I believe," she said, "a bird is beating its wings against the screen." It was difficult in the rain to raise the screen; but we succeeded, and there, clinging to the vines which had clambered over the sill, was my little Robin Redbreast! He fluttered into my outstretched hand. He was limp and dripping wet.

After he dried off a bit, he began to fly about the room. I pictured him as scrutinizing everything with his inquisitive little eyes. When the shower ceased, we took him to the window, but he did not seem to want to leave us. His sharp claws pinched my finger; he tilted his body, as if he would say, "I am satisfied, why do you want me to go?" I put him down on the sill, and he flew back into the room. We managed to catch him, and again I put him outside the screen, and again he flew back into the study. This time he hid under the couch, and we could not find him. We had to get someone with eyes to dig him out. He hopped on the windowsill from one side to the other. I thought, "No doubt he is cocking his head this way and that, soliloquizing in this fashion: 'Oh, which do I prefer? Do I prefer you, or yonder tree? Shall I stay here, or go on and on, away, away, away? Oh my heart aches with such contrary desires!' At last he slowly spread his wings and unwillingly sailed away on the freshly washed air. He has never returned to the dogwood tree, nor to my hand.

Of all things that grow in my garden, I love best the evergreens. What a beautiful way they have of entering into relations with human beings! How readily they harmonize the wild nature of their forest kindred with our domestic habits. And how subtly yet powerfully they influence us while we set bounds to their growth.

The evergreens which grow on one side of my garden walk seem to know me as I know them. They stretch out their branches to me like hands and tease me and pull my hair whenever I pass them. In the springtime, when the world swims with odors of life, they bend toward me like friends full of glad news. They try to tell me what it is, but I cannot always make out what they are saying. I imagine they are asking each other why human creatures move from place to place, unstable as water, and as the wind that is always in motion. "Look!" they say, pointing their sharp little fingers, "look how she is going in and out among flowers; like the mother the wind, she is blowing away out of sight."

If I could fathom that murmur, that sigh, I should fathom the depths of consciousness of my evergreens. I do not know whether they speak of the future, but I am positive they could reveal the past. They could tell me what they have fared through in the immortality that lies behind them. I have felt the rings buried in trees—rings of the many seasons of births and deaths they died to reach this life. Why this thirst to rise higher? Why this love of stars and sun and clouds? Why this sense of duty to the earth, this fixity of purpose, this inward soul that remembers and sighs? As I stand beside my evergreens, they whisper: "All that is you has always been, and will always be. Every atom and every impulse of you began in eternity with us, and with us will return into eternity."

Oh, when my spirit is sore, fretted by the thought of the unhappiness in the world, it soothes me to walk back and forth beside my evergreens. I feel like a flower after a night's frost, when it steadies itself on its stem and looks up again to the sky with brave hope. And ever as I walk round my green circle, I seem to hear the song of the roots down in the ground, cheerily toiling in the dark. They never see the lovely work they have wrought. Hidden away in darkness they bring forth flowers of light! Little and despised are they; but, oh, mighty is their power to create flower and tree!

There are no trees I love more than the redwoods of California. My mother, who was with me when I first went to the west coast, worshipped them. "Nature's monarchs," she called them, and she declared that they were more impressive even than the mountains, "because human faculties can compass them. They are earth's noblest aristocrats."

We went often to the Muir woods on that first trip, and I have visited them many times since. How shall I describe my sensations upon entering that Temple of the Lord? Every time I touch the redwoods, I feel as if the unrest and strife of earth are lulled. I cease to long and grieve—I am in the midst of a Sabbath of repose, resting from human futilities. I am in a holy place, quiet as a heart full of prayer. God seems to walk invisible through the long, dim aisles.

All of us need to go often into the woods alone and sit in silence at the feet of Nature. A few years ago, I persuaded my conscience to turn its back upon prosaic tasks and go pleasuring in the open for two months. My teacher, Mrs. Macy, and a friend went with me. Our automobile was equipped with a tent, a small gasoline stove, an ice box, and last but not least, my beautiful great Dane, Sieglinde, whose business it was to strike terror into the hearts of wandering Robin Hoods and other intruders.

One of our camping spots was a pasture in the Berkshires, where a brook laughed and romped. We were awakened in the morning by a herd of cows. I touched their glossy coats and wet noses as they investigated our bivouac; if they objected to this familiarity; they kept their thoughts to themselves. Another spot I loved was a pine wood near Lake Champlain. One night, we pitched our tent in a great hayfield out of Montreal which we called Stormfield because just after we had settled for the night a tempest burst upon us. We followed the St. Lawrence from Montreal to Quebec. From Quebec, we came down through Maine and camped on the Kennebec River. My teacher told me that logs were being floated down from Moosehead Lake to sawmills farther along. In order to get a sense of what the river was like, I crawled into it, keeping my body out of reach of the logs and clinging to the rocks. The current turned me over and over like a leaf, but I managed to touch some of the logs as they shot past, and the sense of the adventure was delightful.

When I am in the woods, I love to put out my hand and catch the rustling tread of small creatures in the leaves.

I love to follow dark roads that smell of moss and wet grasses, hill roads and deep valley roads so narrow that the trees and bushes touch me as I pass.

I love to stand on a little bridge and feel the brook flowing under it with minnows in her hands.

I love to sit on a fallen tree so long that the shy wood-things forget that it may be imprudent to step on my toes, and the dimpling cascade throws water-spray in my face. With body still and observant, I hear myriad sounds that I understand—leaf sounds, grass sounds, and twigs creaking faintly when birds alight on them, and grass swaying when insects' wings brush it, and the thistle's silvery flutter. These sounds I hear, yet my way is still.

Sometimes when I am at home and the house is all asleep, I steal out into the garden, silent and dim, where lilies and roses grow together. In the delicate dusk of dawn I stand with the shadow-forms of the flowers, waiting expectant the mystery of the birth of day. The earth's breast is sweet with leaf-hidden violets. The skies grow bright—with lifted head I see my lover, the sun, raise his beautiful face above a silvery, misty sea; and I find the thing I have long sought and hoped for—the light!

Three Days to See

The Atlantic Monthly, January 1933, pp. 35-42

I

All of us have read thrilling stories in which the hero had only a limited and specified time to live. Sometimes it was as long as a year; sometimes as short as twenty-four hours. But always we were interested in discovering just how the doomed man chose to spend his last days or his last hours. I speak, of course, of free men who have a choice, not condemned criminals whose sphere of activities is strictly delimited.

Such stories set us thinking, wondering what we should do under similar circumstances. What events, what experiences, what associations, should we crowd into those last hours as mortal beings? What happiness should we find in reviewing the past, what regrets?

Sometimes I have thought it would be an excellent rule to live each day as if we should die to-morrow. Such an attitude would emphasize sharply the values of life. We should live each day with a gentleness, a vigor, and a keenness of appreciation which are often lost when time stretches before us in the constant panorama of more days and months and years to come. There are those, of course, who would adopt the epicurean motto of "Eat, drink, and be merry," but most people would be chastened by the certainty of impending death.

In stories, the doomed hero is usually saved at the last minute by some stroke of fortune, but almost always his sense of values is changed. He becomes more appreciative of the meaning of life and its permanent spiritual values. It has often been noted that those who live, or have lived, in the shadow of death bring a mellow sweetness to everything they do.

Most of us, however, take life for granted. We know that one day we must die, but usually we picture that day as far in the future. When we are in buoyant health, death is all but unimaginable. We seldom think of it. The days stretch out in an endless vista. So we go about our petty tasks, hardly aware of our listless attitude toward life.

The same lethargy, I am afraid, characterizes the use of all our faculties and senses. Only the deaf appreciate hearing, only the blind realize the manifold blessings that lie in sight. Particularly does this observation apply to those who have lost sight and hearing in adult life. But those who have never suffered impairment of sight or hearing seldom make the fullest use of these blessed faculties. Their eyes and ears take in all sights and sounds hazily, without concentration and with little appreciation. It is the same old story of not being grateful for what we have until we lose it, of not being conscious of health until we are ill.

I have often thought it would be a blessing if each human being were stricken blind and deaf for a few days at some time during his early adult life. Darkness would make him more appreciative of sight; silence would teach him the joys of sound.

Now and then I have tested my seeing friends to discover what they see. Recently I was visited by a very good friend who had just returned from a long walk in the woods, and I asked her what she had observed. "Nothing in particular," she replied. I might have been incredulous had I not been accustomed to such responses, for long ago I became convinced that the seeing see little.

How was it possible, I asked myself, to walk for an hour through the woods and see nothing worthy of note? I who cannot see find hundreds of things to interest me through mere touch. I feel the delicate symmetry of a leaf. I pass my hands lovingly about the smooth skin of a silver birch, or the rough, shaggy bark of a pine. In spring I touch the branches of trees hopefully in search of a bud, the first sign of awakening Nature after her winter's sleep. I feel the delightful, velvety texture of a flower, and discover its remarkable convolutions; and something of the miracle of Nature is revealed to me. Occasionally, if I am very fortunate, I place my hand gently on a small tree and feel the happy quiver of a bird in full song. I am delighted to have the cool waters of a brook rush through my open fingers. To me a lush carpet of pine needles or spongy grass is more welcome than the most luxurious Persian rug. To me the pageant of seasons is a thrilling and unending drama, the action of which streams through my finger tips.

At times my heart cries out with longing to see all these things. If I can get so much pleasure from mere touch, how much more beauty must be revealed by sight. Yet, those who have eyes apparently see little. The panorama of color and action which fills the world is taken for granted. It is human, perhaps, to appreciate little that which we have and to long for that which we have not, but it is a great pity that in the world of light the gift of sight is used only as a mere convenience rather than as a means of adding fullness to life.

If I were the president of a university I should establish a compulsory course in "How to Use Your Eyes." The professor would try to show his pupils how they could add joy to their lives by really seeing what passes unnoticed before them. He would try to awake their dormant and sluggish faculties.

II

Perhaps I can best illustrate by imagining what I should most like to see if I was given the use of my eyes, say, for just three days. And while I am imagining, suppose you, too, set your mind to work on the problem of how you would use your own eyes if you had only three days to see. If with the oncoming darkness if the third night you knew that the sun would never rise for you again, how would you spend those three precious intervening days? What would you most want to let your gaze rest upon?

I, naturally, should want most to see the things which have become dear to me through my years of darkness. You, too, would want to let your eyes rest long on the things that have become dear to you so that you could take the memory of them with you into the night that loomed before you.

If, by some miracle, I were granted three seeing days, to be followed by a relapse into darkness, I should divide the period into three parts.

On the first day, I should want to see the people whose kindness and gentleness and companionship have made my life worth living. First I should like to gaze long upon the face of my dear teacher, Mrs. Ann[e] Sullivan Macy, who came to me when I was a child and opened the outer world to me. I should want not merely to see the outline of her face, so that I could cherish it in my memory, but to study that face and find in it the living evidence of the sympathetic tenderness and patience with which she accomplished the difficult task of my education. I should like to see in her eyes that strength of character which has enabled her to stand firm in the face of difficulties, and that compassion for all humanity which she has revealed to me so often.

I do not know what it is to see into the heart of a friend through that "window of the soul," the eye. I can only "see" through my finger tips the outline of a face. I can detect laughter, sorrow, and many other obvious emotions. I know my friends from the feel of their faces. But I cannot really picture their personalities by touch. I know their personalities, of course, through other means, through the thoughts they express to me, through whatever of their actions are revealed to me. But I am denied that deeper understanding of them which I am sure would come through sight of them, through watching their reactions to various expressed thoughts and circumstances, through noting the immediate and fleeting reactions of their eyes and countenance.

Friends who are near to me I know well, because through the months and years they reveal themselves to me in all their phases; but of casual friends I have only an incomplete impression, an impression gained from a handclasp, from spoken words which I take from their lips with my finger tips, or which they tap into the palm of my hand.

How much easier, how much more satisfying it is for you who can see to grasp quickly the essential qualities of another person by watching the subtleties of expression, the quiver of a muscle, the flutter of a hand. But does it ever occur to you to use your sight to see the inner nature of a friend or acquaintance? Do not most of you seeing people grasp casually the outward features of a face and let it go at that?

For instance, can you describe accurately the faces of five good friends? Some of you can, but many cannot. As an experiment, I have questioned husbands of long standing about the color of their wives' eyes, and often they express embarrassed confusion and admit that they do not know. And, incidentally, it is a chronic complaint of wives that their husbands do not notice new dresses, new hats, and changes in household arrangements.

The eyes of seeing persons soon become accustomed to the routine of their surroundings, and they actually see only the startling and spectacular. But even in viewing the most spectacular sights the eyes are lazy. Court records reveal every day how inaccurately "eyewitnesses" see. A given event will be "seen" in several different ways by as many witnesses. Some see more than others, but few see everything that is within the range of their vision.

Oh, the things that I should see if I had the power of sight for just three days!

The first day would be a busy one. I should call to me all my dear friends and look long into their faces, imprinting upon my mind the outward evidence of the beauty that is within them. I should let my eyes rest, too, on the face of a baby, so that I could catch a vision of the eager, innocent beauty which precedes the individual's consciousness of the conflicts which life develops.

And I should like to look into the loyal, trusting eyes of my dogs—the grave, canny little Scottie, Darkie, and the stalwart, understanding Great Dane, Helga, whose warm, tender, and playful friendships are so comforting to me.

On that busy first day I should also view the small simple things of my home. I want to see the warm colors in the rugs under my feet, the pictures on the walls, the intimate trifles that transform a house into a home. My eyes would rest respectfully on the books in raised type which I have read, but they would be more eagerly interested in the printed books which seeing people can read, for during the long night of my life the books I have read and those which have been read to me have built themselves into a great shining lighthouse, revealing to me the deepest channels of human life and the human spirit.

In the afternoon of that first seeing day, I should take a long walk in the woods and intoxicate my eyes on the beauties of the world of Nature, trying desperately to absorb in a few hours the vast splendor which is constantly unfolding itself to those who can see. On the way home from my woodland jaunt my path would lie near a farm so that I might see the patient horses ploughing in the field (perhaps I should see only a tractor!) and the serene content of men living close to the soil. And I should pray for the glory of a colorful sunset.

When dusk had fallen, I should experience the double delight of being able to see by artificial light, which the genius of man has created to extend the power of his sight when Nature decrees darkness.

In the night of that first day of sight, I should not be able to sleep, so full would be my mind of the memories of the day.

III

The next day—the second day of sight—I should arise with the dawn and see the thrilling miracle by which night is transformed into day. I should behold with awe the magnificent panorama of light with which the sun awakens the sleeping earth.

This day I should devote to a hasty glimpse of the world, past and present. I should want to see the pageant of man's progress, the kaleidoscope of the ages. How can so much compressed into one day? Through the museums, of course. Often I have visited the New York Museum of Natural History to touch with my hands many of the objects there exhibited, but I have longed to see with my eyes the condensed history of the earth and its inhabitants displayed there—animals and the races of men pictured in their native environment; gigantic carcasses of dinosaurs and mastodons which roamed the earth long before man appeared, with his tiny stature and powerful brain, to conquer the animal kingdom; realistic presentations of the processes of evolution in animals, in man, and in the implements which man has used to fashion for himself a secure home on this planet; and a thousand and one other aspects of natural history.

I wonder how many readers of this article have viewed this panorama of the face of living things as pictured in that inspiring museum. Many, of course, have not had the opportunity, but, I am sure that many who have had the opportunity have not made use of it. There, indeed, is a place to use your eyes. You who can see can spend many fruitful days there, but I, with my imaginary three days of sight, could only take a hasty glimpse, and pass on.

My next stop would be the Metropolitan Museum of Art, for just as the Museum of Natural History reveals the material aspects of the world, so does the Metropolitan show the myriad facets of the human spirit. Throughout the history of humanity the urge to artistic expression has been almost as powerful as the urge for food, shelter, and procreation. And here, in the vast chambers of the

Metropolitan Museum, is unfolded before me the spirit of Egypt, Greece, and Rome, as expressed in their art. I know well through my hands the sculptured gods and goddesses of the ancient Nile-land. I have felt copies of Parthenon friezes, and I have sensed the rhythmic beauty of charging Athenian warriors. Apollos and Venuses and the winged victory of Samothrace are friends of my finger tips. The gnarled, bearded features of Homer are dear to me, for he, too, knew blindness.

My hands have lingered upon the living marvel of Roman sculpture as well as that of later generations. I have passed my hands over a plaster cast of Michelangelo's inspiring and heroic Moses; I have sensed the power of Rodin; I have been awed by the devoted spirit of Gothic wood carving. These arts which can be touched have meaning for me, but even they were meant to be seen rather than felt, and I can only guess at the beauty which remains hidden from me. I can admire the simple lines of a Greek vase, but its figured decorations are lost to me.

So on this, my second day of sight, I should try to probe into the soul of man through his art. The things I knew through touch I should now see. More splendid still, the whole magnificent world of painting would be opened to me, from the Italian Primitives, with their serene religious devotion, to the Moderns, with their feverish visions. I should look deep into the canvases of Raphael, Leonardo Da Vinci, Titian, Rembrandt. I should want to feast my eyes upon the warm colors of Veronese, study the mysteries of El Greco, catch a new vision of Nature from Corot. Oh, there is so much rich meaning and beauty in the art of the ages for you who have eyes to see!

Upon my short visit to this temple of art I should not be able to review a fraction of that great world of art which is open to you. I should be able to get only a superficial impression. Artists tell me that for a deep and true appreciation of art one must educate the eye. One must learn through experience to weigh the merits of line, of composition, of form and color. If I had eyes, how happily would I embark upon so fascinating a study! Yet I am told that, to many of you who have eyes to see, the world of art is a dark night, unexplored and unilluminated.

It would be with extreme reluctance that I should leave the Metropolitan Museum, which contains the key to beauty—a beauty so neglected. Seeing persons, however, do not need a Metropolitan to find this key to beauty. The same key lies waiting in smaller museums, and in books on the shelves of even small libraries. But naturally, in my limited time of imaginary sight, I should choose the place where the key unlocks the greatest treasures in the shortest time.

The evening of my second day of sight I should spend at a theatre or at the movies. Even now I often attend theatrical performances of all sorts, but the action of the play must be spelled into my hand by a companion. But how I should like to see with my own eyes the fascinating figure of Hamlet, or the gusty Falstaff amid colorful Elizabethan trappings! How I should like to follow each movement of the graceful Hamlet, each strut of the hearty Falstaff! And since I could see only one play, I should be confronted by a many-horned dilemma, for there are scores of plays I should want to see. You who have eyes can see any you like. How many of you, I wonder, when you gaze at a play, a movie, or any spectacle, realize and give thanks for the miracle of sight which enables you to enjoy its color, grace, and movement?

I cannot enjoy the beauty of rhythmic movement except in a sphere restricted to the touch of my hands. I can vision only dimly the grace of a Pavlowa [sic], although I know something of the delight of rhythm, for often I can sense the beat of music as it vibrates through the floor. I can well imagine that cadenced motion must be one of the most pleasing sights in the world. I have been able to gather something of this by tracing with my fingers the lines in sculptured marble; if this static grace can be so lovely, how much more acute must be the thrill of see-ing grace in motion.

One of my dearest memories is of the time when Joseph Jefferson allowed me to touch his face and hands as he went through some of the gestures and speech-es of his beloved Rip Van Winkle. I was able to catch thus a meager glimpse of the world of drama, and I shall never forget the delight of that moment. But, oh, how much I must miss, and how much pleasure you seeing ones can derive from watching and hearing the interplay of speech and movement in the unfolding of a dramatic performance! If I could see only one play, I should know how to picture in my mind the action of a hundred plays which I have read or had transferred to me through the medium of the manual alphabet.

So, through the evening of my second imaginary day of sight, the great figures of dramatic literature would crowd sleep from my eyes.

IV

The following morning, I should again greet the dawn, anxious to discover new delights, for I am sure that, for those who have eyes which really see, the dawn of each day must be a perpetually new revelation of beauty.

This, according to the terms of my imagined miracle, is to be my third and last day of sight. I shall have no time to waste in regrets or longings; there is too much to see. The first day I devoted to my friends, animate and inanimate. The second revealed to me the history of man and Nature. To-day I shall spend in the workday world of the present, amid the haunts of men going about the business of life. And where one can find so many activities and conditions of men as in New York? So the city becomes my destination.

I start from my home in the quiet little suburb of Forest Hills, Long Island. Here, surrounded by green lawns, trees, and flowers, are neat little houses, happy with the voices and movements of wives and children, havens of peaceful rest for men who toil in the city. I drive across the lacy structure of steel which spans the East River, and I get a new and startling vision of the power and ingenuity of the mind of man. Busy boats chug and scurry about the river—racy speed boats, stolid, snorting tugs. If I had long days of sight ahead, I should spend many of them watching the delightful activity upon the river.

I look ahead, and before me rise the fantastic towers of New York, a city that seems to have stepped from the pages of a fairy story. What an awe-inspiring sight, these glittering spires, these vast banks of stone and steel—structures such as the gods might build for themselves! This animated picture is a part of the lives of millions of people every day. How many, I wonder, give it so much as a second glance? Very few, I fear. Their eyes are blind to this magnificent sight because it is so familiar to them.

I hurry to the top of one of those gigantic structures, the Empire State Building, for there, a short time ago, I "saw" the city below through the eyes of my secretary. I am anxious to compare my fancy with reality. I am sure I should not be disappointed in the panorama spread out before me, for to me it would be a vision of another world.

Now I begin my rounds of the city. First, I stand at a busy corner, merely looking at people, trying by sight of them to understand something of their lives. I see smiles, and I am happy. I see serious determination, and I am proud. I see suffering, and I am compassionate.

I stroll down Fifth Avenue. I throw my eyes out of focus, so that I see no particular object but only a seething kaleidoscope of color. I am certain that the colors of women's dresses moving in a throng must be a gorgeous spectacle of which I should never tire. But perhaps if I had sight I should be like most other women—too interested in styles and the cut of individual dresses to give much attention to the splendor of color in the mass. And I am convinced, too, that I should become an inveterate window shopper, for it must be a delight to the eye to view the myriad articles of beauty on display.

From Fifth Avenue I make a tour of the city—to Park Avenue, to the slums, to factories, to parks where children play. I take a stay-at-home trip abroad by visiting the foreign quarters. Always my eyes are open wide to all the sights of both happiness and misery so that I may probe deep and add to my understanding of how people work and live. My heart is full of the images of people and things. My eye passes lightly over no single trifle; it strives to touch and hold closely each thing its gaze rests upon. Some sights are pleasant, filling the heart with happiness; but some are miserably pathetic. To these latter I do not shut my eyes, for they, too, are part of life. To close the eye on them is to close the heart and mind.

My third day of sight is drawing to an end. Perhaps there are many serious pursuits to which I should devote the few remaining hours, but I am afraid that on the evening of that last day I should run away to the theatre, to a hilariously funny play, so that I might appreciate the overtones of comedy in the human spirit.

At midnight my temporary respite from blindness would cease, and permanent night would close in on me again. Naturally in those three short days I should not have seen all I wanted to see. Only when darkness had again descended upon me should I realize how much I had left unseen. But my mind would be so crowded with glorious memories that I should have little time for regrets. Thereafter the touch of every object would bring a glowing memory of how that object looked.

Perhaps this short outline of how I should spend three days of sight does not agree with the programme you would set for yourself if you knew that you were about to be stricken blind. I am, however, sure that if you actually faced that fate your eyes would open to things you had never seen before, storing up memories for the long night ahead. You would use your eyes as never before. Everything you saw would become dear to you. Your eyes would touch and embrace every object that came within your range of vision. Then, at last, you would really see, and a new world of beauty would open itself before you.

I who am blind can give one hint to those who see—one admonition to those who would make full use of the gift of sight: Use your eyes as if to-morrow you would be stricken blind. And the same method can be applied to other senses. Hear the music of voices, the song of a bird, the mighty strains of an orchestra, as if you would be stricken deaf to-morrow. Touch each object you want to touch as if to-morrow your tactile sense would fail. Smell the perfume of flowers, taste with relish each morsel, as if to-morrow you could never smell and taste again. Make the most of every sense; glory in all the facets of pleasure and beauty which the world reveals to you through the several means of contact which Nature provides. But of all the senses, I am sure that sight must be the most delightful.

Sense and Sensibility

The Century Magazine, 1908

Some months ago, in a newspaper which announced the publication of the "Matilda Ziegler Magazine for the Blind," appeared the following paragraph:

"Many poems and stories must be omitted because they deal with sight. Allusions to moonbeams, rainbows, starlight, clouds, and beautiful scenery may not be printed, because they serve to emphasize the blind man's sense of his affliction."

That is to say, I may not talk about beautiful mansions and gardens because I am poor. I may not read about Paris and the West Indies because I cannot visit them in their territorial reality. I may not dream of heaven because it is possible that I may never go there. Yet a venturesome spirit impels me to use words of sight and sound whose meaning I can guess only from analogy and fancy. This hazardous game is half the delight, the frolic, of daily life. I glow as I read of splendors which the eye alone can survey. Allusions to moonbeams and clouds do not emphasize the sense of my affliction: they carry my soul beyond affliction's narrow actuality.

Critics delight to tell us what we cannot do. They assume that blindness and deafness sever us completely from the things which the seeing and the hearing enjoy, and hence they assert we have no moral right to talk about beauty, the skies, mountains, the song of birds, and colors. They declare that the very sensations we have from the sense of touch are "vicarious," as though our friends felt the sun for us! They deny *a priori* what they have not seen and I have felt. Some brave doubters have gone so far even as to deny my existence. In order, therefore, that I may know that I exist, I resort to Descartes's method: "I think, therefore I am." Thus I am metaphysically established, and I throw upon the doubters the burden of proving my nonexistence. When we consider how little has been found out about the mind, is it not amazing that any one should presume to define what one can know or cannot know? I admit that there are innumerable marvels in the visible universe unguessed by me. Likewise, O confident critic, there are a myriad sensations perceived by me of which you do not dream.

Necessity gives to the eye a precious power of seeing, and in the same way it gives a precious power of feeling to the whole body. Sometimes it seems as if the very substance of my flesh were so many eyes looking out at will upon a world new created every day. The silence and darkness which are said to shut me in, open my door most hospitably to countless sensations that distract, inform, admonish, and amuse. With my three trusty guides, touch, smell, and taste, I make many excursions into the borderland of experience which is in sight of the city of Light. Nature accommodates itself to every man's necessity. If the eye is maimed, so that it does not see the beauteous face of day, the touch becomes more poignant and discriminating. For this reason the blind often hear with greater ease and distinctness than other people. The sense of smell becomes almost a new faculty to penetrate the tangle and vagueness of things. Thus, according to an immutable law, the senses assist and reinforce one another.

It is not for me to say whether we see best with the hand or the eye. I only know that the world I see with my fingers is alive, ruddy, and satisfying. Touch brings the blind many sweet certainties which our more fortunate fellows miss, because their sense of touch is uncultivated. When they look at things, they put their hands in their pockets. No doubt that is one reason why their knowledge is often so vague, inaccurate, and useless. It is probable, too, that our knowledge of phenomena beyond the reach of the hand is equally imperfect. But, at all events, we behold them through a golden mist of fantasy.

There is nothing, however, misty or uncertain about what we can touch. Through the sense of touch I know the faces of friends, the illimitable variety of straight and curved lines, all surfaces, the exuberance of the soil, the delicate shapes of flowers, the noble forms of trees, and the range of mighty winds. Besides objects, surfaces, and atmospherical changes, I perceive countless vibrations. I derive much knowledge of everyday matter from the jars and jolts which are to be felt everywhere in the house.

FOOTSTEPS AND VIBRATIONS

Footsteps, I discover, vary tactually according to the age, the sex, and the manners of the walker. It is impossible to mistake a child's patter for the tread of a grown person. The step of the young man, strong and free, differs from the heavy, sedate tread of the middle-aged, and from the step of the old man, whose feet drag along the floor, or beat it with slow, faltering accents. On a bare floor a girl walks with a rapid, elastic rhythm which is quite distinct from the graver step of the elderly woman. I have laughed over the creak of new shoes and the clatter of a stout maid performing a jig in the kitchen. One day, in the dining room of a hotel, a tactual dissonance arrested my attention. I sat still and listened with my feet. I found that two waiters were walking back and forth, but not with the same gait. A band was playing, and I could feel the music-waves along the floor. One of the waiters walked in time to the band, graceful and light, while the other disregarded the music and rushed from table to table to the beat of some discord in his own mind. Their steps reminded me of a spirited war-steed harnessed with a cart-horse.

Often footsteps reveal in some measure the character and the mood of the walker. I feel in them firmness and indecision, hurry and deliberation, activity and laziness, fatigue, carelessness, timidity, anger, and sorrow. I am most conscious of these moods and traits in persons with whom I am familiar.

Footsteps are frequently interrupted by certain jars and jerks, so that I know when one kneels, kicks, shakes something, sits down, or gets up. Thus I follow to some extent the actions of people about me and the changes of postures. Just now a thick, soft patter of bare, padded feet and a slight jolt told me that my dog had jumped on the chair to look out of the window. I do not, however, allow him to go uninvestigated; for occasionally I feel the same motion, and find him, not on the chair, but trespassing on the sofa.

When a carpenter works in the house or in the barn nearby, I know by the slanting, up-and-down, toothed vibration, and the ringing concussion of blow upon blow, that he is sawing or hammering. If I am near enough, a certain vibration, traveling back and forth along a wooden surface, brings me the information that he is using a plane.

A slight flutter on the rug tells me that a breeze has blown my papers off the table. A round thump is a signal that a pencil has rolled on the floor. If a book falls, it gives a flat thud. A wooden rap on the balustrade announces that dinner is ready. Many of these vibrations are obliterated out of doors. On a lawn or the road, I can feel only running, stamping, and the rumble of wheels.

By placing my hand on a person's lips and throat, I gain an idea of many specific vibrations, and interpret them: a boy's chuckle, a man's "Whew!" of surprise, and the "Hem!" of annoyance or perplexity, the moan of pain, a scream, a whisper, a rasp, a sob, a choke, and a gasp. The utterances of animals, though wordless, are eloquent to me—the cat's purr, its mew, its angry, jerky, scolding spit; the dog's bow-wow of warning or of joyous welcome, its yelp of despair, and its contented snore; the cow's moo; a monkey's chatter; the snort of a horse; the lion's roar, and the terrible snarl of the tiger. Perhaps I ought to add, for the benefit of the critics, and doubters who may peruse this essay, that with my own hand I have felt all these sounds. From my childhood to the present day I have availed myself of every opportunity to visit zoological gardens, menageries, and the circus, and all the animals, except the tiger, have talked into my hand. I have touched the tiger only in a museum, where he is as harmless as a lamb. I have, however, heard him talk by putting my hand on the bars of his cage. I have touched several lions in the flesh, and felt them roar royally, like a cataract over rocks.

To continue, I know the *plop* of liquid in a pitcher. So if I spill my milk, I have not the excuse of ignorance. I am also familiar with the pop of a cork, the sputter of a flame, the tick-tack of the clock, the metallic swing of the windmill, the labored rise and fall of the pump, the voluminous spurt of the hose, the deceptive tap of the breeze at door and window, the crash of thunder, and many other vibrations past computing.

There are tactual vibrations which do not belong to skin-touch. They penetrate the skin, the nerves, the bones, like pain, heat, and cold. The beat of a drum smites me through from the chest to the shoulder-blades. The din of the train, the bridge, and grinding machinery retains its "old man of the sea" grip upon me long after its cause has been left behind. If vibration and motion combine in my touch for any length of time, the earth seems to run away while I stand still. When I step off the train, the platform whirls round, and I find it difficult to walk steadily.

Every atom of my body is a vibroscope. But my sensations are not infallible. I reach out, and my fingers meet something furry, which jumps about, gathers itself together as if to spring, and acts like an animal. I pause a moment for caution. I touch it again more firmly, and find it is a fur coat fluttering and flapping in the wind. To me, as to you, the earth seems motionless, and the sun appears to move; for the rays of the afternoon withdraw more and more, as they touch my face, until the air becomes cool. From this I understand how it is that the shore seems to recede as you sail away from it. Hence I feel no incredulity when you say that parallel lines appear to converge, and the earth and sky to meet. My few senses long ago revealed to me their imperfections and deceptivity.

Not only are the senses deceptive, but numerous usages in our language indicate that people who have five senses find it difficult to keep their functions distinct. I understand that we hear views, see tones, taste music. I am told that voices have color. Tact, which I had supposed to be a matter of nice perception, turns out to be a matter of taste. Judging from the large use of the word, taste appears to be the most important of all the senses. Taste governs the great and small conventions of life. Certainly the language of the senses is full of contradictions, and my fellows who have five doors to their house are not more surely at home in themselves than I. May I not, then, be excused if this account of my sensations lacks precision?

The Enjoyment of Music

I have spoken of the numerous jars and jolts which daily minister to my faculties. The loftier and grander vibrations which appeal to my emotions are varied and abundant. I listen with awe to the roll of the thunder and the muffled avalanche of sound when the sea flings itself upon the shore. And I love the instrument by which all the diapasons of the ocean are caught and released in surging floods—the many-voiced organ. If music could be seen, I could point where the organ notes go, as they rise and fall, climb up and up, rock and sway, now loud and deep, now high and stormy, anon soft and solemn, with lighter vibrations interspersed between and running across them. I should say that organ-music fills to an ecstasy the act of feeling.There is tangible delight in other instruments, too. The violin seems beautifully alive as it responds to the lightest wish of the master. The distinction between its notes is more delicate than between the notes of the piano. I enjoy the music of the piano most when I touch the instrument. If I keep my hand on the piano case, I detect tiny quavers, returns of melody, and the hush that follows. This explains to me how sounds can die away to the listening ear:

> . . . How thin and clear.
> And thinner, clearer, farther going!
> O sweet and far from cliff and scar
> The horns of Elfland faintly blowing!

I am able to follow the dominant spirit and mood of the music. I catch the joyous dance as it bounds over the keys, the slow dirge, the reverie. I thrill to the fiery sweep of notes crossed by thunderous tones in the "Walkure," where *Wotan* kindles the dread flames that guard the sleeping *Brunhild*. How wonderful is the instrument on which a great musician sings with his hands! I have never succeeded in distinguishing one composition from another. I think this is possible; but the concentration and strain upon my attention would be so great that I doubt if the pleasure derived would be commensurate to the effort.

Nor can I distinguish easily a tune that is sung. But by placing my hand on another's throat and cheek, I enjoy the changes of the voice. I know when it is low or high, clear or muffled, sad or cheery. The thin, quavering sensation of an old voice differs in my touch from the sensation of a young voice. A Southerner's drawl is quite unlike the Yankee twang. Sometimes the flow and ebb of a voice is so enchanting that my fingers quiver with exquisite pleasure, even if I do not understand a word that is spoken.

On the other hand, I am exceedingly sensitive to the harshness of noises like grinding, scraping, and the hoarse creak of rusty locks. Fog-whistles are my vibratory nightmares. I have stood near a bridge in process of construction, and felt the tactual din, the rattle of heavy masses of stone, the roll of loosened earth, the rumble of engines, the dumping of dirt-cars, the triple blows of vulcan hammers. I can also smell the firepots, the tar and cement. So I have a vivid idea of mighty labors in steel and stone, and I believe that I am acquainted with all the fiendish noises which can be made by man or machinery. The whack of heavy falling bodies, the sudden shivering splinter of chopped logs, the crystal shatter of pounded ice, the crash of a tree hurled to the earth by a hurricane, the irrational, persistent chaos of noise made by switching freight-trains, the explosion of gas, the blasting of rock, and the terrific grinding of rock upon rock which precedes the collapse—all these have been in my touch-experience, and contribute to my idea of Bedlam, of a battle, a waterspout, an earthquake, and other enormous accumulations of sound.

Town and Country

Touch brings me into contact with the traffic and manifold activity of the city. Besides the bustle and crowding of people and the nondescript grating and electric howling of street-cars, I am conscious of exhalations from many different kinds of shops; from automobiles, drays, horses, fruit stands, and many varieties of smoke.

> Odors strange and musty,
> The air sharp and dusty
> With lime and with sand.
> That no one can stand,
> Make the street impassable,
> The people irascible,
> Until every one cries,
> As he trembling goes
> With the sight of his eyes
> And the scent of his nose
> Quite stopped—or at least much diminished—
> "Gracious! when will this city be finished?"[1]

The city is interesting; but the tactual silence of the country is always most welcome after the din of town and the irritating concussions of the train. How

1. George Arnold

noiseless and undisturbing are the demolition, the repairs and the alterations, of nature! With no sound of hammer or saw or stone severed from stone, but a music of rustles and ripe thumps on the grass come the fluttering leaves and mellow fruits which the wind tumbles all day from the branches. Silently all droops, all withers, all is poured back into the earth that it may recreate; all sleeps while the busy architects of day and night ply their silent work elsewhere. The same serenity reigns when all at once the soil yields up a newly wrought creation. Softly the ocean of grass, moss, and flowers rolls surge upon surge across the earth. Curtains of foliage drape the bare branches. Great trees make ready in their sturdy hearts to receive again birds which occupy their spacious chambers to the south and west. Nay, there is no place so lowly that it may not lodge some happy creature. The meadow brook undoes its icy fetters with rippling notes, gurgles, and runs free. And all this is wrought in less than two months to the music of nature's orchestra, in the midst of balmy incense.

The thousand soft voices of the earth have truly found their way to me—the small rustle in tufts of grass, the silky swish of leaves, the buzz of insects, the hum of bees in blossoms I have plucked, the flutter of a bird's wings after his bath, and the slender rippling vibration of water running over pebbles. Once having been felt, these loved voices rustle, buzz, hum, flutter, and ripple in my thought forever, an undying part of happy memories.

Between my experiences and the experiences of others there is no gulf of mute space which I may not bridge. For I have endlessly varied, instructive contacts with all the world, with life, with the atmosphere whose radiant activity enfolds us all. The thrilling energy of the all-encasing air is warm and rapturous. Heat-waves and sound-waves play upon my face in infinite variety and combination, until I am able to surmise what must be the myriad sounds that my senseless ears have not heard.

Wind and Rain

The air varies in different regions, at different seasons of the year, and even different hours of the day. The odorous, fresh sea-breezes are distinct from the fitful breezes along river banks, which are humid and freighted with inland smells. The bracing, light, dry air of the mountains can never been mistaken for the pungent salt air of the ocean. The rain of winter is dense, hard, compressed. In the spring it has new vitality. It is light, mobile, and laden with a thousand palpitating odors from earth, grass, and sprouting leaves. The air of midsummer is dense, saturated, or dry and burning, as if it came from a furnace. When a cool breeze brushes the sultry stillness, it brings fewer odors than in May, and frequently the odor of a coming tempest. The avalanche of coolness which sweeps through the low-hanging air bears little resemblance to the stinging coolness of winter.

The rain of winter is raw, without odor and dismal. The rain of spring is brisk, fragrant, charged with life-giving warmth. I welcome it delightedly as it visits the earth, enriches the streams, waters the hills abundantly, makes the furrows soft with showers for the seed, elicits a perfume which I cannot breathe deep enough. Spring: rain is beautiful, impartial, lovable. With pearly drops it washes every leaf on tree and bush, ministers equally to salutary herbs and noxious growths, searches out every living thing that needs its beneficence.

The senses assist and reinforce each other to such an extent that I am not sure whether touch or smell tells me the most about the world. Everywhere the river of touch is joined by the brooks of odor-perception. Each season has its distinctive odors. The spring is earthy and full of sap. July is rich with the odor of ripening grain and hay. As the season advances, a crisp, dry, mature odor predominates, and golden-rod, tansy, and everlastings mark the onward march of the year. In autumn, soft, alluring scents fill the air, floating from thicket, grass, flower, and tree, and they tell me of time and change, of death and life's renewal, desire and its fulfillment.

SMELL IS A FALLEN ANGEL

For some inexplicable reason the sense of smell does not hold the high position it deserves among its sisters. There is something of the fallen angel about it. When it woos us with woodland scents and beguiles us with the fragrance of lovely gardens, it is admitted frankly to our discourse. But when it gives us warning of something noxious in our vicinity, it is treated as if the demon had got the upper hand of the angel, and is relegated to outer darkness, punished for its faithful service. It is most difficult to keep the true significance of words when one discusses the prejudices of mankind, and I find it hard to give an account of odor-perceptions which shall be at once dignified and truthful.

In my experience smell is most important, and I find that there is high authority for the nobility of the sense which we have neglected and disparaged. It is recorded that the Lord commanded that incense be burnt before Him continually with a sweet savor. I doubt if there is any sensation arising from sight more delightful than the odors which filter through sun-warmed, wind-tossed branches, or the tide of scents which swells, subsides, rises again wave on wave, filling the wide world with invisible sweetness. A whiff of the universe makes us dream of worlds we have never seen, recalls in a flash entire epochs of our dearest experience. I never smell daisies without living over again the ecstatic mornings that my teacher and I spent wandering in the fields, while I learned new words and the names of things. Smell is a potent wizard that transports us across a thousand miles and all the years we have lived. The odor of fruits wafts me to my Southern home, to my childish frolics in the peach orchard. Other odors, instantaneous and fleeting, cause my heart to dilate joyously or contract with remembered grief. Even as I think of smells, my nose is full of scents that start awake sweet memories of summers gone and ripening grain fields far away.

The faintest whiff from a meadow where the new-mown hay lies in the hot sun displaces the here and the now. I am back again in the old red barn. My little friends and I are playing in the haymow. A huge mow it is, packed with crisp, sweet hay, from the top of which the smallest child can reach the straining rafters. In their stalls beneath are the farm animals. Here is Jerry, unresponsive, unbeautiful Jerry, crunching his oats like a true pessimist, resolved to find his feed not good—at least not so good as it ought to be. Again I touch Brownie, eager, grateful little Brownie, ready to leave the juiciest fodder for a pat, straining his beautiful, slender neck for a caress. Nearby stands Lady Belle, with sweet, moist mouth, lazily extracting the sealed-up cordial from timothy and clover, and dreaming of deep June pastures and murmurous streams.

The sense of smell has told me of a coming storm hours before there was any sign of it visible. I notice first a throb of expectancy, a slight quiver, a concentration in my nostrils. As the storm draws nearer, my nostrils dilate the better to receive the flood of earth-odors which seem to multiply and extend, until I feel the splash of rain against my cheek. As the tempest departs, receding farther and farther, the odors fade, become fainter and fainter, and die away beyond the bar of space.

I know by smell the kind of house we enter. I have recognized an old-fashioned country house because it has several layers of odors, left by a succession of families, of plants, perfumes, and draperies.

In the evening quiet there are fewer vibrations than in the daytime, and then I rely more largely upon smell. The sulphuric scent of a match tells me that the lamps are being lighted. Later, I note the wavering trail of odor that flits about and disappears. It is the curfew signal; the lights are out for the night.

Wayside Scents

Out of doors I am aware by smell and touch of the ground we tread and the places we pass. Sometimes, when there is no wind, the odors are so grouped that I know the character of the country, and can place a hayfield, a country store, a garden, a barn, a farm-house with the windows open, a grove of pines.

The other day I went to walk toward a familiar wood. Suddenly a disturbing odor made me pause in dismay. Then followed a peculiar, measured jar, followed by dull, heavy thunder. I understood the odor and the jar only too well. The trees were being cut down. We climbed the stone wall to the left. It borders the wood which I have loved so long that it seems to be my peculiar possession. But today an unfamiliar rush of air and an unwonted outburst of sun told me that my tree friends were gone. The place was empty, like a deserted dwelling. I stretched out my hand. Where once stood the steadfast pines, great, beautiful, sweet, my hand touched raw, moist stumps. All about lay broken branches, like the antlers of stricken deer. The fragrant, piled-up sawdust swirled and tumbled about me. An unreasoning resentment flashed through me at this ruthless destruction of the beauty that I love. But there is no anger, no resentment in nature. The air is equally charged with the odors of life and of destruction, for death equally with growth forever ministers to all-conquering life. The sun shines as ever, and the winds riot through the newly opened spaces. I know that a new forest will spring where the old one stood, as beautiful, as beneficent.

Touch sensations are permanent and definite. Odors deviate and are fugitive, changing in their shades, degrees, and location. There is something else in odor which gives me a sense of distance. I should call it horizon—the line where odor and fancy meet at the farthest limit of scent.

Smell gives me more idea than touch or taste of the manner in which sight and hearing probably discharge their functions. Touch seems to reside in the object touched, because there is a contact of surfaces. In smell there is no notion of relievo, and odor seems to reside not in the object smelt, but in the organ. Since I smell a tree at a distance, it is comprehensible to me that a person sees it without touching it. I am not puzzled over the fact that he receives it as an image on his retina without relievo, since my smell perceives the tree as a thin sphere with no fullness or content. By themselves, odors suggest nothing. I must learn by association to judge from them of distance, of place, and of the actions or the surroundings which are the usual occasions for them, just as I am told people judge from color, light, and sound.

THE ELUSIVE PERSON-ODOR

From exhalations I learn much about people. I often know the work they are engaged in. The odors of wood, iron, paint, and drugs cling to the garments of those that work in them. Thus I can distinguish the carpenter from the iron worker, the artist from the mason or the chemist. When a person passes quickly from one place to another I get a scent impression of where he has been—the kitchen, the garden, or the sick-room. I gain pleasurable ideas of freshness and good taste from the odors of soap, toilet water, clean garments, woolen and silk stuffs, and gloves.

I have not, indeed, the all-knowing scent of the hound or the wild animal. None but the halt and the blind need fear my skill in pursuit; for there are other things besides water, stale trails, confusing cross tracks to put me at fault. Nevertheless, human odors are as varied and capable of recognition as hands and faces. The dear odors of those I love are so definite, so unmistakable, that nothing can quite obliterate them. If many years should elapse before I saw an intimate friend again, I think I should recognize his odor instantly in the heart of Africa, as promptly as would my brother that barks.

Once, long ago, in a crowded railway station, a lady kissed me as she hurried by. I had not touched even her dress. But she left a scent with her kiss which gave me a glimpse of her. The years are many since she kissed me. Yet her odor is fresh in my memory.

It is difficult to put into words the thing itself, the elusive person-odor. There seems to be no adequate vocabulary of smells, and I must fall back on approximate phase and metaphor.

Some people have a vague, unsubstantial odor that floats about, mocking every effort to identify it. It is the will-o'-the-wisp of my olfactive experience. Sometimes I meet one who lacks a distinctive person-scent, and I seldom find such a one lively or entertaining. On the other hand, one who has a pungent odor often possesses great vitality, energy, and vigor of mind.

Masculine exhalations are as a rule stronger, more vivid, more widely differentiated than those of women. In the odor of young men there is something elemental, as of fire, storm, and salt sea. It pulsates with buoyancy and desire. It suggests all things strong and beautiful and joyous, and gives me a sense of physical happiness. I wonder if others observe that all infants have the same scent—pure, simple, undecipherable as their dormant personality. It is not until the age of six or seven that they begin to have perceptible individual odors. These develop and mature along with their mental and bodily powers.

What I have written about smell, especially person-smell, will perhaps be regarded as the abnormal sentiment of one who can have no idea of the "world of reality and beauty which the eye perceives." There are people who are color-blind, people who are tone-deaf. Most people are smell-blind-and-deaf. We should not condemn a musical composition on the testimony of an ear which cannot distinguish one chord from another, or judge a picture by the verdict of a color-blind critic. The sensations of smell which cheer, inform, and broaden my life are not less pleasant merely because some critic who treads the wide, bright pathway of the eye has not cultivated his olfactive sense. Without the shy, fugitive, often unobserved, sensations and the certainties which taste, smell, and touch give me, I should be obliged to take my conception of the universe wholly from others. I should lack the alchemy by which I now infuse into my world light, color, and the Protean spark. The sensuous reality which interthreads and supports all the gropings of my imagination would be shattered. The solid earth would melt from under my feet and disperse itself in space. The objects dear to my hands would become formless, dead things, and I should walk among them an invisible ghost.

RELATIVE VALUES OF THE SENSES

I was once without the sense of smell and taste for several days. It seemed incredible, this utter detachment from odors, to breathe the air in and observe never a single scent. The feeling was probably similar, though in a less degree, to that of one who first loses sight and cannot but expect to see the light again any day, any minute. I knew I should smell again sometime. Still, after the wonder had passed off, a loneliness crept over me as vast as the air whose myriad odors I missed. The multitudinous subtle delights that smell makes mine became for a time wistful memories. When I recovered the lost sense, my heart bounded with gladness. It is a fine dramatic touch that Hans Andersen gives to the story of Kay and Gerda in the passage about flowers. Kay, whom the wicked magician's glass has blinded to human love, rushes away fiercely from home when he discovers that the roses have lost their sweetness.

The loss of smell for a few days gave me a clearer idea than I had ever had what it is to be blinded suddenly, helplessly. With a little stretch of the imagination I knew then what it must be when the great curtain shuts out suddenly the light of day, the stars, and the firmament itself.

I see the blind man's eyes strain for the light, as he fearfully tries to walk his old rounds, until the unchanging blank that everywhere spreads before him stamps the reality of the dark upon his consciousness.

My temporary loss of smell proved to me, too, that the absence of a sense need not dull the mental faculties and does not distort one's view of the world, and so I reason that blindness and deafness need not pervert the inner order of the intellect. I know that if there were no odors for me I should still possess a considerable part of the world. Novelties and surprises would abound, adventures would thicken in the dark.

In my classification of the senses, smell is a little the ear's inferior, and touch is a great deal the eye's superior. I find that great artists and philosophers agree with me in this. Diderot says:

> *Je trouvais que de tous les sens, l'oeil était le plus superficiel; l'oreille, le plus orgueilleux; l'odorat, le plus voluptueux; le gout, le plus superstitieux et le plus inconstant; le toucher, le plus profound et le plus philosophe.*[2]

A friend whom I have never seen sends me a quotation from Symond's "Renaissance in Italy": Lorenzo Ghiberti, after describing a piece of antique sculpture he saw in Rome adds, "To express the perfection of learning, mastery, and art displayed in it is beyond the power of language. Its more exquisite beauties could not be discovered by the sight, but only by the touch of the hand passed over it." Of another classic marble at Padua he says, "This statue, when the Christian faith triumphed, was hidden in that place by some gentle soul, who, seeing it so perfect, fashioned with art so wonderful, and with such power of genius, and being moved to reverend pity, caused a sepulchre of bricks to be built, and there within buried the statue, and covered it with a broad slab of stone, that it might not in any way be injured. It has very many sweet beauties which the eyes alone can comprehend not, either by strong or tempered light; only the hand by touching them finds them out."

Hold out your hands to feel the luxury of the sunbeams. Press the soft blossoms against your cheek, and finger their graces of form, their delicate mutability of shape, their pliancy and freshness. Expose your face to the aerial floods that sweep the heavens, "inhale great draughts of space," wonder, wonder at the wind's unwearied activity. Pile note on note the infinite music that flows increasingly to your soul from the tactual sonorities of a thousand branches and tumbling waters. How can the world be shriveled when this most profound, emotional sense, touch, is faithful to its service? I am sure that if a fairy bade me choose between the sense of sight and that of touch, I would not part with the warm, endearing contact of human hands or the wealth of form, the nobility and fullness that press into my palms.

---

2. I found that of the senses, the eye is the most superficial, the ear the most arrogant, smell the most voluptuous, taste the most superstitious and fickle, touch the most profound and the most philosophical.

PART II

The poets have taught us how full of wonders is the night; and the night of blindness has its wonders, too. The only lightless dark is the night of ignorance and insensibility. We differ, blind and seeing, one from another, not in our senses, but in the use we make of them, in the imagination and courage with which we seek wisdom beyond our senses.

It is more difficult to teach ignorance to think than to teach an intelligent blind man to see the grandeur of Niagara. I have walked with people whose eyes are full of light, but who see nothing in wood, sea, or sky, nothing in city streets, nothing in books. What a witless masquerade is this seeing! It were better far to sail forever in the night of blindness, with sense and feeling and mind, than to be thus content with the mere act of seeing. They have sunset, the morning skies, the purple of distant hills, yet their souls voyage through this enchanted world with a barren stare.

The calamity of the blind is immense, irreparable. But it does not take away our share of the things that count—service, friendship, humor, imagination, wisdom. It is the secret inner will that controls one's fate. We are capable of willing to be good, of loving and being loved, of thinking to the end that we may be wiser. We possess these spirit-born forces equally with all God's children. Therefore we, too, see the lightnings and hear the thunders of Sinai. We, too, march through the wilderness and the solitary place that shall be glad for us, and we pass, God maketh the desert to blossom like the rose. We, too, go in unto the Promised Land to possess the treasures of the spirit, the unseen permanence of life and nature.

The blind man of spirit faces the unknown and grapples with it, and what else does the world of seeing men do? He has imagination, sympathy, humanity, and these ineradicable existences compel him to share by a sort of proxy in a sense he has not. When he meets terms of color, light, physiognomy, he guesses, divines, puzzles out their meaning by analogies drawn from the senses he has. I naturally tend to think, reason draw inferences as if I had five senses instead of three. This tendency is beyond my control; it is involuntary, habitual, instinctive. I cannot compel my mind to say "I feel" instead of "I see" or "I hear." The word "feel" proves on examination to be no less a convention than "see" and "hear" when I seek for words accurately to describe the outward things that affect my three bodily senses. When a man loses a leg, his brain persists in impelling him to use what he has not and yet feels to be there. Can it be that the brain is so constituted that it will continue the activity which animates the sight and the hearing after the eye and the ear have been destroyed?

The Senses Complementary

It might seem that the five senses would work intelligently together only when resident in the same body. Yet when two or three are left unaided, they reach out for their complements in another body, and find that they yoke easily with the borrowed team. When my hand aches from overtouching, I find relief in the sight of another. When my mind lags, wearied with the strain of forcing out thoughts about dark, musicless, colorless, detached substance, it recovers its elasticity as soon as I resort to the powers of another mind which commands light, harmony, color. Now, if the five senses will not remain disassociated, the life of the deaf-blind cannot be severed from the life of the seeing, hearing race.

The deaf-blind person may be plunged and replunged like Schiller's diver into seas of the unknown. But, unlike the doomed hero, he returns triumphant, grasping the priceless truth that his mind is not crippled, not limited to the infirmity of his senses. The world of the eye and the ear becomes to him a subject of fateful interest. He seizes every word of sight and hearing because his sensations compel it. Light and color, of which he has no tactual evidence, he studies fearlessly, believing that all humanly knowable truth is open to him. He is in a position similar to that of the astronomer who, firm, patient, watches a star night after night for many years and feels rewarded if he discovers a single fact about it. The man deaf-blind to ordinary outward things, and the man deaf-blind to the immeasurable universe, are both limited by time and space; but they have made a compact to wring service from their limitations.

The bulk of the world's knowledge is an imaginary construction. History is but a mode of imagining, of making us see civilizations that no longer appear upon the earth. Some of the most significant discoveries in modern science owe their origin to the imagination of men who had neither accurate knowledge nor exact instruments to demonstrate their beliefs. If astronomy had not kept always in advance of the telescope, no one would have thought a telescope worth making. What great invention has not existed in the inventor's mind long before he gave it tangible shape?

A more splendid example of imaginative knowledge is the unity with which philosophers start their study of the world. They can never perceive the world in its entire reality. Yet their imagination, with its magnificent allowance for error, its power of treating uncertainty as negligible, has pointed the way for empirical knowledge.

In their highest creative moment the great poet, the great musician cease to use the crude instruments of sight and hearing. They break away from their sense-moorings, rise on strong, compelling wings of spirit far above our misty hills and darkened valleys into the region of light, music, intellect.

What eye hath seen the glories of the New Jerusalem? What ear hath heard the music of the spheres, the steps of time, the strokes of chance, the blows of death? Men have not heard with their physical sense the tumult of sweet voices above the hills of Judea nor seen the heavenly vision; but millions have listened to that spiritual message through many ages.

Our blindness changes not a whit the course of inner realities. Of us it is as true as it is of the seeing that the most beautiful world is always entered through the imagination. If you wish to be something that you are not,—something fine, noble, good,—you shut your eyes, and for one dreamy moment you are that which you long to be.

INWARD VISIONS OF BEAUTY

According to all art, all nature, all coherent human thought, we know that order, proportion, form, are the essential elements of beauty. Now order, proportion, and form, are palpable to the touch. But beauty and rhythm are deeper than sense. They are like love and faith. They spring out of a spiritual process only slightly dependent upon sensations. Order, proportion, form, cannot generate in the mind the abstract idea of beauty, unless there is already a soul intelligence to breathe life into the elements. Many persons, having perfect eyes, are blind in their perceptions. Many persons, having perfect ears, are emotionally deaf. Yet these are the very ones who dare to set limits to the vision of those who, lacking a sense or two, have will, soul, passion, imagination. Faith is a mockery if it teaches us not that we may construct a world unspeakably more complete and beautiful, than the material world. And I, too, may construct my better world, for I am a child of God, an inheritor of a fragment of the Mind that created all worlds.

There is a consonance of all things, a blending of all that we know about the material world and the spiritual. It consists for me of all the impressions, vibrations, heat, cold, taste, smell, and the sensations which these convey to the mind, infinitely combined, interwoven with associated ideas and acquired knowledge. No thoughtful person will believe that what I said about the meanings of footsteps is strictly true of mere jolts and jars. It is an array of the spiritual in certain natural elements, tactual beats, and an acquired knowledge of physical habits and moral traits of highly organized human beings. What would odors signify if they were not associated with the time of the year, the place I live in, and the people I know?

The result of such a blending is sometimes a discordant trying of strings far removed from a melody, very far from a symphony. (For the benefit of those who must be reassured, I will say that I have felt a musician tuning his violin, that I have read about a symphony, and so have a fair intellectual perception of my metaphor.) But with training and experience the faculties gather up the stray notes and combine them into a full, harmonious whole. If the person who accomplishes this task is peculiarly gifted, we call him a poet. The blind and the deaf are not great poets, it is true. Yet now and again you find one deaf and blind who has attained to his royal kingdom of beauty.

Blind Poets

I have a little volume of poems by a deaf-blind lady, Madame Bertha Galeron. Her poetry has versatility of thought. Now it is tender and sweet, now full of tragic passion and the sternness of destiny. Victor Hugo called her "*La Grande Voyante*." She has written a comedy and two dramas which have been acted in Paris. The French Academy has crowned her work.

The infinite wonders of the universe are revealed to us in exact measure as we are capable of receiving them. The keenness of our vision depends not on how much we can see, but on how much we feel. Nor yet does mere knowledge create beauty. Nature sings her most exquisite songs to those who love her. She does not unfold her secrets to those who come only to gratify their desire of analysis, to gather facts, but to those who see in her manifold phenomena suggestions of lofty, delicate sentiments.

Am I to be denied the use of such adjectives as "freshness" and "sparkle," "dark" and "gloomy"? I have walked in the fields at early morning. I have felt a rose-bush laden with dew and fragrance. I have felt the curves and graces of my kitten at play. I have known the sweet, shy ways of little children. I have known the sad opposites of all these, a ghastly touch picture. Remember, I have sometimes traveled over a dusty road as far as my feet could go. At a sudden turn I have stepped upon starved, ignoble weeds, and reaching out my hands, I have touched a fair tree of which a parasite had taken the life like a vampire. I have touched a pretty little bird whose soft wings hung limp, whose little heart beat no more. I have wept over the feebleness and deformity of a child, lame, or born blind, or, worse still, mindless. If I had the genius of Thomson, I, too, could depict a "City of Dreadful Night" from mere touch sensations. From contrasts so irreconcilable can we fail form an idea of beauty and know surely when we meet with loveliness?

Here is a sonnet eloquent of a blind man's power of vision.

THE MOUNTAIN TO THE PINE

Thou tall, majestic monarch of the wood,
  That standest where no wild vines dare to creep,
  Men call thee old, and say that thou has stood
  A century upon my rugged steep;
Yet unto me thy life is but a day,
  When I recall the things that I have seen,—
  The forest monarchs that have passed away
  Upon the spot where first I saw thy green;
For I am older than the age of man,
  Or all the living things that crawl or creep,
  Or birds of air, or creatures of the deep;
I was the first dim outline of God's plan:
  Only the waters of the restless sea
  And the infinite stars in heaven are old to me.

I am glad my friend Mr. Stedman knew that poem while he was making his anthology, for knowing it, so fine a poet and critic could not fail to give it a place in his treasure-house of American poetry. The poet, Mr. Clarence Hawkes, has been blind since childhood; yet he finds in nature hints of combinations of his mental pictures. Out of the knowledge and impressions that come to him he constructs a masterpiece which hangs upon the walls of his thought. And into the poet's house come all the true spirits of the world.

It was a rare poet who thought of the mountain as "the first dim outline of God's plan." That is the real wonder of the poem, and not that a blind man should speak so confidently of sky and sea. Our ideas of the sky are an accumulation of touch-glimpses, literary allusions, and the observations of others, with an emotional blending of all. My face feels only a tiny portion of the atmosphere; but I go through continuous space and feel the air at every point, every instant. I have been told about the distances from our earth to the sun, to the other planets, and to the fixed stars. I multiply a thousand times the utmost height and width that my touch compasses, and thus I gain a deep sense of the sky's immensity.

Move me along constantly over water, water, nothing but water, and you give me the solitude, the vastness of ocean which fills the eye. I have been in a little sailboat on the sea, when the rising tide swept it toward the shore. May I not understand the poet's figure: "The green of spring overflows the earth like a tide?" I have felt the flame of a candle blow and flutter in the breeze. May I not then, say: "Myriads of fireflies flit hither and thither in the dew-wet grass like little fluttering tapers"?

Combine the endless space of air, the sun's warmth, the prevalence of fitful odors, the clouds that are described to my understanding spirit, the frequent breaking through the soil of a brook or the expanse of the wind-ruffled lake, the tactual undulation of the hills, which I recall when I am far away from them, the towering trees upon trees as I walk by them, the bearings that I try to keep while others tell me the directions of various points of the scenery, and you will begin to feel surer of my mental landscape. The utmost bound to which my thought will go with clearness is the horizon of my mind. From this horizon I imagine the one which the eye marks.

Touch cannot bridge distance,—it is fit only for the contact of surfaces,—but thought leaps the chasm. For this reason I am able to use words descriptive of objects distant from my senses. I have felt the rondure of the infant's tender form. I can apply this perception to the landscape and to the far-off hills.

Analogies in Sense Perception

I have not touched the outline of a star nor the glory of the moon, but I believe that God has set two lights in my mind, the greater to rule by day and the lesser by night, and by them I know that I am able to navigate my life-bark, as certain of reaching the haven as he who steers by the North Star. Perhaps my sun shines not as yours. The colors that glorify my world, the blue of the sky, the green of the fields, may not correspond exactly with those you delight in; but they are none the less color to me. The sun does not shine for my physical eyes, nor does the lightning flash, nor do the trees turn green in the spring; but they have not therefore ceased to exist, any more than the landscape is annihilated when you turn your back on it.

I understand how scarlet can differ from crimson because I know that the smell of an orange is not the smell of a grape-fruit. I can also conceive that colors have shades, and guess what shades are. In smell and taste there are varieties not broad enough to be fundamental; so I call them shades. There are half a dozen roses near me. They all have the unmistakable rose scent; yet my nose tells me that they are not the same. The American Beauty is distinct from the Jacqueminot and the La France. Odors in certain grasses fade as really to my sense as certain colors do to yours in the sun. The freshness of a flower in my hand is analogous to the freshness I taste in an apple newly picked. I make use of analogies like these to enlarge my conceptions of colors. Some analogies which I draw between qualities in surface and vibration, taste and smell, are drawn by others between sight, hearing, and touch. This fact encourages me to persevere, to try to bridge the gap between the eye and the hand.

Certainly I get far enough to sympathize with the delight that my kind feel in beauty they see and harmony they hear. This bond between humanity and me is worth keeping, even if the ideas on which I base it prove erroneous.

Sweet, beautiful vibrations exist for my touch, even though they travel through other substances than air to reach me. So I imagine sweet, delightful sounds, and the artistic arrangement of them which is called music, and I remember that they travel through the air to the ear, conveying impressions somewhat like mine. I also know what tones are since they are perceptible tactually in a voice. Now, heat varies greatly in the sun, in the fire, in hands, and in fur of animals. Indeed, there is such a thing for me as a cold sun. So I think of the varieties of light that touch the eye, cold and warm, vivid and dim, soft and glaring, and I imagine their passage through the air to an extensive sense, instead of to a narrow one like touch. From the experience I have had with voices I guess how the eye distinguishes shades in the midst of light. While I read the lips of a woman whose voice is soprano, I note a low tone or a glad tone in the midst of a high, flowing voice. When I feel my cheeks hot, I know that I am red. I have talked so much and read so much about colors that through no will of my own I attach meanings to them, just as all people attach certain meanings to abstract terms like hope, idealism, monotheism, intellect, which cannot be represented truly by visible objects, but which are understood from analogies between immaterial concepts and the ideas they awaken of external things. The force of association drives me to say that white is exalted and pure, green is exuberant, red suggests love or shame or strength. Without the color or its equivalent, life to me would be dark, barren, a vast blackness.

How Concepts Are Completed

Thus through an inner law of completeness my thoughts are not permitted to remain colorless. It strains my mind to separate color and sounds from objects. Since my education began I have always had things described to me with their colors and sounds by one with keen senses and a fine feeling for the significant. Therefore I habitually think of things as colored and resonant. Habit accounts for part. The soul sense accounts for another part. The brain with its five-sensed construction asserts its rights and accounts for the rest. Inclusive of all, the unity of the world demands that color be kept in it, whether I have cognizance of it or not. Rather than be shut out. I take part in it by discussing it, imagining it, happy in the happiness of those near me who gaze at the lovely hues of the sunset or the rainbow.

My hand has its share in this multiple knowledge, but it must never be forgotten that with the fingers I see only a very small portion of a surface, and that I must pass my hand continually over it before my touch grasps the whole. It is still more important, however, to remember that my imagination is not tethered to certain points, locations, and distances. It puts all the parts together simultaneously as if it saw or knew instead of feeling them. Though I feel only a small part of my horse at a time,—my horse is nervous and does not submit to manual explorations,—yet, because I have many times felt hock, nose, hoof and mane, I can see the steeds of Phoebus Apollo coursing the heavens.

With such a power active it is impossible that my thought should be vague, indistinct. It must needs be potent, definite. This is really a corollary of the philosophical truth that the real world exists only for the mind. That is to say, I can never touch the world in its entirety; indeed, I touch less of it than the portion that others see or hear. But all creatures, all objects, pass into my brain entire, and occupy the same extent there that they do in material space. I declare that for me branched thoughts, instead of pines, wave, sway rustle, make musical the ridges of mountains rising summit upon summit. Mention a rose too far away for me to smell it. Straightway a scent steals into my nostril, a form presses against my palm in all its dilating softness, with rounded petals, slightly curled edges, curving stem, leaves drooping. When I would fain view the world as a whole it rushes into vision—man, beast, bird, reptile, fly, sky, ocean, mountains, plain, rock, pebble. The warmth of life, the reality of creation is over all—the throb of human hands, the glossiness of fur, lithe windings of long bodies, poignant buzzing of insects, the ruggedness of the steeps as I climb them, the liquid mobility and boom of waves upon the rocks. Strange to say, try as I may, I cannot force my touch to pervade this universe in all directions. The moment I try, the whole vanishes; only small objects or narrow portions of a surface, mere touch-signs, a chaos of things scattered at random, remain. No thrill, no delight is excited thereby, Restore to the artistic, comprehensive internal sense its rightful domain, and you give me joy which best proves the reality.

Before the Spiritual Awakening

Before my teacher came to me, I did not know that I am. I lived in a world that was a no-world. I cannot hope to describe adequately that unconscious, yet conscious time of nothingness. I did not know that I knew aught, or that I lived or acted or desired. I had neither will nor intellect. I was carried along to objects and acts by a certain blind natural impetus. I had a mind which caused me to feel anger, satisfaction, desire. These two facts led those about me to suppose that I willed and thought. I can remember all this, not because I knew that it was so but because I have tactual memory. It enables me to remember that I never contracted my forehead in the act of thinking. I never viewed anything beforehand or chose it. I also recall tactually the fact that never in a start of the body or a heart-beat did I feel that I loved or cared for anything. My inner life, then, was a blank without past, present, or future without hope or anticipation, without wonder or joy of faith.

> It was not night—it was not day,
>
> . . .
>
> But vacancy absorbing space,
> And fixedness, without a place;
> There were no stars—no earth—no time—
> No check—no change—no good—no crime.

My dormant being had no idea of God or immortality, or fear of death.

I remember, also through touch, that I had a power of association. I felt tactual jars like the stamp of a foot, the opening of a window or its closing, the slam of a door. After repeatedly smelling rain and feeling the discomfort of wetness, I acted like those about me: I ran to shut the window. But that was not thought in any sense. It was the same kind of association that makes animals take shelter from the rain. From the same instinct of "aping" others, I folded the clothes that came from the laundry, and put mine away, fed the turkeys, sewed bead-eyes on my doll's face, and did many other things of which I have tactual remembrance. When I wanted anything I liked,—ice-cream, for instance, of which I was very fond,—I had a delicious taste on my tongue (which, by the way, I never have now), and in my hand I felt the turning of the freezer. I made the sign, and my mother knew I wanted ice-cream. I "thought" and desired in my fingers. If I had made a man, I should certainly have put the brain and soul in his finger-tips. From reminiscences like these I conclude that it is the opening of the two faculties, freedom of will, or choice, and rationality, or the power of thinking from one thing to another, which makes it possible to come into being first as a child, afterward as a man.

Since I had no power of thought, I did not compare one mental state with another. So I was not conscious of any change or process going on in my brain when my teacher began to instruct me. I merely felt keen delight in obtaining more easily what I wanted by means of the finger motions she taught me. I thought only of objects, and only objects I wanted. It was the turning of the freezer on a larger scale. When I learned the meaning of "I" and "me" and found that I was something, I began to think. Then consciousness first existed for me. Thus it was not the sense of touch that brought me knowledge. It was the awakening of my soul that first rendered my senses their value, their cognizance of objects, names, qualifications, and properties. Thought made me conscious of love, joy, and all the emotions. I was eager to know, then to understand, afterward to reflect on what I knew and understood, and the blind impetus, which had before driven me hither and thither at the dictates of my sensations, vanished forever.

I cannot represent more clearly than any one else the gradual and subtle changes from first impressions to abstract ideas. But I know that my physical ideas, that is, ideas derived from material objects, appear to me first in ideas similar to those of touch. Instantly they pass into intellectual meanings. Afterward the meaning finds expression in what is called "inner speech." When I was a child, my inner speech was inner spelling. Although I am even now frequently caught spelling to myself on my fingers, yet I talk to myself, too, with my lips, and it is true that when I first learned to speak, my mind discarded the finger-symbols and began to articulate. However, when I try to recall what some one has said to me, I am conscious of a hand spelling into mine.

The World Alive

It has often been asked what were my earliest impressions of the world in which I found myself. But one who thinks at all of his first impressions knows what a riddle this is. Our impressions grow and change unnoticed, so that what we suppose we thought as children may be quite different from what we actually experienced in our childhood. I only know that after my education began the world which came within my reach was all alive. I spelled to my blocks and my dogs. I sympathized with plants when the flowers were picked, because I thought it hurt them, and that they grieved for their lost blossoms. It was years before I could be made to believe that my dogs did not understand what I said, and I always apologized to them when I ran into or stepped on them.

As my experiences broadened and deepened, the indeterminate, poetic feelings of childhood began to fix themselves in definite thoughts. Nature— the world I could touch—was folded and filled with myself. I am inclined to believe those philosophers who declare that we know nothing but our own feelings and ideas. With a little ingenious reasoning one may see in the material world simply a mirror, an image of permanent mental sensations. In either sphere self-knowledge is the condition and the limit of our consciousness. That is why, perhaps, many people know so little about what is beyond their short range of experience. They look within themselves—and find nothing! Therefore they conclude that there is nothing outside themselves, either.

However that may be, I came later to look for an image of my emotions and sensations in others. I had to learn the outward signs of inward feelings. The start of fear, the suppressed, controlled tensity of pain, the beat of happy muscles in others, had to be perceived and compared with my own experiences before I could trace them back to the intangible soul of another. Groping, uncertain, I at last found my identity, and after seeing my thoughts and feelings repeated in others, I gradually constructed my world of men and of God. As I read and study, I find that this is what the rest of the race has done. Man looks within himself and in time finds the measure and the meaning of the universe.

THE UNITY OF THE RACE

So, in the midst of life, eager, imperious life, the deaf-blind child, fettered to the bare rock of circumstance, spider-like, sends out gossamer threads of thought into the measureless void that surrounds him. Patiently he explores the dark, until he builds up a knowledge of the world he lives in, and his soul meets the beauty of the world, where the sun shines always, and the birds sing. To the blind child the dark is kindly. In it he finds nothing extraordinary or terrible. It is his familiar world; even the groping from place to place, the halting steps, the dependence upon others, do not seem strange to him. He does not know the countless pleasures that the dark shuts out from him. Not until he weighs his life in the scale of others' experience does he realize what it is to live forever in the dark. But the knowledge that teaches him this bitterness also brings its consolation—spiritual light, the promise of the day that shall be.

The blind child—the deaf-blind child—has inherited the mind of seeing and hearing ancestors—a mind measured to five senses. Therefore he must be influenced, even if it be unknown to himself, by the light, color, song which have been transmitted through the language he is taught, for the chambers of the mind are ready to receive that language. The brain of the race is so permeated with color that it dyes even the speech of the blind. Every object I think of is stained with the hue that belongs to it by association and memory. The experience of the deaf-blind person, in a world of seeing, hearing people, is like that of a sailor on an island where the inhabitants speak a language unknown to him, whose life is unlike that he has lived. He is one, they are many; there is no chance of compromise. He must learn to see with their eyes, to hear with their ears, to think their thoughts, to follow their ideals.

If the dark, silent world which surrounds him were essentially different from the sunlit, resonant world, it would be incomprehensible to his kind, and could never be discussed. If his feelings and sensations were fundamentally different from those of others, they would be inconceivable except to those who had similar sensations and feelings. If the mental consciousness of the deaf-blind person were absolutely dissimilar to that of his fellows, he would have no means of imagining what they think. Since the mind of the sightless is essentially the same as that of the seeing in that it admits of no lack, it must supply some sort of equivalent for missing physical sensations. It must perceive a likeness between things outward and things inward, a correspondence between the seen and the unseen. I make use of such a correspondence in many relations, and no matter how far I pursue it to things I cannot see, it does not break under the test.

Unity of the Inner and Outer Worlds

As a mere hypothesis, correspondence is adequate to all life, through the whole range of phenomena. The flash of thought and its swiftness explain the lightning flash and the sweep of a comet through the heavens. My mental sky opens to me the vast celestial spaces, and I proceed to fill them with the images of my spiritual stars. I recognize truth by the clearness and guidance that it gives my thought, and, knowing what that clearness is, I can imagine what light is to the eye. It is not a convention of language, but a forcible feeling of the reality, that at times makes me start when I say, "Oh, I see my mistake!" or "How dark, cheerless is his life!" I know these are metaphors. Still, I must prove with them, since there is nothing in our language to replace them. Deaf-blind metaphors to correspond do not exist and are not necessary. Because I can understand the word "reflect" figuratively, a mirror has never perplexed me. The manner in which my imagination perceives absent things enables me to see how glasses can magnify things, bring them nearer, or remove them farther.

Deny me this correspondence, this internal sense, confine me to the fragmentary incoherent touch-world, and lo, I become as a bat which wanders about on the wing. Suppose I omitted all odds of seeing, hearing, color, light, landscape, the thousand phenomena, instruments and beauties connected with them. I should suffer a great diminution of the wonder and delight in attaining knowledge; also—more dreadful loss—my emotions would be blunted, so that I could not be touched by things unseen.

Has anything arisen to disprove the adequacy of correspondence? Has any chamber of the blind man's brain been opened and found empty? Has any psychologist explored the mind of the sightless and been able to say, "There is no sensation here"?

I tread the solid earth; I breathe the scented air. Out of those two experiences

I form numberless associations and correspondences. I observe, I feel, I think, I imagine. I associate the countless varied impressions, experiences, concepts. Out of these materials Fancy, the cunning artisan of the brain, welds an image which the skeptic would deny me, because I cannot see with my physical eyes the changeful, lovely face of my thought-child. He would break the mind's mirror. This spirit-vandal would humble my soul and force me to bite the dust of material things. While I champ the bit of circumstance, he scourges and goads me with the spur of fact. If I heeded him, the sweet-visaged earth would vanish into nothing, and I should hold in my hand nought but an aimless, soulless lump of dead matter. But although the body physical is rooted alive to the Promethean rock, the spirit-proud huntress of the air will still pursue the shining, open highways of the universe.

MENTAL VISION NOT LIMITED BY BLINDNESS

Blindness has no limiting effect upon mental vision. My intellectual horizon is infinitely wide. The universe it encircles is immeasurable. Would they who bid me keep within the narrow bound of my meager senses demand of Herschel that he roof his stellar universe and give us back Plato's solid firmament of glassy spheres? Would they command Darwin from the grave and bid him blot out his geological time, give us back a paltry few thousand years? Oh, the supercilious doubters! They ever strive to clip the upward daring wings of the spirit.

A person deprived of one or more senses is not, as many seem to think, turned out into a trackless wilderness without landmark or guide. The blind man carries with him into his dark environment all the faculties essential to the apprehension of the visible world whose door is closed behind him. He finds his surroundings everywhere homogeneous with those of the sunlit world; for there is an inexhaustible ocean of likenesses between the world within, and the world without, and these likenesses, these correspondences, he finds equal to every exigency his life offers.

The necessity of some such thing as correspondence or symbolism appears more and more urgent as we consider the duties that religion and philosophy enjoin upon us.

THE SANCTION OF RELIGION AND PHILOSOPHY

The blind are expected to read the Bible as a means of attaining spiritual happiness. Now, the Bible is filled throughout with references to clouds, stars, colors, and beauty, and often the mention of these is essential to the meaning of the parable or the message in which they occur. Here one must needs see the inconsistency of people who believe in the Bible, and yet deny us a right to talk about what we do not see, and for that matter what *they* do not see, either. Who shall forbid my heart to sing: "Yea, he did fly upon the wings of the wind. He made darkness his secret place; His pavilion round about him were dark waters and thick clouds of the skies."

Philosophy constantly points out the untrustworthiness of the five senses and the important work of reason which corrects the errors of sight and reveals its illusions. If we cannot depend on five senses, how much less may we rely on three! What ground have we for discarding light, sound, and color as an integral part of our world? How are we to know that they have ceased to exist for us? We must take their reality for granted, even as the philosopher assumes the reality of the world without being able to see it physically as a whole.

Ancient philosophy offers an argument which seems still valid. There is in the blind as in the seeing an Absolute which gives truth to what we know to be true, order to what is orderly, beauty to the beautiful, touchableness to what is tangible. If this is granted, it follows that this Absolute is not imperfect, incomplete, partial. It must needs go beyond the limited evidence of our sensations, and also give light to what is invisible, music to the musical that silence dulls. Thus mind itself compels us to acknowledge that we are in a world of intellectual order, beauty, and harmony. The essences, or absolutes of these ideas, necessarily dispel their opposites which belong with evil, disorder, and discord. Thus deafness and blindness do not exist in the immaterial mind, which is philosophically the real world, but are banished with the perishable material senses. Reality, of which visible things are the symbol, shines before my mind. While I walk about my chamber with unsteady steps, my spirit sweeps skyward on eagle wings and looks out with unquenchable vision upon the world of eternal beauty.

Nature's Storehouse of Health

Good Housekeeping, January 1933, pp. 38-39, 140-142.

Editor's note: Helen Keller attended the Wright-Humason School for the Deaf in New York City from 1894-1896.

I like to tell new friends about the day I "saw" the Duke of Marlborough arrested for speeding on his bicycle. I was riding horseback in Central Park, New York City, with my teacher, Mrs. Anne Sullivan Macy, when we suddenly came upon an excited crowd. In the center was a policeman talking to a handsome man who was holding on to a bicycle.

In those days of the middle nineties it was not unusual for a cyclist to be arrested for speeding by some watchful park policeman eager to protect the public from those dangerous wind-scorchers. But this seemed to be something special.

As teacher related it to me, the policeman said in a rather broad brogue:

"And what do you mean endangering the lives and limbs of pedestrians by whirling along here at such a rate of speed? Say, where's the fire? And who do you think you are, anyway?"

"Why—er—I'm the Duke of Marlborough," stammered the lawbreaker, embarrassed and ill at ease.

"So, you're the Duke of Marlborough, are you?" the patrolman smiled cynically. "And here I thought sure you was the Queen of Sheba. Well, you'll have to tell it to the judge."

But, sure enough, it was the Duke of Marlborough, who was in this country for his marriage to Miss Consuela Vanderbilt. The crisp morning had given him an excess of exuberance which he had transferred to the pedals of his bicycle.

Perhaps, through the years, I have come to exaggerate the repartee of the noble guardian of the law, but the essential facts are true. At any rate, I have always thought it an amusing story because of the rank of the gentleman involved, and because of the rather striking contrast with our own motor age. But when I tell it, my new friends pass over these points and ask in great surprise,

"But, Miss Keller, did we understand you to say you were riding horseback in Central Park?"

I can understand their amazement, for it is rather strange that one who is blind should choose horseback riding as a sport.

I am partial to those forms of physical exercise and recreation which bring me into direct contact with nature. I have always the feeling that nature has the power to renew and refresh our minds, our bodies, and our spirits. One of the few quarrels I have with modern life is that it has removed us too far from a direct contact with nature. That, I am afraid, is particularly true in the case of women— in smaller communities as well as in cities. A large amount of freedom has come to women through the simplification of household tasks, but I believe that too much of this leisure flows into purely social, and even intellectual, activities. Bridge parties, club meetings, community service certainly should occupy an important part of a woman's life, but not to the exclusion of those physical activities which mean so much to bodily and mental health.

I am myself a sociable creature. I like parties and companionship and mental activity. I like the few competitive games in which I can indulge—chess and checkers, for instance, which I play with special sets. And I like my own little private card parties—a game of solitaire with marked cards. I like to sit with friends about a pot of tea. But periodically I feel that tug toward nature— the call of meadow and woods and flowing water, the friendly beckoning of dogs and horses and all that host of nature's creatures more primitive than ourselves.

The tug of nature that I feel is not unusual in view of the fact that until I was seven years old I was a primitive creature. I could neither see nor hear. Human qualities in me were not highly developed. So many of my contacts were with the manifestations of nature, and with the animals on our Alabama farm—with the fowls of the barnyard, the horses, the dogs, with trees and fields and meadows. And these were as real to me as human beings. When my teacher began to teach me language, and to explain the marvels around me, my friendship for all phases of nature kept pace with my curiosity. This interest inspired me to scurry about, even to the point of climbing trees, and made my little body strong and active. And I am convinced that it is my abiding friendship with nature which has kept me unusually healthy throughout my life, for this fellow feeling with nature enters into most of my physical activities.

When I ride horseback, it is not merely as a sport, but also as a sort of communion with nature. I feel about me the beauties of the park or the quiet country road. I like to place my hand on my horse's neck and feel the powerful ripple of his muscles. My mind is transported back to the pony of my childhood. (It is one of the compensations of blindness that sight can not interfere with imaginings.) I am imbued with a sense of physical and mental well-being.

So, in walking or swimming or rowing, I am always conscious of that oneness with nature, and this feeling is a beautiful complement to the sense of health and physical well-being which I derive from exercise. I know people who walk or swim or ride as a social activity or as a burdensome duty to their bodies. If only they could see in these physical activities a soothing union with Mother Nature, they would gain in mind and spirit as well as health, and a task would become a keenly anticipated pleasure.

There was a day not so long ago when the duties of housekeeping provided strenuous physical activity for women, but the demands of household duties are gradually becoming fewer, so that the problem of physical exercise is growing increasingly important. The younger generation, of course, has a penchant for athletics, but mothers of this younger generation are inclined to be neglectful except when the looming specter of increasing avoirdupois sends them scampering into a series of calisthenic contortions designed to lay the ghost.

So I take up the cudgels for the natural forms of physical exercise, which carry with them a strong mental and physical medicine. Perhaps I am prejudiced in their favor because my own participation in such exercises gives me peculiar satisfaction.

The fact that I am possessed of only three of the five senses really makes me even more eager to engage in normal physical activities and thus reduce the margin which separates me from the world of other people. Furthermore, living as I do in silent darkness, cut off from all sensations of light and sound, my recreational requirements are perhaps greater than those of normal persons.

The handicapped, particularly those without sight and hearing, are inclined to live too much in the mind, too much within themselves. They are imprisoned, and necessarily restricted in their contacts with the workaday world. That is why so many of them are drawn to brooding; their attention is centered so largely on the narrow world of themselves. They have fewer means of distraction and recreation. That is all the more reason why physical activities and well-being should play so large a role in the lives of those who do not see and hear.

It is difficult for those who see to realize the part sight plays in keeping the mind resilient. You walk down the street. You see people moving about; your eye beholds a pretty girl, a handsome man, the smiling face of a baby, a frisky dog, or a beautiful tree. Your mind is distracted and refreshed. The blind are led down the same street, and their minds go along at the same level. So they must find other means of ripping away the bars which shut them off from the physical world. They must touch, or taste, or smell. But the two senses which I do not have—sight and hearing—are those which are most used to maintain contact with the world and keep the mind healthy. Therefore, to the blind, some form of physical activity is necessary, not only for its healthful effect on the body, but to keep the mind bright and active as well.

When I ride horseback, or when I swim, my whole being is thrown eagerly into these sports. They mean complete mental relaxation as well as physical exercise.

We who live in darkness and silence are very appreciative of those contacts we have. The physical world is perhaps more wondrous to us than to those who see it and take it for granted. In like manner, the glow of health, the activity of the body in exercise, is perhaps more keenly felt by us than by those who have so many other interests in this fascinating world. At least we can enjoy the same physical vitality and well-being as other people.

But even in our exercise we are in some degree restricted. The whole interesting range of competitive sports which require sight are closed to us, as participants or spectators. We are limited to those forms of physical activity which we can perform ourselves. But it is really no great problem for a blind and deaf person to obtain enough exercise to keep in good health if he can conquer the timidity and fear which so often accompanies his condition.

The most obvious means, of course, is calisthenics. Here again, however, we are restricted to those which do not involve that part of the sense of equilibrium dependent upon sight. But we are not hindered from such exercises as lying frontward on the floor and lifting ourselves by pushing on the hands; lying on our backs and lifting first our legs, then our torsos; and similar movements. Then there are such effective devices as rowing machines and electric horses, but I prefer the more natural methods of rowing in real water and riding a real horse.

Rowing is one of my favorite sports, even if I am inclined to splash my companions now and then. Of course, I must have at least one companion to take care of the intricacies of navigation while I furnish the power. My teacher was the martyr to my first splashings. It required a little time to learn the proper angle at which to hold and dip the oars. There were many stops while Teacher patiently corrected my awkwardness. But soon I got the stroke rhythm, and when I was able to propel the boat smoothly, I experienced that thrilling sense of freedom in which the blind delight.

If I am left to my own devices, I naturally row in a circle, but with another rower to correct the errors of my circular navigation, I can do quite well. I am fond of rowing, and I take every opportunity to do it. My favorite rowing place is Long Lake in the Adirondacks.

There is really no logical reason why I should have any favorite place, for the blind are fortunate in the condition that one place is much like another, and they can imagine what they please about any place. On a prosaic pond I can imagine myself in the most beautiful and romantic surroundings, and there is no disillusionment. I can "see" the banks lined with tall trees and fascinatingly dark undergrowth. I can "see" the flashing glint of sun on water, and I can "see" the scurrying of graceful fish even where no fish exist. Now and then I rest my oars and trail my hand in the delightful coolness of rippling water; and I feel the soothing breeze on my cheek. I like to feel the play of my muscles as I row. I am filled with a sense of physical power and well-being. I experience a sense of freedom, and of oneness with the primitiveness of man and nature.

I have something of the same sort of feeling when I swim and ride horseback. My first swimming lessons were at Wrentham when I was twelve years old. My friends were surprised, and even a bit alarmed, when I expressed the desire to learn to swim, but I was determined to learn to do as many as possible of the things that normal people did. I went through the usual stages of the beginner, except that I had to be informed more fully of just what I was supposed to do, for I had never seen any one swim. Then I had to demonstrate just what I had learned by going through the motions on land. For a long time after I had mastered the strokes in the water, a rope was kept tied around me so that I could be hauled in at any moment. And even after I was graduated from this stage, it was necessary to have a long rope strung on poles or floats along my swimming course. Most people exert more pressure on one side than another, and without sight one soon loses direction and swims in a circle. But with the rope alongside me, I can reach out to touch it from time to time and thus hold my course. Once I stepped off into deep water and became confused, and had to be dragged in.

To me there is an inspiring exultation in swimming. One seems to be conquering an element which seems at once strange and natural. The water admits you to itself, enfolds you, embraces you so gently, but it remains a constant challenge to your strength and skill. If you can not meet the test, you die. But I have never been afraid of water. It has always been friendly to me. It has provided me with thrilling pleasure and a sense of tingling health. My fondest memories of swimming are connected with the delightful vacations I spent years ago with Dr. Alexander Graham Bell and his daughters on the coast of Nova Scotia.

It was while I was preparing to enter Radcliffe College, Cambridge, Massachusetts, that I learned to ride a bicycle—a bicycle built for two. Naturally the blind can not ride a single seater bicycle. The tandem bicycle of those long ago years was a blessing to me. It was one of the few methods in those days by which one could get the feeling of speed which is so exhilarating to mankind.

I was taught to ride by Angelo, a famous trick bicycle rider of the vaudeville stage. I have often wondered what he did after his art became historical. Angelo and I did not try any tricks. We were quite happy to "burn the wind" at the terrific rate of twenty miles an hour.

It was not simple for me to learn. Many times Angelo had to exert all his skills to prevent the machine from toppling and flinging us into a ditch. I had to learn to balance myself properly, which is not easy because balance depends upon sight, and to accommodate myself to the motion. We adopted a series of signals by which Angelo informed me of sharp curves, stops and other maneuvers, but soon I was able to sense just what had to be done. I had several falls on the rough country roads of that day.

I am sorry that bicycle riding as a sport has passed. It was marvelous exercise, although it was an invented rather than a natural sport.

Horseback riding, however, which formerly was a means of getting some place, now survives almost entirely as a sport. I did my first real horseback riding in Central Park, New York City, thirty-five years ago. I was then attending the Wright-Humason School on 75th Street.

At that time, the principles of physical culture were not so well known as they are today; and women particularly, with the many restrictions that encompassed us, were behind in physical development. But I felt a real need of strenuous physical activity. Most of my days were spent in mental pursuits and in the exasperating process of learning to speak. It was a nerve-racking task, fatiguing to the mind. I craved the relaxation which comes through bodily activity, and frankly I preferred something with a slight measure of danger.

I persuaded Teacher to allow me to take riding lessons. Mr. Wright and Dr. Humason thought it dangerous for a deaf-blind girl to go cantering about the bridle paths of Central Park, but when they saw me ride on the tanbark they changed their minds, and it was arranged that Dr. Humason, who was a fine horseman, should accompany me during the trial period. Every morning, the two of us, usually accompanied by Teacher, would set out from Durland's Riding Academy at Columbus Circle, Broadway and 59th Street.

I had some practice in sitting a horse as a child when my father used to put me astride a pony on our Alabama farm. I liked to touch the silky coat of the pony and to feel him swaying rhythmically under me. I seemed to have some sort of bond of understanding with horses. They were my friends. So I was not long in feeling secure on a horse, even in those days of the side-saddle when a women rider repaired a good sense of equilibrium.

Naturally I did not ride high-strung horses, but I could handle a horse of some spirit reasonably well. Either Dr. Humason or Teacher held the leading rein, the only requirement being that the horses trot or gallop at about the same pace. Dr. Humason continued to ride with Teacher and me long after my novitiate was ended.

Those first rides in Central Park made a confirmed equestrienne of me, and after I left New York I always took every opportunity to ride. When we went to Hollywood in 1918 to make "Deliverance," which pictured the story of my life, I was delighted to find that in one sequence I was to ride a great white horse named Sligo. And during the making of the picture, which required six months, I had a horse named Peggy to ride, a sleek, spirited chestnut.

In these days I do not ride so frequently as I should like, but I devote myself more thoroughly to other forms of exercise. I am particularly fond of my early morning walk in the meadows near our home in Forest Hills, Long Island. That is a happy part of the day for me. Polly Thomson, my secretary, accompanies me. And as we walk, our dogs swarm about us. Yes, swarm—although there are only two dogs, the Great Dane, Helga, and Darkie, whose family shrine is enveloped by the heather of Scotland. Between them, with their racing and tumbling and leaping and chasing, they manage to give an authentic imitation of a considerable swarm. And at intervals, just to show that they are not allowing their exuberance of spirits to make them forgetful of loyalty, the low-slung, elongated Darkie will dash up and rub his nose against my ankle, and the noble Helga will ease her great head into my hand. Then they're off again for a romp, while Polly and I walk vigorously onward.

Perhaps there is no thrill so great as that which comes with a walk in the freshness of morning air. Though I do not see, I can feel earth's eager awakening after a night of rest. I can feel the first gentle rays of the sun, smiling, "Here we are again." I can feel the yielding softness of dew-freshened soil. The keen sweet smells of nature-in-the-morning stream about me. And the acuteness of smell so noticeable in the blind is some compensation for their sightlessness. (Luther Burbank was kind enough to tell me once that by touch and smell I could recognize and name plants and flowers more readily than most experts who had the use of their eyes as well.) Now and then I pick a flower or a stalk of grass and examine it with my fingers. Each is a new revelation of the wonders of nature.

It is so easy to begin the day's work after one of these stirring morning walks and a hearty breakfast. After lunch I often take a short nap, for I firmly believe that adequate sleep is one of the great medicines. Wholesome food (with a three-day diet of orange juice now and then), plenty of sleep in a well-ventilated room, invigorating exercise, and joy in work—these, in my opinion, are the elements which go to make up good health. It is no new formula, certainly, but apparently it is an often-neglected formula. Perhaps it is easier for me to follow the rules of health than it is for normal persons, because I do not have so many outside distractions to lead me astray.

To me it is so strange that many normal persons, particularly women, who have so much in life fail to abide by their part of the bargain which nature makes with them. Health follows the laws of balance and compensation. Nature makes a standing bargain with us. She says in effect:

"If you pay a reasonable amount of attention to your body, I shall give you a credit memorandum for health in precise proportion to your own efforts."

It is a fair bargain, but so many people try to cheat—they want something for nothing. Nature does not work on that plan. She is a stern and just creditor.

My own adherence to the plan of nature has proved its value. I enjoy far better health than that enjoyed by the average person. And it is this glowing physical health which has contributed so much to my mental health. It is so easy for the handicapped to become depressed, but there is no finer preventive for mental depression than physical well-being.

If I had neglected my body, I should have been conquered long ago. I am convinced that only because of my vigorous health have I been able to preserve a wholesome optimism in my world of darkness and silence.

The World Through Three Senses

Ladies' Home Journal, March 1951, pp. 54, 223-227

People often express surprise that I find life great and wonderful, when I have only three senses. From others' testimony I know that at the age of nineteen months I was exploring the world with five senses, playing, laughing and learning a few words. Then came the illness which deprived me of sight and hearing, and as a result of deafness I lost the ability to speak.

It was not possible for me to develop my remaining senses to a high degree without the stimuli that spring from speech and language, and that means that I was completely isolated. We use sight and hearing principally because from them we learn at once what goes on around us. Through the eye man acquires nine tenths of his experience. Through the spoken word and literature, hearing quickens his mental growth with information and ideas. In my case I was literally unworlded. Smell enabled me to find the fruit I especially loved—bananas; it directed me to the boxwood hedge out in my mother's garden. My nose could distinguish my clothes from those of the family when the laundry was brought home every week, and from imitation I put them away in the bureau. Wherever there was any cake or candy or ice cream I was sure to devour it. My mother wisely let me move about the house and the kitchen, and thus she preserved my health and appetite.

But, untaught, unstimulated, I acted and thought like a mere animal. I cannot convey verbally the state I was in—wrapped in a double silence, my own and that of others to me. I was not merely alone, I was a wild little creature.

The change which occurred after Anne Sullivan began my education still causes me to thrill and glow. It was not a child that confronted her, but an animal utterly ignorant of itself, its feelings and its place among human beings. For some time I was still devoid of a world—I had no sense of my own identity or time or unity or diversity, but Anne Sullivan did not let such details discourage her. She treated me exactly like a seeing, hearing child, substituting hand-spelling for the voice and the eye from which other children learn language. She encouraged me to observe all objects I could reach with my three senses, so that I could relate them bit by bit with the things which surrounded me and gain from them analogies with sight and hearing. She helped me to enrich my vocabulary through the flow of words from her fingers, through association and books to build a world in which color and sound took their place, even though I could not perceive them. That is how it happens that I am aware of sympathies with the seeing, hearing race.

Ideas constitute the world each of us lives in, and impressions are a wellspring of ideas. My outer world, wrought out of the sensations of touch, smell and taste, breathes and throbs because I have a thinking mind and a feeling soul. While others look and listen, I use my tactile faculty to secure information, entertainment and activity in which I have a share. In all I do and think I am conscious of a hand. People dependent upon their eyes and ears seldom realize how many things are tangible. Objects that can be touched are round or flat, broken or symmetrical, flexible or stiff, solid or liquid, and these qualities are modified ad infinitum.

Also I perceive the flow of straight and curved lines and their endless variety on all surfaces—regular or uneven, swelling, rough or smooth. In rocks full of grooves, jagged edges and lichens, in the queenliness of the rose and the velvet of a well-groomed horse's neck, the manifold shapes of young tress, bushes and grasses I find eloquent witness to the glory that once trickled into the seeing hand of the Greek, the Japanese and the South Sea Islander.

Again, with the skin of my face and nose I notice different atmospherical conditions according to the season, even at various hours of the same day and in different regions. For instance, in wintertime I recognize a cold sun, and the rain is chill and odorless. The rain of spring is warm, vital and fragrant. The air of midsummer is heavy and damp or dry and burning, and so the changes of weather go on.

Besides objects, surfaces and the weather, I perceive countless vibrations from which I learn much about everyday happenings. In the house I feel footsteps, noises of the broom, the hammer and the saw, the dishes as they are removed from the table, the excited bark of big Et Tu, my Alsatian, when somebody comes to the door. Footsteps vary tactually according to the age, the sex and the manners of the walker. The child's patter is unlike the tread of a grown person. The springy step of youth differs from the sedate walk of the middle-aged and from the gait of the old man whose feet drag along the floor. In persons whom I know well I detect many moods and traits in their walk—energy or laziness, firmness or hesitation, weariness, impatience or distress. Thus I am aware to some extent of the actions of those about me.

Perhaps I am working at the desk. A sportive breeze blows some papers off, and I jump up to recapture them, guided by the direction from which their flutter on the rug reaches me. A flat thud warns me that a book has fallen. The ring of an electric bell on the desk informs me that I am wanted downstairs. Other vibrations past enumerating speak to my fingers: the wind or rain rattling against the windows as I open or close them; the ring of the telephone when I am close to it; the tic-tac of a clock I touch; the swallowed gurgle of the playing hose; the pop of a champagne bottle opened quite near to me.

There are other vibrations which do not reach me through skin-touch. They enter my nerves and bones loudly or softly. The beat and roll of drums pass through me from the chest to the shoulder blades. The rhythmic vibration of a well-made train over a smooth road is pleasing to my body. There is fascination for me in the echoing thunder and the tremendous booming of the ocean upon the shore. And the organ, whose harmony resembles the onrush and retreat of sea waves, swells my act of feeling to rapture. What I said in The World I Live In is still true: "If music could be seen, I could point where the organ notes go, as they rise and fall, climb up and up, rock and sway, now loud and deep, now high and stormy, anon soft and solemn."

On the other hand, I am annoyed by discords like scraping, the creaking of old floors, and foghorns. I have had contacts with bridges which were being built, and I felt the blows of giant hammers, the rattle of masses of stone and other materials, the rumble of engines and the dumping of dirt cars. I have visited factories and war plants and sensed the clangor and uproar of machines horrible and brutal. I have been shaken by the crash of giant trees as they were felled to the earth, the concussion of huge logs sawed at lumber mills, explosions that follow blasting rocks in mines, the enormous clamor of switching freight trains and the roar of the airplane starting on its flight. At sea I have been pitched to and fro in a storm on a ship as it plowed foaming furrows through the water, and liquid mountains lashed its sides and tossed it aloft like a child's toy, it seemed to me, with devilish exultation. From all these vibrations I have gained my conception of war, earthquakes, tidal waves and raging forest fires.

Through touch, also, I know the gigantic traffic of New York, the grating of electric cars and busses, the tramping and pushing of crowds, the never-ceasing turmoil of the elevated railways and the subways. As I walk along, I am conscious, too, of exhalations from various shops—leather, new fabrics, hardware and drugs—from automobiles, fruit and vegetable stands, people and restaurants. By the odors of fresh lumber, stone and metal, I perceive that a new building is going up. For a while the city is full of interest and excitement for me, but after its enveloping noise and restlessness it is a physical relief to get back to the tactual quietness and peace of my country home.

When I work in my garden early mornings in spring and summer, my sensations are wide open to the "brightness, the spark and flame of the quick forge" of Nature's wonders. It is easy to trim by touch the grass down the driveway and around the trees, to remove stones that press upon the roots and to cut away vines that threaten to strangle other plants. I do not have to worry for fear my shears will murder the lusty pachysandra border, it is so unlike the slender blades of grass I cut. Having felt vines sprawling along the ground or seizing hold of any support with their tendrils, I do not mistake one of them for the foliage of a shrub. The tall, square-stemmed, coarse-leafed, rank weeds I pull up are not to be confused with ferns or delicate, feathery grasses through which the wind pipes tenderly. The malodorous ironweed is an enemy to which I give no quarter. But there are friendly messengers from the wild I love—black-eyed Susans, Queen Anne's lace and the clean, pungent tansy. It is to my sorrow that I have to clear them away from a flower bed or a border of mint. The clover is adorable and a welcome visitor on the lawn, but left too long in one spot, it builds exquisite yet formidable layers of root and stem, and reluctantly I sever it from the young grasses which must be given a chance.

The seasons always charm me as a succession of surprises. No matter how attentively I watch for their signs, they are never the same in odor or temperature. One day when I go out to clip grass it is frosty, and buds on tree and bush are still small and hard. A few days later I am at my outdoor work again, and lo, the maples are in leaf, the evergreens are beginning to put out soft new tips, the turf palpitates with promises of clover and dandelion. Soon the rosebushes and lilac trees are aflutter with fragrant little leaves that seem to my fingers cool distillations of dew and air. The time that passes varies before I discover one bush in flower, and, like wildfire, the blossoming spreads until the entire garden is a vast bouquet of indescribable loveliness. I cannot hear the orchestra of bird voices that those who have ears observe, but the trees and flowers amaze me with their endless changes. The pines and spruces from which I pluck away dead herbage drop pitch upon my hand, and I take that as tidings that summer is near. These palpable phenomena awaken in me a train of happy memories, so that the seasons of each year mean more to me than those of the year before. I can remember moments when I feel young azaleas atremble under my palm or sniff hyacinths, but it takes an evocative touch or scent for me to recover the emotion fully. Truly, as the carefree morning hours slip by, it is a heavenly privilege for me to exercise the faculties of meditation and understanding that empower one to live in the universe.

During the day I am absorbed by intense concentration on work at the desk and the sameness that ever-recurring demands for similar services create. It is to preserve my individuality and keep my three senses alert that I escape into the garden at dawn or soon afterward. Just to have the sweet soil, the grass and dew between my fingers refreshes and clears my mind.

On my walk by the cedar railing at home I have noticed that the pine emits different scents—one wet with rain, one dry in midsummer. Mosses have a distinct olfactory character hard to define.

"But how can you take such pleasure in walking?" I hear someone who has all of his faculties say. "We have all the colors of the landscape, the songs of birds, the ripple of streams, but you have only motion—placing one leg before the other, putting your feet on the ground in turn, lifting them again and stepping forward until intelligence revolts, and the motion ceases, as Rose Macaulay has written."

"Far from it!" I reply, amused.

The chief advantage of walking is the freedom of my mind to go on long excursions into philosophy. This is not a misfortune, I think, as several friends have said to me. It is as natural to man, even in a primitive state, to philosophize as it is to speak. I happen to be among those who can think most effectively on their legs. Happy solutions of my perplexities have sprung up spontaneously on a stroll, after vain attempts to disentangle them indoors. Braille is none other than a brave blind man's philosophy put into practice of overcoming obstacles.

My brain and three senses, certainly, are needed to note every detail of interest in a ramble—whether the path is hilly or flat, grass or gravel, rocks or sand or soft soil. By the shade on my face I can tell when I come to a wood or a thicket. A rush of warm air indicates that I am in an open, sunny glade. Where the road is familiar to me, I hold out my hand to examine the bark and foliage of trees, or gather wild flowers or pick berries.

There is for me a wind-sweet, high resonance in the thin, narrow leaves of willows, agitation in the fussy motions of birches and poplars and a rich, musical depth in the foliage of oaks. Firs and spruces impart to me serenity in the thought that, though the winds from every direction bend them this way and that, yet the straining roots do not loose their hold upon the rock, and I lean against them sustained by their might, drawn from victorious combat.

In walking I also read the weather—and by the weather I mean the outdoors. I have a reasonably tough skin that welcomes most kinds of weather, and I am determined not to succumb to the allurements of a shielded old age. Often I fight a rough wind foot by foot as I struggle down the road, then it veers and pushes me forward like a leaf. Once I was caught in the terrifying clutches of a cyclone, and only by bending very low I managed to follow my companion as we ran to a building nearby for shelter. Again a gentle breeze wavers on my cheek, quivers and shambles like the sea and drops into stillness like a bird descending to its nest.

Without trouble I distinguish the hammering sleet and piercing wind from a still snowfall that has a scent of purity unlike any other element in the sky. Before a thunderstorm the fragrances from garden, field and wood swarm about me, then disappear as the rain falls. The climate of the mountains differs from that of the ocean, which I identify by its salt dampness. In their turn these are utterly dissimilar to the breadth and sweep of the grain-scented, sunflower-flecked prairies on which I have walked during my journeyings out west. Always on my rambles it is a race for me to recognize a crowd of odors as they fleet by. It is fugitive and dependent upon the condition of the air on which it is borne. Smell is also subject to temperature. For instance, in cold weather there are few odors, while heat brings them forth abundantly. From smell I gain a sense of distance, ubiquity and unlimited variety that suggests analogically what people mean by colors and their shades. I can imagine that blue differs from red as widely as an orange does in scent from an apple. The melon has a scent of its own, yet I can distinguish different kinds of melons, and I can understand that roses, while retaining the unmistakable rosaceous smell, have widely varied shades.

It has pleased me especially to learn that, from regarding smell as a sort of fallen angel, an unwelcome monitor of disagreeable objects or danger from fire or escaping gas, society is slowly accepting it as a priceless enrichment of experience. Not only is my olfactive joy in the earth's growth complete, I also recapture whole epochs of my life. Every time I smell daisies I am radiantly happy little girl in the dew-drenched fields, walking with my teacher. A whiff from a meadow where hay has been cut transports me back to the big New England barn where my little friends and I used to play in a huge haymow. The days brimful of adventures, work and beauty I spent in California return to me whenever I catch the odor of a pepper tree, a eucalyptus or a citrus grove.

Never have I had a group of smell memories more delectable than those of Portofino, Italy, where Polly Thomson and I found rest on a mountaintop overlooking the Mediterranean last May. I reveled in the Italian sunshine and fragrances, which thronged upon me from all directions. The salt air streamed in a warm current, side by side with the boxwood hedges. The breath from the orange and lemon groves was an ecstasy, whether lingering lazily on a damp day or animated and strong in dry weather. There was a curious phenomenon which I observed at the lunch table: I could not easily distinguish the blossom of the orange from the fruit I was eating, or the strawberrylike smell in the honeysuckle from the wild berries on my tongue! In and out, all around, delicate grasses and leaves as unlike as the blossoms drifted among the floral odors, and formed an indescribable symphony of their own. The refreshment of mind and body which has invigorated me for my work I owe quite as much to those many well-defined, yet harmoniously blended fragrances as to the tranquility of the weeks at San Sebastiano.

Last Autumn I attended a gathering in Westport, Connecticut, where a professional perfumer talked most interestingly about the distillation of flower fragrances. He gave us all what he called the "blind test" to see how many floral perfumes we could identify. He presented to each of us eight fragrances on little blotters, or "whiff sachets"—rose, carnation, honeysuckle, lily of the valley, lilac, gardenia, jasmine and violet. Everyone complimented me on my ability to name correctly seven out of the eight flower fragrances. I found out that most women can identify only one or two. This is a sad comment indeed on their neglect of a faculty which would repay them a hundredfold for some patience in its development.

To my teacher's indefatigable vigilance that kept the fires of thought and observation burning in me I owe the wealth of experience I have gained through only three bodily faculties. This moves me to remind parents and teachers of their power to train children from the earliest years in the right use of their five senses. The surest hope of culture renewal is always the child. In order to attain his highest education he must be persistently encouraged to extract joy and constructive interest from sight, hearing, touch, smell and taste. Like all forms of education, the child's senses should be aroused by techniques suited to his individuality.

I am not a teacher or an educator, but I have always believed that infants should be taught as soon as possible, before they speak, to notice objects pretty or delightful or unusual. I have noticed the wholesome effect upon a baby of fixing his eyes upon a pleasing color or a delicately carved shell, listening to music that soothes or enchants him, touching a face he loves or smelling a flower at which he smiles. If the mother puts as much gentle art into this delicate fostering of all his physical powers as she does into the task of preserving his health, her reward will be past calculating. The child's five senses are the faithful fairies who, if cherished and heeded, will surrender to him their priceless tokens of royalty—the splendor at the rainbow's end, the seven-league boots of imagination, lovely dreams fulfilled. He will always be charmed or comforted by sky, earth and sea. Not only will he reach a well-ordered stewardship of his senses, he will also have the best chance of spiritual maturity. For there is, I am convinced, a correspondence between the powers of the body and those of the spirit, and when the five senses—or whatever of them there are—serve as entrances into an inner world, the individual attains his or her fullest capacity of pleasure as well as self-mastery. Every person, every group thus excellently equipped for living is the greatest possible contribution to humanity. That is why I like to celebrate the accomplishments of the handicapped whom necessity drives to use all the faculties that remain. They show what normal beings can and should do with a complete set of faculties Once parents and teachers realize the tremendous potencies of good folded up in sense-life and set about developing them in children, they will confer upon the coming generation a blessing that will carry through untold ages its multiplying harvest of alertness, strength and beauty of life.

My Animal Friends

Zoological Society Bulletin, Sept. 1923, pp. 111-118

PART 1
MY ACQUAINTANCE WITH DOMESTIC ANIMALS

I cannot remember a time in my life when animals and I were not the best of friends. I emerged from babyhood clinging frantically to the rough coat of my father's favorite hunting dog, a beautiful Llewellyn setter. Together Belle and I explored the garden. Together we fought our way through box hedges and rose trees. I am sure Belle was often puzzled to account for my peculiarities. She would watch me fall over objects with a troubled expression in her kind eyes. With remarkable intelligence she did her best to keep me out of trouble. She knew perfectly well that rose bushes have thorns, and that thorns scratch children and tear their frocks. She would push and pull in her efforts to dissuade me from going where it was not safe, but when I persisted, despite her most energetic resistance, she gave in and faithfully kept her place at my side, poking out her head in front to take observations and prevent, if possible, a bump or a tumble.

I loved Belle dearly. She was almost human in her patience and forbearance with me when I was only a little savage, more ignorant and apparently less capable of learning than my faithful companion in the great darkness.

No sooner had I learned to spell a word on my fingers than I was seized with the idea of imparting this new accomplishment to Belle. I found her asleep on the shady side of the piazza. I sat down beside her and began to manipulate her blunt toes. She seemed embarrassed, she smelt her feet anxiously and whimpered a little resentfully. I kept on, determined to teach her to make the letters d-o-l-l. Realizing that further objection would be useless, she watched the performance with stolid indifference, as much as to say, "Do as you please, but I'd like to see any one teach me to spell!" Poor Belle, I grew angry at her clumsiness, and pulled her toes so hard that at last she howled. But she bore me no malice, and was ready to play with me as soon as I had varied [sic] of the lesson.

I was fortunate enough to be born on a southern farm, and I grew up among a multitude of domestic animals. It is no exaggeration to say that I spent the greater part of the years before my education began in the company of my barnyard contemporaries. My keen interest in everything that had life led my teacher to use the animals on the farm as object lessons. I absorbed language satisfying my curiosity about living creatures. Hunting for the guinea hens' hidden nests, touching the cool, moist noses and threatening horns of the cows, holding the young pigs in my arms, feeding the great, strutting turkeys and feeling their feathers rise, like a flock of birds hovering close to the ground, being held on the back of a mule by one of the darky farmers when he ploughed the cornfield,— all these experiences imparted the liveliest reality to the words I learned. As I zigzagged my way from the kitchen door to the paddock at the end of the lane, I drank in knowledge with delight. I had a miscellany of small pets. One of them was a racoon [sic], a plump little rascal. He was inquisitive and acquisitive. He had no principles to speak of. The family called him a thief and a nuisance, but to me he was a darling.

I had no end of rabbits, but they did not interest me greatly. They never once had a thought in their wee heads; nothing but downy fur, long ears and wobbly noses.

I recall with creeping thrills of agreeable horror an experience I once had with a magnificent Angora cat. He was sleeping quietly on my knee when something startled him. He stood up humping his back, angrily stretching his body, tensely alert, waiting to leap. His throat began to palpitate. Hungrily, stealthily he reached out one paw. An electric flame seemed to pass through his silken fur. I guessed he saw a bird through the open window. I tried to hold him back, but he darted out the window like a thought charged with an evil intent. I could not see what happened with my physical eyes, but the mental picture I had of the denouement still grieves my soul. In that moment a thing of joy and beauty was snatched from the earth, a lovely voice was stilled, and happy wings ceased to soar in the sunlight. The incident has always been to me a symbol of the ageless tragedy of life.

I had many bird friends,—pretty elves that opened many of the unseen gates of Fairyland for me. A flock of pigeons came to the dining room window every morning for crumbs. They nudged and elbowed each other for standing room on the sill, cooling softly. Three of them became so friendly, they would take bits of muffin from my lips and fight each other for a place on my shoulder or wrist.

A pair of red bantams was the delight of my heart. They were so tame, they would stand on my knees billing and crowing, as much at home as if they were on the ground. One day the lady bantam most amazingly laid an egg on my lap.

One of my feathered flock was a cockatoo which Dr. Alexander Graham Bell gave me for a birthday present. I called him Jonquil because he had a glorious yellow crest which, unfurled, was a sign of wrath. Jonquil was a wicked elf, a menace masked in white and gold feathers. There was no limit or bound to his perversity. He would sit perched on my foot while I read, rocking back and forth as I turned the pages. Every few minutes he would hop up on my shoulder, kiss my ear and cheek, and put his long, sharp, hooked bill in my mouth, a token of his affection which sent tiny ripples of terror down my spine. Suddenly he would dart off screeching fiendishly, to alight on the back of a dog, or any human being who came near. So my happiness in his adoration was not unmixed with fear and dismay. Because of his countless misdemeanors, I had to let him go. My father tried to give him to various people, but Jonquil's evil fame had spread far and wide, and every one declined the gift with thanks. Finally he was given shelter in a saloon, where he acted as a sort of special policeman. Whenever a person became intoxicated or otherwise objectionable, Jonquil drove him out into the street. I do not know what became of him after the passing of the Eighteenth Amendment. Possibly he became the mascot of the Anti-Saloon League.

Then there was a canary which would sit on my finger and sing as if his little heart would burst in a flame of song. People often expressed surprise that I have such a tender feeling for birds. It is true, I cannot see them winging their way through the light, or hear their love calls in the spring-time. Nevertheless, to me they are part of life's dear intimacies. Their delicate endearments, when one is fortunate enough to win their confidence, are like the fragrance of flowers received from a beloved hand. Although I may touch them seldom, yet I sense them as a sweet influence, a hovering presence like the air. In my thoughts they are one with everything beautiful,—sunlight, youth, spring blossoms and the laughter of little children.

When I was ten years old, Mr. William Wade of Oakmont, Pennsylvania, presented me with a beautiful pony. I had just read "Black Beauty," which had been put into raised print, and of course I named the pony Black Beauty. I learned afterwards that he was not black but that did not matter a whit. Our negro cook's little girl's name was Lily, and nobody objected.

To this day I tremble when I recall Black Beauty's pranks. He knew that I could not see, and he took advantage of me in every imaginable way. When I was on his back, he did exactly as he pleased if some grown-up person was not near to discipline him. He would stop to eat grass by the roadside, or rear up on his hind legs to snatch a pear or apple from a tree, nearly pitching me out of the saddle. Indeed, I stayed on only by clinging desperately to his mane. He seemed to think I was bent on breaking my neck, and he aided and abetted me to the utmost of his ingenuity. Nevertheless, we were great pals, and I loved him passionately.

Black Beauty was kept in a paddock, which was surrounded by a wire fence and entered though a high gate. I would find my way to the gate with sugar, but I could not reach the bolt that's secured it. Black Beauty was crazy for the sugar. He would sniff at it greedily, I would push my hand though the bars, and he would take the sugar and gallop away. One day I thought I would tease him. Every time he reached for the sugar, I pulled my hand back. He nosed the gate impatiently, stood up on his hind legs to bite the handle of the wooden bar and finally jerked it up and down. He repeated this biting and jerking of the handle until the bar slid out, and the gate swung open. After that it was almost impossible to keep him in the paddock. His cleverness and initiative usually enabled him to find a way through almost any barricade.

I cannot leave the subject of my childhood pets without a word about Neddy, my wee donkey friend. I think he had lived many years before he came to me. At any rate he seemed to take life philosophically. He subdued himself to its restraints without protest. He was more interested in something to eat than in making progress. It made no difference to him how long it took to go from one point to another, and sometimes he remained deaf to all entreaties to proceed. He viewed the birch switches we cut by the roadside unperturbed. I never knew him to harbor a feeling of resentment or to complain about anything. Sometimes I thought I detected a shade of dejection in the droop of his long ears when he saw a tomato can on the other side of the wire fence, obviously out of reach.

One day my baby sister was riding behind me on Neddy's back. Suddenly, in the middle of the muddy lane, Neddy made a queer, bucking movement with his hind legs, which caused the baby to slip off. I knew she was sprawling in the mud and yelling, but the donkey refused to stop, though I jerked the reins with all my strength. He held his head down and kept on his way resistless as fate itself.

Neddy was kept in the paddock with Black Beauty. He paid not the slightest attention to his handsome companion in captivity. Black Beauty, on the other hand, conceived a half-humorous contempt for Neddy. He would dash up to the donkey, give him a quick nip and gallop off to a distance, where he waited for another opportunity to steal upon his stolid victim. Only once in years did Neddy "get his Jim Crow up" to the fighting pitch. Then he made his heels felt in a way that Black Beauty did not soon forget. That one supreme kick made him a sadder and wiser pony.

To the grown-up mind it may seem a long way from a donkey to a butterfly, but to the eager mind of a child it may be but a single step, just as Wonderland seemed to Alice only a step from home. I imagine God is as much interested in that tiny being composed of one cell called the amoeba as in the kitten and the bird which have countless millions of cells to perform the various functions of their bodies. Even this speck of life is immortal in the scientific sense, for it will live as long as the earth continues to support life.

Nothing I learned about living things as a child excited my imagination so profoundly as the metamorphosis of a butterfly,—first an egg, then a caterpillar, then a motionless, mummy-like form, then a winged creature. I watched the process from day to day with delighted wonder. Never shall I forget the thrill of intense excitement that shot through my body when I found the cocoon empty, and the butterfly drying its wings on a bunch of trailing arbutus in the May sunshine! It looked at the great, bright world with the velvety eyes which adorned its wings, and seemed contented with its bed of flowers. I took it lightly on my palm and marveled at the miracle that had taken place. Where were the clumsy feet and the horny jaws? There was no trace of them left. The delicate creature I held was made to tread on air and blossoms. Gone was the cutting, grinding mouth. Instead, there was a thread-like tube, coiled up like a watch spring, to be uncoiled and daintily thrust into a flower-cup to extract nectar. For a brief time this exquisite creature was one with joy and light and beauty. It could rise from the earth and sip the honey of flowers. In its glorified state it seemed almost to transcend physical existence.

Part II
My Acquaintance with Zoological Park Animals

On my first visit to Boston, soon after my eighth birthday, I was taken to a menagerie, and formally introduced to an elephant, a cageful of monkeys and three baby lions. The monkeys were very mischievous. They pulled my hair and snatched at the flowers in my hat. Their queer, cold hands made me shiver, and I did not like their teasing antics a bit.

The elephant was an enormous fellow with a breath like the blast from a furnace. He helped himself to a bag of peanuts I held in my hand, and swallowed them, bag and all. When I tried to feel his trunk, he objected and lifted it out of reach. His keeper assisted me to climb up on Jumbo's back, where I sat frightened, but proud of the adventure. I felt like a little boat afloat upon a great sea, and secretly I was glad to climb back to the firm earth again.

The young lions were docile and playful. They rolled over on their backs and purred like kittens. I could not believe they would grow up into ferocious beasts of prey. But when I saw two of them years later, I was convinced. As I stood by their cage, I realized that my innocent, pretty, good-natured lion kittens had undergone a great change, not only in their physical appearance, but also in mind and disposition. The lioness was still slender, and more quiet than the male, which had developed into a powerful, aggressive creature with an imposing mane. His baby purr was now a roar that terrified me. I was not permitted to touch him even through the bars.

I have, however, touched two grown lions since then, also Trilby, the famous lioness in the Washington Zoological Park. She was as gentle and as beautiful as a great Dane. She pressed her body against me affectionately and licked my hand. One lion, a splendid fellow, held out a huge paw to me in a friendly manner, let me feel his great head and even growled amiably for my entertainment. His keeper made him walk up and down the cage so that I might feel his stride.

I cannot help thinking, however, that these noble creatures resent our timid familiarity. In the presence of the wild captives from the jungle and forest I always sense the suppressed, fierce discord in the pipes of Pan. I know that the lion and the tiger have been snared from their natural environment into man's world. They submit themselves to the tyrant who walks upright, issues arbitrary commands and prohibits many pleasant things. They endure his laws and bear his yoke, but secretly they rebel, and when opportunity offers, they betray him. They never recognize his superiority or surrender themselves completely to his will. In their mysterious hearts they yield allegiance only to the primal laws of nature. They fear human beings and tolerate their caresses because they are afraid of punishment. Who had not observed the insolent bearing of the tiger toward the people who coddle him with words while fearing him even behind iron bars? Who has not sensed the distrustful bewilderment in the eyes of the deer, and even of the horse, which has for thousands of years responded to the lightest touch of a man's hand! By dint of patience and intelligence man succeeds in trapping and confining the wild beasts of the earth, but they hear his voice only when he brings them food or threatens them. I suspect that if they once regained their liberty, all of them would take reprisals of him, and I am sure some of them would devour him without a prick of conscience. Hagenbeck says in his fascinating book on animals that to win the affection of wild animals is so rare a gift, it seems almost superhuman. The dog is the only animal in nature's annals which has made friends with man. Only the dog draws close to him and to some extent shares his joys and sorrows. The dog, alone of the animal kingdom, acknowledges man's superiority and thinks only of being useful to him, lives only to serve him with unquestioning devotion.

All my life I have been interested in animals. Since my early childhood the circus has fascinated me. I have visited nearly all the important zoological parks and menageries in this country. I have made the acquaintance of African buffaloes, hippopotami, sea-lions, camels (and wondered how anyone ever thought of swallowing one!) I have touched a prairie wolf and a Colorado coyote. When I lived in Wrentham, Massachusetts, wild deer frequently ventured into our garden to eat lettuce and other vegetables. They had been protected by law from hunters so long that they had almost lost their fear of man. I could never get close enough to touch them, but if I sat under the old apple tree at the end of the garden where it joined the hayfield, until they had finished their salad, I could feel their hoof beats as they charged across the field into the woods beyond.

All these contacts with wild animal life have helped to make the world I live in real and vastly interesting. I am sorry for any one who had never known the sheer pleasure of meeting face to face a wild creature of the forest. There is a wealth of adventure in watching the drama of wild life that is always going on in the woods or in one of the zoological parks. When people I meet admit that they have never been to a "zoo," I am tempted to exclaim, "Is it possible that your city has gathered from the four quarters of the earth such a collection of wonders, and you have never seen them? Go at once to your zoological park, it will give you a variety of experiences you have missed. Besides, it is one of the most delightful means of gaining health of body and mind. A ramble in the park will renew your youth. The springtide of new life that flows through every path and green alley will bring a fresh thrill of life and love into your heart."

It was a visit to the Zoological Park of New York City that inspired the idea of this article. One day last summer I took my three little nieces from Alabama, who were visiting me, to see the animals. A blazing sun glared in the deep blue heavens, but the children did not mind that. Anyway, the Park was full of cool, shady spots where a great many people from the city sat indolently, enjoying their beautiful surroundings. For the three little southern girls there was indefinable spirit of adventure in the air. (The Country of Children's Land is always full of surprises.) Pat, Mildred and Katharine were as full of suppressed excitement as Alice in Wonderland when she popped down the rabbit-hole, and they were as greedy to discover new worlds as Columbus himself. They did not fall into a Pool of Tears that I know of, they did not run a race with a lory, a dodo, an eaglet and a mouse, but the furry and feathered folk of the Park were just as magical. Their insatiate curiosity and outbursts of joy carried me back on the wings of memory to the time when I was more interested in the wild folk I met than in human beings.

Spellbound the children watched some seals gambolling in the water, climbing rocks, barking in the sunshine, tumbling off again and swimming about, as happy as if they were off on a holiday, instead of at home, doing the same things every minute of their lives.

A solemn brown bear performed a clumsy dance for them; they laughed delightedly and clapped their hands. Then we were taken to the snake house, and the little girls played with a handsome Texas snake. He was most friendly and I felt him hiss softly with pleasure as he coiled round the warm body of the smallest child. There were many snakes, all interesting each after his fashion. The keeper, a fearless man wise in the ways of serpents, brought a rattlesnake for me to touch, grasping his head firmly in his strong hand, so that I might feel the rattle,—a sound terrible to all living creatures, yet sweet as waters in a desert to his mate when he calls her!

On our way to the monkey house we stopped to look at the strangest mammal imaginable, the Australian platypus,—the first one which had ever been brought to America alive. It was in the water, and came near enough for me to touch its wet furry coat. This animal lives on a certain kind of worm which boys collect for him at a cost of eight dollars per breakfast. Its nondescript appearance suggests that it is one of nature's discarded experiments. Or is it just a little joke? One has the same feeling about the bat with his wings and head like a mouse, the armadillo with a turtle-like covering, the porcupine, so like a pin cushion, the anteater, a mammal with a bill, and the whale making believe he is a fish.

Windy, the great Orang-utang [sic], received us with rough cordiality. She held out two hairy hands to us, and after looking me over critically she climbed into my lap and put her shaggy arms around my neck. The children were delighted, and danced about us with glee. All at once Windy caught sight of a rain coat hanging up in a corner, and she was after it like a shot. It was very amusing to watch her try to put the coat on. She struggled with it half an hour vainly. She pulled it over her head, tugging and twisting but it never occurred to her to put her arms though the sleeves! At last she began to pant and scold furiously, tearing the coat to pieces in her wrath. Then she dropped it and dived under a table, obviously ashamed of her failure. However, when I took her hand and coaxed her to come with me, she smiled affably and marched beside me with heavy tread to face a camera, which she eyed suspiciously. But she submitted good-naturedly to the ordeal of being photographed. When we took leave of Windy, each one of the party shaking her two hands in turn, she smiled in a peculiar way. You know the kind of smile I mean, if you have ever watched a hostess when her society friends tell her what a delightful affair it has been, and what a wonderful time they have had.

The next animals to entertain us were two giraffes. The children gazed at the strange, timid, sad-eyed creatures in speechless amazement. We fed them with biscuits, and they followed us about sighing softly. I wondered if it would make any difference to a giraffe whether his tea was strong or hot. I was sure that it would lose its strength and arrive in his stomach as iced tea, no matter how hot it started. We all thought the giraffes the saddest creatures under the sun. Perhaps they are sensitive about their shape,—poor things.

The climax of happiness came when we all climbed up on the massive back of Alice, the kindliest of elephants, and she carried us round the ring, her long, swinging, heaving, pounding stride filling us with delicious anxiety. It took a good deal of persuasion to make the children dismount. They adored Alice. They wanted to pat her broad forehead, which she wrinkled thoughtfully when she looked at us. She took the bread we gave her indifferently, as much as to say, "I am not hungry, but I will eat it to show my appreciation of your kindness." She seemed to realize that I was different from the others. Elephants are very intelligent. I suppose Alice observed the uncertain movement of my hands. At any rate, she scrutinized me intently, and caressed my face, my shoulder and even my foot lightly with her trunk! Everyone was surprised at her affectionate manner towards me, although they knew she was kindly disposed and trustworthy.

All too soon the time came for saying goodbye to the friends who had done so much to make our visit to the Zoological Park a memorable event in our lives. The children were very tired, but bubbling over with the joy of their discoveries.

"It's just like Noah's Ark," said one. "What a jolly time the animals must have had visiting one another!" exclaimed another. "I suppose they did, but really I wasn't there, you know," said Katherine, the eldest. "Perhaps the little animals were frightened when the lions and bears thought about their supper," suggested the youngest child. "I like the Zoo better than the circus because the animals look so happy in their pretty houses," declared Pat, "and besides, it's more fun than all the rest of New York put together."

As the children chattered, I realized as never before what an important part of the educational system of New York the Zoological Park is. It is crammed with instruction and entertainment for young and old. For the city child it is the very breath of the woods. There he may observe animals gathered from all over the world. There he may study, not only what is going on at the present day, but also what has been evolved through vast periods of time. There the thoughtful catch glimpses of the immensity and wonder of life which lie close to our feeble senses unapprehended. It stimulates a desire for knowledge, it fosters an inquiring spirit and inculcates a less arrogant attitude in the face of the great Unknown. To the investigator it says, "Push the infinite as far as you can. You can always push it farther. Do not fear.

'Veil after veil will lift, but there must be
Veil after veil behind.'"

A Chat About the Hand

The Century Magazine, 1905, pp. 455-465

I have just touched my dog. He was rolling on the grass, with pleasure in every muscle and limb. I wanted to catch a picture of him in my fingers, and I touched him as lightly as I would cobwebs; but lo, his fat body revolved, stiffened and solidified into an upright position, and his tongue gave my hand a lick! He pressed close to me, as if he were fain to crowd himself into my hand. He loved it with his tail, with his paw, with his tongue. If he could speak, I believe he would say with me that paradise is attained by touch; for in touch is all love and intelligence.

This small incident started me on a chat about hands, and if my chat is fortunate I have to thank my dog-star. In any case, it is pleasant to have something to talk about that no one else has monopolized; it is like making a new path in the trackless woods, blazing the trail where no foot has pressed before. I am glad to take you by the hand and lead you along an untrodden way into a world where the hand is supreme. But at the very outset we encounter a difficulty. You are so accustomed to light, I fear you will stumble when I try to guide you through the land of darkness and silence. The blind are not supposed to be the best of guides. Still, though I cannot warrant not to lose you, I promise that you shall not be led into fire or water, or fall into a deep pit. If you will follow me patiently, you will find that "there's a sound so fine, nothing lives 'twixt it and silence," and that there is more meant in things than meets the eye.

My hand is to me what your hearing and sight are together are to you. In large measure we travel the same highways, read the same books, speak the same language, yet our experiences are different. All my comings and goings turn on the hand as on a pivot. It is the hand that binds me to the world of men and women. The hand is my feeler with which I reach through isolation and darkness and seize every pleasure, every activity that my fingers encounter. With the dropping of a little word from another's hand into mine, a slight flutter of the fingers, began the intelligence, the joy, the fullness of my life. Like Job, I feel as if a hand had made me, fashioned me together round about and molded my very soul.

In all my experiences and thoughts I am conscious of a hand. Whatever touches me, whatever thrills me, is as a hand that touches me in the dark, and that touch is my reality. You might as well say that a sight which makes you glad, or a blow which brings the stinging tears to your eyes, is unreal as to say that those impressions are unreal which I have accumulated by means of touch. The delicate tremble of a butterfly's wings in my hand, the soft petals of violets curling in the cool folds of their leaves or lifting sweetly out of the meadow-grass, the clear, firm outline of face and limb, the smooth arch of a horse's neck and the velvety touch of his nose—all these, and a thousand resultant combinations, which take shape in my mind, constitute my world.

Ideas make the world we live in, and impressions furnish ideas. My world is built of touch-sensations, devoid of color and sound; but without color and sound it breathes and throbs with life. Every object is associated in my mind with tactual qualities which, combined in countless ways, give me a sense of power, of beauty, or of incongruity: for with my hands I can feel the comic as well as the beautiful in the outward appearance of things. Remember that you, dependent on your sight, do not realize how many things are tangible. All palpable things are mobile or rigid, solid or liquid, big or small, warm or cold, and these qualities are variously modified. The coolness of a water-lily rounding into bloom is different from the coolness of an evening wind in summer, and different again from the coolness of the rain that soaks into the hearts of growing things and gives them life and body. The velvet of the rose is not that of a ripe peach or of a baby's dimpled cheek. The hardness of the rock is to the hardness of the wood what a man's deep bass is to a woman's voice when it is low. What I call beauty I find in certain combinations of all these qualities, and is largely derived from the flow of curved and straight lines which is over all things.

"What does the straight line mean to you?" I think you will ask.

It means several things. It symbolizes duty. It seems to have the quality of inexorableness that duty has. When I have something to do that must not be set aside, I feel as if I were going forward in a straight line, bound to arrive somewhere, or go on forever without swerving to the right or left.

That is what it means. To escape this moralizing you should ask, "How does the straight line feel?" It feels, as I suppose it looks, straight—a dull thought drawn out endlessly. It is unstraight lines, or many straight and curved lines together, that are eloquent to the touch. They appear and disappear, are now deep, now shallow, now broken off or lengthened or swelling. They rise and sink beneath my fingers, they are full of sudden starts and pauses, and their variety is inexhaustible and wonderful. So you see I am not shut out from the region of the beautiful, though my hand cannot perceive the brilliant colors in the sunset or on the mountain, or reach into the blue depths of the sky.

Physics tells me that I am well off in a world which knows neither color nor sound, but is made in terms of size, shape, and inherent qualities; for at least every object appears to my fingers standing solidly right side up, and is not an inverted image on the retina which, I understand, your brain is at infinite though unconscious labor to set back on its feet. A tangible object passes complete into my brain with the warmth of life upon it, and occupies the same place that it does in space; for, without egotism, the mind is as large as the universe. When I think of hills, I think of the upward strength I tread upon. When water is the object of my thought, I feel the cool shock of the plunge and the quick yielding of the waves that crisp and curl and ripple about my body. The pleasing changes of rough and smooth, pliant and rigid, curved and straight in the bark and branches of a tree give the truth to my hand. The immovable rock, with its juts and warped surface, bends beneath my fingers into all manner of grooves and hollows. The bulge of a watermelon and the puffed-up rotundities of squashes that sprout, bud, and ripen in that strange garden planted somewhere behind my fingertips are the ludicrous in my tactual memory and imagination. My fingers are tickled to delight by the soft ripple of a baby's laugh, and find amusement in the lusty crow of the barnyard autocrat. Once I had a pet rooster that used to perch on my knee and stretch his neck and crow. A bird in my hand was then worth two in the—barnyard.

My fingers cannot, of course, get the impression of a large whole at a glance; but I feel the parts, and my mind puts them together. I move around the house, touching object after object in order, before I can form an idea of the entire house. In other people's houses I can touch only what is shown to me—the chief objects of interest, carvings on the wall, or a curious architectural feature, exhibited like the family album. Therefore a house with which I am not familiar has for me, at first, no general effect or harmony of detail. It is not a complete conception, but a collection of object-impressions which, as they come to me, are disconnected and isolated. But my mind is full of associations, sensations, theories, and with them it constructs the house. The process reminds me of the building of Solomon's temple, where was neither saw, nor hammer, nor any tool heard while the stones were being laid one upon another. The silent worker is imagination which decrees reality out of chaos.

Without imagination what a poor thing my world would be! My garden would be a silent patch of earth strewn with sticks of a variety of shapes and smells. But when the eye of my mind is opened to its beauty, the bare ground brightens beneath my feet, and the hedge-row bursts into leaf, and the rose-tree shakes its fragrance everywhere. I know how budding trees look, and I enter into the amorous joy of the mating birds, and this is the miracle of imagination.

Twofold is the miracle when, through my fingers, my imagination reaches forth and meets the imagination of an artist which he has embodied in a sculptured form. Although, compared with the life-warm, mobile face of a friend, the marble is cold and pulseless and unresponsive, yet it is beautiful to my hand. Its flowing curves and bendings are a real pleasure; only breath is wanting; but under the spell of the imagination the marble thrills and becomes the divine reality of the ideal. Imagination puts a sentiment into every line and curve, and the statue in my touch is indeed the goddess herself who breathes and moves and enchants.

It is true, however, that some sculptures, even recognized masterpieces, do not please my hand. When I touch what there is of the Winged Victory, it reminds me at first of a headless, limbless dream that flies toward me in an unrestful sleep. The garments of the Victory thrust stiffly out behind, and do not resemble garments that I have felt flying, fluttering, folding, spreading in the wind. But imagination fulfils [sic] these imperfections, and straightway the Victory becomes a powerful and spirited figure with the sweep of sea-winds in her robes and the splendor of conquest in her wings.

I find in a beautiful statue, beside perfection of bodily form, the qualities of balance and completeness. The Minerva, hung with a web of poetical allusion, gives me a sense of exhilaration that is almost physical; and I like the luxuriant, wavy hair of Bacchus and Apollo, and the wreath of ivy, so suggestive of pagan holidays.

So imagination crowns the experience of my hands. And they learned their cunning from the wise hand of another, which, itself guided by imagination, led me safely in paths that I knew not, made darkness light before me, and made crooked ways straight.

The warmth and protectiveness of the hand are most homefelt [sic] to me who have always looked to it for aid and joy. I understand perfectly how the Psalmist can lift up his voice with strength and gladness, singing, "I put my trust and gladness in the Lord at all times, and his hand shall uphold me, and I shall dwell in safety." In the strength of the human hand, too, there is something divine. I am told that the glance of a beloved eye thrills one from a distance; but there is no distance in the touch of a beloved hand.Even the letters I receive are

> Kind letters that betray the heart's deep history,
> In which we feel the presence of a hand.

It is interesting to observe the difference in the hands of people. They show all kinds of vitality, energy, stillness, and cordiality. I never realized how living the hand is until I saw those chill plaster images in Mr. Hutton's collection of casts. The hand I know in life has the fullness of blood in its veins, and is elastic with spirit. How different dear Mr. Hutton's hand was from its dull, insensate image! To me the cast lacks the very form of the hand. Of the many casts in Mr. Hutton's collection I did not recognize any, not even my own. But a loving hand I never forget. I remember in my fingers the large hands of Bishop Brooks, brimful of tenderness and a strong man's joy. If you were deaf and blind, and could hold Mr. Jefferson's hand, you would see in it a face and hear a kind voice unlike any other you have known. Mark Twain's hand is full of whimsies and the drollest humors, and while you hold it the drollery changes to sympathy and championship.

I am told that the words I have just written do not "describe" the hands of my friends, but merely endow them with the kindly human qualities which I know they possess, and which language conveys in abstract words. The criticism implies that I am not giving the primary truth of what I feel; but how otherwise do descriptions in books I read, written by men who can see, render the visible look of a face? I read that a face is strong, gentle; that it is full of patience, of intellect; that it is fine, sweet, noble, beautiful. Have I not the same right to use these words in describing what I feel as you have in describing what you see? They express truly what I feel in the hand. I am seldom conscious of physical qualities, and I do not remember whether the fingers of a hand are short or long, or the skin is moist or dry. No more can you, without conscious effort, recall the details of a face even when you have seen it many times. If you do recall the features, and say that an eye is blue, a chin sharp, a nose short, or a cheek sunken, I fancy that you do not succeed well in giving the impression of the person,—not so well as when you interpret at once to the heart the essential moral qualities of the face—its humor, gravity, sadness, spirituality. If I should tell you in physical terms how a hand feels, you would be no wiser for my account than a blind man to whom you describe a face in detail. Remember that when a blind man recovers his sight, he does not recognize the commonest thing that has been familiar to his touch, the dearest face intimate to his fingers, and it does not help him at all that things and people have been described to him again and again. So you, who are untrained of touch, do not recognize a hand by the grasp; and so, too, any description I might give would fail to make you acquainted with a friendly hand which my fingers have often folded about, and which my affection translates to my memory.

I cannot describe hands under any class or type; there is no democracy of hands. Some hands tell me that they do everything with the maximum of bustle and noise. Other hands are fidgety and unadvised, with nervous, fussy fingers which indicate a nature sensitive to the little pricks of daily life. Sometimes I recognize with foreboding the kindly but stupid hand of one who tells with many words news that is no news. I have met a bishop with a jocose hand, a humorist with a hand of leaden gravity, a man of pretentious valor with a timorous hand, and a quiet, apologetic man with a fist of iron. When I was a little girl I was taken to see a woman who was blind and paralyzed. I shall never forget how she held out her small, trembling hand and pressed sympathy into mine. My eyes fill with tears as I think of her. The weariness, pain, darkness, and sweet patience were all to be felt in her thin, wasted, groping, loving hand.

Few people who do not know me will understand, I think, how much I get of the mood of a friend who is engaged in oral conversation with somebody else. My hand follows his motions; I touch his hand, his arm, his face. I can tell when he is full of glee over a good joke which has not been repeated to me, or when he is telling a lively story. One of my friends is rather aggressive, and his hand always announces the coming of a dispute. By his impatient jerk I know he has argument ready for someone. I have felt him start as a sudden recollection or a new idea shot through his mind. I have felt grief in his hand. I have felt his soul wrap itself in darkness majestically as in a garment. Another friend has positive, emphatic hands which show great pertinacity of opinion. She is the only person I know who emphasizes her spelled words and accents them as she emphasizes and accents her spoken words when I read her lips. I like this varied emphasis better than the monotonous pound of unmodulated people who hammer their meaning into my palm.

Some hands, when they clasp yours, beam and bubble over with gladness. They throb and expand with life. Strangers have clasped my hand like that of a long-lost sister. Other people shake hands with me as if with the fear that I may do them mischief. Such persons hold out civil fingertips which they permit you to touch, and in the moment of contact they retreat, and inwardly you hope that you will not be called upon again to take that hand of "dormouse valor." It betokens a prudish mind, ungracious pride, and not seldom mistrust. It is the antipode to the hand of those who have large, lovable natures.

The handshake of some people makes you think of an accident and sudden death. Contrast this ill-boding hand with the quick, skillful, quiet hand of a nurse whom I remember with affection because she took the best care of my teacher. I have clasped the hands of some rich people that spin not and toil not, and yet are not beautiful. Beneath their soft, smooth roundness, what a chaos of undeveloped character!

All this is my private science of palmistry, and when I tell your fortune it is by no mysterious intuition or Gipsy witchcraft, but by natural, explicable recognition of the embossed character in your hand. Not only is the hand as easy to recognize as the face, but it reveals its secrets more openly and unconsciously. People control their countenances, but the hand is under no such restraint. It relaxes and becomes listless when the spirit is low and dejected; the muscles tighten when the mind is excited or the heart glad; and permanent qualities stand written on it all the time.

As there are many beauties of the face, so the beauties of the hand are many. Touch has its ecstasies. The hands of people of strong individuality and sensitiveness are wonderfully mobile. In a glance of their finger-tips they express many shades of thought. Now and again I touch a fine, graceful, supple-wristed hand which spells with the same beauty and distinction that you must see in the handwriting of some highly cultivated people. I wish you could see how prettily little children spell in my hand. They are wild flowers of humanity and their finger motions wild flowers of speech.

Look in your "Century Dictionary," or if you are blind, ask your teacher to do it for you, and learn how many idioms are made on the idea of hand, and how many words are formed from the Latin root manus—enough words to name all the essential affairs of life. "Hand," with quotations and compounds, occupies twenty-four columns, eight pages of this dictionary, in all ten times as long as this essay. The hand is defined as the "organ of apprehension." How perfectly the definition fits my case in both senses of the word "apprehend!" With my hand I seize and hold all that I find in the three worlds—physical, intellectual, and spiritual.

Think how man has regarded the world in terms of the hand. All life is divided between what lies *on one hand* and on the other. The products of skill are *manu*factures. The conduct of affairs is *man*agement. History seems to be the record—alas for our chronicles of war!—of the *man*oeuvers of armies. But the history of peace, too, the narrative of labor in the field, the forest, and the vineyard, is written in the victorious sign *manual*—the sign of the hand that has conquered the wilderness. The laborer himself is called a *hand*.

The minor idioms are myriad; but I will not recall too many, lest you cry, "Hands off!" I cannot desist, however, from this word-game until I have set down a few. Whatever is not one's own by first possession is *second-hand*. That is what I am told my knowledge is. But my well-meaning friends come to my defense, and, not content with endowing me with natural *first-hand* knowledge which is rightfully mine, ascribe to me a preternatural sixth sense and credit to miracles and heaven-sent compensations all that I have won and discovered with my good right hand. And with my left hand too; for with that I read, and it is as true and honorable as the other. By what half-development of human power has the left hand been neglected? When we arrive at the acme of civilization shall we not all be ambidextrous, and in our *hand-to-hand* contests against difficulties shall we not be doubly triumphant? It occurs to me, by the way, that when my teacher was training my unreclaimed spirit, her struggle against the powers of darkness, with the stout arm of discipline and the light of the manual alphabet, was in two senses a hand-to-hand conflict.

No essay would be complete without quotations from Shakspere [sic]. In the field which, in the presumption of my youth, I thought was my own he has reaped before me. In almost every play there are passages where the hand plays a part. Lady Macbeth's heartbroken soliloquy over her little hand, from which all the perfumes of Arabia will not wash the stain, is the most pitiful moment in the tragedy. Mark Antony rewards Scarus, the bravest of his soldiers, by asking Cleopatra to give him her hand: "Commend unto his lips thy favoring hand." In a different mood he is enraged because Thyreus, whom he despises, has presumed to kiss the hand of the queen, "my playfellow, the kingly seal of high hearts." When Cleopatra is threatened with the humiliation of gracing Caesar's triumph, she snatches a dagger, exclaiming, "I will trust my resolution and my good hands." With the same swift instinct, Cassius trusts to his hands when he stabs Caesar: "Speak, hands for me!" "Let me kiss your hand," says the blind Gloster [sic] to Lear." "Let me wipe it first," replies the broken old king; "it smells of mortality." How charged is this single touch with sad meaning! How it opens our eyes to the fearful purging Lear has undergone, to learn that royalty is no defense against ingratitude and cruelty! Gloster's exclamation about his son, "Did I but live to see thee in my touch, I'd say I had eyes again," is as true to a pulse within me as the grief he feels. The ghost in "Hamlet" recites the wrongs from which springs the tragedy:

> Thus was I, sleeping, by a brother's hand
> At once of life, of crown, of queen dispatch'd.

How that passage in "Othello" stops your breath—that passage full of bitter double intention in which Othello's suspicion tips with evil what he says about Desdemona's hand; and she in innocence answers only the innocent meaning of his words: "for 't was that hand that gave away my heart."

Not all of Shakspere's great passages about the hand are tragic. Remember the light play of words in "Romeo and Juliet" where the dialogue, flying nimbly back and forth, weaves a pretty sonnet about the hand. And who knows the hand, if not the lover?

The touch of the hand is in every chapter of the Bible. Why, you could almost rewrite Exodus as the story of the hand. Everything is done by the hand of the Lord and of Moses. The oppression of the Hebrews is translated thus: "The hand of Pharaoh was heavy upon the Hebrews." Their departure out of the land is told in these vivid words: "The Lord brought the children of Israel out of the house of bondage with a strong hand and a stretched-out arm." At the stretching out of the hand of Moses the waters of the Red Sea part and stand all on a heap. When the Lord lifts his hand in anger, thousands perish in the wilderness. Every act, every decree in the history of Israel, as indeed in the history of the human race, is sanctioned by the hand. Is it not used in the great moments of swearing, blessing, cursing, smiting, agreeing, marrying, building, destroying? Its sacredness is in the law that no sacrifice is valid unless the sacrificer lay his hand upon the head of the victim. The congregation lay their hands on the heads of those who are sentenced to death. How terrible the dumb condemnation of their hands must be to the condemned! When Moses builds the altar on Mount Sinai, he is commanded to use no tool, but rear it with his own hands. Earth, sea, sky, man, and all lower animals are holy unto the Lord because he has formed them with his hand. When the Psalmist considers the heavens and the earth, he exclaims: "What is man, O Lord, that thou art mindful of him? For thou hast made him to have dominion over the works of thy hands." The supplicating gesture of the hand always accompanies the spoken prayer, and with clean hands goes the pure heart.

Christ comforted and blessed and healed and wrought many miracles with his hands. He touched the eyes of the blind, and they were opened. When Jairus sought him, overwhelmed with grief, Jesus went and laid his hands on the ruler's daughter, and she awoke from the sleep of death to her father's love. You also remember how he healed the crooked woman. He said to her, "Woman, thou art loosed from thine infirmary," and he laid his hands on her and immediately she was made straight, and she glorified God.

Look where we will, we find the hand in time and history, working, building, inventing, bringing civilization out of barbarism. The hand symbolizes power and the excellence of work. The mechanic's hand, that minister of elemental forces, the hand that hews, saws, cuts, builds, is useful in the world equally with the delicate hand that paints a wild flower or molds a Grecian urn, or the hand of a statesman that writes a law. The eye cannot say to the hand, "I have no need of thee." Blessed be the hand! Thrice blessed be the hands that work!

Summer Day in Scotland

The Home Magazine, August 1934, p. 50

In Scotland there is a proverb: Wish for a Silken Gown, and you may get the sleeve of it.

One who journeys through life in this spirit will pick up many comfortable bits of heaven on the way. And there are more wee patches of heaven in Scotland than in any place I know.

If you enjoy the water, you can have the sailor's delight in wind and wave in a small row-boat.

Imagine setting out on a bright summer day just for the joy of catching glimpses of lovely islands far out on pearly seas. As we row in perfect happiness out and still farther out, we get a clearer view of the picturesque Scottish coast. It looks as if someone had gone round it with a jigsaw and let the water into every corner of the land. Look where we will, we see a river, a loch, a mountain cascade.

One of these mountain waterfalls is known as MacLean's Towel, which pours seaward, a surging white flood.

Puffing and blowing, we breathe out joy and breathe in buoyancy with each stroke of the oar. Without doubt we have the Sleeve of the Silken Gown between us, and we are content. Forward dip! Backward pull! We set a course for the Infinite!

Beautiful shining yachts pass swiftly by, they are the Silken Gowns but the winds of heaven can equally fill a Silken Sleeve and the lungs of adventurous lovers of the sea.

We steer closer to the shore where the land odors are sweet and pungent. We get sudden glimpses into deep glens where history was made, and many a man and woman met death long ago. For every hollow and promontory of Scotland tells a tale of dark deeds, high courage and strong faith which were not quenched by the passing we call death.

Always the shore is impressive with hills and green spreading trees and vast stretches of purple moorland. As we row along in silence, our feeling too deep for words, the historian of the party exclaims, "There, behind those jagged rocks, is the Cairn where Red Colin of Glen Ure was killed two hundred years ago by a mysterious enemy with a gun which the old people of the Glen still speak of as the Black Gun of Misfortune." The wind that surges up the Narrows and the mists that crowd in upon the hills still tell of the tragedy.

Just beyond can be seen the road dipping down to the sea before it winds into a sheltered and wooded country which is the setting for an ancient ruined castle.

Close by is the seat of the Pictish Monarchy which is now called Beregonium. It stands on a small green hill at the edge of the sea-shore.

But it is getting late, some of us are hungry, and we have a long row back. As we start homeward, we can see the white wings of a yacht bowling along with every sail spread to catch the evening breeze. "That is the Silken Gown!" we in the Silken Sleeve murmur. We watch it go by, the sea curling in jade green patterns from the keel, the foam from the wash knocking our boat gally [sic] west.

Two hours later, weary, but exultant, we pull in beside the Silken Gown. Her white wings are folded on the quiet waters. The gaskets are tied, the cover is put on, every rope is coiled.

After a good supper at a hospitable little old inn, we climb to the top of a jagged rock, from which we look down upon the ship at rest. There in the purple night lies the Silken Gown, her riding-light making a long golden road through the still waters, and there too lies the little row-boat—our Silken Sleeve—like a dove in the velvety dark.

As I stand there, I reflect that when it comes to sailing the seas of life, there is perhaps as much happiness in the Silken Sleeve as in the Gown itself.

My Dreams

The Century Magazine, November 1908, pp. 69-74

Everybody takes his own dreams seriously, but yawns at the breakfast-table when somebody else begins to tell the adventures of the night before. I hesitate, therefore, to enter upon an account of my dreams; for it is a literary sin to bore the reader, and a scientific sin to report the facts of a far country with more regard to point and brevity than to complete the literal truth. The psychologists have trained a pack of theories and facts which they keep in leash, like so many bulldogs, and which they let loose upon us whenever we depart from the strait and narrow path of dream probability. One may not even tell an entertaining dream without being suspected of having liberally edited it, as if editing were one of the seven deadly sins, instead of a useful and honorable occupation. Be it understood, then, that I am discoursing at my own breakfast-table, and that no scientific man is present to trip the autocrat.

I used to wonder why scientific men and others were always asking me about my dreams. But I am not surprised now, since I have discovered what some of them believe to be the ordinary waking experience of one who is both deaf and blind. They think that I can know very little about objects even a few feet beyond the reach of my arms. Everything outside of myself, according to them, is a hazy blur. Trees, mountains, cities, the ocean, even the house I live in, are but fairy fabrications, misty unrealities. Therefore it is assumed that my dreams should have peculiar interest for the man of science. In some undefined way it is expected that they should reveal the world I dwell in to be flat, formless, colorless, without perspective, with little thickness and less solidity—a vast solitude of soundless space. But who shall put into words limitless, visionless, silent void? One should be a disembodied spirit indeed to make anything out of such insubstantial experiences. A world, or a dream, for that matter, to be comprehensible to us, must, I should think, have a warp of substance woven into the woof of fantasy. We cannot imagine even in dreams an object which has no counterpart in reality. Ghosts always resemble somebody, and if they do not appear themselves, their presence is indicated by circumstances with which we are perfectly familiar.

During sleep we enter a strange, mysterious realm which science has thus far not explored. Beyond the border-line of slumber the investigator may not pass with his common-sense rule and test. Sleep with softest touch locks all the gates of our physical senses and lulls to rest the conscious will, the disciplinarian of our waking thoughts. Then the spirit wrenches itself free from the sinewy arms of reason and, like a winged courser, spurns the firm, green earth and speeds away upon wind and cloud, leaving neither trace nor footprint by which science may track its flight and bring us knowledge of the distant, shadowy country that we nightly visit. When we come back from the dream-realm, we can give no reasonable report of what we met there. But once across the border, we feel at home, as if we had always lived there and had never made any excursions into this rational, daylight world.

My dreams do not seem to differ very much from the dreams of other people. Some of them are coherent and safely hitched to an event or a conclusion; others are inconsequent and fantastic. All attest that in Dreamland there is no such thing as repose. We are always up and doing, with a mind for any adventure. We act, strive, think, suffer, and are glad to no purpose. We leave outside the portals of Sleep all troublesome incredulities and vexatious speculations as to probability. I float wraithlike upon clouds, in and out among the winds, without the faintest notion that I am doing anything unusual. In Dreamland I find little that is altogether strange or wholly new to my experience. No matter what happens, I am not astonished, however extraordinary the circumstances may be. I visit a foreign land where I have not been in reality, and I converse with peoples whose language I have never heard. Yet we manage to understand one another perfectly. Into whatsoever situation or society my wanderings bring me, there is the same homogeneity. If I happen into Vagabondia, I make merry with the jolly folk of the road or the tavern.

I do not remember ever to have met persons with whom I could not at once communicate, or to have been shocked or surprised at the doings of my dream-companions. In its strange wanderings in those dusky groves of Slumberland, my soul takes everything for granted and adapts itself to the wildest phantoms. I am seldom confused. Everything is as clear as day. I know events the instant they take place, and wherever I turn my steps, mind is my faithful guide and interpreter.I suppose every one has had in a dream the exasperating, profitless experience of seeking something urgently desired at the moment, and the aching, weary sensation that follows each failure to track the thing to its hiding-place. Sometimes with a singing dizziness in my head I climb and climb, I know not where or why. Yet I cannot quit the torturing, passionate endeavor, though again and again I reach out blindly for an object to hold to. Of course, according to the perversity of dreams, there is no object near. I clutch empty air, and then I fall downward, and still downward, and in the midst of the fall I dissolve into the atmosphere upon which I have been floating so precariously.

Some of my dreams seem to be traced one within another like a series of concentric circles. In sleep I think I cannot sleep. I toss about in the toils of tasks unfinished. I decide to get up and read for a while. I know the shelf in my library where I keep the book I want. The book has no name, but I find it without difficulty. I settle myself comfortably in the Morris-chair, the great book open on my knee. Not a word can I make out, the pages are utterly blank. I am not surprised, but keenly disappointed. I finger the pages, I bend over them lovingly, the tears fall on my hands. I shut the book quickly as the thought passes through my mind, "The print will be all rubbed out if I get it wet." Yet there is no print tangible on the page!

This morning I thought that I awoke. I was certain that I had overslept. I seized my watch, and, sure enough, it pointed to an hour after my rising time. I sprang up in the greatest hurry, knowing that breakfast was ready. I called my mother, who declared that my watch must be wrong. She was certain it could not be so late. I looked at my watch again, and, lo! the hands wiggled, whirled, buzzed, and disappeared. I awoke more fully as my dismay grew, until I was at the antipodes of sleep. Finally my eyes opened actually, and I knew that I had been dreaming. I had only waked into sleep. What is still more bewildering, there is no difference between the consciousness of the sham waking and that of the real one.

It is fearful to think that all that we have ever seen, felt, read, and done, may suddenly rise to our dream-vision, as the sea casts up objects it has swallowed. I have held a little child in my arms in the midst of a riot and spoken vehemently, imploring the Russian soldiers not to massacre the Jews. I have relived the agonizing scenes of the Sepoy Rebellion and the French Revolution. Cities have burned before my eyes, and I have fought the flames until I fell exhausted. Holocausts overtake the world, and I struggle in vain to save my friends.

Once in a dream a message came speeding over land and sea that winter was descending upon the world from the North Pole, that the Arctic zone was shifting to our mild climate. Far and wide the message flew. The ocean was congealed in midsummer. Ships were held fast in the ice by thousands, the ships with large, white sails were held fast. Riches of the Orient and the plenteous harvests of the golden West might no more pass between nation and nation. For some time the trees and flowers grew on, despite the intense cold. Birds flew into the houses for safety, and those which winter had overtaken lay on the snow with wings spread in vain flight. At last the foliage and blossoms fell at the feet of Winter. The petals of the flowers were turned to rubies and sapphires. The leaves froze into emeralds. The trees moaned and tossed their branches as the frost pierced them through bark and sap, pierced into their very roots. I shivered myself awake, and with a tumult of joy I breathed the many sweet morning odors wakened by the summer sun.

One need not visit an African jungle or an Indian forest to hunt the tiger. One can lie in bed amid downy pillows and dream tigers as terrible as any in the pathless wild. I was a little girl when one night I tried to cross the garden in front of my aunt's house in Alabama. I was in pursuit of a large cat with a great, bushy tail. A few hours before he had clawed my little canary out of its cage, and crunched it between his cruel teeth. I could not see the cat; but the thought in my mind was distinct: "He is making for the high grass at the end of the garden. I'll get there first." I put my hand on the box border and ran swiftly along the path. When I reached the high grass, there was the cat gliding into the wavy tangle. I rushed forward and tried to seize him and take the bird from between his teeth. To my horror, a huge beast, not the cat at all, sprang out from the grass, and his sinewy shoulder rubbed against me with palpitating strength! His ears stood up and quivered with anger. His eyes were hot. His nostrils were large and wet. His lips moved horribly. I knew it was a tiger, a real live tiger, and that I should be devoured—my little bird and I. I do not know what happened after that. The next important thing seldom happens in dreams.

Some time earlier I had a dream which made a vivid impression upon me. My aunt was weeping because she could not find me; but I took an impish pleasure in the thought that she and others were searching for me, and making great noise, which I felt through my feet. Suddenly the spirit of mischief gave way to uncertainty and fear. I felt cold. The air smelled like ice and salt. I tried to run; but the long grass tripped me, and I fell forward on my face. I lay very still, feeling with all my body. After a while my sensations seemed to be concentrated in my fingers, and I perceived that the grass blades were as sharp as knives, and hurt my hands cruelly. I tried to get up cautiously, so as not to cut myself on the sharp grass. I put down a tentative foot, much as my kitten treads for the first time the primeval forest in the back yard. All at once I felt the stealthy patter of something creeping, creeping, creeping purposely toward me. I do not know how at that time the idea was in my mind,—I had no words for intention or purpose,—yet it was precisely the evil intent, and not the creeping animal, that terrified me. I had no fear of living creatures. I loved my father's dogs, the frisky little calf, the gentle cows, the horses and mules that ate apples from my hand, and none of them had ever harmed me. I lay low, waiting in breathless terror for the creature to spring and bury its long claws in my flesh. I thought, "They will feel like turkey-claws." Something warm and wet touched my face. I shrieked, struck out frantically, and awoke. Something was still struggling in my arms. I held on with might and main until I was exhausted, then I loosed my hold. I found dear old Belle, the setter, shaking herself and looking at me reproachfully. She and I had gone to sleep together on the rug, and had naturally wandered to the dream-forest where dogs and little girls hunt wild game and have strange adventures. We encountered hosts of elfin foes, and it required all the dog tactics at Belle's command to acquit herself like the lady and huntress that she was. Belle had her dreams, too. We used to lie under the trees and flowers in the old garden, and I used to laugh with delight when the magnolia leaves fell with little thuds, and Belle jumped up, thinking she had heard a partridge. She would pursue the leaf, point it, bring it back to me, and lay it at my feet with a humorous wag of her tail, as much as to say, "This is the kind of bird that waked me." I made a chain for her neck out of the lovely blue Paulownia flowers and covered her with the great heart-shaped leaves.

Dear old Belle, she has long been dreaming among the lotus-flowers and poppies of the dogs' paradise.

Certain dreams have haunted me since my childhood. One which recurs often proceeds after this wise: A spirit seems to pass before my face. I feel an extreme heat like the blast from an engine. It is the embodiment of evil. I must have had it first after the day that I nearly got burned.

Another spirit which visits me often brings a sensation of cool dampness, such as one feels on a chill November night when the window is open. The spirit stops just beyond my reach, and sways back and forth like a creature in grief. My blood is chilled, and seems to freeze in my veins. I try to move, but my body is still, and I cannot even cry out. After a while the spirit passes on, and I say to myself shudderingly: "That was Death. I wonder if he has taken her." The pronoun stands for my teacher.

In my dreams I have sensations, odors, tastes, and ideas which I do not remember to have had in reality. Perhaps they are the glimpses which my mind catches, through the veil of sleep of my earliest babyhood. I have heard "the trampling of many waters." Sometimes a wonderful light visits me in sleep. Such a flash and glory as it is! I gaze and gaze until it vanishes. I smell and taste much as in my waking hours; but the sense of touch plays a less important part. In sleep I almost never grope. No one guides me. Even in a crowded street I am self-sufficient, and I enjoy an independence quite foreign to my physical life. Now I seldom spell on my fingers, and it is still rarer for others to spell into my hand. My mind acts independent of my physical organs. I am delighted to be thus endowed, if only in sleep; for then my soul dons its winged sandals and joyfully joins the throng of happy beings who dwell beyond the reaches of bodily sense.

The moral inconsistency of dreams is glaring. Mine grow less and less accordant with my proper principles. I am nightly hurled into an unethical medley of extremes. I must either defend another to the last drop of my blood or condemn him past all repenting. I commit murder, sleeping, to save the lives of others. I ascribe to those I love best acts and words which it mortifies me to remember, and I cast reproach after reproach upon them. It is fortunate for our peace of mind that most wicked dreams are soon forgotten. Death, sudden and awful, strange loves and hates remorselessly pursued, cunningly plotted revenge, are seldom more than dim, haunting recollections in the morning, and during the day they are erased by the normal activities of the mind. Sometimes, immediately on waking, I am so vexed at the memory of a dream-fracas that I wish I may dream no more. With this wish distinctly before me I drop off again into a new turmoil of dreams.

Oh, dreams, what opprobrium I heap upon you—you, the most pointless things imaginable, saucy apes, brewers of odious contrasts, haunting birds of ill omen, mocking echoes, unseasonable reminders, oft-returning vexations, skeletons in my Morris-chair, jesters in the tomb, death's-heads at the wedding feast, outlaws of the brain that every night defy the mind's police service, thieves of my Hesperidean apples, breakers of my domestic peace, murderers of sleep! "Oh, dreadful dreams that do fright my spirit from her propriety!" No wonder that Hamlet preferred the ills he knew rather than run the risk of one dream-vision.

Yet remove the dream-world, and the loss is inconceivable. The magic spell which binds poetry together is broken. The splendor of art and the soaring might of imagination are lessened because no phantom of fadeless sunsets and flowers urges onward to a goal. Gone is the mute permission or connivance which emboldens the soul to mock the limits of time and space, forecast and gather in harvests of achievement for ages yet unborn. Blot out dreams, and the blind lose one of their chief comforts; for in the visions of sleep they behold their belief in the seeing mind and their expectation of light beyond the blank, narrow night justified. Nay, our conception of immortality is shaken. Faith, the motive-power of human life, flickers out. Before such vacancy and bareness the shock of wrecked worlds were indeed welcome. In truth, dreams bring us the thought independently of us and in spite of us that the soul

> may right
> Her nature, shoot large sail on lengthening cord,
> And rush exultant on the Infinite.

Dreams and Reality

It is astonishing to think how our real wide-awake life revolves around the shadowy unrealities of Dreamland. Despite all that we say about the inconsequence of dreams, we often reason by them. We stake our greatest hopes upon them. Nay, we build upon them the fabric of an ideal world. I can recall few fine, thoughtful poems, few noble works of art, or any system of philosophy, in which there is not evidence that dream-fantasies symbolize truths concealed by phenomena.

The fact that in dreams confusion reigns and illogical connections occur gives plausibility to the theory which Sir Arthur Mitchell and other scientific men hold, that our dream-thinking is uncontrolled and undirected by the will. The will—the inhibiting and guiding power—finds rest and refreshment in sleep, while the mind, like a bark without rudder or compass, drifts aimlessly upon an uncharted sea. But, curiously enough, these fantasies and intertwistings of thought are to be found in great imaginative poems like Spenser's "Faerie Queene." Lamb was impressed by the analogy between our dream-thinking and the work of the imagination. Speaking of the episode in the cave of Mammon, Lamb wrote:

> It is not enough to say that the whole episode is a copy of the mind's conceptions in sleep; it is, in some sort—but what a copy! Let the most romantic of us that has been entertained all night with the spectacle of some wild and magnificent vision, recombine it in the morning and try it by his waking judgment. That which appeared so shifting and yet so coherent, while that faculty was passive, when it comes under cool examination shall appear so reasonless and so unlinked, that we are ashamed to have been so deluded, and to have taken, though but in sleep, a monster for a god. But the transitions in this episode are every whit as violent as in the most extravagant dream, and yet the waking judgment ratifies them.

Perhaps I feel more than others the analogy between the world of our waking life and the world of dreams because before I was taught I lived in a sort of perpetual dream. The testimony of parents and friends who watched me day after day is the only means that I have of knowing the actuality of those early, obscure years of my childhood. The physical acts of going to bed and waking in the morning alone mark the transition from reality to Dreamland. As near as I can tell, asleep or awake, I felt only with my body. I can recollect no process which I should now dignify with the term of thought. It is true that my bodily sensations were extremely acute; but beyond a crude connection with physical wants, they were not associated or directed. They had little relation to one another, to me, or to the experience of others. Idea—that which gives identity and continuity to experience— came into my sleeping and waking existence at the same moment with the awakening of self-consciousness. Before that moment my mind was in a state of anarchy in which meaningless sensations rioted, and if thought existed, it was so vague and inconsequent that it cannot be made a part of discourse. Yet before my education began, I dreamed. I know that I must have dreamed because I recall no break in my tactual experiences. Things fell suddenly, heavily. I felt my clothing afire, or I fell into a tub of cold water. Once I smelled bananas, and the odor in my nostrils was so vivid that in the morning, before I was dressed, I went to the sideboard to look for the bananas. There were no bananas, and no odor of bananas anywhere. My life was in fact a dream throughout.

The likeness between my waking state and the sleeping one is still marked. In both states I see, but not with my eyes. I hear, but not with my ears. I speak, and am spoken to, without the sound of a voice. I am moved to pleasure by visions of ineffable beauty which I have never beheld in the physical world. Once in a dream I held in my hand a pearl. I have no memory-vision of a real pearl. The one I saw in my dreams must, therefore, have been a creation of my imagination. It was a smooth, exquisitely molded crystal. As I gazed into its shimmering deeps, my soul was flooded with an ecstasy of tenderness, and I was filled with wonder, as one who should for the first time look into the cool, sweet heart of a rose. My pearl was dew and fire, the velvety green of moss, the soft whiteness of lilies, and the distilled hues and sweetness of a thousand roses. It seemed to me, the soul of beauty was dissolved in its crystal bosom. This beauteous vision strengthens my conviction that the world which the mind builds up out of countless subtle experiences and suggestions is fairer than the world of the senses. The splendor of the sunset my friends gaze at across the purpling hills is wonderful; but the sunset of the inner vision brings purer delight because it is the worshipful blending of all the beauty that we have known and desired.

I believe that I am more fortunate in my dreams than most people; for as I think back over my dreams, the pleasant ones seem to predominate, although we naturally recall most vividly and tell most eagerly the grotesque and fantastic adventures in Slumberland. I have friends, however, whose dreams are always troubled and disturbed. They wake fatigued and bruised, and they tell me that they would give a kingdom for one dreamless night. There is one friend who declares that she has never had a felicitous dream in her life. The grind and worry of the day invade the sweet domain of sleep and weary her with incessant, profitless effort. I feel very sorry for this friend, and perhaps it is hardly fair to insist upon the pleasure of dreaming in the presence of one whose dream-experience is so unhappy. Still, it is true that my dreams have uses as many and sweet as those of adversity. All my yearning for the strange, the weird, the ghostlike is gratified in dreams. They carry me out of the accustomed and commonplace. In a flash, in the winking of an eye, they snatch the burden from my shoulder, the trivial task from my hand, and the pain and disappointment from my heart, and I behold the lovely face of my dream. It dances round me with merry measure, and darts hither and thither in happy abandon. Sudden, sweet fancies spring forth from every nook and corner, and delightful surprises meet me at every turn. A happy dream is more precious than gold and rubies.

I like to think that in dreams we catch glimpses of a life larger than our own. We see it as a little child, or as a Savage who visits a civilized nation. Thoughts are imparted to us far above our ordinary thinking. Feelings nobler and wiser than any we have known thrill us between heart-beats. For one fleeting night a princelier nature captures us, and we become as great as our aspirations.

3

Moral Character and Spirituality

A large number of Helen Keller's *Home Magazine* columns, which ran 1930-1935, dealt with the theme of moral uplift and optimism. It was clear that this was her way of helping her readers deal with the Great Depression. In one of Keller's columns published less than a year after the 1929 stock market crash, she sent a message about learning to cope with hardships. She wrote: "What really counts in life is the quiet meeting of every difficulty with the determination to get out of it all the good there is. I am not advocating a passive resignation to things as they are, but a cheerful resolve to make the best of them."[1] That column also quotes President Herbert Hoover's thoughts about solitude being a way to refresh a person's mind. Keller asks her readers to look inward to see that they do have the character to deal with bad times: "The realization that we have infinite resources within ourselves would strengthen us to wrestle with any fate."[2]

Keller also takes the United States to task for not being a thoughtful and peace-loving world power. As she writes in 1931, "If we do not accept our responsibilities toward world affairs in the right spirit, we shall soon degenerate as world power."[3] She advocates for the cancellation of war debts and the fostering of a spirit of cooperation among nations. She says America has many good attributes, but that Americans' values focus on frivolous and shallow concerns. Keller says of post-World War I America, "The prosperity we have enjoyed has nourished our vanity until it has obscured our vision of essential values."[4]

Keller's early *Home* columns were accompanied by a large picture of Keller as a young woman reading in braille. The photo has an almost religious quality: her eyes are turned heavenward and she is dressed in clothes of the early 20th century that are reminiscent of a Rembrandt painting. Her hand is on an open book, and because her eyes are cast upward, it is clear she is reading braille. This dramatic photo was used with her first columns in 1930 and reinforced the power of her byline with a reminder of her disabilities.

The illustrations and photos are an interesting aspect of Keller columns in *Home Magazine*. From 1930 through 1932, they are accompanied by a variety of photos of the writer, ranging from the fairly mundane—of her reading a braille page, of which there are several versions—to the instructional, showing how she lip-reads a speech with her hand on the face of a judge. A 1931 photo depicts Keller with her dogs.

By mid-1932, however, the magazine had begun using drawings to illustrate the columns. By early 1933, the famed illustrator Robert Fawcett (1903-1967) was creating all the drawings for the columns. Most are beautiful and captivating; some illustrations dominated the columns, much larger than Keller's text. Fawcett was known as an "illustrator's illustrator" because of his attention to detail and his integrity. He once said, "We represent the only view of art, of beauty, to millions of people. If we do less than our best, we cheat them."[5] His attitude made him a good match for Keller's column because as she was trying to inspire during difficult times, his drawings were trying to give readers an inspirational, aesthetic pleasure.

Notes:

1. Helen Keller, "Know Thyself," *The Home Magazine*, September 1930, p. 6.

2. Helen Keller, "Know Thyself," *The Home Magazine*, September 1930, p. 6.

3. Helen Keller, Love Ye One Another," *The Home Magazine*, May 1931, p. 6.

4. Helen Keller, Love Ye One Another," *The Home Magazine*, May 1931, p. 6.

5. Illustration House website. Robert Fawcett biography. http://www.illustration-house.com/bios/fawcett_bio.html. No date.

Know Thyself

The Home Magazine, September 1930, pp. 6, 117

President Hoover said recently, "Solitude offers the only opportunity for refreshment and clarification of the mind." These words can be confirmed by many quotations from the philosophers and writers of all ages. I wish those who read this would shut themselves away from all distraction a little while each day and "listen in" on their thoughts. If we would only approach our minds with curiosity, we would discover a new world of interest and delight. The realization that we have infinite resources within ourselves would strengthen us to wrestle with any fate.

Most of us believe that could we choose our environment, we should be perfectly happy. We think of environment in terms of money, power, fame, having a good time, sight, hearing, health. My experience is that happiness has little to do with outward circumstances.

I once lived in a dark, soundless, hopeless world. I fretted and beat myself against the walls that imprisoned me. No one, not even my mother, could communicate with me, and I could not speak one word. Then a great teacher came and helped me to conquer my limitations. She succeeded because she loved me and believed I could be taught. She was not discouraged by difficulties. Patiently she broke one fetter after another that held me captive. With a little word spelled into my hand she led me out into the sunshine of life, and I found myself, I found friends and work I could do within my limitations.

This convinces me that no matter what our outward lot may be, we can do anything we want if we have a reasonable, steadfast purpose. There is a place for every one of us to fill in the world. Let us resolve to fill it honorably. Recently Dr. Kitson, Professor of Psychology and Education at Columbia University, found that few people are content with their life-work, that many stated bluntly their interest was at zero point. This attitude of mind seems to me most unfortunate. If we do not like our work, and do not try to get happiness out of it, we are a menace to our profession as well as to ourselves. What really counts in life is the quiet meeting of every difficulty with the determination to get out of it all the good there is.

I am not advocating a passive resignation to things as they are, but a cheerful resolve to make the best of them. While recognizing the situation as it is, and admitting that circumstance has us by the collar, we can keep on our guard and break loose when the waited-for moment comes. In the meantime we can wring from it treasures of knowledge, thought and strength. Too many of us long for a different environment without striving to attain it. The prospect of sustained effort frightens us. We make out of our discontent, complaints or idle dreams. There is something subversive of the finer qualities of our nature in crying out against our destiny. We want prosperity and success. Very good! Let us work for these things.

To imagine a world with no hardships to encounter, no dangers to meet, no obstacles to overcome is to picture a society wearisome and deadly monotonous. The joy of living is in venturing[,] in doing, in dreaming. There is in each one of us the urge to test our powers against adverse circumstances. We could smooth out our difficulties ourselves if we would take a little time to study the possibilities of the environment in which we are placed. But we seldom sit down and get acquainted with our true selves.

We live in a restless, noisy age. There are so many places to go to, and it is so easy to get there, the almost universal cry is, "Let us go somewhere, and let us go at top speed!" Doing nothing is unthinkable, the idea of being alone with our thoughts is almost terrifying. We take twice as much trouble as is necessary to attain happiness, and miss it in the end.

Many of my friends marvel when I tell them I am happy. They imagine my deprivations weigh heavily on my spirit and chain me. I wonder if their eyes and ears are joy-bringers! With eyes full of light, color and joyous motion they are dissatisfied, eager for amusement and exciting adventures. To me, alone with silence, my thoughts are beautiful realities. It is in silent communion with themselves that great men create works that live forever. We may not be endowed with the divine spark of genius. The vital thing is not that we have many talents, but it is the practical use we make of the talent we have, and we can all use our minds to explore the inner world and learn to hear wisdom in

> The winged silences that fly
> Like homing birds
> From human heart to human heart
> When undisturbed by words.

126

A Christmas Challenge

The Home Magazine, December 1930, p. 8

The ringing declaration of Field Marshal Haig, "It is the business of Christians to make my business impossible," is a challenge which Christian people cannot ignore. Nor can they close their ears to the terrible arraignment of the churches by Brigadier-General Crozier. In his book, "The Brass Hat in No Man's Land," he says, "The churches are the finest blood-lust creators, and of them we have made free use."

On December 25th the Christian world will celebrate the nineteen hundred and thirtieth anniversary of the birth of Him who came upon earth that all men might have life, and have it more abundantly. There will be a joyous pealing of bells. Away in the blue there will appear a vision of a lowly manger where the infant Savior lies, while angel voices are singing peace on earth, good will to men.

That vision will awaken in our hearts tender emotions which have been dormant for a year. For a brief season we shall allow our kindlier impulses to have their way. For one day we shall live as Christians should live, loving one another.

Wonderful! The doors that were closed stand open! The will to give, to make happy, to rejoice streams out upon the world!

All this we do on Christmas Day; but the morning after our homage to the Prince of Peace wanes. Our joyful good will to all men fizzles out more or less. There is cynicism in our attitude toward the sentiments we uttered the day before.

The truth is, when we face the facts of existence, we find that we were not born anew on Christmas Day. Our ideals were not vitalized. We merely exhausted our energies in giving and receiving, not so much in the spirit of Jesus of Nazareth as in a sort of competition to outdo each other. Our Christmas friendliness proves to be part of the hypocrisy and lip worship which have brought us to the brink of an abyss.

We call ourselves Christians, but in our every-day lives we are not Christians. Two contrary attitudes prevail today in our civilization. One believes in the inevitability of blood and death. This belief finds expression in daily inventing new means of killing. It obliges the nations to be ever preparing for war.

The other is an attitude of peace, of labor, of salvation. One would sacrifice hundreds of thousands of lives for the ambition of a few selfish individuals who want their country to be supreme; the other strives to deliver man from the scourges that afflict him.

In women exists the impulse to conserve, to protect, to create harmony. The age is coming when women will more and more resist man's inherent will to dominate, and women will exercise their natural bent for peace.

Then let women speak with a million tongues, calling upon the peoples to put an end to war and the expectation of wars. Let them summon all nationalities to join in a glad song of peace on earth, good will to men, and Christians shall be the most beautiful of realities because it is the Spirit of Christ incarnate.

Marks

The Home Magazine, July 1930, p. 6

Much of the good work of the world is done by those who as students failed in their examinations, or at least passed with very low marks. Many a student has thought himself mediocre, and has been humiliated because he could not answer certain questions satisfactorily.

Now success and happiness should not depend on marks. The one who works hard and carries in his soul a vision of service, but who receives low marks, may prove to be no less necessary to the world than the self-possessed student who receives high marks. If from our studies, the books we read, the friends we cultivate, we learn understanding, sympathy and helpfulness, we need have no concern about the marks on our examination papers. It may be more important to talk for an hour with an intelligent, broad-minded person than to receive the approval of high marks.

It is a great mistake to attach too much significance to examinations. It is natural to feel proud when we acquit ourselves well in an ordeal of any kind; but it would be a grievous evil if all the school work of the single year were to depend on the marks given in a single examination. Questionnaires of any sort are apt to create an anxious, confused state of mind, and fail of the very object of the test—to find out the natural endowment of the student. If in our school years we learn to think and form our own judgments, we are a hundred times better off than if we had come out of an examination with flying colors.

An institution of learning is honored in the highest degree by the men and woman it sends out into the world able to cope with the real problems of life. That is the true fruit of education—the only mark worth striving for. To give importance to marks indicates a slight knowledge of the true nature of character-building and a doubtful respect for the worth and dignity of man's spirit. A test or a reward held out in order to stimulate attention and ambition invariably fails of its purpose. When an external stimulus is used, no matter how spiritual it appears, we leave undeveloped the active, independent inward force which is latent in each one of us. We dwarf and degrade human nature when we dangle before it a bait to good action, even though the bait be a high mark culminating in a college degree. Diligence, faithfulness, devotion to knowledge are at all times the most potent methods of attaining satisfying human aspirations.

The marking system is another ancient idol that must come down from its pedestal. Marks have no intrinsic value. It is not marks that are important to the world, but character, thoughts and deeds. Great men and women, we shall find, were not bent on high marks.

A Thought for the New Year

The Home Magazine, January 1931, p. 17

I t may make a difference to all eternity whether we start 1931 right or wrong. Let us begin the new year by looking for the opportunities it contains, and approaching them with fresh minds and ready hands.

It is chiefly by what are regarded as misfortunes that we gain power and initiative. Prosperity unalloyed dulls our faculties and keeps us preoccupied with selfish pursuits; it produces a false confidence and self-pride, and makes those of us who enjoy affluence and honor forget the hands by which they are bestowed.

It is seldom otherwise than by adversity that we are made to see our folly, and how little all our acquisitions contribute to safety, peace of mind or happiness. In our vanity we consider the profits that cause our bank accounts to mount ever higher as the result of our own policy and courage. Hard times teach us that we live by each other and for each other; that, to achieve success, even average success, we must know thoroughly about some one thing, and utilize our knowledge, not only for ourselves, but also for the benefit of others.

When money is easy, as the saying is, there is a lack of initiative and perseverance. It is good to have money and the things that money can buy, but it is good also to check up once in a while and make sure that we haven't lost the things which money can't buy—the will to serve, to love, to create beauty and joy.

Again I repeat, misfortunes, hard times and greater difficulties to overcome develop more power and initiative, just as a falling body generates greater momentum with each foot of the fall. If falling stocks and falling bank accounts make us wiser, manlier, more worthy of God's gifts of life, health and sound faculties, blessed be the failures that put such precious spiritual wealth into our hands! Let us hasten to Wall Street and hang laurel wreaths upon the barred and bolted doors of the Stock Exchange.

We are living in troublous times. Prices are low, production has fallen off, profits are cut down. Yet I dare strike a positive note of hopefulness.

Adversity has its uses. It necessitates the tense bracing of the will and mental resourcefulness which differentiate us from the cat by the fire when there is no more wood to burn. Let us begin the new year by looking for the opportunities it contains.

My friends, let us begin today by putting out of our minds the idea that the world owes us anything. The world doesn't owe us even a living unless we work for it. There is a kind of prosperity that may justly be regarded not only as a spendthrift, but also as a robber of human happiness. Let us seek rather the mutual advantage and welfare of all our fellow-men, in which there shall be scope for every fine quality to grow, and every noble impulse to be embodied in constructive achievement. Courage, initiative and patient work are forces before which difficulties disappear.

Love Ye One Another

The Home Magazine, May 1931, pp. 6, 115

No people can live unto themselves and fulfill a worthy destiny. Our own problems offer but a limited scope for statesmanship, and we cannot solve them satisfactorily by patriotism, chauvinism, constitutionalism or more and more laws. The time has come to shake off our provincialism.

Through the entanglements of the World War we are today involved in the problems of mankind. Most of us have yet to learn what these problems are and how to approach them. Our ignorant attitude towards them is fraught with immense danger. If we do not accept our responsibilities toward world affairs in the right spirit, we shall soon degenerate as a world power. We could easily become the leader in international amity and cooperation. What would do more to bring all nations together than the cancellation of war debts? Coming from us, what a noble gesture!

But before this can happen, we must adopt a different attitude toward other people, a less arrogant and contemptuous point of view of the older civilizations and a more critical attitude towards ourselves. Our love of freedom, love of justice, love of truth, love of beauty will have to stand the test of comparison with some of the nations we despise.

We shall have to face the unpleasant fact that our cities are for the most part ugly, noisy and lacking in refinements and intellectual satisfactions. We shall have to ask ourselves whether in our haste to get rich we have not sacrificed beauty. For art requires patience, leisure and serenity.

The prosperity we have enjoyed has nourished our vanity until it has obscured our vision of essential values. We have attained phenomenal success, but we are not a great nation in the sense that little Greece was great.

We have paved roads, lighted streets, pleasant parks, sanitation and as good schools as we can understand for our children. For the average American expects the school to train them only along lines that yield immediate results. We have learned accuracy, observation and quickness of action, but we have not learned to think. Thus our schools have failed to broaden or enrich our minds, and true greatness depends upon how we use our minds—upon things that endure—love, faith, right living, imagination, beauty. The practical knowledge of which we boast will become our destroyer unless it is supplemented by understanding and appreciation.

We have more newspapers than any other country on earth, yet we are uninformed. Why? Because we read the sport news first, the crimes next and then the comic page. At election time we read the editorials in the paper on our side and ignore those on the other side.

As people we do not read serious books. We dismiss as "highbrow stuff" thoughtful consideration of any important subject. We are for peace in times of peace. We talk about disarmament—and build another frightful machine.

We are very proud of our civilization, but will posterity feel that we have builded well? I think that in this period of economic depression we are being confronted with the faultiness of our foundations.

However, I have great faith in America. It is like the sun—it can be clouded, but not extinguished. I believe the cloud which is now darkening the sky has a silver lining. It is making us pause and ask ourselves where we are going, and if the goal we are striving for is worthy of a great nation. We are finding out that we need the spiritual magnanimity which enables men to come nearer to one another. Perhaps the commandment, "Love ye one another" is being uttered in whispers behind closed doors, and will grow in volume and strength until it becomes a shout that shall forever still brute force and the greed that makes slaves of men.

The Great Choice

The Home Magazine, January 1932, p. 8

The beginning of the new year seems the right moment to give thought to a problem that concerns the whole world. The responsibility of a great choice rests with us women.

We can build up a world of beauty and humanity or we can let the politicians and the profiteers plunge us into another world cataclysm. Let all of us reflect earnestly on this choice. If we decide that we will have peace, permanent peace, the next thing is to consider how to work most effectively for it.

The most fundamental way to work for peace is to begin with our children. We can see to it that hatred is not fostered between them and the children of other lands in the teaching of history and literature. Military heroes must not be held up for their admiration, but rather the common adventures of men in all lands who have won victories over darkness within and the forces of nature without.

We cannot start too early to develop world friendship in children. Their reading is a very important factor in cultivating universal good-will. From books that give a vivid description of life in other nations they catch the spirit and humanity of civilizations that would otherwise seem to them strange and hostile. More than a century ago George Washington said that extremes of antipathy and attachment towards particular nations are inimical to progress and must be eliminated.

Our children must be made to feel that heroes in the work of peace exist and that the heroism of peace is the highest courage. We have war medals and decorations. Why not have medals and decorations for those who show talent, imagination and initiative in peace promotion?

We must have peace organizations that do more than talk. We have pacts, leagues and protocols of peace which spend their time swapping old troubles for new ones or scrapping only armaments that will not be needed in the next war.

Any intelligent person can see that peace cannot be left to governments. Governments are founded on force, and in order to defend and extend their power they inevitably resort to militarism.

One of the most effective methods against war is to refuse to have anything to do with the production of munitions and armaments. Let us insist that the building of submarines and the manufacture of gas be stopped, also the establishment of air forces intended to destroy human life.

Our greatest need at present is a peace formula that means something. This formula must be short, a flash in darkness. It must have in it the spirit of the commandment, "Thou shalt not kill."

Permanent peace and prosperity will come only when we realize and incorporate into our lives the truth that we live by each other and for each other and not unto ourselves. We must work all together for a world organized for peace. Never was there a better end to strive for. The alternative is the most appalling catastrophe mankind has ever faced. Never did the possibility of war in the future hold such horror as it does today to those who realize the type of munitions and weapons of warfare being gathered through research and manufacture throughout the world.

Then let us women throw our weight in the scale on the side of peace. Women can be a greater power for world peace than they realize. We not only can teach our children ideals of peace, but we can influence others around us. We shall thus contribute most of the enduring glory of our country. Let us turn our backs upon the blood-soaked path by which we came and face towards peace, for thus alone can our feet be lighted along the roadway of the future.

Let Us Create Beauty

The Home Magazine, March 1932, p. 6

Editor's note: French painter Jean-François Millet, who died in 1875, helped found the Barbizon school in rural France.

I believe if we took up some handicraft in our free moments we would be happier. There are many kinds of embroidery, weaving, leather and brass work that we could master, and I feel sure such occupation would prove far more interesting than speeding somewhere and back again in an automobile. It could be work into which we could put a spirit of play, and that is what we so sadly need in this age of machinery and monotonous routine.

The best work is that which we do when we experience the joy of creation—when we feel that it is a part of ourselves, our child as it were, which we are proud to show to others. Millet, the French artist, was obliged to paint signs to earn a living, but that was not his best work. In his leisure hours he painted his masterpieces, "The Angelus" and "The Gleaners," for the sheer love of painting.

All of us are not as gifted as Millet, but I think if we would only try, we should be surprised to find how many touches of loveliness we could impart to the prosaic, work-a-day life about us.

If we could become more aware of the power within us to give form and color to our individuality, we should have a joyous sense of creating beauty in common things. There is an individuality, a friendliness in things made by hand that are not to be found in the perfect machine product.

Things we do with our hands develop us. The perfect way to spoil a child is to do everything for him.

Who has not noticed that when a child is left to himself he is always doing something? He is a little mechanic fashioning the world to his own fancy.

Let us learn from our children and do things with our own hands for the mere joy of it. Making things opens the mind as naturally as extracting food from the soil opens the flowers.

The forms of life change from age to age, but fundamental human needs never change. We must, by all means, give vent to our creative faculties and try to develop our sense of color, form and design. The thought I am anxious to express and have understood is this—things we do ourselves make us happy. All sound handiwork is beautiful and has joy in it. Work that has not joy in it is drudgery and slavery.

We often say that we would do these delightful things if it were not for the ever-present, stern necessity of earning our daily bread. But there are always hours or half hours when we might turn our thoughts away from this necessity and find rest in some expression of ourselves. How wonderful it would be if we should breathe into the dull substance of life the breath of a vivid personality!

We have been led to think so much of great things and great performances that we have gone far towards drying up the fresh wells in our souls from which the more specialized arts flow. When we look at common things with seeing eyes, we shall discover in them the magic of poetry.

Both plain sewing and weaving are foundational arts. In ancient times weaving was the typical art of the peoples. Into fabrics that still excite admiration after thousands of years they wove their faith, their songs, their love of flowers and birds. This occupation had a wholesome effect upon woman, it kept her fingers busy, her movements placid and her thoughts free to wander at will, or rest upon some loved object.

Mothers, older sisters and teachers can do much now and here if they encourage children in their natural inclination towards drawing or some other handicraft. If this is done, a generation will grow up that is more easily entertained and wiser in the art of being happy.

Easter

The Home Magazine, April 1932, p. 6

P raise the Lord, all ye things that die! Ye die that ye may live again."
This is the Resurrection Season, and that glad word shall be my theme. I love to say it over and over, and to listen to the sweet reverberations of thought it wakes—thoughts of Spring, of life, of friends who are waiting for me in the Spring of Eternity. What makes this miracle of Spring—this unfailing resurrection of life from death?

Behold how the tide of green comes up from the south again, climbing the hills and pouring through the valleys! Almost while we watch, invading every inch of the ground! The sap sings in the trees, and soon the branches are full of crinkled young leaves and blossoms. No place is left hidden from the gentle inundation of Spring, all hear her whisper, "Come forth," feel her touch and rise again. Her victory is visible in the waving leaf and flower and dancing stream.

Death is but the beginning of a new life. Death is the condition of life, just as the fading of the sunset and the withering of the flower are the condition of renewed beauty. Nothing in death is stranger than everything in life! Everywhere we sense the joy of the Resurrection. The sun is blazing it, the winds are shouting it, the birds are singing it, our thoughts are ringing gladly, and our hearts open wide to the new life of earth and sky.

Let us now turn from the fields, woods and streams to the world of men. Here our thoughts are crowded with human resurrections. History shows us how one nation blots out another by conquest, and how the vanquished nation rises again in the new.

One day we discover that we have been living selfish, useless lives. With deep heart-searchings and contrition we cast aside our old thoughts and ambitions and consecrate our energies to the service of others. This is the noblest of all resurrections.

Happy are they who can think of death as re-birth! The joyous feeling that the thought of Resurrection brings is a good feeling. It releases us, lifts us, gives us a fresh impulse and a new power. It is in happy accord with the resurrection of Spring and the renewals of human nature. Man is so completely a part of all things, and all things are so completely represented in man, he cannot escape the universal law that life shall change from one form to another more wonderful, more perfect.

Let us, then, take the thought of a new life into our souls as joyously as we take the sunshine into our bodies and move forward to new adventures. Let us live every moment as fully as we can on earth, and then all the beauty we have created will be part of our resurrection to a more glorious world.

The Goddess Who Knows Not Pity

The Home Magazine, August 1932, p. 6

Editor's note: Dr. Johnson is Samuel Johnson, the distinguished and prolific 18th-century British writer.

D r. Johnson once said, speaking of death, "Let it alone. It matters not how a man dies, but how he lives." The modern woman would probably say, "It matters not how a woman dies, but how she presents a handsome appearance while alive."

And after all, there is not such a wide chasm of meaning between these two simple statements. The first is a little more general in its scope, perhaps, but each admits that Life is the most important thing. Life and all it embodies. Death is a mere slipping on into a new sphere, a drifting over into a new horizon. But life is an eager, throbbing present to which we must give our attention. It makes its claims and we must heed them. And one of life's greatest claims is beauty.

Beauty has received a rather twisted meaning in modern times. To many it is judged by the comparison of a favorite movie star's languid eyes, her tilted nose or her dimpled cheek. A mere surface beauty. And real beauty is more than that.

One of my braille definitions proves what I am trying to say. It claims that beauty is an assemblage of graces, satisfying the eye, the ear, the intellect, the aesthetic faculty and the moral sense.

Whenever I hear people make the remark, "She is so beautiful," I wonder just how they are looking at the one described. Are they looking at her with their outer eye, or are they seeing, realizing what makes her beautiful? True beauty comes from the heart. It is a shining thing and reflects in the face the beauty of thought.

Often I have heard people say, "I never realized how pretty she was until I began to know her." They do not realize it, but association has created a new vision. The first impression was a misty film. But the new vision lasts. This beauty of character is not a temporary thing. It grows, and its growth does something to the face. And as we know the person better her sweetness and fine qualities blur our first impression. We do not see the blemishes, but we notice the kindly eye, the sympathetic smile and the generous spirit. And how happy this picture makes us! We, in turn, react and carry away with us a happy feeling that "God's in his heaven, all's right with the world."

To have beauty, one must live it, not just when company comes, to be put on and off as we do our guest silver. If we could only remember that every thought, every gesture is registering, and the repetition of that thought, good or bad, is going to lead us down the path of beauty or toward the mire of ugliness, how simple it all would be!

Happiness gives forth a strange vapor that is a powerful aid to the beauty specialist. It brightens the eye, and brings the needed color into the cheeks. The step becomes lighter and the air becomes electrified with good-will signals. Then it is that real beauty that shines forth. A little child is quick to sense this quality of good looks. That is why he sees his mother as "the prettiest lady." He feels the warmth of love. It dazzles his eyes until his probably plain little mother, becomes the queen of one of his story books. He sees the beauty of her soul, and in his appreciation is created an individual phase of feeling—the beauty of mother love.

The love of beauty is not a modern appreciation. The Greeks worshiped beauty and grace and spent their time developing the body into a rhythmic demonstration of fine living and thinking. They realized that beauty of mind and body produced a beauty that would defy the passing of years. And it has. The inspiration and its origin is never forgotten.

I think I will leave the summary of this little thought on beauty to John Keats who writes:

> A thing of beauty is a joy forever;
> Its loveliness increases; it will never
> Pass into nothingness!

The True Religion

The Home Magazine, October 1932, p. 6

I read much these days about skepticism among the young; and young girls often call on me whose frivolous attitude towards spiritual questions troubles me deeply.

What we believe is a serious matter, even if there were no life beyond the grave. Young girls make a great mistake to think that it is clever to doubt everything and assume a cynical outlook on life. They are like foolish virgins carrying lamps without oil to the House of the Next Generation. They are unconsciously jeopardizing the spiritual light which alone can guide themselves and their children through the increasingly difficult days of a changing world.

It is necessary only to listen to the talk of young people to realize that the more serious-minded among them are perplexed as to what to believe and what to reject. The dense materialism of today raises almost insurmountable obstacles to spiritual expansion, it narrows experience and sympathy, and cripples the imagination.

This is very different from doubting dogma and authority. One may doubt constructively and try to make one's thoughts conform to truth and the spiritual needs of the present. There is nothing more harmful to one's development than to sink into a welter of hypocrisy and cant.

I have much more sympathy for those who cannot believe all the circumstances of Jesus's life recorded in the Gospels—His birth and resurrection and the miracles He wrought—than for those who believe in all these details and in His teaching, and yet trample them under-foot when they interfere with material gain. The belief in immortality involving the survival of personality and individual recognition, while a source of joy to me, may be a stumbling-block to others. There are those who passionately believe in the Divine ordering of the universe; others that mankind is slowly emerging from the slough of ignorance through human knowledge of good and evil, and onward to ultimate choice of the good. One may believe that by God's Good Grace humanity shall one day become perfect if this faith ennobles one's life. It is then like a golden mesh in the fabric of character. Certainly one should not believe what one cannot understand or live.

To change from one faith to another or from habitual doubt to an earnest attitude towards the problems of the spirit is not easy. Progress towards any new expressions of faith may bring distress to somebody near us, but we must each read the riddle of the universe and answer it in her own way. What is deadly is indifference or insincerity. Youth can be forgiven everything else. Almost everyone has an honest respect for white-hot convictions. It is the lukewarm mind in religious faith that leaves us cold.

Hypocrisy is our national sin. We profess one thing and do another. In fact, our most sacred shibboleths are words of a thousand meanings or meanings of a thousand words. We have acquired a pharisaic morality. More and more we are forgetting the Law of Life. The red tide of crime flows on in the dark places of our cities. The cruel passions that create war are still unrestrained. Divorces are multiplying, child labor, lynching and mob violence remain to dishonor our civilization. Bigotry, racial hatred and political cant still put an appalling distance between us and the really united, progressive nation we can become.

Does not all this prove that young women need to believe genuinely in something great and live it with all their strength, heart and mind if they wish to see the next generation freer, happier, going forward to higher achievement? Young woman here and everywhere need less dogma and fewer observances, more religion of the head and the heart, a stronger social unity to make their country great in the future.

One thing personal religion should never do is to fetter the mind with fears. Fear can take us only a little way in character-forming. The most it can do is to fill life with inhibitions. Positive goodness demands a more adequate motive. Love is the strongest motive between man and God as well as between man and man. When love has become the dominant force of a human life without hypocrisy, without pose or pretense, without false sentimentality, we have found the true religion.

A Thanksgiving Prayer

The Home Magazine, November 1932, p. 6

We habitually thank God for material blessings—abundant crops, good health and prosperity. We think of illness, failure and hard times as wholly evil, and we pray fervently to be delivered from them. But banishing them would not be good for us, even if it could be done. We should try to think of them as endurance tests which develop our powers, strengthen our wills and invigorate our minds.

The worst sorrows in life are not its losses and misfortunes, but its fears. Often a misfortune turns out to be a new prospect of life because it calls forth new interests and sympathies of which we were not aware before.

There are many of us who have an impediment—a something wanting—withheld—that prevents our inner existence from flowering out into visible fact and deed—flowers that require the rain of tears to bring them to bloom. I like to think our individual trials are unfolding our characters all the while and preparing us for the service which God has reserved for us in His infinite wisdom.

Let us try changing our thanksgiving and prayer this year. Let us give thanks to God for the heavy blows of adversity that drive us back from wrong ways into harmony with the laws of our being. Let us thank Him for the stinging whips of pain and privation that urge us on to bitter strivings and high achievement, for the steep climb and the roughness of the road that make us staunch and fearless, for hardship and stumbling through darkness and sloughs of discouragement by which we blaze new trails along which many feet shall pass to a richer life, for the blight of confidence betrayed that makes us more discerning and just.

Let us strive to keep our eyes toward the east, toward the dawn of a new confidence that will make us better able to combat the struggles of the day. Let us not waste too much time pining for the glories that are past, victories that have been won, fortunes that have been made. Rather let us peer with uplifted faces into the mysterious challenge of the future, the great unexplored tomorrow.

Let us pray: We pray not, God, for the removal of our cross, but for better understanding, to the end that when failure and disappointment are ours, when again and again we are defeated and humbled, we may be saved from complaining. Burn out of us, O God, all thoughts of easy victory! Toughen our spirits for longer marches and fiercer battles over our selfish desires! Make us conscious of our neighbor's dependence on our thoughtfulness. Help us to know that now, as never before, we need the cheer and kindness of a friendly greeting. Keep our hearts from gazing into the grim sadness of circumstances, and may we find rainbows of faith making a colorful bridge over our dark grievances. Teach us how to learn from our mistakes the lessons of humility and patience. As little rivulets creep from mountain heights into parched valleys, even so cause love and hope to flow into our hearts. Discomfort us that our sight may be clearer to others' needs, and our hearing keener to their sighs. As the frail, yet indomitable voice of the captain makes itself heard above the tempest steering the ship, so teach us who are little, Lord, to go far though great difficulties. Make true progress more precious to us than our sheltering traditions and prejudices.

The lives of great men teach us that we grow to our full stature only on the bread of hard days.

Let us, in the spirit of proud acquiescence, thank God for Tears—Tears that wash away the mire of gain and the stain of hate, tears that give us a vision of the common good and human brotherhood. Tears that soften us towards the weaknesses and failings of our neighbors and quicken our perception of their better nature. Tears that broaden us and deepen our sympathy. Tears that drive from the mind many strange and peevish things—ambition, pride and greed, with all their accompanying appetites. Tears that usher in love, treading softly like a bird when young ones fill her nest. Yea, Thank Thee, Lord, for Thy Gift of Tears.

Are We Wasters of Time?

The Home Magazine, January 1933, p. 6

On the first of the New Year, when good resolutions are in order, it might be well for us to consider whether we have been time-wasters, and what is to be done about it.

Time is one of the things we possess. Our success depends on the right use of it.

The difficulty of the right use of time lies in the nature of time itself. It is not easy to make the best use of anything without knowing how much of it there is to use. We know that we have only a limited time at our life's disposal, but we have no means of discovering where the limit lies; so we are apt to spend our time extravagantly on trivialities, as if our portion of it were unlimited.

The bulk of our time is mapped out for us by circumstance. After eight hours have been given for the task of earning our daily bread, eight hours for sleep and two or three more for meals, there is not much of a day left that we may call our own to do with as we like. All the more careful should we be in the use we make of the precious remnant.

But what about the odd moments? Some of the men who have moved the world forward were men who used the odd moments wisely. Edison, for instance, was hammering away at a telegraph key-board when he was a telegraph operator on a small salary. He did not waste the odd moments; he thought and planned and tried between messages to perfect the instrument.

Benjamin Franklin, in his autobiography, tells how in a hundred different ways he made the odd moments useful and profitable.

Charles Darwin's ill-health rendered it impossible for him to work more than half an hour at a time. Yet in many half-hours he laid the foundations of a new philosophy that has changed the thought of the world.

What we do in the odd moments is not only likely to be pleasant, it is likely also to stimulate our minds and bring to us out of the every-day routine new ideas that may be turned to our profit or to the benefit of others.

Of course there is another side to the proper use of time. There are many more ways than one of wasting time. Doing too much may be as spendthrift of it as doing too little. Feverish activity, without due regard to quality or relevance, may be as great a waste of time as idleness. The fussy woman not only does needless things, she also does things that must be done over.

Time can be active as well as passive. It can waste was well as be wasted. It is capable of ravages, and its revenges are very cruel. But I think we shall all

147

agree that we should not "kill time" or spend it in anything that conscience or common sense tell us is sheer frivolity or meanness. At least we should endeavor to use our leisure time so as to get all we possibly can out of life. The persistent time-waster must not be surprised if sooner or later she finds herself echoing the lamentation of Tithonus.

Thy strong Hours indignant work'd their wills,
And beat me down and marr'd and wasted me.

The Simplest Way to Be Happy

The Home Magazine, February 1933, p. 6

My theme is that happiness is not the work of magic. Happiness comes under the law of seed and blossom. Happiness is the final and perfect fruit of obedience to the laws of life. One who lives in accordance with these laws has a talisman of happiness always at hand.

I know no study that will take you nearer the way to happiness than the study of nature—and I include in the study of nature not only things and their forces, but also mankind and their ways, and the molding of the affections and the will into an earnest desire not only to be happy, but to create happiness.

A happy life consists not in the absence, but in the mastery of hardships. Happiness is not for wild animals who can only oscillate between hunger and repletion. To be happy we must exercise our reasoning faculty and be conscious of our will and powers. In other words, we must have learned the secret of self-discipline. To be happy we must do those things which produce happiness.

Happiness is one of the slowest ripening fruits in the Garden of Life, and, like all fruits, it must be grown. There is a very clever trick in India. A mango-seed is put in the ground, and after divers incantations a full-blown mango-bush appears within five minutes! I have never met any one who knew how the thing was done, but I have never met any one who believed it to be anything else than a conjuring trick. We may never have planted a tree, but we know that it cannot grow in five minutes.

Some of us have not one plant in our lives on which to grow the fruit of happiness. We have not planted one sound seed in our hearts, and when we do plant a seed, it gets so little sunshine that it can never come to maturity.

The vine was the Eastern symbol of joy. It was its fruit that made glad the heart of man. The juice of the grape was the common drink at every peasant's meal. The gladness was the innocent gladness of satisfying the need of the body. This is not the truest happiness, and the vine of the Palestine vineyards was but a symbol of fruit-bearing and the act of sharing which implies inspiration to live and work for others with all that that brings of selflessness and joy in others' good.

It all comes to this: the simplest way to be happy is to do good. This is instant and infallible happiness. The surest proof that this is the law of cause and effect is, we may try every other conceivable way of being happy, and they will all fail. We cannot gather figs from thorns or grapes from thistles. The tree bears fruit after its kind both in the soil and in the soul. If we spend the time we waste in sighing for the perfect golden fruit in fulfilling the conditions of its growth, happiness will come, must come. It is guaranteed in the very laws of the universe. If it involves some chastening and renunciation, well, the fruit will be all the sweeter for this touch of holiness.

Vision of Service

The Home Magazine, May 1933, p. 6

I cannot look at myself in a mirror, but a mirror has a strange fascination for me. During the five dreary years that followed the loss of my sight and hearing, before I was taught, my mother said I often went to the dressing-table, apparently making believe that I saw my reflection in the glass. I would cock my head on one side then on the other. Once I put on my aunt's bonnet and hurried to the mirror, as if I wanted to see the effect. My mother thought I remembered being held up as a baby to look at myself.

I have wondered many times what made me do that. I have also wondered what other people really see in a mirror. Do they always see the same person? Or do they feel that they are meeting a new person? Does a woman ever really see herself? Might it not be a good idea for her to scrutinize herself consciously and critically as others look at her when she is unaware?

What do they see? Many of them, I suppose, do not see far below the surface. They look at one and say, "She's so conceited!" "She looks older, don't you think?" "She's rather pretty, but very shallow." Remarks like that should make one look closely and earnestly at oneself. To say we don't care what other people think about us does not help our feelings or our character.

We can have the highest beauty such as goes along with being a great individual only by having wide thoughts and much feeling for the rest of the world as well as ourselves. We must learn to endure what is hard and painful to our egotism. There are so many things wrong in this world that we can hardly keep ourselves from selfishness and pride if we care a great deal about our own pleasures. Let us remember that if the emphasis is put on physical and material things, old age comes just the same, and when it comes it comes down upon an empty mind, and that is the one form of sorrow that has no balm.

As I write, there comes to my mind the fable of a beautiful princess, the walls of whose palace were mirrors of her own charms. In these mirrors she beheld herself to right-hand and herself to left-hand; always her own self-seeking, solitary face looked back at her. The years passed until the reflections of her mirrors became monotonous, and she longed to escape from herself.

One day while the Princess was out riding, the longing within her opened her eyes, and for the first time in her life she discovered that everything she saw seemed to be contributing to the growth and welfare of something beside itself, and in that service to find its fulfillment. The flowers were busy furnishing sugar for the bees, fragrance for the atmosphere and garlands for homes. The bees were making honey for their offspring and also for the Princess's table, and wax for the artist. The dew and the rain supplied nourishment to the gardens and fields and quenched the thirst of every living thing. The meadows, orchards and forests in their turn supplied grass, corn and oats, fruits and vegetables for princesses and peasants alike. When the Princess returned to her palace full of this wondrous vision of service, she was surprised to find that the mirrors on the walls had all disappeared.

The Christmas Vision

The Home Magazine, December 1933, pp. 12, 71

The shepherds said one to another, "Let us go even unto Bethlehem and see this thing which is come to pass. They went, and made known the saying which was told them concerning the child."

It is Christmas Eve! Bells and carols everywhere are bringing back to us the wonderful Christ story which the shepherds heard and believed.

For many of us Christmas is a festival of candles which throw their little rays upon happy family reunions, happy, laughing children and evergreen tress bearing fascinating garlands of gold and green and stars which repeat the blue that Mary wore.

Was there ever a greater or grander message proclaimed to humanity than Christ's Nativity and the song of the angels, "Peace on earth and good-will to men?" Christmas Day with the Babe in the manger is a bright spot in an age over which materialism casts its cold gray shadow.

This magnificent vision is not merely something about which to theorize. Let us go to Bethlehem with the shepherds and see the new-born Child beneath his mother's smiling face. Let each of us, like them, approach, examine and discover love new-born in the heart of man.

Not until the shepherds had gone and seen the mystery of love revealed in the lowly manger did they become possessed of a new sense of the Lord's nearness and their own powers. The Vision was made still more their own when through them other people beheld it and rejoiced. Like them, we must realize within ourselves the ecstasy of the Vision . . . the Heavenly host, the song of gladness and the Star of Light that shall lead us on to a fairer life. We need to listen in simple, fervent faith to the Christ story and let it live in us.

On Christmas Day we are, as it were, in a high tower where we have a wide outlook on the ideal life, but when we try to live it we find ourselves too close to fettering circumstances and personalities. We feel that Christianity cannot be lived on earth.

But have we ever really made an honest effort to live it all together? Christianity is a social and emotional experience, and the great movements of the human race have originated in the deep, compelling, emotions of the heart. Once a year we Christians surrender for a brief season to the law of the heart. We cast out fear, and love becomes the driving force of conduct. Every man is our brother and friend. We let ourselves think more of the happiness we are able to create for others than of our own pleasures.

But when Christmas passes, we let ourselves fall back into fear and inhibition. The fixed idea that what is, will always be, settles upon us again like a dismal fog, checking imagination and generous desires. We return to the distressful spectacle of men fighting new ideas, scoffing at new visions and obstructing progress with ignorant selfishness.

The time has come for us to break away from inhibiting traditions. We are living in the midst of events more charged with wonderful possibilities of life than mankind has yet known.

At present the effort to see the Christmas Vision realized in the world is like looking through the boughs of a tree with dense foliage for a particular star. The happy world Christianity presupposes is hidden by a branch and peace on earth by a leaf. We require a spiritual attitude that will enable us to distinguish between a leaf and the Vision. When that happens, we shall cease to look in one direction and work in another.

Many men of great learning and wisdom lived in ancient times, but, lacking a lens and not understanding how to use a prism, they could only conjecture imperfectly as to the rays beyond the light in their eyes. Even so, is it with faith applied to every day life. Beyond our present lip-worship of Jesus there is an infinity of splendid living. What we need to realize this Christmas is that only by bravely accepting the Christ-ideal as a law of life can we face courageously the age of change and upturning which even now is upon us. Let us resolve to carry the Christmas vision into the dark which stretches before us. Then with that sure guiding light we shall create a new world where human beings will be free and happy and at peace with one another.

We Can Do More

The Home Magazine, February 1934, p. 12

O ver the gate of an ancient castle in France is the motto, *"Plus est en vous*—There is more in you." When those words carved in stone centuries ago were spelled into my hands, my spirit responded eagerly, "True—true every one of us."

There are infinite resources and powers within us if we will only search them out. Let us affirm this over and over to ourselves at the beginning of the new year, and keep on until the truth it contains has illumined our minds and quickened our spirits. Then it will indeed be a new year for us.

We are apt to think humbly of ourselves. Too readily we acquiesce in the attitude of those who stand and wait and receive from other hands. We imagine we cannot do anything important because we are not fitted like the great men and women about whom we read.

But if we examine ourselves diligently, we may discover that we possess a talent with which we can create beauty or joy, or assist somebody else to achieve something fine.

The woods would be very silent if no bird sang but those who have prima donna voices. It takes a multitude of little birds to make up the music of the Summer. Likewise it takes a multitude of small accomplishments to make up a rich life.

I repeat, there is more in you than you know. Look into your mind as a naturalist studies a plant, and you may be surprised at what you find.

The heather which covers the hills and moors of Scotland is a very coarse plant. Yet viewed under a microscope, it proves to be an exquisite thing. Its tiny bells reveal a delicacy of color and tracery upon which one gazes until one loses count of time. One day a scientist met an old highland shepherd and handed him a sprig of heather and a microscope. He peered at the blossoms intently, and was silent. Then, handing back the heather and the instrument, he said, "Ay, man, I wish ye had never shown me that." "Why?" asked the botanist. "Because my rude feet have trodden and broken so many of them."

Even so is it with our minds. What we regard in ourselves as commonplace and uninteresting may have charm and nobility if we look through the lens of a strong desire to make the most of the faculties God has given us. It is this desire that unveils capacity.

I am thinking of a woman who began life poor, friendless, uneducated, almost blind. For a long time she thought there was nothing in the world she could do.

She said, "I do not know enough to teach. I am too handicapped by imperfect sight to engage in occupations taken up by other girls. I have no talent for music or writing or dramatics." To the few people who thought about her at all her future looked very dark.

Then there came a letter from the father of a deaf, blind and mute child in Alabama, inquiring if it were possible to have her taught. The poor, half blind young woman heard the cry of the little spirit in prison and said, "Here am I, send me." Everyone knows the story—how Anne Sullivan, with the most unpromising equipment, released a child-soul from darkness and led her along the ways of happiness and accomplishment.

There is the story too, of the old miner who was left alone after the gold rush was over. He had come a long way, too late to share in the others' rich strike. He stayed and worked what appeared to be a worn-out vein. And at last he found gold. He had believed in the earth's endless possibilities and had profited by his faith.

Truly there is more in us than we dream; for we are parts or shadows of something more intense and greater. We know ourselves only imperfectly. We never fully realize our possibilities, but very near us, touching every one of us, is the Source of all Light, the Sovereign Alchemist who will enable us to transmute the lead of life into gold if we desire it with our whole being, and are willing to work faithfully for its realization.

"There is more in us." Let us carve this thought over the gate in the new year.

Easter Message

The Home Magazine, April 1934, p. 6

Teach it again to us, O living God! Teach us to renew ourselves, O Jesus, who wept bitter tears in Gethsemane.

Help us to forget the long way of pain and strife we have come, each of us dragging a cross to some Calvary in our hearts. Help us to forget the hours of utter darkness when we have lost the way. Help us to forget our hates, fears and the bitter thoughts that divide us.

Help us to remember the upclimbing will that is a staff unto our feet. Nourish in us every tiny impulse to help each other. Give us more love, more compassion, more sincerity one to another.

Help us appreciate the present moment and to search out its advantages that we may be glad for the todays of life, leaving the tomorrows in Thy Hand.

Steady us to do our full stint of work. Help us to rise each day with new sympathies, new thoughts of unity and joy.

Great need have we, this year of all years, to seek the garden where Thou, O risen Lord, shalt lay on each heart Thy healing Hand.

Give to those who feel down-trodden and neglected the spirit to look up to the sun, to feel its warmth and to appreciate its bright rays. Let them see rainbows in the murky pools, and help them to feel that they are not alone, that Thou from Thy Heavenly Home are watching over them.

Let us be thankful for the resurrection season which revives in us the faith that this circumscribed world in which we live, with its partial visions and unfulfilled dreams, its wearisome struggles and frustrations, is not all there is to life. There is so much to live for! There is the courageous, useful and unselfish life.

There is so much to be thankful for! The feeling of springtime promise in the air after the cold grayness of the winter season; the drops of rain that take on new meaning. They are not the dull accompaniment to a somber, gray sky and a relentless chill, but bear the promise of new life and renewed energy to the rootlets and buds.

There is much to strive for—to make our cities clean and pleasant, to keep our children healthy, and teach them the honor of work that is worthy of the finest manhood and womanhood, to eradicate from all the fountains of our national life everything that is corrupt. When these commandments of life are kept, there will be resurrection in our souls and in our nation, and our days of tribulation will not have been in vain.

Well may the earth rejoice, lift her head and turn her face to the sun! The sun! The sun that mounts the heavens and makes all things new again!

How punctually Nature keeps her Easter! Out of the sod climb the flowers we love—the snowdrop, the violet and the trailing arbutus. The old trees know it is Easter-time, and put forth new-budded leaves. The pussy-willows reach out their velvety paws, the twigs of the larches are gilded, and the birches don their purple. The frankincense and myrrh of the world are laid at the feet of Life, new-born in myriads of blossoms. The brook, released from its icy shell of Winter, gurgles in glad abandon and brings the news of the hillsides of [sic] the waiting valleys. The cowslips along the way make gay golden patches of sunshine and listen to the brook's merry whisperings of the glad tidings of new life and resurrected joy. The birds sing again as if they had never sung before, all with joy deep as the life-giving warmth of the sun. In every nook and cranny life is more abundant, as He said.

Let us not miss the long-waited joy of that promise fulfilled.

The Spirit of Easter

The Youth's Companion, March 1904

Oh, give thanks unto the Lord, for He is good, and His mercy endureth forever. Sing unto Him a new song, for He causeth the desert to put forth blossoms, and the valleys He covereth with greenness. Out of the night He bringeth day, out of death life everlasting. On this day a new light is upon the mountains; for life and the resurrection are proclaimed forever.

The bands of winter are broken in sunder, and the land is made soft with showers. Easter day bringeth the children of men near to the source of all light; for on this day the Lord declareth the permanence of His world, and maketh known the immortality of the soul. He hath revealed the life everlasting, and His goodness endureth forever.

Easter is the promise of the Lord that all the best and noblest in man shall be renewed, even as growth and bloom and ripening shall not cease. The bars of winter are broken, and the iron bands of death are riven. The bird is on the wing, and the flight of the soul shall know no weariness. The lilies lift their holy white grails, brimmed with the sunshine of God's love. For has not the Lord manifested His love in flowers and in the upspringing of green things? They are sweet interpreters of large certainties. Each year the winter cuts them down, and each spring they put forth again. Every spring is a new page in the book of revelation, wherein we read that life is an eternal genesis, and its end is not; for it endureth forever.

The festival of the springtime is as old as the hope of man. The Jews had their feast of the Passover. The Romans celebrated the Megalensia in honor of mother earth. But not the Jews nor the Romans interpreted the whole message of spring. To the regeneration of earth Christ has added the new birth and eternal youth of the soul. We know that our branch grows in the physical life, but in the soul bears fruit that shall endure forever.

Belief in eternal life compels us to believe in good deeds and honest thoughts. The good man toils not for to-day, nor for to-morrow alone, but because he knows that his labor shall survive long after his hand has fallen from the plow. The good man pours himself into the world and makes it new. He is among the blessed who win sight out of blindness, order out of chaos and life out of death. Since the first Easter morning the soul of man has shone with unwasting light; for then he looked into the radiant face of the risen Christ, and knew that God's universe shapes itself not to destruction, but to a yet more glorious genesis; yea, it endureth from everlasting to everlasting.

A Christmas Thought

The Home Magazine, December 1932, pp. 6, 87

O nce more Christmas brings to our hearts a brief season of happiness and participation in the creation of joy for others.

How many dormant sympathies and generous impulses Christmas-time awakens! We write words of greeting to friends scattered far and wide. We use our ingenuity to devise gifts that will bring delight to children. Happy, happy Christmas that can win us back to love and simplicity of heart!

Why should this beautiful spirit of friendliness end with the Christmas season? Why cannot we keep it all the year round, as the fir keeps its green? That the Christmas spirit should always vanish with ringing of Christmas bells, has always bewildered and saddened me. Christianity overflows with the noblest words in the language expressive of love, peace, faith, light. These precious words persist in humans and prayers. Why do they not persist in our daily actions also?

We think of Christmas as a festival of joy that comes once a year when we should think of it as an every-day Christian experience. Much of our life is made up of phrases that fall upon unheeding ears because there is nothing behind them—no vital purpose, no spontaneous outpouring from the heart. Indeed, to some of us the true Christmas message has less meaning than when we first heard it. There are times when a wave of Christ-love strays into our spirits, but these experiences are not as frequent as they should be.

Christianity is a livable philosophy and a sure remedy for most of the ills flesh is heir to, if we only think so. I do not believe the difficulty lies in the fact that we are not in earnest. It is one of the most touching facts of life that spiritual longing runs deep in the hearts of unnumbered millions of people, as is manifest at Christmas time.

I think the cause of our failure to live the Christian life is lack of faith. We do not truly believe that the fulfillment of the Teaching of Jesus is possible. We put our Christian ideals on one side of the fence and practical living on the other, as we continually see-saw between the spiritual and the material.

What we need is a more thorough realization of the Teaching of Christ in our daily life. "The brotherhood of man"—what a phrase, what a noble slogan for Christians to inscribe on their banner!

Let us begin this Christmas to replace a social life in which division, falsehood and violence are all-powerful with a new order in which humanity, truth and brotherhood shall reign. Let us give ourselves up absolutely to the Christmas spirit of love and fellowship, and we shall find our mental barriers crumbling away as the year circles round to another Christmas.

Let us resolve here and now to banish our prejudices and put ourselves in sympathetic touch with all men. It should be remembered, it is only by the whim of fate, the chance of birth in one land or another, that we are black or yellow or white or brown. Men and races should be judged not by the tint of their skin or the gods they worship, but by the quality of the thoughts they think and the deeds they do. Christ teaches that God hath made all nations of one blood and one spirit.

Let us then carry with us, love and tolerance from this Christmas into the coming year. We must if we are to remake the paths of civilization and bind the world together in peace and good-will, and make the angel song of two thousand years, a reality. Then, only then, will Christmas be Christmas indeed.

4

Socialism

Her socialism might have been controversial had she not been Helen Keller. Apparently, though, the only real controversy was about who may have influenced her to become socialist. Some believed she was "brainwashed" by John Macy, the Radcliffe instructor who was briefly married to Anne Sullivan. He went on to travel to Russia with John Reed, the American who sympathetically chronicled the Bolshevik Revolution.[1] But however she got to socialism, Keller maintained her commitment to it, even when faced with angering industrialist Andrew Carnegie, who was offering her a semi-annual stipend. After she told him, "You believe in the brotherhood of man, in peace among nations, in education for everybody. All those are Socialist beliefs,"[2] he agreed to fund her.

In the columns, topics such as world peace or the problems of child labor reflected her socialism. She wrote about a White House conference on the topic of child labor and urged states to enact laws mandating that children stay in school until a certain age. "Child labor has wrought a double harm," she wrote, "first, by robbing children of the education which the state should guarantee them; second, by taking from adults work that rightfully belongs to them."[3] She added that women have a responsibility to protect children and should take a leadership role in stopping child labor.

A few months later she took on childhood poverty. She didn't ask for more social programs, however. She encouraged women to seek solutions through education and prevention. "It is up to women to try to understand

163

why there is so much preventable wretchedness and find methods of preventing it," she wrote.[4]

Keller's socialist background led to strong support of newly-inaugurated President Roosevelt and his social programs, which she voiced in several columns. In a Thanksgiving column, she said his leadership was reason for nationwide hopefulness. "He roused us to a sense of our responsibility and revived in us the American spirit of self-help and optimism. Eagerly we accepted his leadership, and the whole country rang with brave words of gladness."[5] Her strongest socialist rhetoric came in an Independence Day column also in support of FDR. "He is setting up a humane order in the midst of ruthless, self-seeking, reckless greed and economic anarchy," she wrote. "He is using all the powers at his command to compel the selfish few to play the game of business fairly. Never again, he says, shall we permit unsocial conditions in the United States which have heretofore allowed the maldistribution of wealth and power by a small minority."[6]

It was clear from many of Keller's columns during the Great Depression that she felt materialistic behavior was immoral and blamed it for the economic crisis. "It has become necessary—or so it seems—to make more and more money at any cost of principles or ideals. Out of this unnatural situation have grown the economic and political dilemmas we are contending with today," she said. "The motives for buying which [advertisers] stressed most were snobbishness, vanity, the wish to have some article because another has it, fear of what a neighbor might think, the desire to make a show, whether there is anything substantial behind it or not. This is a regrettable testimony to the spiritual decadence which has made inroads into our national life."[7]

Keller typically merged her socialism with democratic ideals. In 1935 she wrote about her concerns that New York City children did not have safe playgrounds. "Experience has proved that human beings do not develop healthily in overcrowded tenements and surroundings ill-conditioned for play," she explained. "The test of democracy is not the magnificence of buildings or the speed of automobiles or the efficiency of air transportation, but rather the care given to the welfare of *all* the people."[8] Her columns tried to inspire action to right social ills, without blaming any specific group such as the city government. Her message was one of social responsibility—that all citizens in a democracy should do their part to improve society.

Notes:

1. Paula Marantz Cohen, "Helen Keller and the American Myth," *The Yale Review*, Vol. 85, No. 1. January 1977, p. 13.

2. Helen Keller, *Midstream* (NY: Greenwood Pres, 1929), p. 141.

3. Helen Keller, "Crushing Out Our Children's Lives," *The Home Magazine*, August 1931, p. 10.

4. Helen Keller, "The Unprivileged," *The Home Magazine*, November 1931, p. 8.

5. Helen Keller, Thanksgiving Thoughts," *The Home Magazine*, November 1933, p. 8.

6. Helen Keller, "Independence Day," *The Home Magazine*, July 1934, p. 6.

7. Helen Keller, "Our Coming Great Adventure," *The Home Magazine*, August 1935, p. 40.

8. Helen Keller, "Try Democracy," *The Home Magazine*, April 1935, p. 11.

Crushing Out Our Children's Lives

The Home Magazine, August 1931, p. 10

Editor's note: This column refers to the U.S. Children's Bureau's efforts to stop child labor, led by Grace Abbott from 1921 to 1934. The Children's Bureau is a division of the U.S. Department of Health and Human Services. In November 1930, the White House held a conference on Child Health and Protection.

I wonder how many of you have Miss Abbott's annual report of the Children's Bureau. The part relating to child labor is distressing.

Miss Abbott tells us that there was a steady increase in child labor during the three years preceding the present period of depression and unemployment. According to reports from sixty cities in thirty-three states, 220,000 full-time working certificates were issued to children between fourteen and eighteen years of age in 1929, as against 150,000 in 1928.

It is well to note that New York state issued 72,536 certificates to children under sixteen years for full-time work in all types of occupation during the year ending August 31, 1930. New York City alone employs 35,628.

One of the aims to which the White House Conference pledged itself is protection for every child against labor that stunts growth, either physical or mental, that limits education, that deprives the child of the right of comradeship, of play and of joy.

One means of accomplishing this is to insure to every child in the United States a period of education that will enable him not only to learn what the race has to teach him out of its experience, but also to live as a child. It is in childhood that we acquire the knowledge that will fit us for life's responsibilities and to develop us healthily and happily.

To this end, a bill has been introduced into the New York Legislature raising the minimum age when children may leave school.

Let us stop a minute and think what it would have meant to large numbers of anxious, thinly-clad bread-liners this Winter if their children between fourteen and seventeen years of age—130,000 in all—had remained at school and left their jobs to be filled by their elders! Child labor has wrought a double harm to society; first, by robbing children of the education which the state should guarantee them; second, by taking from adults work that rightfully belongs to them.

It is true, the bill does not propose to raise the child's time for leaving school all the way up to seventeen, but it will cover the fourteen and fifteen-year group, and it will in time lift it up with the group of those who are not allowed to leave the schools so soon on account of their mental backwardness. There is really a steady, but too slow, increase of compulsory school attendance going on throughout the country.

I look to women to be leaders in this important and vital movement. No state that wrings profits out of the health and the laughter of little children is civilized. The longer I live, the more amazed I am at the peculiar mental constitution of anyone who dares to be a parent and lets young lives be crushed in order to create wealth for him and his children.

I have no patience with women who say, "Oh, I can't do anything about solving this problem. Time adjusts all things."

That is not true. Wrong things cannot work themselves right. We ourselves, must always work them right.

Let us each one be a law unto herself, and refuse to allow the evil she deplores to exist in her own life or her dealing with the community. Then we shall not have to wait centuries for results.

What are we all here for? What are we given children for? This question is being seared into our consciousness daily, and will not rest until we all rise to meet its challenge:

"The greatest enterprise, both for splendor and for vastness, is the building up of a man."

The Unprivileged

The Home Magazine, November 1931, p. 8

I wonder if you have tried to imagine what unemployment does to boys and girls in families of comfortable circumstances—children who have had good food, clothing and warm beds, who have gone to school and enjoyed the companionship of other children.

These children are suddenly transported to an impoverished home, they go to bed hungry and sleep in unwholesome, overcrowded quarters; they run errands and peddle papers for a few pennies to buy bread; and all this through no fault of their parents who are willing and anxious to work, but they tramp the streets all day and find no work!

This disaster may happen to any worker under our modern industrial system. The children of any respectable working-man's family are faced with these hardships when the small savings of the parents are used up by illness or lack of work.

One terrible result of these wrong life conditions became evident last year when 37,000 boys under sixteen years of age were brought before our juvenile courts, and it is a fact that our penal institutions are fed largely from this class of young delinquents, who commit about forty-four per cent of the crimes in New York City! This should cover the face of Manhattan with shame. For it means that every boy there has a one-to-three chance that his name will find its way into the criminal records before he is sixteen years old. Is not this a special problem for women, since they have to mold the minds and keep pure the souls of the young?

As you realize that in New Jersey there are now 2715 feeble-minded children being cared for in institutions, and there are still 814 on the waiting list, let it be remembered, there is no state in the Union more advanced or earnest in its care and training of mental defectives than New Jersey.

There are also in New Jersey 11,681 crippled children, and in New York City 30,000 under eighteen years of age!

Our tuberculosis hospitals are filled to the limit with patients, and still they come. Very young workers contract this disease working and living under conditions which inevitably produce invalids by the thousands. Any one who makes a study of this appalling situation knows that wrong industrial conditions are responsible, and that only by removing these conditions can this menace to public welfare be checked.

Again, in Greater New York there are a million and five hundred thousand children, of whom a very large part—perhaps about five hundred thousand—are underprivileged, suffering from malnutrition or physical defects. They grow up in an environment that in the nature of things breeds more poverty and more defectives.

It is urgent that women should take hold of these questions and seek a commonsense solution. It is not more relief that is needed so much as more education, more preventive measures. It is up to women to try to understand why there is so much preventable wretchedness and find methods of preventing it.

Thanksgiving Thoughts

The Home Magazine, November 5, 1933, p. 8

For more than a hundred years we Americans have gathered about the festive board on Thanksgiving Day, following a custom of the Founders of this nation. With grateful hearts we have thanked God for the golden corn, dropping kernels beside our plates, symbols of the early days when food was scarce. Happily we have lifted to our lips the sweet juice from the fruit of the apple trees and rejoiced in the bounty with which the world is nourished.

But the past four years there has been a shadow upon us. It has not been possible for us to rejoice whole-heartedly in the blessings we still enjoyed when many in the land went hungry. We have said in our hearts, "What can we do about it as individuals? Are not our hands tied? Are not circumstances stronger than we are?"

However, when President Roosevelt took the helm of state last March, he showed us in his courageous way that we COULD do something about it. He roused us to a sense of our responsibility and revived in us the American spirit of self-help and optimism. Eagerly we accepted his leadership, and the whole country rang with brave words of gladness. Men began to think more hopefully, whereupon the heavy clouds of depression started to drift away.

Business is looking up, and unemployment is perceptibly declining. Each month since the Inauguration, March 4th, has shown a substantial improvement in the employment figures.

Then let us take this auspicious moment, when friends and family are gathered in the home circle, and hearts are drawn closer to hearts, to consider the tremendous problems which the nation is now facing. Let us ask ourselves: Are we sincere and brave enough to go forward with our President and build up a nation that shall bring to all men their share of advantage and happiness?

Surely, that is a noble nationalism for which to strive and pray. On the Day of the Pilgrim Fathers let us resolve to think more, to feel more, to love more and to be more in the service of one another and the world.

Our Coming Great Adventure

The Home Magazine, August 1935, p. 40

As we approach Independence Day, it seems fitting that we should give a thought to the problems which confront us as individuals and as a nation.

It must be obvious to anyone who thinks at all that as a people we are passing through a grave crisis. There are three fundamental aspects of this crisis—the political, the economic and the moral. We read a great deal about the first two aspects, but not nearly enough about the third. Yet it is the moral force which must transform the other two if we are to come out of our national ordeal triumphant.

If we had held fast to the great simplicities and the hardihood of our fathers, we should have avoided the demoralizing effects of war and resisted the tendency to create a false prosperity through mad speculation. The leaders upon whom we depended failed us, and we lost confidence in ourselves, and years of corruption ensued.

Not so very long ago a group of advertising men gave away the secret of success in salesmanship in America. The motives for buying which they stressed most were snobbishness, vanity, the wish to have some article because another has it, fear of what a neighbor may think, the desire to make a show, whether there is anything substantial behind it or not. This is a regrettable testimony to the spiritual decadence which has made inroads into our national life.

It is easy to see that we are not the strong, simple, courageous Americans who can meet and surmount obstacles, look depression in the face and rise after each fall. It should be helpful to us to consider what has wrought such a change in the past generation. First of all, our individual lives have been affected by time-saving inventions and the luxuries and idleness consequent upon them. It is true that only a small minority of the people have had the luxuries and the idleness, but these subversive things have been desired by all to such an extent it has come to pass that the dragon of extravagant selfishness has devoured the substance of the people. It has become necessary—or so it seems—to make more and more money at any cost of principles or ideals.

Out of this unnatural situation have grown the economic and political dilemmas we are contending with today. In the effort of the few to keep what they have got and the effort of the many to exist, every appetite, every emotion, good or bad, social or personal, is being played upon, and class antagonism is spreading throughout the land.

The question now is, what are we going to do about it? Is our situation hopeless? I refuse to believe so. One cannot lose faith in social regeneration any more than one can lose faith in one's friends or in God without serious spiritual loss.

One thing is certain, if there is to be a rebirth of the national character it can come about only through the regeneration of each of us as individuals. It is not a matter of committees or machinery or recovery programs. It can come only from some change in the American heart.

This change will not make life any easier, but it will make life more decent and honest. There must be struggles and victories of the spirit—something to look back to with pride and something to look forward to with enthusiasm. This land, which was so fair that men looked upon it as a pleasant place to build homes and live and die in security shall not perish from the earth if we again assert our individuality, not in the sense of seeking profit at the expense of society, but saving ourselves from the deadening effects of conformity and false ideals.

Heroism

The Home Magazine, September 1933, pp. 8, 75

Editor's note: This column refers to the Frontier Nursing Service, founded by Mrs. Mary Breckinridge in Kentucky in 1925 to care for rural children living in poverty. The Frontier Nursing Service, www.frontiernursing.org, still exists. Martha Berry, 1866-1942, founded schools for poor children in the rural South.

Down in the South, where I have been trying to make friends for the blind, I had some exciting adventures last Spring. We (my friends, the automobile and I) would set out early in the morning to reach some place where I was to speak that evening. Usually the mornings were exquisitely beautiful, especially in Kentucky, where the marvelous blue grass stretches for leagues upon leagues along the highway. My friends were always watching the sloping pastures for the blue hue, which is only seen by the uninitiated in a certain slant of light. I used to wonder why they were more interested in the blue grass than in the frolicking colts digging their heels into the turf. Everywhere forsythia waved its golden sprays, coquetting with the breezes, and on wall and tree the wisteria hung out its bright treasure to decoy bees into its honeyed clusters.

Then I would feel the car slowing down and smell a spring freshet tumbling down the mountainside. The mighty rush of it warned us to go cautiously; somewhere there would be a washout, and the water would hold us up like an army with banners. Sometimes it was necessary to make long detours in order to avoid the washouts. Sometimes we would cross an old-fashioned covered bridge on which the spring rain would beat like horses' feet. As we approached the opposite bank I could smell the wet clover and the blossoming trees.

As we raced along, always there was in my mind a vivid picture of two brave Southern women who often traverse these mountains and the mountains of Georgia to succor the sick and the injured and bring the light of knowledge to people buried alive in remote hamlets.

Mrs. Breckinridge began her work with two nurses. Riding horseback in all weather, they found their way to rough cabins, made friends with the children, took care of the sick, helped and advised weary mothers and brought their babies into the world with skillful treatment unknown up there before. Today twenty-eight nurses and three supervisors, with headquarters at Lexington, serve a region in seven counties that cannot be reached except by mountain trails. These women are ready at a moment's notice to face any danger on expeditions of aid. A mountaineer need only send in a distress call and a nurse is on her way—a messenger of comfort—to render whatever service may be needed. In Winter, that means hard riding on rocky trails, up icy slopes where one must get off his horse and cut a way through the ice. In the floods of early Spring, the nurses may have to swim their horses over swollen rivers and creeks.

Mary Breckinridge tells this story: She found among her patients several who needed hospital care. Just at that time the Middle Fork River rose in a surging, muddy tide, burying the wagon road, but undaunted, Mary Breckinridge managed to crowd a woman, some children and herself into a small flatboat, piloted by a tall mountaineer. Standing with a long pole in his hand, he steered the whirling craft for ten hours down that terrific tide, avoiding rocks and shooting many rapids, finally bringing his little craft to a safe landing.

Martha Berry is another heroic woman who has made her life a wellspring of blessing to the mountain people of Georgia. Her family were wealthy aristocrats. Beyond their great plantation rose the picturesque mountains of the Blue Ridge, barely supporting a forlorn, despised people on small, rough clearings who could not read or write. They lived eight or ten to a cabin, under-nourished and without medical aid.

Alone of her family and caste, Martha Berry had faith in the capabilities of those humble folk and the will to develop them. She left finishing school and gave up all the gaieties of plantation society. She refused suitors who offered her luxury and elegance and gave up the joy of motherhood so that ten thousand Georgian girls might have a chance in life. She withdrew to a cabin retreat to read and study, make friends with the half wild mountaineers, young and old, and taught them. She rode on horseback, carrying her torch of knowledge and comfort ever farther into the mountains, and often it was necessary to spend the night in one of the cabins, sleeping with the girls, three to four to a bed.

There, in that remote region of the southern Appalachians, she found more than a million victims of poverty, ignorance and ill-health needing her help. For thirty years she had devoted herself tirelessly to their welfare, and today she is still laboring without letup or rest in their behalf. She deeded her inheritance to her schools, she plunged into debt recklessly, scrubbing, toiling, teaching, taking more children and still more into the schools each year. She has begged for money during thirty years throughout America until she has raised twenty-seven million dollars! But she has kept none of it for endowment, she has used every cent to teach one more girl or boy, and to equip her students for a life of usefulness and self-respect.

Of course all of us cannot engage on such high adventure, but each one of us can do her bit, and oh, how much there is to be done! The world is crying aloud for women to dare hardship and poverty, to work with sincerity of mind and singleness of purpose.

Our holiday is over, and September has come with its tasks and cares. Let us dare to choose the difficult road, and learn from such women as Mary Breckinridge and Martha Berry how we can leave the world in a better condition than we find it.

The Common Good

The Home Magazine, November 1934, p. 13

On Thanksgiving Day Americans commemorate the triumph of a little group of men and women who believed in God, and that His Kingdom would prevail upon the earth.

Inspired by this belief, they endured unimaginable privations and dangers, and surmounted the greatest obstacles. Ungrudgingly they labored that the nation they were founding might grow and become a wide and fair habitation of men. They had brought from the Old World a determination to live the Christian Life.

For nearly a hundred years their descendants followed with some measure of fidelity the ideals of their fathers. But, unfortunately, from the beginning the canker-worm of slavery had crept into the heart of the new nation. The war between the South and the North brought to a head the division and strife engendered by this violation of human liberty.

When the Civil War was ended, a profound change took place in the American people. They departed from the faith and simple ways of the Founders and started on the perilous road of material prosperity, and a period of economic serfdom began.

Dazzled by inventions and exploitation of the vast resources in which the country abounded, the people lost the vision of the Kingdom of God. The time came when almost every American was afraid to be poor, and despised anyone who elected to remain poor in order to simplify his life and save his conscience. They lost even the power of imagining what their ideal of a nation of God-fearing men had been. They could not conceive liberation from the material things or the unbribed soul and manly indifference to personal gain. They thought not of paying their way through life by what they were or what they did, but by what they wrested from others in one way or another.

This unethical prosperity has broken down. A flood of adversity has swept over us which has opened our eyes to many things. Already changes have occurred in the United States that seem almost incredible.

Much of this change has been effected on the basis of the surrender of individualism and the acceptance of a leadership of men who believe that it is not a time to try and patch up things as they were and pretend they were right. What thoughtful men want is not a breaking up of all our institutions and laws, but a new social order of cooperation and willing assistance by all the people. Thus once more the adversity of a nation is creating an attitude which will regenerate its ideals.

Let us on this day of national thanksgiving rejoice that an ever increasing number of Americans will never again give thanks for anything which will make others poorer or divide and darken humanity.

There is only one true kind of national greatness, and that is to hold fast to, and conscientiously work for the ideal of the Common Good which is mightier than any man and worthy of all men.

Try Democracy

The Home Magazine, April 1935, p. 11

Editor's note: Anne Sullivan, Helen Keller's teacher, companion and interpreter, died Oct. 20, 1936 in Forest Hills, NY.

Last November I spent some time in the Doctor's Hospital where my teacher was being treated after a year's illness. Every morning I took an early walk along the East River front. I was glad to get out and refresh my mind during the weary days of waiting.

That part of New York City was most interesting. On bright mornings I was filled with wonder as my friend described to me the rising sun making a path of glory through the water and turning thousands of windows to gold.

As we walked through the streets, I noted with pleasure that people came out to exercise their dogs at that early hour. There were all kinds of dogs—Scotties, English Bull Terriers, Airedales, Alsatians and tiny Toy dogs. It was delightful to see their joyousness as they ran and jumped, exchanging barks and wags. And how anxiously their masters guarded them against the rushing automobiles and the juggernaut trucks that thundered by at every crossing! The thought entered my mind like pain that those dogs were being watched with more solicitude than many of the city children. I often ran into little groups playing on the pavements.

Surely, every child has the right to a decent playground away from danger and harmful excitement. Experience has proved that human beings do not develop healthily in overcrowded tenements and surroundings ill-conditioned for play.

The test of a democracy is not the magnificence of buildings or the speed of automobiles or the efficiency of air transportation, but rather the care given to the welfare of all the people. We should look about us and see what there is to do for the good of our neighbors and find ways to accomplish it.

It is a marvel what attention is given to the sick. Everywhere huge hospitals, laboratories and clinics—piles of beneficence—pierce the sky. Every facility known to science is placed at the disposal of physicians.

Would it not be wise to employ some of this science in safeguarding the health of those who are well?

What have we done to lessen the terrific noises of traffic and machinery which are shattering nerves and causing much deafness?

The ideal of democracy bequeathed to us by the founders of this nation included in its benevolent purposes all these public services, and much more.

Indeed, they set forth in the Declaration of Independence the principle that it is the function of government to ensure for all, life, liberty and the pursuit of happiness

Put Your Husband in the Kitchen

The Atlantic Monthly, August 1932, pp. 140-47

I

In my childhood, even before my education had been begun, I was allowed to take part in the elaborate ritual which, in those days, marked the making of a fruit cake at Christmas time. Although I was blind, deaf, and speechless, the thrill of the occasion communicated itself to me. There were all sorts of pungent and fragrant ingredients to collect and prepare—orange and lemon peel, citron, nuts (which had to be cracked), apples, currants, raisins (which had to be seeded), and a host of other things. The family encouraged me to assist in these preparations, for they discovered that this was one means of keeping me, at least temporarily, out of mischief; and I, for my part, was just as eager to help, because I was always permitted to claim my wages in raisins.

All in all, this concoction of a fruit cake was a long and complicated task. If there had been some oversight in the preliminary planning and an important ingredient was missing, someone had to make a trip to town to fetch it. While the mixing process was being carefully attended to, a roaring fire was built in the stove. At last, when everything was ready and the fire was giving off just the right degree of heat, the great pan was placed reverently in the oven. The climax of the ritual was now at hand. The temperature had to be maintained for several hours with the utmost precision, and everybody had to walk about on tiptoe lest some unguarded step shake the floor and cause the precious batter, swelling with the heat, to fall. In the end, if all went well, we were rewarded with a very miracle of a fruit cake, without which Christmas would not have been Christmas.

To-day this ritual, so delightful to children, so exacting to the mothers who superintended it, is fast becoming a lost art. The modern housewife has only to go to her compact kitchen cabinet to assemble the ready-prepared ingredients, even to shelled nuts. If one should be lacking, she telephones to the corner grocery. The cake almost bakes itself in an automatically regulated gas stove, while the lady of the house goes about her other duties. Or perhaps she achieves her fruit cake by buying it in a tin container at her grocer's. Whether she bakes it or buys it, her labor in either case is simple and quick compared to what it was even a few years ago.

The same thing may be said of almost every other phase of household work. Our grandmothers had to perform a tremendous amount of dreary drudgery in managing their homes. They were kept busy from morning till night, for those were the days when a woman's work was never done. Since then, however, the machine age has come upon us, the transforming the home no less surely than the factory. The housewife of today finds that many heavy responsibilities which she would have had to assume in any other age, such as the baking of bread and the weaving of cloth, have been lifted from her, and scores of other tasks which still remain in her province have been so simplified that they can now be performed with a great saving of time and effort. Electricity and gas and innumerable mechanical devices have reduced household labor to a fraction of its former burden. In consequence, the modern woman enjoys a degree of leisure which her grandmother could hardly have dared to dream of.

Whether women are using their new-found leisure to its full advantage is a debatable question, and one which I shall not attempt to discuss here. The point that I want to emphasize is that they have it—and they have it because of these countless machines and clever contrivances which have been invented to save them time and labor.

This, of course, is a very familiar observation, and I claim no credit for originality in mentioning it. But recently, as I was turning over in my mind the tragic muddle of present economic conditions, it suddenly occurred to me that this commonplace is not nearly as hackneyed as it may seem. Few of us seem to have grasped the significance of this new leisureliness which has come to grace our households. As a matter of plain fact, what women have done with labor-saving machinery in the home is exactly the reverse of what men have done with it in their factories and offices. The captain of industry seizes upon improved tools as means to increase production, and now he finds the channels of trade clogged with more goods than can be sold; his wife uses them to produce leisure, of which she can never have too much.

The average woman is not very familiar with the complexities of economics, but it seems that she has ordered her household economy upon a more solid basis than that upon which men have arranged the affairs of their larger world. In industry, the amazing increase in the use of labor-saving machinery has brought about overproduction, unemployment, and widespread suffering. Either women are wiser, or they have a sounder instinct for economics. At any rate, they use labor-saving devices for the heretical purpose of saving labor, and in doing so they have, I think, demonstrated in their homes a practical object lesson in economics which their husbands would do well to master. While theorists are still searching for the causes of the depression, and politicians remain at loggerheads in their effort to conjure remedies, I am tempted to think that the perplexed business man might discover a possible solution of his troubles if he would just spend a few days in his wife's kitchen.

Let us see what would happen if he did.

II

Mr. Jones, let us say, is a modern captain of industry. Mrs. Jones is an intelligent woman who knows more than the average about economics, and has the knack of seeing things through to their essentials. She had often discussed business problems with her husband, and had endeavored without success to win him to her point of view. At last she decided to try an experiment. She persuaded her husband that he owed it to humanity to demonstrate the correctness of his ideas by applying them to the home—the one field which men had not yet touched with their organizing genius. Mr. Jones accepted the challenge and agreed to serve for a term as cook, maid, and household manager. He promised to see what improvements he could effect by directing all domestic activities in precisely the same way that he conducted his own business.

Mr. Jones had grown up on a farm. The chores that fell to his lot as a boy made him familiar with the drudgery of household work in former days. Although he was vaguely aware that the home had kept pace with the mechanical age, he did not know what a startling revolution had taken place in the economy of the household until he surveyed his wife's model kitchen, with its gas range, its dishwashing machine, its electric mixer, and its various other labor-saving appliances. He investigated the interior of the compact kitchen cabinet, containing all sorts of prepared foods. He was particularly impressed by the special cake flour and the shelled nuts.

"Ah, the wonders of science and modern efficiency!" he said to himself. "I remember the fine nut cakes my mother used to make. What a job it was in those days! But now, with all these prepared ingredients, with the electric mixer and the automatically regulated gas range, I ought to be able to make ten cakes in less time and with less trouble than my mother required to make one in her primitive household."

So, true to the ideas which had made him captain of industry, Mr. Jones proceeded to transform potential power into actuality. When the family assembled at the dinner table that evening, the new household manager could hardly restrain his enthusiasm. Laughingly, he said to his wife: "See now, Mary, what I have done. Ten cakes. Ten! When you were running the house we had only one, or two at most. Ah, the logical, orderly, efficient brain of a man is needed even in the kitchen, that sacred province of woman. In one day I have revolutionized the business of cooking, and have put it on a sound basis."

The cakes were good, and the family ate almost a whole one with relish. They

were persuaded to finish it. But there were still nine left. By good salesmanship
the industrialist-turned-cook induced the family to eat another, which they did
to please him, but they had no relish for it. At this point Mr. Jones found himself confronted with the same problem which he had to face every day in his
business—he would have to sell more. Inventory would have to be reduced, unit
costs slashed. That could be done only by stimulating demand and increasing
consumption. So he employed the cash rebate system, offering small William a
dime to place his order for a large section of the third cake. William saw that it
was a consumer market; he knew that such wonders are unnatural and imperma-
nent, and could not resist stocking up. In the end, by using every known trick of
the salesman's art, Mr. Jones coaxed, wheedled, and bribed the family to dispose
of the third cake. By this time everybody had arrived at a stage of acute discomfort and complete indifference to his further entreaties, and he recognized the
symptoms of a saturated market.

That night the family physician was kept busy ministering to varying degrees
of indigestion from mild to acute. The care with which Mrs. Jones had nurtured
the family stood them in good stead, however, and all were fairly well recovered
by morning.

At breakfast Mrs. Jones said to her husband: "Of course you realize that the
doctor's fees will have to come out of your budget. It was all your fault."

"But I have no reserves set aside for that," replied Mr. Jones. "You know that
before we changed places I always paid the doctor. His bill shouldn't be charged
against the household budget."

"Just the same," said Mrs. Jones "I'm afraid you'll have to add it to your production costs. Then next time you'll know better than to glut the market."

For once Mr. Jones had nothing to say, and his wife continued: "Fortunately,
we shall not want any more cake for a long time to come. But when we do, you
can bake ten, if you must, and then throw away nine. You can't object to that. I
understand that such methods are common in your economic world. "Maintaining the market"—isn't that what you call it? It won't be the first time food has
been destroyed to maintain the market. And, of course, you manufacturers are
constantly producing goods that go to waste because of lack of demand. So I
shouldn't dare suggest that you bake only one cake merely because that is all we
need. That would be heresy. It would be inefficient. It would be criminal failure
to take advantage of "plant capacity." The gas stove will easily hold ten cakes,
and the same gas that will bake one will bake the others too. The electric mixer
also represents an investment. You should not let it stand idle, for the overhead
will ruin us. So go ahead with your plans, John. I just know you are going to do

remarkable things in increasing production and cutting unit costs—but don't forget to dispose of your surplus."

"Getting sarcastic, aren't you?" replied Mr. Jones. "Well, perhaps I did make a mistake. Anyway, let's forget it. If you want to be helpful, tell me what I can do with these seven cakes left over from yesterday. It seems a pity to throw them away."

Mrs. Jones was helpful. She took the remaining cakes in her car and distributed them among her friends. She knew that it would not be long before her friends would bring her a few glasses of jelly or some other homemade delicacy in return.

Mr. Jones did not like his wife's solution of the problem, but he was not in a position to protest. Such friendly bartering of goods struck him as very primitive, a reversion to economic methods of savage tribes. He thought of economics in terms of money, vast organizations, complicated financial structures, stocks and bonds, banking and credits, and a hundred and one other intricate devices. All these he contemplated with pride, as evidence of the lofty plane upon which our civilization moves. But in this imposing forest he lost sight of the trees. He forgot that the sole purpose of any economic system is to facilitate the manufacture and exchange of the necessities and luxuries of life, in order that life may be made easier and finer. Like many another captain of industry, he had come to consider business, not as a means toward this end, but as an end in itself. No wonder he was having difficulty accommodating himself to the elementary principals of household economy, the sole purpose of which is to promote the welfare and happiness of the family.

III

When Mrs. Jones returned from her little tour of barter, her husband was busy with the vacuum cleaner and was putting the finishing touches on the living room rug.

"Why," she cried, "you've practically completed the cleaning! What will you do then? With a broom it would have taken you four times as long. Here you've used the vacuum cleaner only a few minutes, and you're almost through. Then the machine will have to lie idle until tomorrow. Heavens, you could have cleaned a house twice as large! I suppose there is really nothing for us to do but buy a larger house. It is really a shame to waste all the time that is saved by this electric sweeper. Then there is the investment in the machine; you can't afford to let it stand idle. That is not efficiency. Yes, I can see the vacuum cleaner will have to give a better account of itself in future. It must be used more, and the only way to make sure of that is to get a larger house."

"Have you gone completely out of your senses?" asked the astonished Mr. Jones.

"Not at all," replied his wife. "I'm just beginning to understand your way of looking at things. We must go in for 'plant expansion'—isn't that what you business men call it? We must realize the productive potentialities of our vacuum cleaner. It cries out for new carpets to sweep, and of course the new house will need lots of new rugs. Just think, John! We shall immediately create a vast, untouched market for the services of our electric sweeper. How foolish I have been all these years! How inefficient! Why, that silly old vacuum cleaner has been in the closet for years, idle practically all of the time except for a few minutes a day, and I never realized until now how wasteful it was."

"Please, Mary, don't be ridiculous," Mr. Jones snapped.

"Oh, was I being ridiculous? Why, I thought I was following your business logic. Have you forgotten the time, two years ago, when your foreman invented that labor-saving device which made it possible for a man to tend two machines instead of one? You expanded the plant, put in twice as many machines, and doubled production. You said then that it wouldn't be long before I could have a new car and a new fur coat and all sorts of things, because profits would be more than doubled. Production was doubled, just as you planned, but at the end of the year you had half of the goods in the warehouse and you closed the factory while the machines and the new plant 'ate their heads off,' as you so quaintly put it."

Mrs. Jones smiled sweetly, but Mr. Jones stammered and rushed away to his new sanctum—the kitchen.

Early that afternoon when Mrs. Jones came downstairs on her way to a meeting of her church club, she found her husband seated before the living room fireplace smoking a fragrant cigar and contentedly immersed in a book. He looked up guiltily as she entered.

"Is something wrong, John?" she asked. "It isn't at all like you to be wasting time in this fashion. Surely you don't sit in your office and read a book in the middle of the afternoon! Even when you have nothing to do, you at least try to appear busy."

"I won't need to start dinner for another hour," Mr. Jones explained, "and everything else has been attended to."

"Have you finished the luncheon dishes? Yes, I suppose you have. It takes very little time with the new dishwasher. But, really, I don't know how to suggest making efficient use of the time you save. I don't know how to provide more raw material for a machine which transforms soiled dishes into clean ones. I hope you won't be driven to the extremity of having to invent a dish-soiling machine so that the dishwasher may be kept operating at capacity."

Mr. Jones's cigar turned bitter in his mouth and he lost interest in his book, but his wife hurried out the door and went her way.

IV

When Mrs. Jones returned from her club meeting she brought news to cheer her husband. The women of the church were to give a large charity dinner, and Mr. Jones saw in this event an opportunity to demonstrate his methods of efficiency, organization, and mass production in a real test. He sprang to the telephone and immediately began placing orders for hams and chicken, jellies and pickles, and scores of other things that would be needed to feed the hundred people who were to be invited.

That evening Mrs. Smith came in to talk over arrangements for the dinner, but Mrs. Jones referred the embarrassed caller to the new director of cuisine and household economics. Mr. Jones was pleased to have this chance to spread his gospel of efficiency, and he launched at once upon a technical outline of his plans for preparing the whole affair according to the most improved factory methods.

"I am sure," he concluded, "that by proper organization and mass production I can bring the unit cost per dinner down to a record minimum. I think I can guarantee that the cash contribution from each member of the club will be smaller than has ever before been possible."

Mrs. Smith interrupted him. "But, Mr. Jones," she said, "Your proposal would upset all our arrangements. You see, each of our members has her own specialty to supply. Every summer when I put up jelly, for example, I always set aside a few extra jars for the church dinner. Mrs. Doe does the same with chowchow and pickles. Mrs. Roe supplies chickens from her own barnyard, and Mrs. Franklin furnishes potatoes from her farm. Very little actual money goes into the dinner. Each of us donates what she is best equipped to give."

"You see, John," spoke up Mrs. Jones with an indulgent smile, "none of us tries to capture the whole dinner market. We plan and cooperate. We don't go about it as you manufacturers do when a new field is opened up, and every manufacturer sets out to capture the market in toto. If we did that, we should find ourselves spreading a dinner for a thousand people instead of a hundred. Mrs. Roe might make a full supply of potato salad, while Mrs. Doe, convinced that her own potato salad was far better, might make a full supply and place it in competition with Mrs. Roe's product. Then we should have over-production, and all of us would lose by it. We avoid this by estimating our market as closely as possible, we plan and cooperate to supply the demand. I suppose, John, that this will strike you as very primitive indeed, but somehow it seems to accomplish our purpose with a minimum of waste."

In the end Mr. Jones had nothing for it but to sneak away to the telephone and cancel the orders he had placed.

Thereafter he seemed a much chastened man. He did not again make himself the butt of his wife's irony by producing more things than his family could use, just to demonstrate the efficiency of his household machinery. In a few days he took to spending an occasional afternoon at his club. He began playing golf, and devoted many of his leisure hours exploring the rather large library, which had hitherto been merely an unused collection of books. He found himself becoming interested in all sorts of fascinating subjects. He was really enjoying himself immensely, although he had a guilty look on his face whenever Mrs. Jones caught him at any of these diversions during working hours.

One day she said to him, "Perhaps you can see now, John, that the purpose of labor-saving devices is really to save labor, so that more time can be devoted to pleasant and stimulating living."

Not long after this, Mr. Jones decided that his business again required his attention. His wife is convinced that he returned to his office with a few elementary but enlightening lessons in economics well mastered.

V

No one, of course, would act as foolishly in the realm of household economics as did this mythical Mr. Jones, but there are many Mr. Joneses who have acted no less foolishly in their own sphere of large-scale industry, expanding plants and piling up goods with complete disregard of market demand. It may be argued that the parallel I have drawn is not a fair one because the family unit is so small and static that its requirements can be easily gauged, while there is no element of competition in supplying these requirements. But the nation, after all, is only the sum of these small units, and with proper cooperation it should not be impossible to estimate, within certain limits, the amount of goods the nation needs.

Here, of course, arises the question of whether we are at present suffering from overproduction or underconsumption—the question, in short, of purchasing power. This is a large subject which I do not have space to deal with in this article, but I hope to write about it some other time. The only point I want to make here is this: that it is about time for us to begin using our labor-saving machinery actually to save labor instead of using it to flood the nation haphazardly with surplus goods which clog the channels of trade. That will presuppose, to be sure, some cooperative effort to determine the needs of the people and to produce accordingly.

In the allegory of Mr. Jones, perhaps Mrs. Jones came off better than she should. She has obtained leisure, certainly, but it is doubtful whether the hundreds of thousands of Mrs. Joneses throughout the land are making the best use of the new wealth of hours which the labor-saving devices in their homes have made possible. But at least the opportunity is there. Women have won the first skirmish, whereas in the industrial world—the world of men—the machine is battering at the very livelihood of our beleaguered people. If we are to win this larger battle, we must adopt a new collective view of the machine and the complex economic structure which had been erected upon it.

I am convinced that the machine has taken something out of life. We have paid, and are still paying a great price for the benefits it has given us. But the fault lies with us. We have not used it properly. If the progress of the mechanical age should suddenly cease now, I should say that its disadvantages had outweighed its benefits. But further developments are certain to come. We cannot now throw the machine overboard. It is with us to stay, and our task is to turn it to our proper need. In the machine, rightly controlled, lies the hope of reducing human drudgery to the minimum—not merely that we may be free of drudgery, but that every individual may have the opportunity for a happy life, for a leisure which, under wise guidance, may lead to mental and spiritual growth.

I do not set myself up as an expert economist, but from my detached position I have tried to examine the whole problem from a humanitarian and common-sense point of view. It is evident to me, as it must be to all thinking people, that the manufacturer and exchange of goods constitute the preponderant influences in modern life. That is a false emphasis. Now, at last, we have an opportunity gradually to shift that emphasis by using labor-saving machinery for its ostensible purpose of saving labor. This will mean a reduction in the hours of toil for the great masses of people. The trend is already in that direction, as an emergency measure, and I am convinced that the pressure toward this end will outlast the emergency, for it is a logical result of the flowering of the mechanical age. This new orientation is by no means impossible. If I thought it were, I should lose my faith in humanity.

After all, is it too much to expect that our ingenuity can reorganize our economic system to take advantage of the machines which we have created? It is largely up to the men—the statesmen and the captains of industry; and, if they are unable to accomplish the task, we women shall have to send them into the kitchen for a few lessons in common-sense economics.

5

Women's Issues

When Keller began writing a regular column for *The Home Magazine*, a number of her columns focused on women's issues—an apt topic since the magazine was geared toward women and homemakers, and the column began with an explicit focus on women as readers. Many of the columns on women's rights and education/children appeared in 1930-31.

Keller's first *Home* column, "Women and Peace," was on the topic of women's responsibility to the world. She called for women worldwide to "make the idea of peace live in their home talk, their books, their art and their lives."[1] A few months later she combined a women's-rights theme with motherhood, telling women that, now that they have more access to knowledge, they can raise intelligent and moral children. "Such children, when the opportunity comes, will shape to higher ends the new order of society that is now emerging from the chaos of the world. Yes, new times demand new measures, new women and a new education."[2]

Keller continued this theme the next month by defending the girls of that time who were breaking free of traditional clothes and customs. "She is not consciously defiant, but simply obeying the urge of evolutionary forces that are shaping a new society," Keller wrote.[3] In other venues such as *McClure's Magazine* and *The Metropolitan*, she also defended the right of women to become college educated, as she had done for herself. She explained in *McClure's:*

> For the first time in the history of the world, women are expected
> to have an intelligent understanding of business, of politics, of all
> the practical problems of our modern life. . . . By throwing herself
> into college affairs, she acquires the habit of rendering intelligent
> and efficient service to others; so that when she graduates, she
> becomes a practical force in the world, and a responsible member
> of society.[4]

Her women's rights themes continued in *Home* columns such as those about Emmeline Pankhurst, a British suffragist[5]; American suffragists Susan B. Anthony, Lucy Stone, and Elizabeth Cady Stanton[6]; women's role in preventing poverty[7]; and marriage as a choice, not an obligation.[8]

Keller had long supported women's rights; in 1909, after she joined the Socialist Party, she became a supporter of women's suffrage and birth control.[9] Calling herself a "militant suffragist" in 1913, she attended suffrage parades and rallies of the National Women's Party, which was considered a radical suffrage group.[10]

In her writings about women's issues, she took the somewhat contradictory stance (in modern terms) that women should be in charge of the household, but also needed a voice in the larger societal "household"; women should be able to vote and should be involved in social issues that affected everyone. In her article, "The Modern Woman," in *The Metropolitan* magazine in December 1912, she wrote:

> Women's place is still the household. But the household is more
> spacious than in times gone by. Not all the changes of modern
> life have changed her duties essentially. Her work as a spin-
> ner, breadgiver, helper of the helpless, mother and teacher of
> children is nowise different today but is immensely increased
> and intensified. Too often confused by the dazzle and uproar of
> modern life she is the primal woman still, the savior and shaper
> of the race.[11]

It is clear from her writings that she was in line with other socialists and suffragists, but most people could never get past Keller's disabilities and saw her only as an inspirational icon rather than a political thinker. She often tried to confront a society that questioned her "civic fitness," Keller biographer Kim Nielsen says.[12] In her book, *Out of the Dark*, Keller explains that blindness and deafness do not prevent her from keeping up with what is happening around her. In the AFB publication, *The Outlook*, she wrote that her disabilities gave her unique perspectives that non-disabled people did not have. Her willingness to continue to write about her way of interacting with the world, when it wasn't her favorite topic, was primarily a response to those who continually questioned how she perceived politics and social issues, Nielsen says.[13]

But Nielsen believes that, although Keller wrote about women's issues and social reform regarding women and children, she still remained an outsider to much of the women's movement of the early 20th century.

> What differentiated her was her relative lack of involvement in the networks of club women, settlement house workers, peace advocates, union organizers, social scientists, and legislative campaigners. She met political women, corresponded with them, and occasionally spoke in public forums but remained on the sidelines of the rich emotional and organized public work of radical and reformist women.[14]

In fact, Nielsen argues that many movements, such as the suffragist movement, used Keller for her role as an inspirational icon, which helped these movements solicit funds, garner media attention, gather an audience to an event, and generally draw attention to a cause.[15]

Even if Keller knew she was being "used," she did not veer from her support of women, especially poor women or blind women. She wrote in a 1944 letter about finally meeting with birth control advocate Margaret Sanger: "She is indeed a truly great soul. Her instructive talk confirms my ideal as I picture her, despite imprisonment and calumny, choosing her own destiny and enabling unnumbered women to take independent charge of their lives and ensure the improved health and joy of their children."[16]

Keller lent her ability to bring attention to women's issues to groups worldwide. When she traveled in Egypt and Syria in the early 1950s, she said that tea at the Feminist Union in Egypt was a favorite event; and in Damascus, because no schools for deaf or blind children existed for her to visit, she visited women's groups that worked on social welfare issues.[17] It is clear Keller's "miracle status" and ability to direct media attention benefited many efforts on behalf of women anywhere she spoke or wherever she was published. So although she may not have been embraced by women's organizations directly, her journalistic writings on women's issues helped keep these organizations' agenda in the minds of newspaper and magazine readers.

Notes:

1. Helen Keller, "Women and Peace," *The Home Magazine*, February 1930, p. 6.

2. Helen Keller, "Women and Peace," *The Home Magazine*, February 1930, p. 6.

3. Helen Keller, "The Modern Girl," *The Home Magazine*, June 1930, p. 6.

4. Helen Keller, "An Apology for Going to College," *McClure's Magazine*, June 1904, p. 193.

5. Helen Keller, "Something to Think About," *The Home Magazine*, August 1930, p. 13.

6. Helen Keller, "Great American Women," *The Home Magazine*, February 1932, p. 8.

7. Helen Keller, "What Are Women Interested in?" *The Home Magazine*, September 1931, p. 8.

8. Helen Keller, "Is Marriage the Highest Fulfillment of a Girl's Life?" *The Home Magazine*, November 1930, p. 6.

9. Kim E. Nielsen, *The Radical Lives of Helen Keller* (NY: NYU Press, 2009), p. 7.

10. Philip S. Foner, (Ed.), *Helen Keller, Her Socialist Years* (New York: International Publishers, 1967), p. 33.

11. Helen Keller, "The Modern Woman," *The Metropolitan*, Dec. 1912, p. 23.

12. Nielsen, *op. cit.*, p. 43.

13. Nielsen, *op. cit.*, p. 44.

14. Nielsen, *op. cit.*, pp. 45-6.

15. Nielsen, *op. cit.*, p. 46.

16. Kim E. Nielsen (Ed.), *Helen Keller, Selected Writings* (NY: NYU Press, 2005), p. 233.

17. Nielsen, *The Radical Lives of Helen Keller*, pp. 108-9.

Women and Peace

The Home Magazine, February 1930, p.6

We are standing on the threshold of the New Year. The world goes on from year to year with its burden of suffering and misery that need not be.

Some of us are asking ourselves if the time has not come for women to put the world-house in order. We are weary of groping among the shadows of old sins! We want more light, more life, more love! Above all, we want peace—peace of mind, peace in the world.

Since the beginning of history women have dreamed of a day when the Dove of Peace should descend upon the world, and no one should make them afraid. That day has always been postponed, defeated, the lovely vision retreating with their retreat and advancing with their advance. Always the women, the sweethearts, the young wives and mothers have looked forward to that day, mocked at by the old, the politicians, the militarists. The sacred, perfect world of love and harmony has ever seemed like a spirit without a body; but it has lived on in the hearts of prophets, seers and women, and that which liveth shall take shape and stand forth incarnate, manifest unto all eyes.

I believe that the idea of peace is more alive in our hearts today than ever before. We do not need to go to the Scriptures or the sages of a thousand years to find it. It is within us. We contain all things—the past with its hate, cruelty and greed; the future radiant with the hope of a world where the nations shall be in love with each other, without fear and without danger; and the present in which to work, and bring strong desire to renew and reorganize our habits. Ours is the mission of universal peace, since in us alone is the life of the generations. Let us, then, resolve, while we ache with the memory of lovers, husbands and sons dead, that no more battlefields shall be covered with their young bodies. Peace will not begin until women everywhere make the idea of peace live in their home talk, their books, their art and their lives.

She should say not, then, "I am only one woman, I can do nothing. Men make war and peace, it is their affair, not ours." True, men have been the masters of the world—the autocrats of statecraft; but, what have they done to put the world-house in order? Have they not imperilled the human race with their diplomacy?

Let us not be deceived by talk about war to end war. That is propaganda which closes the mind and prevents education from opening it to the facts. Violence does not, and never will, yield to violence. There is a great, vibrant renaissance coming through women. They will not continue to tolerate the old hateful things their eyes have opened upon New Year after New Year.

195

When women in all lands are fully awake to their missions, their efforts will ensure the final triumph of justice. They can do more than any conference of diplomats to help usher in the dawn of a new era of good-will and peace and righteousness. When such patriotism is taught in our schools and churches, there shall arise the warm, throbbing, one-hearted Empire of Brothers.

It is for women to bring this to pass. I call upon them to brush aside all obstructions from their door-sill and step into the open road of peace on earth and good-will among men

Is Marriage the Highest Fulfillment of a Girl's Life?

The Home Magazine, November 1930, p.6

There was a time when everybody thought so. Marriage was regarded by every girl as inevitable. It was her destiny, her career, the reward of her charms. To be well married was the goal of her existence. An unmarried girl was reproached, pitied, even scorned.

Today the unmarried girl no longer calls forth surprise or suspicion.

Marriage is no longer looked upon as a guarantee of respectability or happiness or success.

At present marriage does not offer a girl a permanent position. It does not assure her a home or hedge her about with propriety. Like many another time-honored institution, marriage has been haled before the bar of criticism and stripped of its divinity.

The girl of today, if she is sensible, asks herself some plain questions: "Would I really like to be married? What are the advantages? Would I be happier as wife and mother? How do the advantages of marriage weigh against its disadvantages, its pleasures against its sacrifices, its responsibilities against the freedom I enjoy as a spinster? What will marriage give me in exchange for the energy and liberty it will take from me? Can I have a career quite my own and fulfill the obligations of marriage?"

The modern girl, freed from the trammels of social prejudice about the necessity of marrying, has only one compelling reason for desiring marriage, and that is because she wants to marry; in other words, because she is in love.

Love and romance are naturally desired by the young. They should not be lightly put out of a woman's life. Marriage has advantages for the girl who desires them—the companionship of a husband, a home and children. These are precious. They offer the best prospect of happiness if the contracting parties have the requisite sympathy and understanding to adjust themselves to the trials of married life.

The psychological and intellectual benefits of marriage are undoubtedly great, and any sincere effort on the part of two people to live together harmoniously most certainly brings a rich reward.

It would seem that many persons do not possess the essentials of a happy marriage, if one may draw a conclusion from the ever increasing number of divorces.

The modern girl's training and way of living make it difficult for her to be contented within the limits imposed by marriage. From the day she leaves school she thinks about a career. She finds work. It occupies her thoughts. She has a certain independence of mind and action. She chooses her friends, her amusements and sports.

This independence fosters habits of thought and an egotism which are not as easy to give up as a girl thinks when she is in love. She should therefore ponder deeply on the question of marriage in all its aspects. Should ask herself, "Am I willing to give up my freedom, my individual interests, my work, my whole being? Am I willing to have another dominate me—my emotions, my goings and comings, my life? Shall I be responsible to another's will? Shall I gracefully permit myself to be influenced, guided and directed in every situation and decision of life by another person? If I have children, shall I find happiness in living for them—giving up my leisure, my occupations, my pleasures, as one must do if one is to create a happy home for husband and children?"

It is woman's part to adapt herself to her husband's way of life. If his work takes him to the tropics, she must go with him, and think no more about winter sports at Lake Placid. A husband's work inevitably conditions the wife's life, even if he wants her to live as she likes, see her own friends, think her own thoughts and engage in activities that interest her. It sounds fine, but it does not work. No matter how generous, broad-minded and self-effacing a husband may be, his life must absorb the wife's, or the marriage will not be a success. It will be a kind of partnership which cannot in the nature of things be conclusive and satisfactory.

It may be possible for a man to keep his business activities separate from his domestic life, but a woman cannot do so successfully. Once she is married, her energies, mental, physical and practical, go into the building up of the well-being and happiness of her family. Every girl must face these facts squarely and make her choice.

The more calmly and intelligently she considers her choice, the better will be her chance of a happy life within the bonds of wedlock, or pursuing an independent career. The goal of existence is not marriage or celibacy, but a full-blown personality achieving a lively and fruitful life.

An Apology for Going to College

McClure's Magazine, June 1905, pp. 190-96

I t is heresy in our time to intimate that a young woman may do better than go to college. Five years ago I had to decide whether I should be a heretic, or adhere to the ancient faith that it is the woman's part to lay her hands to the spindle and to hold the distaff. Some of my friends were enthusiastic about the advantages of a college education, and the special honor it would be for me to compete with my fellows who see and hear. Others were doubtful. One gentleman said to me: "I do not approve of college women, because they lose all respect for men." This argument had, however, the opposite effect to what was intended; for I thought if our respect for men could be philosophized, or economized, or debated, or booked away, or by any learning rendered null and void, the men must be at fault, and it was my duty as a woman to try to reestablish them on their ancient pedestal. Fortunately, women are born with a missionary spirit.

The champions of what Bacon calls "she-colleges" gave their persuasions a Baconian turn. "College maketh a full man; conference a ready man; and writing an exact man, and so," said they, "college maketh a full, ready, and exact woman." If I did not confer, I should have a hoar-frost on my wits, and if I did not read under judicious instruction, I should have to pretend to knowledge in the presence of Princess Ida and her "violet-hooded doctors." Then came yet other people who set to work to destroy the arguments of the advocates. "What use is there in your going to college? You will find much drudgery, and you must renounce many of your dearest pleasures. What will come of it? You cannot hope to teach or turn your education to practical account. Why not take life pleasantly? Why not stay at home and read books and develop your individuality? College is only for mediocre people, not for geniuses." (This was music in my fingers!) It grieves me that those who spoke so eloquently should have spoken in vain. But love of knowledge had stopped the ears with which I hear. I felt that all the forces of my nature were cudgeling me to college. It was not in the hope of large scholarship that I made the pilgrimage to this laborious Eldorado. The riches I sought consisted in learning to do something, and do it well. I felt, and still feel, that the demand of the world is not so much for scholarship as for effective service. The world needs men and women who are able to work, and who will work with enthusiasm; and it is to college graduates that this nation has a right to look for intelligent sons and daughters who will return to the state tenfold what the state has given to them.

I realized that the avenues of usefulness opened to me were few and strait.

But who shall set bounds to the aspirations of the mind, or limit that which the Lord hath created in His mercy and goodness? I had a mind to begin with, and two good hands by which I had groped my way to the frontiers of knowledge. Beyond the frontiers there might he stretches of desert; but if you must pass through a desert to reach the smiling land of plenty, set forth bravely, and the hard journey across the waste places shall give strength to your feet. We derive benefit from the things we do not like, and do nevertheless because they have to be done, and done all the more conscientiously because we do not like them. Necessity teaches patience and obedience.

These considerations, then, determined me to take a college course. I suppose I appeared to many of my advisers like the Philistines who went to the wars as men proud of destruction. People are too prone to think that the actual is the limit of possibility. They believe that all that has been done is all that can be done. They ridicule every departure from practice. "No deaf-blind person has ever taken a college course," they say. Why do you attempt what no one else has ventured? Even if you succeed in passing the entrance examinations, you cannot go on after you get into college. You have no books. You cannot hear lectures. You cannot make notes. You are most foolhardy to attempt something in which you are sure to fail." Thus counseled the unadventurous people, to whom the untrodden field is full of traps and pitfalls. Although they are Christians, yet they are possessed of the idea that man does everything, and God does nothing! The argument brought against me, that no deaf-blind person had ever gone to college, was precisely the kind of argument brought a generation ago against any woman's going to college. True, there had been seminaries and academies for girls, but no colleges of an [sic] university standard; and the so-called universities for men showed stern oaken doors to all women. There was no precedent for trying woman's intelligence in a fair contest by the high criterion men had established for themselves; but women created a new precedent.

Before 1878, women, backed by public opinion, were already standing at the door of Harvard demanding higher education, and conservative men felt uneasy lest they should seem selfishly to monopolize knowledge. A few progressive members of the Harvard Faculty agreed to teach women in private classes. There was a precedent for this; for in England women were already receiving instruction from professors of Oxford and Cambridge. The new project in American Cambridge enlisted, between 1879 and 1881, the services of nearly forty Harvard instructors. According to an historian, the few women who availed themselves of this new opportunity were keen, earnest, and capable to such a degree that the only trouble was to satisfy their demands. In 1882 the Society for the Collegiate

Instruction of Women was organized. The next year three young women finished the four years' course, and about fifty were taking partial courses. All had proved their ability to do work at least equal to that of Harvard students. Yet there were no degrees to reward them, only certificates stating that the course they had taken was equal to one at Harvard. Even when Atalanta won the race, the prize went still to a lame Hippomenes!

In 1894 the Society took the name of Radcliffe College, and got its charter from the legislature, which gave it the right to confer its own degree. This degree is countersigned by the president of Harvard, who warrants it equal to a Harvard degree. We owe Radcliffe not to Harvard, but to the success of those first earnest students who proved that they were able to do university work, and to the large-minded professors who, by unofficial and individual devotion to learning, helped the Pilgrim band to found a safe, permanent home where other women could come. That little band has transmitted the torch of learning for women from frontier to frontier, until there is not a state in the Union which does not provide for the higher education of women. Every woman, whether she can go to college or not, owes a great deal to those pioneers who cleared a place in the wilderness of men's prejudice for the lowly walls of the first woman's college.

Radcliffe College was a new and stronger expression of the spirit which had founded several good American colleges for girls. For the first time in America women's educational opportunities were equal to those of men.

Radcliffe College inherits the spirit of the women who, twenty-seven years ago, sought knowledge for its own sake. Radcliffe is still for earnest women who seek knowledge for its own sake. Girls who go there should have some object in view, some standard of excellence, the gift of handling knowledge in a plain, downright way. There is too little teaching at Harvard or Radcliffe, but there is much opportunity to learn. You may take the treasures offered, or leave them. At Radcliffe, I think, the treasures are more highly valued than among the young gentlemen across the street; for young men, I am told, go to college for a variety of reasons, or for no reason at all. But a girl who goes to Radcliffe should be filled with the desire to look behind the forms of things into things themselves, and to add, to beauty and softness, solidity and accuracy of knowledge. Stucco is no more serviceable to woman than to man. A well-trained mind and the ability to grasp the ideas essential to a purpose and carry them out with perseverance—this is the ideal Radcliffe places before women. How far this ideal can be realized appeared at a meeting of Radcliffe alumnae last year, where there were nine speakers—the scholar, the poet, the teacher, the dramatist, the administrative woman, the woman in domestic life. Their success had lain in different directions, and each testified that she owed her success in large part to her training at Radcliffe. Any young woman who acquires the self-control which Radcliffe teaches, and performs her task resolutely, may stand up before the kings of learning and not be ashamed, whether she be a writer, a teacher, a speaker, an administrative woman, a society woman, or a home-maker. Radcliffe strives to give her students the substance of wisdom, and to promote earnest and independent scholarship. In her, discipline, knowledge and self-mastery have replaced the narrow rules of conduct and the prudish dogmatism of the old-fashioned women's academies, just as arbitration and statesmanship are replacing the soldier and the priest. If the classes at Radcliffe which sit under Professor Kittredge and Dr. Royce are not learned, they at least carry away with them a sense of the dignity of scholarship, and do not, like Becky Sharp, when they depart through the college gate, hurl Johnson's dictionary at their preceptor's head.

For the first time in the history of the world, women are expected to have an intelligent understanding of business, of politics, of all the practical problems of our modern life. The college woman learns to cooperate with others, and that means she learns how not to have her own way. Experience in college activities teaches her the right of her companions to freedom of thought and action. By throwing herself into college affairs, she acquires the habit of rendering intelligent and efficient service to others; so that when she graduates, she becomes a practical force in the world, and a responsible member of society.

Like all human institutions Radcliffe falls short of her ideals, and her students, who are also human, do not always achieve theirs. I am acquainted with one who did not. Where I failed, the fault was sometimes my own, sometimes attributable to the peculiar circumstances under which I worked. But my successes were made possible by the spirit and the methods of the college and its unique advantages. And there were many advantages I could not avail myself of. The lectures, libraries, theaters, and museums for which Boston and Cambridge are celebrated, and which largely supplement college work, were not of service to me. The advantages of especial value to me were the excellence of the instruction and the liberality of the elective system. The quality of the instruction at Radcliffe is beyond question; for it is given by the best men at Harvard. The elective system offers a broad variety of courses and freedom of choice. Many subjects were impossible for me on account of my limitations, and I could not have planned my course so as to win a degree but for the scope of the Radcliffe curriculum. The ordinary student, who is not so restricted as I was, has wider opportunities, and she must choose wisely. In her very selection of courses there is a chance to "develop her individuality." And in the exercise of judgment as to the amount of time and energy she will devote to her work, she proves her individuality.

In a college like Radcliffe, where so much depends on individual judgment, the students fall naturally into three classes: first, those who choose their course wisely and pursue it with consistency, without sacrificing other joys and interests; second, "joyless grinds" who study for high marks; and third, those who choose indiscriminately courses that are pleasant, easy, and unrelated.

In the first class are those who realize that to get the greatest benefit from college it is necessary to take one's time, to proceed at an easy gait, and not to hurry or scramble. They know the pleasure of lingering over a subject, of asking questions, and of following an idea as fancy listeth. Happy study is as sweet to the true student as news of his sweetheart to the ardent lover. But the happy following of an interesting idea is not always possible. The arbitrary demands of instructors and the exigencies of a mechanical routine often forbid it. If my college is at fault in not permitting enough leisurely and meditative study, I hereby suggest my panacea—fewer courses, and more time for each.

Every student has a panacea for some weakness of his alma mater. One would have dull professors prohibited, another would have all dates and formulas weeded out, another would have examinations abolished, another would do away with daily themes, extorted from impoverished minds a most tyrannical oppression, taxation without representation, the wrong which lost England her thirteen colonies! If the instructors would only consult the benevolent, reforming student, he could give them valuable points. But instead of consulting the student's profound intuitions, the instructors go forward in a straight, narrow line, never looking to the right or to the left, blind and deaf to the wisdom that crieth on the campus. The younger the student is, the more confident he is that he has found the solution of the problem. He often forgets that his alma mater has given him the very wisdom with which he sharpens his darts against her. The critical student sees that the reformative schemes of his fellow-students are valueless. Their incompetence is glaring! But as he grows older he sees his own folly too. If after his graduation he has tried to plan the curriculum of a small primary school and failed, he too will turn conservative, and leave to time's slow evolution the great problems of education.

To be candid, I have proposed the leisurely, reflective manner of study because I have an indolent, wayward mind which likes to ramble through the garden of knowledge, picking here a leaf, there a blossom, and so off to pastures new. Fortunately, the spirit of Radcliffe and a good conscience forbid that the student shall abuse her liberties. It is good for us to read books we do not like.

The performance of set tasks and work that is not of our choosing are stimulating. Miry ways and rugged mountain-paths mean strength, grip, poise. If they draw out our miles and make them wearisome, it only means that we have new vigor added to us, and that we shall enter into the treasures of endurance. I know not whether I with more delight strapped the knapsack over my shoulder, or set it down at the end of the journey. The mastering of difficulties is followed by a sense of well-being and capacity which is like a river of water in a dry land, like the shadow of a great rock in the heat.

The girl who is not a slave to books, who selects her courses judiciously and gives them a right and proper amount of strength, is not to be confounded with the girl whose independence is mere indifference or egotism. Not such do I admire, and, for all my pet schemes to reform my college, not such am I. I only maintain that we have a right to ourselves, that we should be masters of our books and preserve our serenity. There is no profit where there is no pleasure. College consists of five parts sense and five parts what, from the class-room point of view, would be called nonsense; but nonsense is the very vitality of youth. After all, book-knowledge is not the most important thing to acquire, and perpetual work on five or six courses cannot be sustained without neglect of other important things. Even thoughtful and independent girls try to do so much that they can do nothing thoroughly. They rush, cram, thieve many hours from their nights, and for all their ill-timed industry they hand in next morning papers full of mistakes. Although I always tried to work with a cool head and a steady hand, and sleep according to the law, I too was drawn into this whirlpool of confused, incomplete tasks. I met other girls in the college halls and on the stairs who stopped a moment to greet me, but they were rushing from lecture to examination, from examination to basket-ball practice, from practice to dramatic rehearsal, rehearsal to conference, and there was no time for a pleasant chat. And if the girls who had eyes and ears were overburdened and distraught, I was at least no better off. During four years a torrent of miscellaneous knowledge poured through my fingers, and it fills me with despair to think how much of the choicest matter of this abundant stream dripped and oozed away. I was eager to draw from the living waters of wisdom; but my pitcher must have had a hole in it. I was like the Danaides who poured water eternally into a broken urn.

Once in a while a book or an instructor started a vein of bright thoughts. I caught a glimpse of old truths in a new perspective; but I could not linger. Before I had got a good look, I was hurried away on the current of words, and in the effort to keep from being upset in midstream, I lost sight of the bright idea, and on reaching firm ground I was chagrined to find that it had fallen overboard. The idea thus irrevocably lost was often one on which depended a fortnightly composition, or even a three hours' examination.

I was of course hampered by my limitations, which turned to drudgery much work that might have been delightful; for they imposed upon me tedious methods of study. I was often behind in my work at a distance forbidden by military law; I was never ahead; and once I fell so far behind that it seemed as if I might as well try to keep pace with a shooting star! Experience, however, taught me to tack against wind and tide—the first lesson of life I learned in college. And this was easier with Miss Sullivan at the helm. I would not part with one of those struggles against the gales—"the winds and persecutions of the sky." They tested my powers and developed the individuality which I had been advised to bring up on books at home.

Had I not gone to college, I should have missed some of the authors whose individuality taught me to value my own without isolating myself from the seeing and hearing world. I discovered that darkness and silence might be rich in possibilities, which in my turn I might discover to the world. In other words, l found the treasures of my own island.

Different students seek different treasures. To some the most precious nuggets are high marks. Such plodders as I watch their quest from afar. We hear about them with the wonder with which we listened to the fairy tales of our childhood; but we should not dream of following them any more than we should think of going in search of the singing-tree in the "Arabian Nights." Their high marks are no incentive to us to fill our midnight lamps with oil that we may enter in with the wise virgins. They stuff themselves with dates, and with figs gathered of thistles, and think themselves blessed. They have dyspeptic nightmares of the brain, in which they go through flood and fire, seeking the phantom gold at the rainbow's end.

The court to which they return from a futile quest, or with meager spoil, is a chamber of inquisition. Oh, the examinations! They separate us from our kind. They water our pillows, they drive sleep from our beds, they inspire us with hope, then dash us ruthlessly from our pinnacle, they cross-question us until their martyrs lie in the dust, and their apostasy is the open secret of the universe. Oh, those little crisp sheets of paper written with a pencil of fire which consumeth ideas like chaff! They are the accidents of time and flesh, they are mere conundrums on which we throw away our beauty sleep; and, in the end, all the dull substance of our brains and our ingenious padding dwindle to "a lame and impotent conclusion."

Before an examination we feel delightfully precocious and original. After it we are full of the wise things we did not say. We took twice as much trouble as was necessary to prepare our subject only to miss the essential points after all. The least explicable thing that an examination paper does is to destroy your sense of proportion and reduce everything you have read to a dead level. Like Doctor Johnson you make your little fishes talk like whales, and your whales twitter like canary-birds, and the result is a collision of contrary absurdities!

The chief loss of a girl who "grinds" is that she misses other college activities. It is the light of college education to join with one's fellow-students on class-teams, in college plays, and on the college magazines. For the most part you study by yourself; but in the united activities of class and college you learn the tact and community which are the beginning of useful service to mankind. Of course I had little part in the social life of my college. I enjoyed my share of work; the obstacles which were declared insurmountable came against me one way and retreated seven ways, and that was happiness enough. I had, too, many pleasures, solitary and apart from the other girls, but as genuine as theirs. They often invited me to join their frolics and club-meetings, and it cost me many a twinge of regret not to be able to take part in their affairs; for I was keenly alive to everything that interested them. If I had been of the class of 1906 or 1907, I should have met them oftener in the new Elizabeth Cary Agassiz House, which is to be the social center of Radcliffe, and I should have felt the inspiration of their activities. Nothing encourages us so much as the example of others, nothing stirs our energies more than generous emulation, nothing comforts us so much in discouragement as companionship. My friendships must come through the medium of my hand, and few of the girls knew the manual alphabet; and the conditions under which we shook hands for a moment in the crowded class-room were not favorable to intimacy. They could not reach me through my isolation, and in the midst of my class I could not help at times feeling lonely and sad.

But a happy disposition turns everything to good, yea, the want of one thing, lacking which so many melancholy beings want everything. I forgot my loneliness in the cheerful realities that touched me. I knew there was a rich store of experience outside my comprehension, but the little I could grasp was wonderful enough, and having contentment I was possessed of the boon whereof I had been beggared.

A happy spirit is worth a library of learning. I think I derived from the daily walk to college with Miss Sullivan, more genuine pleasure than comes to many a girl who sits in a corner and works the sunshine, the fresh air, and even good humor out of her morning lessons—all for high marks.

On the other hand, I do not understand the motives of that third class of girls who go to college, apparently, to be entertained. I do not see the use of studies chosen from year to year, without plan or forethought, because this instructor marks easily, or that professor is "so nice," or the conference man is "so polite," or "Doctor G. keeps you so interested"—in himself, that means, not in the subject. These girls dip into all that treat of whatsoever is, the state, the total chronicle of man, chemical and electrical laws, and whatsoever can be taught and known. "General education" is their apology, their rock of defense, their tabernacle from which they shall not be moved. I have known girls who graduated, and with good marks too, whose minds seemed to me undisciplined and crammed with odds and ends of knowledge which they displayed for the enlightenment of their friends. They reminded me of the maidens of old whose accomplishments were feminine and elegant, who brought out a sketch-book to be inspected by admiring friends. The sketches represented nothing that creepeth on the ground, flieth in the air or passeth through the paths of the seas, but they were lady-like all the same. Girls whose education is too general shall prove to have none at all. Their infinite variety will be withered by age and staled by custom.

The ideal of college education is not to give miscellaneous instruction, but to disclose to the student his highest capacities and teach him how to turn them to achievement. By this ideal, those who labor in darkness are brought to see a great light, and those who dwell in silence shall give service in obedience to the voice of love.

Something to Think About

The Home Magazine, August 1930, pp. 13, 116

Editor's note: Emmeline Pankhurst was a British suffragist who fought for women's voting rights in the early 20th century in England. She died in 1928.

Millions of women are living today whose outlook on life and their part in the world drama are different, because Emmeline Pankhurst lived, thought, worked and made sacrifices for the social and political emancipation of woman. The ideas for which she was ridiculed, persecuted and imprisoned are now triumphant on both sides of the Atlantic Ocean. Women exercise the franchise over the greater part of the earth's surface where the electoral system obtains.

Recently, in London, a statue erected to Mrs. Pankhurst's memory was unveiled in the shadow of the Houses of Parliament, a mere stone's throw from the spot where the militant suffragette leader had once been arrested. Homage was paid her by those who had been her bitterest opponents. Mr. Stanley Baldwin said: "I was opposed to her for many years, but it fell to my lot to put the coping-stone on her labors." He was referring to the recent bill extending the franchise to women of twenty-one, from the original age minimum of thirty, set in 1918. How the Goddess Fortune must have laughed when the music on this occasion was played by a police band whose officials had arrested Mrs. Pankhurst and five hundred of her faithful followers!

In the throng gathered to do honor to Mrs. Pankhurst were many women wearing badges with miniature prison-gates and little broken chains hanging from them, which distinguished them as martyrs of Holloway Jail. Others wore badges which showed they had been hunger-strikers. A bar across the ribbon meant that the wearer had been forcibly fed. Undoubtedly the recognition so impressively accorded to Mrs. Pankhurst's achievement is the greatest event in the history of woman. The enthusiasm and indomitable spirit of this fearless leader, inspired women with confidence in themselves and led them to victory over tradition, prejudice and the arrogance of a man-made society.

I met Mrs. Pankhurst twenty years ago when she visited New York. She called on me one day at the Prince George Hotel. She was a gentle, sweet-voiced, gray-haired little woman whom it warms my heart to remember. She told me how some members of her party, the Women's Social and Political Union, had irritated their opponents, attracted the attention of people everywhere and tired out the patience of the statesmen, who had put off granting their demands.

Mrs. Pankhurst did not want violence. Her militancy was engendered by the obtuse indifference and hostility of the public. No one wants violence in the beginning, and in our quiet moments we shun it; but intolerance and persecution produce the violence we deprecate. Force begets force. It is like the obstruction in a stream. When let alone, the stream flows onward peaceably; but when it encounters an obstacle, it uses the power that is in it to tear a channel where there is none.

Down through history we note the transition from martyrdom to the monument that celebrated triumph; but it does not often happen that we witness in our own lifetime the struggle and the victory. But, while rejoicing in Mrs. Pankhurst's achievement, it may be well for us to remind ourselves of what still remains to be accomplished.

Women did not become different human beings as a result of the franchise. They did not show themselves more intelligent or more broad-minded or more just. The vote did not give them a monopoly of righteousness. It did not immediately raise their ideas of living, nor did they gain greater self-control. The vote does not make a good citizen any more than the uniform makes a brave soldier.

The franchise is, however, a stimulant to thinking. It brings to view the problems that would otherwise remain unnoticed. It encourages discussion and criticism, and thereby ideas grow and multiply. Issues are defined, and a sense of responsibility is fostered. In the great School of Citizenship, women are learning to depend upon themselves. What will happen when women really take hold of public affairs, having finished the big job of establishing their political rights? I am hoping they will make the most of their opportunities. They have a chance to do great things. Will they prove equal to the demands of a new age? Make the necessary new adjustment?

If, like Mrs. Pankhurst, women will defy tradition and remain true to their ideals to the end, they will grow even stronger, and make life more worth living for all mankind. The struggle for liberty goes on despite innumerable defeats and repressions. There may not be a woman as strong as Samson or of the same intellectual power as Isaac Newton or the same spiritual elevation as St. Paul; but women in the mass are moving towards the place of wisdom and understanding. Even the women of India, China and Japan are beginning to realize that they have a soul, a self and a part as human beings, in shaping their destiny; and here and there a long step is being taken on the road to progress—all because Emmeline Pankhurst dared to carry the banner of an Idea.

What are Women Interested in?

The Home Magazine, September 1931, p. 8

I am often disturbed when I read magazines devoted to women's affairs. Much space is given to the consideration of dress, personal appearance and habits.

"Do you bob your hair?" "Should young girls smoke?" "How many hours should they sleep?"

A great deal is written about the motion pictures, and as far as I know, they are not less degraded. The endless discussion of the theater does not criticize its tawdry sentimentalism and sensational excitement. It is rare to read an article protesting against the triviality of the subjects supposed to interest women. I should like to see well-written articles on serious questions now and then interspersed between costumes and theater gossip.

It is true that there are many women engaged in social welfare work in New York, but one has to read dry reports for facts and figures gathered by social researchers. I think the facts and figures given by the Social Welfare Council, of which Robert W. De Forest, a wealthy citizen, is president, would surprise women generally.

Despite the oft-repeated boast that New York is the richest city in the world, the report showed there was need for alleviating great suffering here even in the city's most prosperous days. Public and private charities were spending a hundred million dollars a year for relief work before the heavy weight of economic depression settled down upon us. Unorganized philanthropy contributed as much more in order that destitute people of all ages might not starve or be destroyed by preventable disease.

Why is there always unemployment in the large cities in the Winter time? What is poverty? Why are not some women trying to get to the bottom of these questions, instead of adding up their bridge scores day by day?

It is for us women to try to understand what prevention means, and how to apply it to the evils which are sapping the strength of millions of people around us every day.

Blazing the Trail

The Home Magazine, October 1934, p. 8

There has been much argument lately among women, young and old, as to whether the enlarged opportunities and innumerable avenues of adventure open to them that were closed to their grandmothers have stimulated independence and self-expression.

I asked a man I know, "Do modern women think for themselves?" He replied, "Very few women have thought in any age. It is the same now as it always was. Everything depends on the few." This answer faces both ways, and is not very satisfactory.

The gist of my personal observations is that, for the most part, American women imitate male psychology. They content themselves with doing what men do.

It seems to me, there is a field of enterprise which women have neglected, and in which they would meet with little or no competition from men—namely, civilizing themselves.

Why should women make of themselves caricatures of men? If they would only cultivate their own individualities, how much more useful they would be, and how much happier!

Would it not be worth while for women to make a stringent revision of their whole standard of values, and set off some of the stress on the claims of materialism and bring those of the other fundamental instincts into some kind of balance and harmony with them? Does the material life really offer enough to make it worth living even to those who dominate and shape it?

If women truly wish to promote a finer civilization, should they not take a quite different angle—*say, the spiritual angle?* For civilization is an affair of the spirit, and, in the realm of the spirit, organization and getting and spending money count for very little. I only ask whether women would not be happier if something of the sort happened within them.

If women's freedom and greater opportunities are to prove a blessing to humanity, they must work from an inner consciousness.

Then perhaps we should see the beginning of a humane and reasonable society—a society which has work to do that is of real value, a mind unafraid to travel, even though the trail be not blazed, a genuine pleasure in the arts, now and then *a sight of the eternal hills and a sense of the presence of God.*

Great American Women

The Home Magazine, February 1932, pp. 8, 113

I hold in my heart the memory of three loving and courageous women—women who possessed a gracious presence, unusual intelligence and great eloquence. They listened to the "voices" in their youth, like Joan of Arc, and their demands kept Susan B. Anthony, Lucy Stone and Elizabeth Cady Stanton young and beautiful even into old age.

Elizabeth Cady Stanton was born in Seneca Falls, New York, in 1815, and lived to see the century out. Her father was a Supreme Court Judge. At the age of twenty-five she married Mr. Henry Brewster Stanton, a descendant of the Puritan elder. She was not dazzled by this distinction, nor was she much impressed by Puritanism. But Mr. Stanton was a leading abolitionist, and was sent as a delegate to the World's Anti-slavery Convention which met in London in 1840.

Elizabeth was a girl of high spirit, eager to see the world. She married on Friday (the word "obey" was omitted from the ceremony), and on Monday she sailed for England. On this eventful journey she met Lucretia Mott, and shared with her the humiliation of being excluded from the Anti-slavery Convention floor on account of her sex—an act of tactlessness to which we probably owe the Anglo-American movement for women's political equality.

A convention called by Mrs. Stanton and Lucretia Mott in Seneca Falls, 1848, placed her name on the revolutionary roll-call. Not long afterwards she joined Susan B. Anthony and a few kindred spirits to form the first women's rights organization in this country. This was the beginning of the lifelong struggle of these women against repressive laws and traditions affecting women.

Their "wants" were so numerous, just to name them would fill my space! I will mention a few of them. They wanted bloomers, they wanted divorce, they wanted the franchise, they wanted equal pay, they wanted to enter the professions on equal terms with men, they wanted education. They stopped at nothing until the Civil War came along and put an end to their "unseemly practice of public lectures" throughout the country.

Susan B. Anthony was born in South Adams, Mass. Her environment moulded her for the destiny she was to fulfill. She had experience as a teacher and a factory worker. The hard life her mother and neighbors lived kindled in her the flame of the crusader.

She became interested in temperance work. To her surprise and indignation she was denied admission to a meeting of temperance workers because she was a woman.

She was present at the convention called by Mrs. Stanton and Lucretia Mott at Seneca Falls. Mrs. Stanton and Miss Anthony seem to have been created for each other, and certainly they were one in every crisis of their heroic lives. Miss Anthony also met Lucy Stone at the Seneca Falls convention for the first time.

Lucy Stone was born in 1818, on a picturesque, rocky farm near West Brookfield, Mass.

Her mother, a farmer's wife, had milked eight cows the night before Lucy was born, as a sudden shower had obliged all the men of the family to rush to the fields and save the hay. When she was told the sex of the new baby (the eighth of nine children), the mother immediately cried, "Oh, dear, I am so sorry it's a girl. A woman's life is so hard!" I like to think that the baby born of that weary, sad mother was destined to make life less hard for all the generations of women that were to follow.

The world upon which Lucy's bright eyes opened was very different from the world of our day. Women were not admitted to the colleges. No free high school for girls existed. It was generally believed that a woman should receive only enough instruction to enable her to read the Psalms and to keep her household accounts, and that any attempt to give her more knowledge would ruin her as a wife and mother.

Public speaking for women was taboo. Even to write for publication was considered unwomanly. Law, religion and custom affirmed the inferiority of women.

Lucy Stone was the first married woman in America to keep her own name. She was also the first woman to receive a college degree. She converted Susan B. Anthony and Julia Ward Howe to the Suffragists' cause. She was the founder and editor of "The Woman's Journal" in Boston, which was the principal woman suffrage newspaper of the United States for nearly half a century. During their heroic careers these three women champions of women's rights, revealed the qualities of steadfastness, independent thinking and large sympathy.

We of today can have little conception of the difficulties these women encountered, or the brutal prejudice that pursued them ceaselessly. They were accused of being infidels and atheists! They were charged with being free lovers! It was asserted and reiterated that they were bent upon undermining the sacredness of the institution of marriage, breaking up the family and destroying the home! Yet the cause for which those women were slandered is triumphant today.

The Modern Girl

The Home Magazine, June 1930, p. 6

Some people are horrified by the rebellion of the modern girl against authority and tradition. Countless editorials are written for her correction, the pulpit rings with protests; but there is much to be said for the modern girl. Life is self-expression, and each new generation must express itself in its own way, and that is precisely what the modern girl is doing. Everything would be right with her if she were not quite so inclined to disport herself like a goddess exempt from the responsibilities of mortals. But the cause of her waywardness is not far to seek.

World changes have been so rapid that it has been hard for the young woman to adjust her life. She has had only half a century in which to free herself from the ignorance and subjections of past ages and prepare herself for the many new fields of activity now open to her. Everywhere she is shaking herself free of age-long restraint.

"True," her critics affirm with melancholy foreboding, "and of womanliness and modesty as well—and a woman without modesty cannot keep a man's interest. Observe the modern girl. If you wish to know what woman released from all conventions is like, there she is sitting in public, smoking a cigarette, her legs crossed, shamelessly exposing her knees. She spends most of her time making up her face. We invite her to give a little of her time to making up and enriching her mind."

One wonders what all this to-do over a lipstick and a cigarette—trifles as light as air—is about. The modern girl has not lost the grace of blushing. I know, for I enjoy the society of a number of bright young girls who powder their noses and smoke, and in whom there is no lack of delicacy or modesty. As to the kind of mother she will be, time will answer that question; but it should not be forgotten that before or after she is a mother, she is a human being, and neither the motherly nor the wifely destination should overbalance the human.

Custom forbade the grandmother of the modern girl to exercise in the open air on pain of being frowned upon as unladylike. Custom prescribed long, voluminous skirts that swept the ground, and steel-ribbed corsets, and it was a long battle before the girl broke loose from the fetters of clothes and customs.

The conservatives build a wall to halt the modern girl, but she leaps straight over it. She is not consciously defiant, but simply obeying the urge of evolutionary forces that are shaping a new society. She stands between two ages—the dead and the newly born.

We who understand the modern girl and believe in her, see that her spirit is radiant with dawn, that in her hands is beauty, and that the children of the future will rise up and call her blessed.

The Modern Woman

The Metropolitan Magazine, October, November, December, 1912

I
THE EDUCATED WOMAN

What I shall try to say in the following pages is in the nature of a composite reply to letters I receive from young women who ask my advice about the education they should strive for, and the use of the education they have. The prevailing spirit of these correspondents is an eager desire to be of service. Their letters are at once delightful and appalling; they fill me with mingled pride and timidity. They reveal an immeasurable will-to-serve, an incalculable soul-power waiting, like a mountain reservoir, to be released in irresistible floods of righteousness, capable, too, of devastating misdirection. All this power says to me in so many words: "Tell us what to do."

My sense of responsibility is lightened by the consideration that people do not take one's advice, even when it is good, and when they seek it. Human actions are shaped by a thousand forces stronger than the written wisdom of the wisest guide that ever lived. The best that the seers of the race discovered centuries ago has not, it seems, become a controlling motive even in the lives of their followers. If the counsel of the ages is not regarded, an ordinary modern cannot hope that his words will have much influence for good. But a sincere request demands a sincere compliance. Since my correspondents think that my advice may be of use to them, I will suggest some problems for them to study, that they may be better fitted for humanitarian work.

Because I am known to be interested in bettering the condition of the blind, many of my correspondents, whose hearts are stirred by the thought of blindness, offer to help their brothers in the dark, and they ask me how to begin. Of late I have found that my letters, in reply to those who wish to help the blind, contain a paragraph about the sightless, and then pass to other things. I have sometimes wondered if my friends were not puzzled rather than helped by what I wrote. A class of college girls in an institution near great manufacturing cities and coal-mines asked me to initiate them into philanthropic endeavour for the sightless. I told them to study the life that swarms at their very doors—the mill-hands and the miners. I wonder if they understood. I tried to tell them what has been said many times, that the best educated human being is the one who understands most about the life in which he is placed, that the blind man, however poignantly his individual suffering appeals to our hearts, is not a single, separate person whose problem can be solved by itself, but a symptom of social maladjustment.

That sounds discouragingly vague and cosmic. It may have perplexed the girls to whom I wrote it. They asked me how to help the blind, how to educate themselves so that they might be of use to their unfortunate fellowmen, and I offered them the universe—I gravely recommended that they study Industrial Economics. My advice to them to study the life that surrounds them was perhaps the only part of my prescription that was not paradoxical. For the whole situation is paradoxical and confused. Society is a unit; the parts depend on one another; one part of the world suffers because the rest is not right. And yet we can each know only a very little about the whole of society. Moreover, these college girls, living in a life that I do not know, send their questions to me across a thousand miles—to me who must grope about a library of a few hundred books, whereas they have all the books of the world open to them. They can visit and talk with ten human beings while I am spelling out my intercourse with one.

Education? How can any one who has eyes to see and ears to hear and leisure to read and study remain uneducated? Are the "educators" at fault? Is there something lacking in those who administer the schools and colleges? I wonder about these things and puzzle out the details of my message with increasing perplexity.

The unfortunate are not only those whose infirmity appeals to our sympathies by its visible, palpable terror—the blind, the deaf, the dumb, the halt, the crooked, the feeble-minded, the morally diseased. The unfortunate include the vast number of those who are destitute of the means and comforts that promote right living and self-development. The way to help the blind or any other defective class is to understand, correct, remove the incapacities and inequalities of our entire civilization. We are striving to prevent blindness. Technically we know how to prevent it, as technically we know how to have clean houses, pure food, and safe railways. Socially we do not know how, socially we are still ignorant. Social ignorance is at the bottom of our miseries, and if the function of education is to correct ignorance, social education is at this hour the most important kind education.

The educated woman, then, is she who knows the social basis of her life, and of the lives of those whom she would help, her children, her employers, the beggar at her door, and her congressman at Washington. When Shakespeare wrote "Hamlet," or whether he wrote it or not, seems relatively unimportant compared with the question whether the workingwomen in your town receive a living wage and bear their children amid proper surroundings. The history of our Civil War is incomplete, as taught in the schools, if fifty years afterward the daughters and granddaughters of veterans do not understand such a simple proposition as this: "The woman who bears a child risks her life for her country." It is just such fundamental propositions related to the problems of life which school education seems to ignore. In school and college we spend a great deal of time over trivial matters. I cannot recall much that I learned at Radcliffe College, which now stands forth in my mind as of primary importance. The little economic theory that I learned was admirably put; but I have never succeeded in bringing it into harmony with the economic facts that I have learned since. The courses I took were so elementary that I should not presume to judge the opportunities which Radcliffe offers for the study of economics. It simply happens, as it happens in the experience of many students, that such academic wisdom as I was privileged to share in did not touch the problems I met later.

If we women are to learn the fundamental things in life, we must educate ourselves and one another. And we few who are unfairly called educated because we have been to college must learn much, and forget much, if we are not to appear as useless idlers to the millions of workingwomen in America. Any girl who goes to school can study and find out some of the things that an educated American woman ought to know. For instance, why in this land of great wealth is there great poverty? Any intelligent young woman like those who write to me, eager to help the sightless or any other unfortunate class, can learn why such important work as supplying food, clothing, and shelter is ill-rewarded, why children toil in the mills while thousands of men cannot get work, why women who do nothing have thousands of dollars a year to spend.

There is an economic cause for these things. It is for the American woman to know why millions are shut out from the full benefits of such education, art, and science as the race has thus far achieved. We women have to face questions that men alone have evidently not been quite able to solve. We must know why a woman who owns property has no voice in selecting the men who make laws that affect her property. We must know why a woman who earns wages has nothing to say about the choice of the men who make laws that govern her wages. We must know why a hundred and fifty of our sisters were killed in New York in a shirt-waist factory fire the other day, and nobody to blame. We must know why our fathers, brothers, and husbands are killed in mines and on railroads. We women, who are natural conservationists, must find out why the sons we bring forth are drawn up in line and shot. We must organize with our more enlightened brothers and declare a general strike against war. My father was a Confederate soldier, and I respect soldiers. But I grow more and more suspicious of the political powers that take men away from their work and set them shooting one another. Not all the military poems that I have read have roused in me an heroic desire to welcome my brother home with a bullet in his heart. We women have the privilege of going hungry while our men are in battle, and it is our right to be widowed and orphaned by political stupidity and economic chaos. To be sure, we are not allowed to vote for or against the congressman who declares war; but we can instruct ourselves unofficially in these matters.

Does what I mean by an educated woman become clearer? It ought to be clear; for all that I have said was said before I was born, and said by men; so there can be no flaw in the logic. We women must educate ourselves, and that without delay. We cannot wait longer for political economists to solve such vital problems as clean streets, decent houses, warm clothes, wholesome food, living wages, safeguarded mines and factories, honest public schools. These are our questions. Already women are speaking, and speaking nobly, and men are speaking with us. To be sure, some men and some women are speaking against us; but their contest is with the spirit of life. Lot's wife turned back; but she is an exception. It is proverbial that women get what they are bent on getting, and circumstances are driving them toward education.

The other day the newspapers contained an item which is pertinent here, since we are dealing with women and education. The Harvard Corporation has voted that it will not allow any halls of the university to be open to lectures and addresses by women, except when they are especially invited by the Corporation. There was no such rule until an undergraduate club asked Mrs. Pankhurst to speak. Then the rule was made. The Corporation has a right to make such a rule. But why has it discriminated against women? An educated man is one who receives, fosters, and contributes to the best thought of his time. By this definition, are the Harvard Corporation educated men?[1]

Fortunately, education does not depend on educational institutions any more than religion depends on churches. Says Bacon in "Novum Organum": "In the customs and institutions of schools, academies, and colleges, and similar bodies destined for the abode of learned men, and the cultivation of learning, everything is found adverse to the progress of science, for the lectures and exercises are there so ordered that to think or speculate on anything out of the common way can hardly occur to any man, and if one or two have the boldness to use any liberty of judgment, they must undertake the task all by themselves; they can have no advantage from the company of others. And if they can endure this also, they

[1] Since the above was written the Harvard Corporation's ruled that no one, man or woman, shall use the college lecture halls for "persistent propaganda" about social, economic, political or religious questions. In other words, the Harvard Corporation is sole judge of what a lecturer shall talk about.

will find their industry and largeness of mind no slight hindrance to their fortune. For the studies of men in these places are confined and, as it were, imprisoned in the writings of certain authors, from whom, if any man dissent, he is straightway arraigned as a turbulent person, and an innovator."

Perhaps the first lesson to be learned by us women who are bent on educating ourselves is, that we are too docile under formal instruction. We accept with too little question what the learned tell us. Reason, or whatever substitute heaven has given to us, does not stand at the door of receptivity and challenge what seeks admission. I am surprised to find that many champions of woman, upholders of "advanced ideas," exalt the intelligence of the so-called cultivated woman. They portray her as an intellectual prodigy to whom the wisest man would resign his library and his laboratory with a feeling of dismayed incompetence. It is not woman's intelligence that should be insisted upon, but her needs, her responsibilities, her functions. The woman who works for a dollar a day has as much right as any other human being to say what the conditions of her work should be. It is just this, I am sorry to find, which educated women do not always understand. They argue that because George Eliot wrote great novels, and Jeanne d'Arc led armies to victory, therefore, women have as much genius as men; so they go on and on in a course of thought which is beside the point. Those who argue against the rights to which we are plainly entitled do not elude the issue with more wavering uncertainty than we show in defending ourselves.

I am not disposed to praise the educated woman, as we commonly use the term. I find her narrow and lacking in vision. Few women whom I meet take a deep interest in the important questions of the day. They are bored by any problem not immediately related to their desires and ambitions. Their conversation is trivial and erratic. They do not consider a subject long enough to find out that they know nothing about it. How seldom does the college girl who has tasted philosophy and studied history relate philosophy and the chronicles of the past to the terrific processes of life which are making history every day! Her reputed practical judgment and swift sympathy seem to become inoperative in the presence of any question that reaches to a wide horizon. Her mind works quickly so long as it follows a traditional groove. Lift her out of it, and she becomes inert and without resource. She is wanting in reflection, originality, independence. In the face of opposition to a private interest or a primitive instinct she can be courageous and vividly intelligent. But she retreats from general ideas as if they did not concern her, when in point of fact civilized life is comprehended in general ideas.

Such a woman comes to the gravest responsibilities like the foolish virgins who hastened to the marriage with no oil in their lamps. She is not prepared for the battle of life. Before she knows it she may be in the midst of the fight, undisciplined and disorganized, struggling for all that is precious to her against an enemy whose position she has not reconnoitred. She sends her sons and daughters into the streets of life without the knowledge that protects. Ignorance gives her confidence, and she is fearless from want of understanding.

It is not possible to refer a complex difficulty to a single cause. But it sometimes seems that the heaviest shackle on the wrists of delicate, well-nurtured women is a false notion of "purity and womanliness." We are taught, generation after generation, that purity and womanliness are the only weapons we need in the contest of life. With this shield and buckler we are assured of all possible safety in an essentially hard world. But the enemy does not play fair. He disregards womanliness and purity. Women have learned this in lifelong suffering. Yet some of those who have suffered most cling to the ideal and pass it on to their daughters, as slaves teach their children to kiss their chains. About matters that affect our very lives we are cautioned to speak "with bated breath" lest we offend the proprieties and provoke a blushing disapprobation. The ideal of the trustful, pure, and ignorant woman is flattering and sweet to her timid soul. But it is not, I believe, the product of her own imagination. It has grown up in the worshipful fancy of romantic man—her poet and her master. The time has come when woman is subjecting this ideal to shrewd criticism.

II

MY LADY

All things uncomely and broken, all
things worn out and old,
The cry of a child by the roadway,
the creak of a lumbering cart,

The heavy steps of the ploughman
splashing the wintry mould,
Are wronging your image that blossoms
a rose in the deeps of my heart.

The wrong of unshapely things is a wrong
too great to be told;
I hunger to build them anew, and sit on a
green knoll apart.
With the earth and the sky and the water

re-made, like a casket of gold,
For my dreams of your image that blossoms
a rose in the deeps of my heart.

These beautiful verses by Mr. Yeats are the song of the new spirit hymning the mistress of the world. The old chivalry couched a lance against dragons that would devour us, and sang our beauty in unmeasured ecstasy. In some legends it proved its gallantry by kissing an ugly hag, and forthwith she turned into a lovely princess. When we were locked in grim dungeons, chivalry assailed the stronghold and delivered us, especially if we were handsome and of royal blood.

The new chivalry is dressed in working-clothes, and the dragons it must face are poverty, squalor, industrial slavery. The distressed damsel in the moonlit tower has become the girl in the street, the woman prisoned in a dirty kitchen, the wage-earner in the factory. Our champion need not fare forth into far countries to do wonders and attest his prowess. The enemy is here, everywhere—"all things uncomely and broken."

Woman-worship, the central motive of song and legend these many centuries, has been too much inspired by the will to possess and too little by the will to serve. The modern knight *sans peur et sans reproche* must learn that virtues ascribed to his lady to make her a more precious object of desire have not proved good working substitutes for some plainer virtues which he denies her after he has won his suit. It is but niggardly largess to bestow upon her so much education as will make her a witty, pleasant companion and then refuse her access to the wider knowledge of which man is the jealous custodian. We confess our incapacities. We are inconsistent and timid. We hand down from mother to daughter ideals of ourselves which are not in keeping with our experience. We amuse our brothers by irreconcilable and conflicting assertions. Every day of our lives we justify that superior masculine smile which says, "Just like a woman!" We especially justify it by accepting the legendary ideal of us which he has made for his gratification. This ideal has tender and beautiful aspects. But it is full of contradictions and absurdities. It is, on the whole, an obstacle to justice, intervening darkly between the facts of life and a clear, honest vision.

Men assure us that woman is an angel, but has not sense enough to share in the management of common earthly affairs. The standard of good sense which man has in mind is not an absolute standard beyond the reach of human attainment, but the ordinary standard of masculine achievement. Man ascribes to woman a mysterious short-cut method of mind known as "intuition," a cerebral power which guides all her activities from sewing on a button to discharging statesman's duties as Queen of England. Perception, tact, sympathy, nervous rapidity of thought are her age-long attributes. But—she would abuse the ballot. Her judgment is childish, she lacks discrimination and balance. She is frugal, a sharp bargainer in the retail market, a capable partner in a little shop; but she is unable to figure the economy of spending a hundred and fifty millions for battle-ships. She excels in organizing and conducting philanthropic work; but it would be disastrous to allow her an equal voice in determining how much public money should be spent in charitable undertakings.

I was once a member of the Massachusetts Commission for the Blind. We had forty thousand dollars of public money to spend. The work was so new and experimental that the Legislature and other officers of government could not know whether we were using the money wisely or not. There were three men on the commission and one other woman. She and I were in a safe minority, but our voice counted in every expenditure. The money was appropriated by a legisla-ture of men as the result of an investigation and appeal made largely by women. Now note the contradiction. Women were allowed to have authority in spending State money. But no woman had had direct voice in deciding whether or not the money should be appropriated at all. The money was collected from tax-payers, many of whom were women, and it was created in part by the labour of women wage-earners. Once in the hands of the State, it was beyond the control of wom-an's fine, feminine intuition, of her perception, her tact, her other adorable quali-ties. If a woman, unaided and triumphantly irrational, should devise a situation as contradictory as that, the magnificent male would smile in condescension and say: "There you are! You see, women are utterly inconsistent."

For her to answer as she might, I fear, would be "unladylike." True ladies do not argue. They cannot argue because they are women as well as ladies, and lack the reasoning faculties. Moreover, argument is unseemly in them. It only dem-onstrates their proverbial loquacity. It is, in a word, "unladylike." So round and round runs the circle of thought, coming back always to that ideal of the lady; receptive, unquestioning, illogical, charming. While her lord sings to "Highland Mary," to "the angel in the house," to the "phantom of delight," it is not gentle for her to lay her hand across the sweet strings and ask a plain question. Hers is the charm "to haunt, to startle, to waylay," but she must haunt with a smile, she must startle only pleasant sensations, she must waylay her lord's thought only when it is happy, never when it is errant fallacy.

The books of the world have sung woman's praises and placed her a little higher than the angels. But the book of woman is not un-mixed adoration. When desire liberates his generosity and wakes his lyre to rapture, man sets her upon peaks limitlessly high, and if she had true modesty, she would blush with discomfort at his impetuous hyperbole. However, he has his hours of disillusion and takes back everything nice he has said. As long ago as when the Hebrews were making the Bible, when man did all the writing, if not most of the talking, he discovered many faults in woman and set them down in vigorous words. He noted especially her tendency to infringe upon his hours of wordless meditation. Saith Ecclesiasticus: "As the climbing up of a sandy way is to the feet of the aged, so is a wife full of words to a quiet man." St. Paul says: "Let the woman learn in silence with all subjection, but I suffer not a woman to teach, or to usurp authority over the man, but be in silence."

It was St. Paul who insisted on the ideal of celibacy which was taken up by the early fathers of the Roman Church. The ancient Jews had felt the need of sons to make their tribes strong against enemies; so fruitfulness with them was a religious virtue. But the Roman world was densely populated, and the need for individual salvation was more urgent than the need for more people; so single blessedness became a religious virtue among the early Christians. The natural obstacle to celibacy was woman, and the result was that she was held responsible for man's lapses into matrimony. To the more austere fathers of the church she seemed to be man's greatest enemy, his tempter and affliction, the devil's gateway, destroyer of God's image. This idea of her fitted well with the story of her misdeed in the garden of Eden and man's banishment from paradise, for which he bore her a grudge. As a wife she was not worshipped; but her unmarried state became exalted in the figure of the Virgin Mary. Men knelt to her and besought her intercession. While the spirit of the time, embodied in church authority, beautified the mother of Christ, it continued to degrade her sisters. They were shut up in convents and ordered to stay at home, to conceal their beauty as dangerous to the beholder.

The ascetic ideal did not prevail in practice because human nature is against it. The church, which found in the words of St. Paul only a reluctant approval of marriage, finally took marriage under its protection and sanctified it. The romantic spirit grew up through the Middle Ages, and woman again became an object of delight and praise. But priestcraft and statecraft, expressions of man's attitude, kept her subjugated. Man was her sole instructor in religion, and religion comprehended all that she officially learned. He taught her her duties, her needs, and her capacities. He marked out for her the wavering line which delimited her "sphere." The chief content of this "sphere" was her duty to make him happy, to be a proper mate for him. He drilled her in morals, that she might not deceive him; he taught her obedience, that she might be his slave. He celebrated her in song and story because that celebration gave him pleasure. It was an utterance of his artistic sense. He made her laws, constituted himself judge, jury, jailer, and executioner. He had entire charge of her prisons and convents, of her house, her church, and her person. He burnt her, tortured her, gave her to wild beasts and cast her forth to be a pariah when she violated his property title in her. He laid down the measure of her knowledge, the quantity of it that would meet his approval. Through all times he granted her the privilege—of bearing his children. But once born, they were his children, not hers.

One day, when he felt especially good-humoured, he gave her permission to learn to read. "I wish," said Erasmus when he was translating the Greek Testament, "that the weakest women might read the Gospels and the Epistles of St. Paul." The alphabet was her new tree of knowledge. She had made a ruinous blunder at the first tree, but the fruits of the new tree carried no penalty, except the sorrow which knowledge brings to the innocent. It is likely, however, that experience had already taught her the full measure of sorrow. The beginning of literacy among women was the beginning of their emancipation, just as the spread of common school education was the beginning of democracy. The emancipation is not complete, and we have not arrived at democracy. The masters seem instinctively to have felt that some bars should be left up, some gates should be closed against women and against certain classes of men. The professions were placarded, "Dangerous. Women not admitted." Over the pulpit was placed the legend inherited from the Jewish and Roman priesthood, "Woman, be silent."

As late as the nineteenth century John Ruskin, who was thought very radical in his time, confessed how quaintly old-fashioned he was in these words: "There is one dangerous science for women—one which let them beware how they profanely touch—that of theology." As if the relation between God and man were a masculine monopoly! Ruskin's essay on "Queens' Gardens" is an expression of the romantic liberal who dares and retreats, sings brave paeans of deliverance and then shrinks back into a sort of timid severity. He attributes to us almost every admirable quality that a human being could dream of possessing. Indeed, he praises us unfairly at the expense of our brothers; for he says: "Men are feeble in sympathy and contracted in hope; it is you only who can feel the depths of pain and conceive the way of its healing." That is to say, our natures are richer than men's, we suffer more, yet we must not explore the relations between God and man by which our sufferings are explained and assuaged. It is amusing to remember that critics have spoken of Ruskin's genius as "feminine."

The nineteenth century with its tardy medievalism and its return to lights that never were on land or sea, together with its scientific clarity and its economic revolts, has summed up all the confusions of woman's position. Ruskin and Spencer are contemporaries. Mill's "On the Subjection of Women" and Tennyson's "Princess" are fruits of the same nation and the same era.

There is a deeper comedy in the "Princess" than Tennyson intended to put there. The opening scene is on an English lawn, and there is light talk about culture and the nobility of legendary women. One of the guests mocks at the notion of women's colleges:

> Pretty were the sight
> If our old halls could change their sex, and flaunt
> With prudes for proctors, dowagers for deans,
> And sweet girl graduates in their golden hair.
> I think they should not wear our rusty gowns,
> But move as rich as emperor-moths.

Then the poet tells a sweet, fantastic story laid in Fairyland. The mood of the story is expressed in the sad, exquisite interludes, lyrics of tears, of dead warriors, and of soft yieldings to the touch of man. Poetry is timeless; but time brings its revenges even upon poets. Just before Tennyson, who had been a brave democrat in his youth, was made a baron, Newnham College was opened, and "sweet girl graduates" became so familiar that the "Princess" lost its mild point before the author was dead. Tennyson fluttered a little way into the thought of his time, and then fluttered back again. In the second "Locksley Hall," he poetized his Toryism finally and fatally. Meanwhile the world had moved on.

In the nineteenth century Shakespeare was rediscovered and worshipped the other side idolatry. Everything was found in Shakespeare, including much that is not there; for example: his profound psychological knowledge of women. Books were written about his heroines which prove that the ideal of the perfect lady is drawn forever in the Shakespearian drama. In the introductions to the plays that I read at college, Rosalind and Portia are analyzed as if the whole philosophy of womanhood were contained in their poetical fancies, or at least as if we could never thoroughly understand women without knowing what Shakespeare wrote about them. I doubt if the women in Shakespeare's comedies are to be taken seriously. They are pretty creatures intended to be played by boys. They are the vehicle of any more or less fitting strain of poetry which happens to please the poet. Alice in Wonderland is a very real little girl; but one would not make a grave, scholarly analysis of the traits of character which she displays in her encounter with the Mock Turtle. Neither should we press too heavily upon Shakespeare's poetry to extract his beliefs about women. The unrivalled sonnets voice the praise and also the petulant dissatisfaction of a man in love, or pretending to be in love for the purpose of poetry. The woman-worship in the sonnets and in the glowing passages of the plays, spoken by gallants in pursuit of their ladies, is only the conventional romanticism common in mediaeval and renaissance literature.

Shakespeare's phrasing outflies that of all other poets. But his ideas of women are neither original nor enlightened. In studying the social ideas of a writer and his time we often learn more from his unconscious testimony than from his direct eloquence. Portia is wise, witty, learned, especially when disguised as a man; but she is disposed of without protest, through her father's will and its irrational accidents, to a commonplace, bankrupt courtier, and the tacit implication is that she is happily bestowed. Where Shakespeare brings Portia's career to an end, a modern comedy would begin. In the other plays the delightful heroine is hurried off at the close of the fifth act into the possession of a man whom she would not look at if she were as wise and strong and witty as the situations have represented her. Wedlock, no matter what the conditions, or how deep its essential indignity, is good enough for the loveliest Shakespearian maiden, and there is no suggestion that all is not as it should be. Helena, devoted, brave, loyal, is rewarded by being given to a careless worthless youth. In "Twelfth Night," Viola and the sentimental Duke, Olivia and Sebastian, pair off as nimbly as if personality were only a matter of wigs and disguises, of identities easily mistaken and as easily reestablished. Hermione, queenly and gracious, is bound to a person who behaves like a furious spoilt child, and is represented as respecting him and wishing to keep him.

Shakespeare does teach us much about the ideals of women that prevailed in his time. For he regards as a comic situation, to be turned with his magic phrases and concluded with joy-bells, what we should regard as a tragic situation.

The tragedy that lurks behind the false ideal of womanhood is being disclosed in our time. Woman is beginning to say to her master: "Romantic man, cease a while your singing of lays antique and ballads new. We would talk with you in prose. You have dreamed long enough of the lady, who, alas, is in a negligible minority. It is time for you to give your superior intelligence to the well-being of millions and millions of women."

III
THE WOMAN AND HER HOUSE

We women have often been told that the home contains all the interests and duties in which we are concerned. Our province is limited by the walls of a house, and to emerge from this honourable circumscription, to share in any broad enterprise, would be not only unladylike, but unwomanly. I could not help thinking of this the other day when I was asked to go to a far state and take part in some work that is being done for the blind. If I accepted this invitation, should I not be leaving my proper sphere, which is my home? I have thought of it many times since I learned that there are in America over six million women wage-earners. Every morning they leave their homes to tend machines, to scrub office-buildings, to sell goods in department stores. Society not only permits them to leave their proper sphere; it forces them to this unwomanly desertion of the hearth, in order that they may not starve. Oh, my sisters in the mills and shops, are you too tired, too indifferent to read the ridiculous arguments by which your rights are denied and your capacities depreciated in the sacred name of the home and its defence?

Woman's sphere is the home, and the home, too, is the sphere of man. The home embraces everything we strive for in this world. To get and maintain a decent home is the object of all our best endeavours. But where is the home? What are its boundaries? What does it contain? What must we do to secure and protect it?

In olden times the home was a private factory. The man worked in the field or at his handicraft, while the woman made food and clothes. She shared in out-of-door labour; but indoor work naturally became her special province. The household was the centre of production, and in it and about it man supplied himself with all that he needed—or all that he had—by rudimentary hand-processes. The mill to grind corn was not far away. The leather used by the shoemaker was from a beef killed by a neighbour. Over every cottage door the words might have been written: "Mr. and Mrs. Man, Manufacturers and Dealers in General Merchandise." Home life and industrial life were one. To-day they are widely separated. Industries that used to be in the house are spread all over the world. The woman's spinning-wheel and part of her kitchen and dairy have been taken away from her. When she seeks to understand economic affairs, and to exert her authority in their management, she is in reality only following her utensils.

The spinning-wheel, ancient emblem of domestic industry, has been removed to great factories. She has followed it there both as worker and owner. So she still does her part in the great task of clothing the human race. Where the spinning-wheel is, the woman has an ancestral right to be. For no matter how complex wheel and loom have become, she depends on them still to make the blanket that covers her child in its sleep. It is her duty as a house-mother to watch her spinning-wheel, to see that no member of the world-family goes ill-clad in an age when wool is abundant, when cunning machines can make good coats, when a ragged frock on a self-respecting woman is a shame to us all. It is for woman to follow her wheel, to make sure that it is spinning wool and not grinding misery, that no little child is chained to it in a torture of day-long labour. The spinning-wheel has grown a monstrous thing. In order to identify it, one must study wages, tariffs, dividends, the organization of labour and factory sanitation. The woman who studies these problems and insists on having a voice in their solution is in her home as truly as was her grandmother whose tireless foot drove the treadle of the old spinning-wheel. The home is where those things are made without which no home can be comfortable.

Once the housewife made her own butter and baked her own bread; she even sowed, reaped, threshed, and ground the wheat. Now her churn has been removed to great cheese and butter factories. The village mill, where she used to take her corn, is to-day in Minneapolis; her sickle is in Dakota. Every morning the express company delivers her loaves to the local grocer from a bakery that employs a thousand hands. The men who inspect her winter preserves are chemists in Washington, Her ice-box is in Chicago. The men in control of her pantry are bankers in New York. The leavening of bread is somehow dependent upon the culinary science of congressmen, and the washing of milk-cans is a complicated art which legislative bodies, composed of lawyers, are trying to teach the voting population on the farms. It would take a modern woman a lifetime to walk across her kitchen floor; and to keep it clean is an Augean labour. No wonder that she sometimes shrinks from the task and joins the company of timid, lazy women who do not want to vote. But she must manage her home; for, no matter how grievously incompetent she may be, there is no one else authorized or able to manage it for her. She must secure for her children clean food at honest prices. Through all the changes of industry and government she remains the baker of bread, the minister of the universal sacrament of life.

When she demands to be mistress of the national granary, the national kitchen, the national dairy, the national sewing-room, whoever tells her to confine herself to her house is asking her to move forward and backward at the same time. This is a feat which even her inconsistency cannot achieve. The inconsistencies reside not in woman and her relation to her plain duties, but in her circumstances and in some of her critics. She can put a basket on her arm and bargain intelligently with a corner grocer; but she cannot understand the problem of nationalizing the railroads which have brought the food to the grocer's shop. She is clever at selecting a cut of meat; but the central meat-market must not be opened to her investigation; a congressional committee, which she did not choose, is doing its whole duty as father of the house when it tries to find out who owns the packing-houses in Chicago, how much money the owners make out of her dinner, and why thousands of tons of meat are shipped out of the country while her family is hungry.

She opens a can of food which is adulterated with worthless or dangerous stuff. In a distant city a man is building himself a palace with the profits of many such cans. If a petty thief should break into her pantry, and she should fight him tooth and nail, she would be applauded for her spirit and bravery; but when a millionaire manufacturer a thousand miles away robs her by the peaceful methods of commerce, she has nothing to say, because she does not understand business, and politics is not for her to meddle in.

Woman's old "domestic sphere" has become not only an empty shell with much of the contents removed, but a fragile shell in which she is not safe. Beside her own hearth she may be poisoned, starved, and robbed. When shall we have done with the tyranny which applies worn-out formulas to modern conditions? When shall we learn that domestic economy is political economy? The noblest task of woman is to get bread for her children. Whatever touches her children's bread is her business.

Woman from times long gone has been the nurse, the consoler, the healer of pain. To-day the sick-bed is often in a great public hospital. There she has followed it as professional nurse, and her services have been welcomed and acknowledged. In the hospital wards where she moves, deft, cheerful, capable, there are men unnecessarily laid low by the accidents of trade, and children maimed and dying who might be well and playing merrily in the bright morning of life. From the battlefields of industry come the wounded, from the shambles of poverty come the deformed. What enemy has stricken them? How much of all this disease and misery is preventable? Shall the wise nurse stand by the bed of pain and ask no questions about the social causes of ill health? If her own child in her own home is needlessly hurt, she blames herself for her carelessness. In the world-home if a child is needlessly hurt, she is equally responsible. By her vigilance in the world-home woman can help to bring about a civilization in which every preventable disease shall be rooted out, and every condition that causes broken bodies shall be examined and abolished. This is her problem. She is mistress of the sick-room, and the sick-room is world-wide.

The education of children is acknowledged as lying within the scope of maternal care. The mother is the first teacher before the child goes to school, and in the schoolroom her unmarried sister devotes herself as a professional foster-mother to the children of others. The American nursery is a public building with a flag flying over it. If anywhere, woman is mistress in the schoolroom. So evident is this that in relation to schools she has a certain political privilege. She can vote for the school committee and serve on it herself. But even here she is bound by a very short tether. She has nothing official to say about how much money shall be spent for schools. Her freedom in this respect, as in some others, is the form without the substance. For the fundamental question in the public school problem is the question of money. Money must be appropriated by men. Moreover, the laws relating to children, for example, the laws of compulsory education, are made by men. It is not for her to say whether a child shall be taken from school to grind in mill and factory. Yet every child plunged in ignorance, bent by man's work before his time, is a thwarting of her sacred mission to fill the world with children well-born, well-bred, beautiful, wise, strong for the burdens of life! The schoolroom and all that it means belongs to the central intimacy of home, and all that violates the schoolroom violates the sanctity of the woman's hearth.

It is idle to say that woman could not improve the schools, that the schools are already free, and that every child has opportunity for instruction. The efficiency of the school depends upon things outside the schoolroom. It has been found that you must feed your child before you can teach it, and that the poor home defeats the best schoolroom. Behind the free school we must have a free people. What profits it to provide costly school buildings for anemic, under-fed children, to pass compulsory education laws and not secure a livelihood for the families whose children must obey them? What is the common sense of free text-books without wholesome food and proper clothing? Where is the logic—masculine or feminine—of free schools and free child-labour in the same commonwealth? These questions concern the most ignorant woman and the best educated woman, and the solution of them is necessary to the health and comfort of every home.

Woman's place is still the household. But the household is more spacious than in times gone by. Not all the changes of modern life have changed woman's duties essentially. Her work as spinner, bread-giver, helper of the helpless, mother and teacher of children is nowise different to-day but is immensely increased and intensified. Too often confused by the dazzle and uproar of modern life, she is the primal woman still, the saviour and shaper of the race.

In what a grim, strange abode must she often discharge her old-time functions! Some-times it is no home at all, but an overcrowded, sunless lodging; it is not a shelter, but an industrial prison; it is not a nursery, but a lazaretto. Countless mothers of men have no place fit to be born in, to bear others in, to lie in. Packed in tenements forgot of light, unheeded and slighted, starved of eye and ear and heart, they wear out their dull existence in monotonous toil—all for a crust of bread! They strive and labour, sweat and produce; they subject their bodies and souls to every risk, lest their children die for want of food. Their clever hands which have so long been set to the spindle and the distaff, their patience, their industry, their cheapness, have but served to herd them in masses under the control of a growing industrial despotism.

Why is all this? Partly because woman does not own and direct her own share of the national household. True government is nothing but the management of this household for the good of the family. Under what kind of government do we live? To this question, her question, woman must find an answer by following her sisters to their places of sojourn. It is for her to know if their home is home indeed, if their shelter is strong and healthful, if every room—in lodging, shop, and factory—is open to light and air. It is for her to see that every dweller therein has freedom to drink in the winds of heaven and refresh his mind with music, art, and books; it is for her to see that every mother is enabled to bring up her children under favourable circumstances.

The greatest change is coming that has ever come in the history of the world. Order is evolving out of the chaos that followed the breaking up of the old system in which each household lived after its own manner. By using the physical forces of the universe men have replaced the slow hand-processes with the swift power of machines. If women demand it, a fair share of the machine-products will go to them and their families, as when the loom stood at hand in their dwellings. They will no more give all their best years to keep bright and fair the homes of others while their own are neglected. They will no more consume all their time, strength, and mental capacity in bringing up the rosy, laughing children of others while their own sweet children grow up pitiful and stunted. There is motherhood enough in the world to go round if it is not abused and wasted.

Yes, the greatest change is coming that has ever come in the history of the world. The idea that a higher power decrees definite stations for different human beings—that some are born to be kings and others to be slaves—is passing away. We know that there is plenty of room in the world and plenty of raw material in it for us all to be born right, to be brought up right, to work right, and to die right. We know that by the application of ordinary intelligence and common good-will, we can secure to every one of our children the means of culture, progress, and knowledge, of reasonable comfort, health, and happiness, or, if not happiness, at least freedom from the unnecessary misery which we all suffer to-day. This is the new faith that is taking the place of the faith in blind, selfish, capricious powers. Religion, the life of which is to do good, is supplanting the old servile superstitions. The spirit of the time we are in has been eloquently described by Henry Demarest Lloyd:

"It is an ethical renaissance, and insists that the divine ideals preached for thousands of years by the priests of humanity be put into form, now, here, and practically, in farm and mine, stock-market, factory, and bank. It denies point-blank that business is business. It declares business to be business and politics and religion. Business is the stewardship of the commissary of mankind, the administration of the resources upon which depend the possibilities of the human life, which is the divine life."

What is there, then, so cold, sordid, inhuman in economics that we women should shrink from the subject, disclaim all part in it, when we touch it daily in our domestic lives?

Many young women full of devotion and good-will have been engaged in superficial charities. They have tried to feed the hungry without knowing the causes of poverty. They have tried to minister to the sick without understanding the cause of disease. They have tried to raise up fallen sisters without knowing the brutal arm of necessity that struck them down. We give relief to a mother here and there, and still women are worn out at their daily tasks. We attempt social reforms where we need social transformations. We mend small things and leave the great things untouched. We strive after order and comfort in a few households, regardless of the world where distress prevails and loveliness is trodden in the dust.

Our abiding-place will be home indeed when the world outside is a peaceful, bright home for mankind. Woman's happiness depends upon her knowledge of the facts of life as much as upon her lovely thoughts and sweet speech and her faithfulness to small duties. In woman is wrapped the hope of the future. The new child, the new civilization, all the possibilities that sleep in mankind are enfolded in her. In her travail is the resurrection of the human race. All this glorious promise can be brought to naught by ignorance of the world in which it is to be fulfilled. To plead with woman to urge her to open her eyes to the great affairs of life, is merely to bid her make ready her house for the child that is to be born.

6

Children and Education

elen Keller's columns on children and education covered issues such as the importance of reading, nurturing children,[1] and stimulating children's intelligence.[2] Her comments about reading are quite charming, given the context of her disabilities. "Reading has been the chief pleasure of my life," she writes in 1930.[3] "Indeed, reading has meant so much to me that I am in danger of extravagance whenever I speak of it. My joy in books has filled with happiness the chinks created by my limitations. Had I not early learned to relish good books, I tremble to think how desolate my life would have been. In books I have found wise counselors, cheerful friends, unfailing comforters." Even on a simple subject like reading, her messages carried power because of who she was.

From a disability image standpoint, her words also subtly diffused the negative connotations of deafness and blindness when she called them "chinks" and "limitations." That is an interesting aspect to her writing about her disabilities—she never invoked any image of tragedy in her situation. Although non-disabled people may believe deafness or blindness to be a tragic occurrence, Keller's columns counteracted this notion at every turn with her keen intellect, diverse interests, and the obvious joy she gathered from so many activities.

Notes:

1. Helen Keller, "Christmas Day is Children's Day," *The Home Magazine*, December 1931, p. 8.

2. Helen Keller, "Seek the Cause," *The Home Magazine*, March 1933, p. 6.

3. Helen Keller, "The Importance of Reading," *The Home Magazine*, October 1930, p. 6.

Christmas Day Is Children's Day

The Home Magazine, December 1931, p. 8

D uring the Christmas season the minds of parents are especially occupied with their children. Everything that will make them happy is planned. What lovelier sight can be imagined than the family gathered 'round the Christmas tree, the children's faces aglow with eager interest, their hands full of glittering treasures, their voices, like bells, filling the house with joyous music! In a very real sense Christmas Day is Children's Day.

I wonder whether, if parents gave more time to their children on other days, every day would not be fuller of interest and joy for them. Parents can do much to keep their boys and girls interested in their studies by being interested themselves.

I remember how my teacher used to stimulate my desire for knowledge by talking over every lesson as if she were a child herself. It was wonderful to have her work out a sum of arithmetic by my side, or trace in the sand the course of a river, placing big and little stones along its bank to represent cities and towns.

Such companionship of minds is of inestimable value to every child, but particularly to the child of slow mental processes. Left to plod along by himself, he becomes discouraged, especially when he sees other children getting ahead of him. His parents can obviate this difficulty, they can show him how to overcome his handicap and shake off the inhibitions that embarrass him. Often slowness has its advantages over that of a quick, impatient mind.

Busy parents need not sacrifice time for this purpose. The idea is for them to take a thoughtful interest in the endeavors of the backward child. When he comes home from school, let him see that you really want to know what he has been doing. Get him to talk about his studies and his teachers. Do not criticize him openly, and do not pretend interest you do not feel; for he will detect your insincerity and retire into his inferiority complex. But if he sees that you are listening to him sympathetically, he will gain confidence.

Keep in touch with what your children are studying. Ask them questions, not to examine them, but in a pleasant, interested way. Perhaps you have traveled, and can give them a lively description of the places mentioned in their geography lesson. Tell them what you know about the subjects they discuss. Look up words in the dictionary with them, show them how to use the encyclopedia and the atlas.

If you are genuinely interested in the information thus obtained, all the better for your children. They will sense your enthusiasm and talk more, and acquire valuable knowledge with delight. This will be a bond between yourselves and your children which will mean much to you in their advancement and in your understanding of their minds. It amazes me how parents think they can be an influence for good in their children's lives while indifferent to what concerns them, and while frittering away precious time at motion pictures, bridge and gossip parties.

If parents would only be companions to their children, what an enjoyable place the home would be!

Quite as harmful as parental indifference is the shallow, cynical talk children hear in their homes. To speak slightingly of the primary things of life—of the sweet sacredness of family life, of love, of religion and of human nature is a serious offence against childhood. It chokes the seeds of good in the child's heart and distorts his sense of values. He grows up distrusting ideals, and affects skepticism about faith, hope and inspiration.

If you find your young people practicing a kind of topsy-turvy doubting of everything they should hold sacred, consider whether you may not be responsible. You may have lightly spoken blasphemies in their ears.

On this day when man becomes as a child, and so prepared to enter into the Kingdom of God, examine your thoughts, from which your heart speaketh, and give your children only the thoughts that shall keep their lives sweet, sane and strong.

Seek the Cause

The Home Magazine, March 1933, p. 6

How often have we heard it said, "That child can't keep still for two minutes together!" Of course a child can't keep still, it isn't natural. But he doesn't have to be a little "fidget." It is easy enough to stop aimless flitting to and fro. Restlessness is aimless movement, and a healthy child will not move aimlessly unless he is thwarted in some way.

Constant activity is essential to the child's physical development. Of course there are times when it is necessary that he should keep quiet. You have tidied up the house for visitors for instance, and you can't have the little one go tearing through the rooms, scattering his toys on the furniture. Try to remember something he has been especially interested in the past day or two. Perhaps only this morning you saw him fitting a key in the door and turning the lock. Give him the key to your wardrobe or dressing-table and ask him what it is for. In all probability he will immediately take it and begin fitting the key and undoing the catch. You will be surprised to find how long he keeps himself occupied.

There is no fidgeting about the child who is absorbed in some interesting activity. There is no unnecessary fussing, no explosion of temper. Time and again you have noticed how he frets and is troublesome when you try to do things for him. You are in a hurry; so you don't allow him to struggle with the intricacies of buttons and socks and shoes. You put them on, curbing as best you can his impatient jerks and twistings. His aimless resistance is a sign that he is being thwarted.

No indeed, I do not think a child should always have his way. That is not my meaning when I say that it is wrong to thwart the natural instincts of the child.

There are two ways to teach him obedience. One is the old way of compulsion and punishment if he disobeys. The other way is to ask from the child what he can do, that is, to ask obedience in such a way that your child will be glad to obey, and he will form the habit of obedience easily because he learns it naturally. It is just as easy in the beginning to form right habits as wrong ones.

Try to imagine the torture of a small child who is made to sit still at a table while grown-ups talk, or in school while the teacher draws on the blackboard! No wonder he shuffles and wriggles from head to foot.

No child can learn sitting still. He only learns to dislike his teacher and what she tries to teach him. When the restraint is no longer endurable, the child is given exercises which are as unnatural as sitting still. The exercises should be spontaneous, joyous, not simply movements at the word of command. Everything that does not teach self-discipline and self-activity should be avoided in the training of the child.

When the child first goes to school, he should be given things he can do. He can help to look after the school-room—put the desks and chairs in place. There are many little personal things he can do for himself—hang up his coat and cap, wash his hands, brush his hair, tidy his desk. When we do these things for the child, we discourage initiative and prevent him from acquiring the habit of orderliness. It will be found that he takes the greatest interest in performing all the movements of daily life.

I have seen a little girl amuse herself for hours with two pieces of cloth, on one of which she sewed buttons, and on the other she made buttonholes.

When the child acts only in a disorderly, disconnected manner, his nervous force is under a great strain, while on the other hand his nervous energy is positively increased and multiplied by intelligent activity.

It is a pitiful mistake for a parent or teacher to try to force a child into a rigid pattern of behavior. The child becomes negative, or rebellious, refusing to obey the simplest and most necessary commands. It seems to me, "grown-ups" often disguise irritability and impatience under the cloak of discipline.

On the other hand, it is equally bad to try to get the child to obey by threatening him with the loss of love or appealing to his affection. "Mother won't love you if you act like that," is an expression that should never be used to a child. "Your naughtiness breaks mother's heart" and similar phrases put a terrible strain upon the child's emotions and eventually produce very unhappy results.

Those who have to do with young children should develop the habit of seeking the cause of naughtiness and temper. They should treat the cause, not the symptoms. For restlessness and bad temper are manifestations of an emotional upset. Perhaps the child wants more attention or more love, or quieter surroundings and more sleep.

One thing is sure, real discipline is the kind that is developed from within. It is the only lasting kind, and the only discipline that builds character.

The Importance of Reading

The Home Magazine, October 1933, p. 6

We all think we enjoy reading; but when we talk to people, we find that their interest in books does not go very deep. I do not remember anyone ever saying to me: "I don't care for reading, it bores me"; but very many people have said: "I regret extremely that I have never read as much as I should like to because I never have time." As a matter of fact, no one who really cares for reading is deterred from it by want of time.

I find that a very large number of people never read books after leaving school. Our system of education renders it possible for everyone to read, and students read with an object—preparing for their examinations or writing a thesis; but they do not form the reading habit. Prescribed reading seldom, if ever, stimulates a love of books.

When I speak of reading, I mean reading with discrimination and delight. I know people who think they are readers because they glance through books they have heard discussed. But mere browsing is a hindrance to sincere reading. The cursory, haphazard perusal of books tends to fix the attention on their high points and leave the substance of the narrative almost untouched. It is as if a miner should pick up a nugget of gold and go away satisfied, without taking the trouble to dig into the precious vein that runs underground.

Reading has been the chief pleasure of my life. Indeed, reading has meant so much to me that I am in danger of extravagance whenever I speak of it. My joy in books has increased with the years, and filled with happiness the chinks created by my limitations. Had I not early learned to relish good books, I tremble to think how desolate my life would have been. In books I have found wise counselors, cheerful friends, unfailing comforters.

The love of reading is an appetite that grows by what it feeds upon. Every book we read thoughtfully makes us want to read another. We cannot but be ennobled by familiarity with the thoughts of great minds. Such thoughts live forever and keep us young and sensitive to the true values of life. Reading is to the mind what exercise is to the body, it invigorates our mental processes.

Of course, there are preferences in the kinds of books we read. We cannot all like the same writers. We are all more or less limited in our powers of appreciation; but we can try to understand and value the books that competent critics tell us are great literature. It is never difficult to follow our natural inclinations; but it requires patience and perseverance to bend our minds in a somewhat different direction and feel at home in ideas new to us. Sometimes it is necessary to read over and over a book which at first did not interest us, in order to find its treasure. What is important is that the mind should be kept alert, interested, that it should be broadened and quickened by the books we read, that it should have some vital and balanced idea of the myriad factors and forces which make up our modern world.

Someone may ask how we are to know who are the great authors. Until we have developed our own powers of discernment and judgment, we must accept the verdict of experts. The only way to train ourselves to think and judge independently is to read, read, read. Happy are they who persist in cultivating a taste for reading! They win riches that no poverty or care can take from them. They will never say they have no time for reading, they will keep a book by them and snatch it up when they have a moment. That moment will reward them handsomely and minister to their happiness.

Books give us the treasures of earth and heaven for the asking, and the more we read, the better able we are to build with this wealth, spiritual walls and towers of thought that no misfortune can destroy.

Woman and Peace

The Home Magazine, May 1930, p. 6

It is fitting and proper that we should turn our minds to a new way of thinking and feeling in the Springtime—the season of the year that suggests renaissance, youth, vigor. We are symbolists all, and I see in each bud, leaf and blade of grass, life with its new hopes, dreams and aspirations.

That these leaves and buds will pass away ought not to discourage us. Each has played its part, has spent its brief hour in the world, and goes to prepare the way for others. Ideals, if they possess truth and beauty, will grow with time and expand into greater truths with greater beauty.

Down through the ages woman has accepted a sphere of activity far below her intelligence and capacity. Deceived, denied and bullied, she has frittered away her life in trivial pursuits. Only in child-bearing has she seemed to fulfill her destiny. Even in the education of her children she has had little to say. But at last she is beginning to shake herself free from the old laws, old customs and old ideas which our fathers held to be the best of civilization. She is challenging fear and superstition, and facing unashamed, unafraid, the facts that science has discovered.

One of the old ideas that is passing away is the commandment, "Thou shalt not eat of the Fruit of the Tree of Knowledge." This has been the command of man, church and school. Always there have been subjects which convention and prejudice tabooed for woman. Even in my youth it was considered unwomanly to discuss the causes of blindness in the new-born child. At first not one newspaper or magazine would open its pages to the subject. It was years before we broke down the barriers of reserve and prudery that hindered free discussion.

The time has come for woman to open the graves of dead institutions, and breathe new life into them, and thus bring into the land live men and women. The first thing she ought to do is draw aside the curtain of convention and peer with the naked eye of love into the mind of her child. It is her duty to study the child and learn what he really is. In order to do this, it is vital for her to know the facts that are being accumulated in biology, eugenics, psychology, the relation between habits and impulses in human development. On this development depends her efficacy in shaping the child's character.

Tomorrow our children will be sitting where we sit today. They will carry out the policies we lay down, they will bear our influence into their enterprises. They will exercise authority in business, in Congress, on the bench of justice, and many will be on the battlefields of industry. They will control cities and states,

243

and hold in their hands the destiny of their country. They will act according to the character, intelligence and knowledge we have developed in them in their formative years.

Start today, O mother, and understand the laws of your child's growth and happiness. Only through him will come a civilization that shall conform with the highest attributes of human nature.

Obviously, the mother is the first teacher, and the home is the school from which the child receives his earliest and strongest impressions. Happy is the child who grows up in an environment where he hears intelligent conversation and discussion! For such worthwhile talk and exchange of views give balance to his mind and dispose him to noble feelings.

It is in the mother's power to sow in his mind the seeds of future deeds. She can substitute for the football hero that he admires the lives of great men, their lofty thoughts and creative works. By word, story and example she can teach her child that humanity is enriched, not by athletes and money-makers, but by the ideals, the unselfishness and the courage of the Franklins, the Lincolns, the Newtons, the Tolstoys, the Pasteurs and the Einsteins. All these men did their great work for mankind without the help of machinery, intensive production and wealth of which we are so proud.

Again I urge you, study the child, learn to meet with sympathy his reactions to the world about him, and endeavor to create for him an environment favorable to his development. Then he will be able to take charge of himself intelligently, serve his fellowmen with his mind and contribute something to the common good. These are only a few of the things that a mother needs to know if she wants her children to be happy and intelligent. Such children, when the opportunity comes, will shape to higher ends the new order of society that is now emerging from the chaos of the world.

Yes, new times demand new measures, new women and a new education.

Making a Happy Home

The Home Magazine, June 1933, p. 6

Everybody agrees that the American home has changed, and is still changing. Pessimists with a reverence for tradition tell us it will not exist much longer. Optimists contemplate its disappearance with joy. People who have "golden mean" minds survey the changes and study statistics, but refuse to conjecture what developments ten years will bring.

Economic necessity has dictated many of the changes. The home is being ground between two millstones—the tendency of the individual to assert himself and the counter-tendency of a machine society to shape the individual to the mass pattern.

Unless the women of today think deeply on the home problem, they will have a negligible part in the discipline and in forming the ideals that will develop the minds and characters of their children and preparing them for the duties of a changing world.

Modern conditions are generally detrimental to this great source of family happiness. It is for women to study the causes of home disintegration and use their votes and their influence to remove them. Woman must prepare herself for the most important work of life—making a happy home. She must realize that the time to give her children a chance of happiness when they grow up is in their babyhood, in school days and in college years, from the moment the little girl or boy can understand words and transmute them into thoughts and action.

I do not think of home as an economic unit, but as a place dear to our hearts. It may be only a small apartment or cottage, but those who can make it a real home are happy there. Home is a place where young married people begin their life together and share great moments and precious things—the joy of planning for their children, the pleasure of books, the satisfaction of holidays, sympathy in difficulties and successes, in dark days and bright!

Home life brings every faculty and gift into play in degrees and proportions very different from public life or casual intercourse and relations. Blessed is the home where parents know how to soothe, to sympathize, to counsel and to encourage the highest qualities in each other and their children!

The nation which has the best homes will have the brightest future. Boys and girls are the men and women of tomorrow. When well brought up, they grow into men and women who believe in the right things—in the importance of good schools, in the dignity of work with the hands as well as with the head, in the community spirit, in the joy of serving others—in everything beneficial to home and civic life.

Intelligent Reading

The Home Magazine, July 1933, p. 6

Editor's note: British theologian John Wesley, with his brother, founded the Methodist religion in the 18th century.

There is too much scatter-brain reading by both men and women. One sees them reading newspapers and magazines assiduously, but when one enters into conversation with them, it would seem they had digested little of what they had read. We rise from our newspapers and magazines with our appetite for news satisfied, but with no perception of the sequence of events or our relation to them. We scatter abroad disconnected comments and opinions, thus passing on our topsy-turvy way of thinking to others.

I meet many women who read extensively, but their reading seems to limit itself to what is interesting, but not important. This kind of reading enlivens for the moment and deadens afterward. John Wesley refers to it as a "wasteful, unhealthy self-indulgence." Certainly it leaves the mind barren of needful knowledge that should be communicated to the younger generation.

We should read with some sort of system and purpose. We should read for understanding and tolerance, for historical value and critical judgement. When we have read an article or an instructive book attentively, we should try to apply what we have read to the principles of life and the march of events.

No matter what happens, right reading done in season and done with an open mind will render intelligible to us the why and the how of falling empires, changes in governments, events that reduce our means of life or affect our children's welfare, and we shall be able to put ourselves in a position to resist the menacing evil or benefit by the good that comes. For these same questions that disturb and puzzle and confound us today have in their turn occurred to all the wise men.

When we stand up for judgment in the crisis that is even now upon us, it will be of no use to say, "Oh, I did not understand," or "So many things happened, I could not keep up with them, and anyway, what could I do about them?" Unless we are informed we shall be numbered among those who having eyes see not and having ears hear not.

Perhaps we can give only a few minutes to reading each day, but it will steer us through a storm of conflicting ideas and standards and save us some cruel disappointments. For it will keep us clear of some of the pernicious false assertions that work as much havoc in our national life as selfishness. Want of thought is as harmful to us as want of heart. No one who reads attentively is ever quite the same again. He earnestly regrets that he does not know more, and that is at least the beginning of vision that keeps individuals and nations spiritually alive.

Many of the great men today, the men who have accomplished something in the way of science, medicine, exploration have received their inspiration from good reading material. The deeds and hardships of others who have given their thoughts to a great national service have spurred them on.

The kind of reading that counts is that which "doth buckle and bow the mind to the nature of things." Intelligent reading makes of us trail-breakers and lamps to the feet of our children.

Going Back to School

The Home Magazine, June 1930, p. 6

I t is September. Vacation time is over, and the children of the nation are going back to school.

Education has been called "the American passion."

We spend more money on education than any other nation on earth. In the last thirty years the high school enrolment increased fifteen times as fast as the population, and our college students about seven times as rapidly.

Yet thoughtful observers of our national life are appalled by the lack of culture in the people. If this is true, what is wrong with our educational system?

My answer is that parents and teachers have regarded the education of children merely as wage-earners or non-wage-earners in this or that occupation when the emphasis should have been on the ethical values; in other words, the sort of men and women they are to become.

Education should train the child to use his brains, to make for himself a place in the world and maintain his rights even when it seem that society would shove him into the scrap-heap.

Education is not to fit us to get ahead of our fellows and to dominate them. It is rather to develop our talents and personalities and stimulate us to use our faculties effectively.

If our sympathies and understanding are not educated, the fact that we have a college degree, or that we have discovered a new fact in science does not make us educated men and women. The only way to judge the value of education is by what it does.

To be influenced in our school years to love our fellowmen is not sentimentalism. It is quite as necessary to our well-being as fresh air and food to the body, and a feeling for fair play, generosity and consideration can be instilled into every normal child.

Many a child seems stupid because his parents and teachers are too impatient or too busy to care what he is really interested in. If educators tried to find out what the student especially wants to do, how much time would be saved that is now wasted in teaching things which will never mean anything to him!

May I give my personal experience as an illustration of what I mean?

When my teacher began my education, she saw that my physical limitations narrowed the range of studies which might be useful to me. She knew that I could not hope to do everything that a person with his full quota of faculties could do. Therefore she noted carefully the things I could do with some hope of success.

She encouraged me to develop the sense of touch not only in my fingers but in all parts of my body, and to observe every object and sensation accurately and write about it. Every minute of the day, in one way or another, she stressed the importance of self-expression.

I hated writing exercises. Writing was never easy to me. But my teacher pointed out that writing was almost the only game I could play on equal terms with others. "You must learn," she said, "to find joy in self-expression; for that is the only way you can reach the mind and heart of the public."

The simplest thing we learn to do well—even if it is only to sweep a room in a beautiful spirit of service—makes life infinitely worth while, and is true education.

A Vital Responsibility for Teachers

The Instructor, April 1957

My thoughts on education are colored by the blessings I received from my teacher Anne Sullivan. Certainly it seems to me, from my own experience, that there is nothing more magical in education than a teacher who shares children's desires and pleasures and encourages them to explore with their eyes and ears and their hands. For it takes all senses, well trained, to give the fullest measure of knowledge.

The more that children under such a teacher handle objects and learn their uses, the more will be their appreciation of life and its manifold possibilities. When children first have contact with something new they are likely to ask few questions, because their ideas are vague and their vocabulary is not large enough to express their groping thoughts. But the good teacher understands this and knows that as their knowledge increases they find words for their questions, their field of inquiry widens, and they return to the same subjects often, eager for more information. The imaginative teacher enters into the world of the child, thrills him and delights him, and stresses his capacity for originality to prevent him from becoming a victim of the herd mind.

We are living in an age of a fast-enlarging world society. The United States has reached a position where it requires stores of knowledge, wisdom, and understanding for the solution of the colossal problems with which it is confronted, and yet we are surrounded by an atmosphere of mediocrity. Greatness is lacking in government, in legislation, in the press, the pulpit, and the schools, and many people in all these fields seem unconscious of the drab level to which they have descended.

We are deplorably unprepared for our future and it is a vital responsibility for our teachers to understand the changes of our time and to move with them. Teachers must constantly re-examine the specific objectives and the practical methods of education, as experience and study reveal new truths about the child, the adult, and society. They must help prepare young minds for adjustment to multitudinous interactions with people of different views and practices, and guide them towards a composite world of order and mutual service.

Although I am no teacher and cannot measure the difficulties of opening the mind of a child, I have unlimited faith in the capabilities of teachers. If it was possible for a young woman, alone, half-blind, and deficient in education to penetrate my silent night, how much easier it must be for those with all their faculties to help normal children develop their intelligence.

The teacher in my mind is an unfailing battery of enthusiasm and inspiration who never permits children to lose their zest for knowledge as an adventure or a means of accomplishment. When men and women with the "divine fire" teach, there is no calculating the wealth they confer upon their pupils in literature, art, science, and the treasures of the human spirit. It is from the hearts and intellects of our dedicated teachers that a humane, progressive society may rise in the twentieth century.

We Don't Know How to Think

The Home Magazine, March 1930, p. 7

D r. Frederick Tilney, Professor of Neurology at Columbia University, says that the brain of normal people is used to just one-fifth of its possible capacity! The fact that the blind and the deaf can keep informed as to the world about them, can enjoy books, flowers, music, and live as happily as anyone with all his faculties is a challenge to those who have five senses.

Education does not mean teaching people what they do not know, but teaching them how to find out things for themselves. The student who does not learn to think in school or college is not educated.

We know that brain power, like muscle power, can be developed by exercise. Most of us depend upon others to do our thinking for us. We accept their opinions and beliefs without taking the trouble to reason them out. That is one of the chief reasons why racial and social prejudices are so easily formed, and so difficult to eradicate. And we read carelessly, just as we listen.

Now it seems to me we Americans have a rather superficial attitude towards learning. We foster a quality of performance which implies that the end is more important than the means. We admire the ability to achieve quickly and dazzlingly in the public eye. We laud success at any cost. We imagine that a "best seller" is literature, that a newspaper with a great circulation is progressive, and that college men are educated. Such an attitude undermines spiritual values. From it spring false ideals, mental blindness, selfish ambitions and restlessness. It also explains why our spiritual progress is not commensurate with out material achievements. Everyone is impatient of painstaking workmanship. Everyone is in a hurry to finish a task. We demand quick education, quick wealth, quick transportation. Speed, speed, speed is the fixed idea of our people, and many of us delude ourselves into thinking that swiftness is progress, and quick performance genius. Because we do not take the time to develop our faculties, our knowledge on most subjects is ineffective, and what we think is of little value. For speed and impatience are heavy handicaps in the world of the mind. It is these qualities in our national life that make newspapers without ideas, literature without art and churches without religion.

There is a fact which we are apt to disregard, which is that all thing in life are the direct and immediate expression of our minds. Whatever we believe is embodied in our acts. All things in the world are as they are because man's consciousness is what it is. The realization of our dream of a better world is dependent upon right thinking. At present our thinking is so close to that of the barbarous state that when we look about is and see a world of poverty, disease, sin and war, our sensibilities are not shocked. That is because these conditions are the outward expression of an unthinking consciousness. It is futile to attempt to change the world by reform or charity. Therefore it is the first duty of educators to encourage students to think; for thereby we shall build up a world more suitable for our children to be born into. The nation that thinks has a future.

7

Blindness and Deafness

Had she not been the world-famous deaf-blind woman Helen Keller, her early writing about infant blindness might have been controversial because it involved her sounding the alarm about gonorrhea causing blindness in newborns. In 1901 in the *Ladies' Home Journal*, she warned women that they must be assertive in protecting their newborns from preventable blindness. Keller wrote about *ophthalmia neonatorum* in newborns, which results from the infant's mother transferring a gonorrheal infection to the baby during childbirth. *Ophthalmia neonatorum* from gonorrhea will result in blindness if the infant is not treated immediately after birth, and Keller explained that many women probably didn't know that their husbands had transmitted gonorrhea to them. Silver nitrate was introduced as the treatment to prevent blindness in newborns in 1897 but was not in regular use at most hospital births in the United States until 1910. Between 1910 and 1940, many state legislatures mandated silver nitrate be put in all newborns' eyes.[1] Keller knew she was taking a risk by talking about a venereal disease, but said, "If I am to stand as an advocate of the work for the sightless, I cannot, without accusing myself of cowardice, gloss over or ignore the fundamental evil."[2] She begged new mothers to educate themselves about this condition and ask for treatment for it for their babies.

Beginning in 1921, Helen Keller began 40 years of work at the American Foundation for the Blind (AFB) in New York City. Her work for AFB "provided her with a global platform to advocate for the needs of people with vision loss and she wasted no opportunity. As a result of her travels across the

United States, state commissions for the blind were created, rehabilitation centers were built, and education was made accessible to those with vision loss."[3] She definitely saw herself as someone who should use every aspect of what she did, including her writing, to advocate for blind people and deaf people. Early in her writing career, she discussed the training of blind children and adults in articles in *The Outlook* in 1906,[4] *The Youth's Companion* in 1906,[5] and the *Ladies' Home Journal* in 1908.[6]

She also became a kind of product tester for new technologies for the blind, according to several stories in *The New York Times*. She had been written about or been interviewed about these topics in newspapers for years. She ushered in the era of talking books with her endorsement in 1935; a *New York Times* article about the topic was headlined "Helen Keller Hails Aid of Talking Books: Holds Them Greatest Boon to Blind since Introduction of Braille System."[7]

Keller wrote about job training and what would aid deaf people and blind people but only occasionally wrote about what new techniques assisted her. However, as a longtime animal lover, she became an enthusiastic supporter of a new service for blind people that was destined to provide independence to thousands—guide dogs. The first guide dog in the United States was trained in 1929, and by 1931 The Seeing Eye was established in the Morristown, N.J., where it continues today to breed dogs, train dogs, and partner them with blind people.[8]

A 1935 *Home Magazine* column by Keller discussed the early days of The Seeing Eye and its benefit for blind people. "It has been observed that the possession of a 'Seeing Eye' dog makes a great difference in the outlook of the sightless; they become more active, more careful of their appearance and altogether happier," she wrote. Keller had been a dog lover and owner since her Radcliffe days when her classmates gave her a Boston terrier.[10] This affection is obvious in the last line of the column: "May the happiness dogs create shine into every corner of the world."[11]

Keller discussed assistance for blind people much more than for deaf people probably because she herself used many blindness aids but not many deafness aids. In fact, her use of tactile sign language rather than visual sign language meant her communication style was different from that of most deaf people. She became more connected to deafness causes when soldiers returned home with damaged hearing. After visiting Deshon Military Hospital, in Butler, Penn., she wrote an article for *The Rotarian* in 1944 about treatment of deafened soldiers returning from World War II and encouraged them to use the new technologies being developed:

It is essential also to make sure that deafened soldiers do not become sensitive about their infirmity and shrink from wearing valve aids on account of their appearance. It is as unintelligent for any hard-of-hearing person (except in cases of serious poverty) not to help himself by using a hearing aid as it would be for one with impaired vision to refuse glasses prescribed by a responsible ophthalmologist. Deshon Hospital employs the most progressive scientists, and they deserve all honor because of their enthusiasm for humanity in repeating attempt after attempt to improve each instrument which promises results and to assist the partially deaf to retain their life-line of hearing to the last.[12]

In all her writings about blindness and deafness topics, she exudes her usual optimism about what new services and technologies will bring to both blind people and deaf people.

Notes:

1. Ronald B. Standler. *Statutory Law in the USA: Requiring Silver Nitrate in Eyes of Newborns* (2006) http://www.rbs2.com/SilvNitr.pdf.

2. Helen Keller, "I Must Speak: A Plea to American Women," *Ladies' Home Journal*, Jan. 1901

3. American Foundation for the Blind website, "Helen Keller Biography," 2015, http://www.afb.org/info/about-us/helen-keller/biography-and-chronology/biography/1235.

4. Helen Keller, "How to Be Blind," *The Outlook*, April 28, 1906, pp. 983-990.

5. Helen Keller, "What the Blind Can Do," *The Youth's Companion*, Jan. 4, 1906, pp. 3-4.

6. Helen Keller, "The Correct Training of a Blind Child," *Ladies' Home Journal*, April 1908.

7. *The New York Times*, "Helen Keller Hails Aid of Talking Books: Holds Them Greatest Boon to Blind since Introduction of Braille System," June 7, 1935, p. 2.

8. The Seeing Eye website, "Our mission & history," 2015, http://www.seeingeye.org/aboutus/?M_ID=88.

9. Helen Keller, "The Seeing Eye," *The Home Magazine*, September 1935, p. 16.

10. Keller, *Midstream* (NY: Greenwood Press, 1929) p. 19.

11. Helen Keller, "The Seeing Eye," *The Home Magazine*, Sept. 1935, p. 16.

12. Helen Keller, "Deaf but not Down!" *The Rotarian*, Nov. 1944, pp. 15-16.

The Seeing Eye

The Home Magazine, September 1935, p. 16

Editor's note: The Seeing Eye still trains guide dogs in Morristown, N.J. Founded in 1929, it has trained more than 16,000 guide dogs since that time.

All through history the dog has been man's faithful friend, rendering him heroic service in his endless adventures and vicissitudes.

In ancient China dogs were taught to carry lighted lanterns in their mouths to lead their seeing masters home at night.

The monks of the Order of St. Bernard in Switzerland have for centuries trained the noble dog of that name to rescue people perishing of cold in the Alpine snows. The dog story which is oftenest told and draws tears from most eyes is that of Barry, the St. Bernard. He saved forty persons during the seven years he lived, and through a tragic blunder was killed by the forty-first. The lost traveler, frenzied with exposure and hunger, saw a huge dog bounding towards him, was so terrified that he struck Barry on the head with his staff, wounding him mortally. The dog managed to crawl back to the monastery to let the monks know someone needed help, and by following the trail of his blood they found the man.

Something quite as wonderful as the work of the St. Bernards is happening right here and now. Dogs are being trained to be the eyes to the blind.

It often happens in some mysterious way that the things we most desire are to be found in one place. In the case of the blind the most precious things they long for are to be found at a school known as "The Seeing Eye"—a friend, a companion, some measure of independence, adventure and pleasure, nights of quiet sleep, days of confident comings and goings with a trusty guide. Blessings upon the dog!

A "Seeing Eye" school has been established at Morrison, New Jersey. I am sure that if any of the readers of *Home Magazine* are at a loss where to go on a summer day for a pleasant outing they would enjoy a trip to that school.

There they would see young female shepherd dogs being carefully fitted for their work in life. There also they would see a blind person learning to know the dog, and how to keep step with her and direct her intelligently. Before the dog is taken by the blind person, the trainer blindfolds himself and walks through the street traffic with it.

The first thing the dog learns is instant obedience to simple commands such as "Right!" "Left!" "Lie down," "Wait for me." Then she is taught to disobey if obeying a particular command would endanger her master. This development of discretion is a triumph of skill on the part of the trainer.

It has been observed that the possession of a "Seeing Eye" dog makes a great difference in the outlook of the sightless; they become more active, more careful of their appearance and altogether happier. There was a blind man who was very untidy about his clothes. When he was given a dog, a surprising change took place in his ways. "Why are you all dolled up, Jim?" exclaimed one of the attendants at the school. "Oh", he replied, "one must give a little thought to one's looks when one goes out with a lady like this," patting the head of his guide.

Again I say, may the happiness dogs create shine into every corner of the world.

Noise

The Home Magazine, July 1931, p. 8

It may seem strange that I should protest against the terrible noise of the city when I cannot hear. That is because most people do not realize that there cannot be noise without vibration, and I am extremely sensitive to vibration. I am startled by harsh noises like grinding and scraping, fog-whistles, the exasperating din of switching freight trains.

Under an elevated railway the crash of the cars sets every fiber in my body vibrating discordantly. I wonder how people keep their sanity who live close to these thundering monsters of steel and electricity! I cannot see them, but they suggest a terrifying image.

I feel a train coming. The platform shivers and sways, the track seems to stretch back to the sky-line. On comes the train with a rhythmic hissing and zipping. It seems as if a giant beast were tearing and ripping a swath out of space! Then there is a whip-like crack, the doors shoot back—the beast's black mouth is wide open! Trembling I enter the coach and fall into a seat or cling desperately to a swinging strap.

After it is all over, I wonder what such an adventure is worth. I know people (they seem to me abnormal) who like it—the noise; the terror has become such a common experience that they would actually be depressed without it. When they are not catching an express train, they are listening to jazz over the radio.

There are three kinds of people who delight in noise—savages, children and Americans. Physicians say that many Americans have grown so habituated to noise, they cannot sleep in the country, they are restless and unhappy until they get back where they can hear the noise of the city! In fact, they have developed this noise mania to such an extent that they rejoice in noisy demonstrations. I am told they show joyous excitement when horns toot, whistles blow and sirens shriek.

I think this is mostly the fault of the education they received in early years. Children should be taught both in the home and in school the preciousness of silence and of harmonious sounds.

Certainly, it is imperative that drastic measures should be adopted to lessen the uproar of our modern large cities. Noise is on the increase. As a result, city dwellers are growing more nervous and irritable, and it is said that the people on the streets are already from one-third to half deafened by the noise of traffic. What used to be poetically described as the voice of labor is no longer a voice, rather it seems a million-toned cry of pain and discord.

Would that there were a Solomon to build our subways and skyscrapers without the sound of hammer or saw or rivet. It is not the mild noise of hand-swung hammer, saw and axe that now racks our nerves, but the fiendish noise of machinery—rock drills, stone crushers, motor trucks and cranes that lift and let fall with groan and screech.

A subway is being built near my home, and although I am deaf, yet I cannot escape these disturbing vibrations. I do not wonder that hospitals and sanitariums are full of patients whose nervous systems have been deranged by all these torturing sounds. When I reflect upon the noisy inanity of much of American life, I long to retire to the silence which yet reigns in rural England—a silence which is as high as the heavens and as deep as the brown earth.

We cannot be too grateful to those who are waging war upon the noise nuisance. A decided victory will be won if they succeed in getting laws passed to keep our cities quiet from 10 p.m. to 6 a.m. But this is not enough. After five years' study of noise, it is shown that automobile trucks need not be noisy. By denying the streets to any vehicle with a rattling part, the cities can reduce the noise of traffic at least fifty per cent. A few simple regulations, such as the suppression of unnecessary horn-tooting, public loud-speakers and the placing of mufflers on machines would help.

Why should not women take a more active part in this fight against noise? Are they not the natural guardians of the peace and quiet of their homes? And is it not women especially who should guard the health of the young against the evil effects of a noisy environment?

The Mother's Mission

The Home Magazine, October 1931, pp. 12, 93

Through the ages the mother has striven to protect her children against danger, sickness and evil influences. But her beneficence has remained to a large extent ineffective because it has been unorganized, unguided by enlightened methods of promoting child welfare. Denied the knowledge that saves, she has suffered, and still suffers in countless cases the anguish of seeing her children blind or deaf or feeble-minded or crippled when they need never have been plunged into such an abyss of misery. Now, however, science is discovering the laws by which the health of the human race can be conserved, and every mother has it in her power to learn these laws and thus safeguard her home. It is her mission to render life sweeter and safer for the coming generation.

Because I am constantly asked to bring a message of encouragement to the unfortunate, I am apt to stress the thought that obstacles are important in our spiritual development. But there is another aspect of affliction which is just as apparent to me. Much energy and thought and time are necessary to overcome physical handicaps even partially. This time and energy and thought might have gone into constructive achievement and a richer contribution to the common good. There can be no doubt that it is better for us to see than to be blind. The human being can accomplish more if he is sound in mind and body than if he is feeble and infirm. Imperfect faculties limit our usefulness, check right impulses and cause us to limp when the race is to the swift.

Dear Reader, have you ever tried to imagine how you would feel if one of your children lost his sight needlessly? Can you picture him suddenly cut off from all the beauty of life—your smile, his games, his studies and his playmates. Does not such a picture grip your soul and make you want to save other little lives from that calamity? You can do this this, and if you obtain literature on the subject from the National Committee for the Prevention of Blindness, you will find out how simple the means are. You will learn at what comparatively small cost you can accomplish a tremendous saving in human eyesight and happiness of all concerned.

The complications which arise from lack of sight are so great, some of us are asking ourselves if blindness should be tolerated in civilized society. Experience has shown me that the blind are the most difficult group of handicapped people to assist. Their misfortune creates problems entirely different from those of any other class in the community. It calls for almost as many kinds of aid as there are blind people! We are already supporting hundreds of agencies and expensive schools for persons who should never have been blind and this is true also of the deaf, the crippled and the feebleminded.

What we chiefly need is frank discussion in every home of the causes of these evils. Personally, I refuse to accept such evils as a necessary part of existence, and I plead with every mother who reads my words to do what she can to put an end to these irreparable misfortunes. The facts are not pleasant, and often revolting; but it is better that we should be pained than that we should remain ignorant of facts upon which depend the sight, hearing, intelligence and happiness of our children. For instance, there are annually in the United States two hundred thousand industrial accidents which injure the eyes, and in many cases the result is total blindness. It is incumbent upon mothers to demand that all known means be studied and employed to prevent this fearful waste of human eyes. Again, one-tenth of the blindness prevalent in the country would be eliminated if physicians and nurses did their plain duty at every child-birth—applied simple, corrective, prompt measures in the treatment of the baby's eyes. There are many other facts that every mother must know if she is to accomplish her duties to the race. Watchful and informed, she will know the right demands to make upon her physician, she will insist that every measure be taken for the welfare of her children in the state where they must live, grow up and earn their daily bread.

The Beauty of Silence

The Home Magazine, May 1935, p. 8

Editor's note: Novelist Pearl S. Buck won the Pulitzer Prize for The Good Earth *in 1932 and won the Nobel Prize for Literature in 1938.*

Perhaps I have chosen a peculiar subject for this article. How can one who does not hear a sound contrast noise with silence?

Most people use their ears so constantly, they do not realize that the skin of our bodies is so sensitive that we perceive countless vibrations in the air and in objects we touch. For instance, I am extremely susceptible to noises of machinery, whistles and the irritating jar of multitudes out of step. In the peace of my little garden I usually can escape from disturbing vibrations, but at present I am greatly annoyed by the metal hammers pounding on the new subway that is being constructed through Forest Hills.

However, not all vibrations are unpleasant. Music has always been an exquisite joy to me. Although I cannot distinguish the melody, the rhythm delights and soothes me. In seasons of growth and bloom nature sings into my hand with leaves, grasses and the rippling accents of river and stream.

There has been a great deal in the papers recently about the effects of noise upon health. Many physicians maintain that the uproar of our cities is causing many mental disorders and much deafness.

However that may be, I know that silence is essential to the happy development of the human being. In the Montessori schools the period of quiet is a part of the curriculum. Every child sits tranquilly at his task for a certain length of time. When they become obstreperous and interfere with each other's orderly conduct, they are isolated until they regain their composure.

For the most part, we live in an environment that is unfavorable to silence, and we ourselves contribute to the din by too much talking. When two or three women get together, they positively deluge each other with words. Everybody talks, nobody listens.

Good listeners are as rare as white crows. No sooner does one set out to expound a theory or explain a situation than someone breaks in with "That's all nonsense! Such ideas will never be taken seriously in America." How can a fruitful conversation spring from such an attitude?

It is said of Macaulay, who was a great talker, that he had his "brilliant flashes of silence"—that he was much more interesting and a better companion during those silences than when his flood of discourse poured over the whole table.

Many a stupid man has made an enviable reputation for good sense by holding his tongue. Shakespeare wrote: "Some are accounted wise for saying nothing." Such is the merited reward for a good listener.

The Chinese regard silence as so important that for three days after the birth of a child perfect quiet is maintained—even the courtyards are thickly strewn with straw so that no sound may reach mother and child.

There are also eloquent listeners. My friend, Pearl Buck, who has lived in China since she was three years old, has taken on the restful quality of silence that is so much a part of the character of the Chinese people. Callers are embarrassed by her stillness and the steady gaze of her observing eyes. This is the sweet silence of deep woods and placid waters.

Women have for ages been regarded as the supreme offenders against the beauty of silence. The Bible is full of disparaging comments on the mischief that lurks in woman's tongue. "Many words are like a sandy hill to the feet of the aged." "A woman who talks continually is a weariness." In Ireland, fisherman say, "If you want a good catch, have no women around, the clatter of their tongues drives away the fish." How many saints, scientists and sages have taken refuge from the siege of tongues in cells or on the mountaintop or in the desert!

It would be a good thing if women as well as men cultivated the Art of Silence. For silence restores poise and judgment to our fidgety minds. It keeps us serene in the midst of a thousand small distractions. Only in quietness do we truly possess our own minds and discover the resources of the Inner Life.

The Correct Training of a Blind Child

Ladies' Home Journal, April 1908, pp. 12, 76

For many centuries after the coming of Christ, blindness, deafness, and mental defects were regarded as the visitations of Providence, to be borne with meekness and fortitude. This old misreading of the message of Christianity still persists in some unhappy minds. There are mothers who object to having an afflicted child taught, lest the more he knows the less resigned he will be to a divine decree. Recently a case came to my knowledge of a devoted parent who kept a deaf girl out of school in order that she might not lose "her beautiful spirit of resignation." The truer Christianity teaches us that disease and ignorance are not ultimate decrees of Heaven, and that such discontent as the first visions of light bring to the yearning soul is a divine discontent. The finest resignation and submission are not incompatible with heroic contest against the forces of darkness. The old idea was to endure. This was succeeded by a better idea, to alleviate and cure. And that, in turn, has given way to the modern idea, to prevent, to root out diseases that destroy the sight, the hearing, the mind, the life and the morals of men. Physicians like Pasteur and Koch, soldiers like Major Walter Reed, and other men of the American Army who gave their lives in a grim war of extermination against disease—these are the leaders of a new cohort of crusaders who are fighting the true battle of God against the infidel. We know now that hospitals and institutions for defectives are not permanent temples of salvation. They are, rather, like temporary camp-sites along the way upon which the race is journeying toward a city where disease and darkness shall not be.

I have already written about the prevention of unnecessary blindness. We know that much of it can be prevented by simple timely measures. But so long as the laws of health and right living are violated, any mother may have the anguish of seeing her child's beautiful eyes closed to the light forever. Hence, all mothers, nurses, and teachers should have some knowledge of the methods of training blind children. On the American mother the schools for the blind—and for the seeing—depend for support, encouragement, intelligent criticism. Moreover, the work of the schools is helped or thwarted by the care which the children receive before they are old enough to go school.

There are in this country thousands of blind children under school age. Many of them are growing up helpless, untrained, and suffering from want of exercise and play. In order to understand their needs let us imagine what happens when a child loses his sight. He is suddenly shut out from all familiar things, from his games, his studies and the society of other children. The experience and incentive to action that come to us largely through the eye are arrested. The toys that erewhile charmed him with bright colours fall meaningless from his little hands. The picture of tree or bird that he drew in the flush of delight in a newly acquired art is a blank to him. He runs no more to gaze at the changing scenes of the city street or at the sights of the country that fly thick as driving rain. He has lost a world of stimuli, the free motion and the restless outreachings of sense which animate us from the earliest years. He ceases to imitate, because he sees nothing to imitate, and imitation is essential to growth. He no longer plays the king, the soldier, the sailor, the giant.

He was but a recipient of life from life, of impulses that pushed him to action. He listened to life, he saw it gleam, and every instinct within him felt a stir of might, and, grasping at the clews [sic] of sense, embodied itself in his act, his look, his word. This was the natural way of beginning his existence. In those glimpses, those bursts of sound, he grew. They are now withdrawn, and the activity which flooded his being has ebbed away. Small, tottering, bewildered, he must begin life again. A new sense must be developed that shall bring back the stimuli and set aglow again the joy of his heart. The new sense is touch. He must learn to use his hands instead of his eyes. Flung upon a wholly strange world, he must learn to play again, but in the dark; he must grow in the dark, work in the dark, and perhaps die in the dark. We are ready to understand now what must be supplied to him and to the child blind at infancy.

The devices for teaching and amusing a sightless child at home are simple and within the reach of intelligent parents. A blind child should have plenty of objects that he can feel, throw around, hunt for, put in his mouth, if he likes. He will learn their qualities. Touchable qualities are countless; round, flat, smooth, rough, soft and hard, cold and hot, sharp, pointed and blunt, fat, thin, silky, velvety. The elements of beauty, order, form, symmetry, are within his reach. Try to refine his touch, so that he may delight in feeling graceful lines, curves, and motions, and you will thereby refine his mind and tastes.

Encourage him to examine the properties of everything that he can safely touch. He should not, however, be allowed to remain a sedentary investigator, using only the small muscles of his fingers. The wider the range of his explorations the stouter and braver the young navigator will grow. He can go sailing on the wide, wide ocean if he piles up chairs for a ship and hoists a cloth for a sail. A rocking-chair makes a fine locomotive, wherewith to cross continents, but the young engineer should not sit in it; he should push it from behind, that his legs may grow sturdy. Without strength gained from vigorous action he will profit little by the knowledge gained from more delicate activities. There is time enough for these when his legs are weary and he is ready to sit down. Then he can find multifold exercise for his flexible, inquisitive fingers. He can weave tape in and out through the back rods of a chair, cut paper (with blunt-pointed scissors), make chains of spools, beads or daisies. Let him model with clay or putty, put together sliced maps and puzzles. Such play exercises his ingenuity, brings firmness and precision of touch, fosters observation. Teach him to spin tops, for he will find never-ending pleasure in their whirl and hum. I used to love to spin dollars and every other thing that would spin. I remember a set of stone blocks with which I joyed to build cathedrals, castles, houses, bridges. Finally I asked for a toy city, entire, including churches with steeples, a schoolhouse, a hospital, a square full of trees and houses with steep roofs and plenty of doors and windows. Sometimes I flung all the buildings down, pretending it was an earthquake. Then I dropped apples in the midst of the town and cried, "Vesuvius has erupted!"

The toy-shops, with their wonderful mechanical playthings, their ingenious miniatures of all the furniture of life, will supply apparatus enough for the blind child's home school, and, even if the teacher-mother cannot afford to buy toys, she will find suggestions for homemade ones.

But the toy is merely an adjunct. Child and mother can turn the commonest things, indoors and out, into the materials of play. The all-important object is interesting exercise. Do not let your blind child lie on the bed in the daytime or rest in the corner "out of harm's way." Pull the mattress into the middle of the room, and teach him to turn somersaults on it. Let him cling to your dress or your arm as you go about your work. Even if it inconveniences you, it will teach him to walk steadily and to find his way about the house. Encourage him to run, skip, jump, fly in the swing, and give his playmates a push when they take their turn at swinging. Children are sympathetic and quick to learn. They will lead their blind comrade into their games, especially if they receive the right suggestions from the parents. When the blind child wrestles and plays rough-and-tumble with the other children the unwise mother will run to rescue the afflicted contestant; the wise mother will applaud the struggle so long as it is sportsmanlike and good-natured.

When it is possible, the blind child should be taught to swim and to row. If there is a yard or garden with definite boundaries let him be familiar with every part of it. Furnish him with a sandpile, spade, and shovel; show him how to plant, pick flowers, and water them. Before my teacher came to me I used to hang to my mother's skirt or to my nurse, and I picked strawberries, watered the flowers, turned the ice-cream freezer, folded clothes, and helped the cook pluck the fowl—much to the cook's annoyance. This was an ignorant activity on my part, for I had no language, and therefore no knowledge. How much more is open to the blind child who has learned the language of affection and can be stimulated by the thought that he is "helping mother!" This will develop a love of usefulness, the inspiring sense that he is of service to his family.

It is needful that the mother be ever ready with a suggestion of something new, for the child will tire of doing one thing long. If he is in the country he can feed the poultry, the dog and the cat, shell peas, string beans, peel apples, set the table, wipe dishes, dust, put things in place, and some of these activities are possible in the city, too. That day has been well spent which leaves the blind child in state of healthy fatigue ready to go to sleep. A great many blind persons have insomnia due to nervousness and lack of exercise. Indeed—and mark this well—it is not blindness, but the afflictions that accompany it and result from it, that make the blind miserable and inefficient.

The mother who knows that she has it in her power to restore to her blind child almost everything but the mere act of seeing will find in his deprivation, not a calamity to cast her down, but an opportunity to develop her tact, patience, wisdom—an object on which to bestow the highest gifts that have been vouchsafed to her.

Laugh and talk with your blind child as you look and smile at your seeing child. Pass his hand lightly over your features and let him feel, not for long, but attentively, the play of facial expression. The face speaks eloquently by unconscious movements of the muscles, as in the smile, the set grave look, the quiver of the lips. Tears, the hot flush of the cheek, the toss of the head, the look downward or upward, are the true indices of mood and emotion. The child will learn these expressions, come in time to imitate them, and thus show an animated face. It is very necessary for the blind child to have a face which speaks to the world of seeing persons in the language which they are accustomed to read in each other's countenances. Without that he will be isolated and misunderstood. People shrink from a blind-looking face and mistake its blankness for want of interest or stupidity. The child's ability to look his thought, appropriate manners, demonstrative gestures, will help him on his way through a world of seeing men. There are many sightless men who try hard and work faithfully, but who lack the accomplishments and amenities of social intercourse. They do not make friends readily and are much alone. Because they seem spiritless they are not invited out, and thus they do become that which they seem; uninteresting, dispirited, uncompanionable. The blind man's opportunities to mingle with his kind depend largely on whether as a child he has learned attractive ways and manners, on whether his mother has laughed with him and sung to him and let him feel with his hands her smile, her frown, her look of surprised delight. The seeing child observes these things unconsciously. To reveal them to the blind child a little conscious effort is necessary.

For, after all, the whole difference between training a blind child and one who sees lies in a little extra effort. The blind child cannot be deliberately stuffed with information and good morals. Directions must be taught him by indirections. He is a growing human thing, like all the other child-plants in the garden. Only he needs more care. He requires the gardener's best skill. He is to be encouraged, not forced. He can be coaxed, not compelled, to commit poems to memory, to reproduce stories and tell them to his playmates. This should be a pastime and a pleasure, and it will help his progress in composition and reading when he enters school. Throughout life he will find story-telling a welcome diversion for idle hours. Did you ever notice how few seeing people can tell a story? And yet they read so many! Would not a blind man who could tell a story be delightful company by the fireside? The world has not forgotten a blind man who told stories in Greece, centuries ago, or another who sat with closed eyes and read as upon a scroll within his brain the story of creation written anew. The princes and nobles of Japan have heard the wisdom of their ancestors and the history of their country from the eloquent lips of blind men.

There are so many fine and useful things that a blind man can do if he is well brought up, so many disagreeable and debilitating things that he will do if he is left untrained. Like other human beings, he must go forward or he will sink and fall. If his energies are not directed in childhood they will run wild into contortions and perversions. The child not drilled in deportment, not taught to use his hands, will fall into ungainly nervous habits called "blindisms." Left to himself he rocks his body, puts his fingers in his eyes, shakes his hands before his face, sways from one foot to the other, bends forward and back, and develops other uncouth mannerisms. These are frequent among blind children who enter the schools, and the fight to overcome them is much harder than would have been timely discipline at home. In a blind child it is important, first, to beware of bad habits, then to cultivate good ones.

The cultivation of good habits, of right moral and religious ideas, is a delicate and yet natural process. One method that is likely to succeed is to speak the pleasant word of praise at the right moment. Seeing people are subjected to unconscious criticism in the inevitable comparison they make between what they do and what others do. The blind person needs to be told more often and more definitely when he has done well and when he has done ill. Here the parent (and other seeing persons) should guard against the temptation to praise a blind child because he is afflicted. It is harmful, not helpful, to the sightless to be commended for work that is worthless. In this country good people have for years bought cheap beadwork and fancywork from the blind, not because they admired the articles, but because they pitied the makers. This has tended to keep the standard of work low. At present, however, efforts are being made in several States to raise the standard of work and give the blind opportunity to make useful and beautiful things.

It is wonderful what a wise mother can accomplish for her blind child, and the story I shall relate cannot fail to hearten those who have a disaster to right in the lives of their little ones. Dr. F. J. Campbell, who is himself blind, has done more than any other man living for the sightless. He is an American, born in Tennessee, and he founded and has managed for thirty years the Royal Normal College and Academy of Music for the Blind at Norwood, near London. He is a teacher and an exemplar of independence, self-reliance, and dignified industry for the blind. In vacation time, just to show what the blind can do he has climbed Mont Blanc, and in work-time he has educated and placed in positions of competence some of the best musicians of England. He lost his sight when he was between four and five years of age. At that time there were only two or three schools for the blind in America. His father said to the other members of the family: "Joseph will never see again. He is helpless. We must all work for him and take care of him. As long as he lives he must never want for anything that we can give him. We must wait on him and do everything for him."

The family agreed conscientiously—all but the mother. She took her blind son by the hand, led him into another room, and said: "Joseph, don't you pay any attention to what you have heard. You can learn to work, and I will teach you. In fact, you've got to work." She did teach him, and saw to it that he did what the other boys did. But what could a blind boy do? Once he suggested that he might chop kindling-wood for the fire. The father was unwilling to trust a blind boy with an axe. But soon he went away on business for a few days. Then the mother took the boy to the woodpile, gave him an axe and set him to work. When the father returned he found six cords of firewood cut and piled. "Well done, lads," he said to the other boys, and then they told him that Joseph had done it all. The father took the hint and bought the boy a new light axe, and from that time taught him all kinds of work about the farm.

Senator Gore, of Oklahoma, was stricken with blindness when he was eleven years old. His father told him that he must go to an institution for the blind. "No, Father," exclaimed the sturdy little lad, "I will go to school for the seeing, right here." They lived then in Mississippi. The boy was page in the State Senate, and boarded at the house of United States Senator George. So he was brought up in politics and early acquired the love for debating and oratory which led to his success in public life. Mr. Gore's State will not fail to build the fine institution for the blind which some of its citizens are planning, for the welfare of the sightless must be dear to the heart of young Oklahoma, the first American Commonwealth, I believe, to send a blind man to the national Senate.

Doctor Campbell and Senator Gore are men of unusual native power, but their success teaches us surely that ordinary blind children can by careful teaching be fitted for ordinary studies and pursuits. It is significant, I think, that Senator Gore did not go to an institution for the blind, and the question may be raised, though it cannot be easily settled, whether our blind children cannot be taken care of in the ordinary public schools. All the apparatus they need is raised books, raised maps, and a tablet to write on. These can be furnished as well at a regular school as at an institution. The teachers are overworked, it is true, and in the prevailing ignorance about the blind they would expect a blind child to be a difficult burden. But a special teacher could be engaged at less ultimate cost to the community than the cost of existing institutions. The advantage to the blind child would be great. He would be brought up in the midst of seeing children and become a familiar and accepted member of the community in which he must live and work. His presence in the school might have a good effect on popular education by proving that education is a process of mind, and not a matter of apparatus. Solving mathematical problems in his head, he would suggest perhaps to his teachers that arithmetic is an abstraction, and is independent of chalk and blackboard, even of the newest textbook recommended by the school committee.

The reason for the institutions lies in the history of education, not in the essential needs of the blind. Philanthropists saw years ago that blind children were neglected—left out of the race entirely. The first thought, naturally, was to bring them together, in a special institution. So one State after another built its school for the blind, and their education remained a mystery to the general public, surrounded, like most institutional education, by myth and superstition. Even now some parents shrink from sending their afflicted children to an "institution," for the very word suggests a prison or asylum. Under present conditions no parent should deprive a blind child of such opportunities as the schools for the blind afford. The children are well treated, they are not coddled, their blindness is not emphasized, and much is done to make them happy. Whatever the formal schooling of a blind child is to be, his preliminary training and the use he makes of his education depend largely upon his mother. Before he is ready for school she can send to the nearest institution, get an alphabet sheet of embossed characters and teach him his letters. There is the same eagerness for knowledge among blind children as among seeing. Blind boys and girls long to read as their seeing brothers and sisters do. They finger the schoolbooks that the others are studying and feel the blank pages to find the stories that are being read aloud. The first signs of intellectual curiosity will be met by the watchful mother, and she will make her blind child ready for the school that must ere long educate him, ready for the long road of life on which he must set out through the darkness.

My Future as I See It

Ladies' Home Journal, No. 12, 1903, p. 11

When I wrote "The Story of My Life" for THE LADIES' HOME JOURNAL I thought I had told my readers all I knew about myself. But since the publication of my book I have been asked what I am going to do after I graduate from Radcliffe next year. People often ask me what my future is as I see it. I do not intend to follow the example of the peasant girl in La Fontaine, who pictured such a bright future that in her enthusiasm she spilled her milk. Nor am I like the small boys who vie with each other in predicting what they will do when they grow up, and promise to be policemen, doctors, firemen and soldiers.

I used to have all sorts of unrealizable ambitions. Indeed, the only one that has never troubled me is the ambition to be President of the United States. I suppose in youth we are all, as a matter of course, song-birds. The only question of importance which we have to decide is what kind of song-bird we shall be. As we grow older we smile at the eager soarings of our childhood. But I hope we shall never cease to dream out our world, to people it with gods strong of hand and great of soul. I certainly hope I shall never think of the world as the pessimist thinks of it—a commonplace thing shaped like an orange, slightly flattened at the ends!

The only real ambitions spring from the circumstances in which our lives are set. I used to believe that my limitations would prevent me from doing anything beyond improving my mind and accepting the cup of pleasure or sorrow in whatever measure it might be dealt to me. There is no grief deeper than the consciousness that we are isolated, no ache of heart harder to bear than the thought that our fellows are crying in the darkness, and we are so fettered that we may not go to them. This is separation from the social order into which we are born, the agony of thwarted forces, a death in the midst of life. But I have discovered that the material with which we work is everywhere and in abundance. I have felt the joy of the strong man who grasps the reins in his hands and drives the forces that would master him. Our worst foes are not belligerent circumstances, but wavering spirits. As a man thinketh, so is he. The field in which I may work is narrow, but it stretches before me limitless. I am like the philosopher whose garden was small but reached up to the stars.

The occupations I can engage in are few, but into each one I can throw my whole strength. Opportunities to be of service to others offer themselves constantly, and every day, every hour, calls even on me for a timely word or action.

It bewilders me to think of the countless tasks that may be mine. I am at the beginning of my last year at college. I am already looking forward to Commencement Day. In imagination I have passed my last examinations, I have written my last thesis, I have said good-by to my school days, and taken my little canoe and ventured out on unknown seas. I have received the best education my country can give me. Generous friends have assisted me and strewn my path with opportunities. The question now is, what shall I do with this education and these opportunities?

I shall not forget the continuous task which my friends keep before me of improving my mind. I shall try to keep my flower-beds well trimmed and perhaps I may add to my estate. I shall read as extensively as possible and, perhaps, increase my knowledge of the classics. I shall never lose my interest in history and social questions, and I shall continue the studies that please me most as long as I live.

I am much interested in work that woman may do in the world. It is a fine thing to be an American woman. Never in the history of the world has woman held a position of such dignity, honor and usefulness as here and now. We read how nation after nation has reached a certain height of civilization and failed because the women of the nation remained uncivilized. I think the degree of a nation's civilization may be measured by the degree of enlightenment of its women. So I shall study the economic questions relating to woman and do my best to further her advancement; for God and His world are for everybody.

Above all must I interest myself in affairs which concern the deaf and the blind. Their needs have given me another motive for traveling. I used to idle away hours in dreams of sailing on the Rhine, climbing the Alps, and wandering amid the monuments of Greece and Rome. Every tale I read about travelers, every description that friends gave me of their experiences abroad, and especially my visit to the World's Fair at Chicago, added fire to my longing. But now I have another ambition which transcends those imagined pleasures. Travel would, it seems to me, afford valuable opportunities to act as a sort of emissary from the teachers in this county to those of Europe, and to carry a message of encouragement to those who, in face of popular prejudice and indifference, as in Italy and Sweden, are struggling to teach the blind and give them means of self-support.

There are two ways in which we may work: with our own hands and through our fellowmen. Both ways are open to me. With my own hands and voice I can teach; perhaps I can write. Through others I can do good by speaking in favor of beneficent work and by speaking against what seems to me wrong.

I often think I shall live in the country and take into my home a deaf child and teach him as Miss Sullivan has taught me. For years I have observed the details of her method, and her example in word and deed has inspired me so that I feel that I could impart to a child afflicted like myself the power to see with the soul and understand with the heart. All his needs and difficulties would be intelligible to me since I know the darkness he sees and the stillness he hears. The road he must travel I have traveled; I know where the rough places are and how to help him over them. This would be the directest and most joyous way of doing for another what has been done for me.

Whether I teach or not, I shall write. My subject-matter is limited. I have very little that is novel or entertaining to tell those who see and hear, who have a vision that embraces earth and sky and water, whereas I grasp only so much of the world as I can hold in my hand. But I may perhaps translate from the classics and from the modern languages. If opportunity offers I shall certainly write on topics connected with the deaf and the blind. If I see a plan on foot to place the blind in positions of self-support I will advocate it. If there is a good cause that needs a word I will speak it if I can. If an institution is projected for the relief of suffering, and money is needed, I will write a timely appeal. Editors and publishers have already suggested subjects on which I might write, and I find their proposals helpful because they afford a clew [sic] to what others expect of me and indicate the various ways in which I may increase and apply my literary skill. I cannot say, however, to what extent I shall follow those suggestions.

Another way in which I may render service to others with my own hands is to take up settlement work. I suppose, as a friend said, I was fighting with windmills when I said in my story that it seemed wicked that the poor could not live in comfortable homes and grow strong and beautiful. But I hear every day of young girls who leave their homes and pleasures to dwell among the poor, and brighten and dignify their lives, and the impulse within me to follow their example seems at times too strong for me to restrain. The world is full of suffering, it is true, but full, also, of the overcoming of it. As I reflect on the enormous amount of good work that is left undone I cannot but say a word and look my disapproval when I hear that my country is spending millions upon millions of dollars for war and war engines—more, I have heard, than twice as much as the entire public school system of the United States costs us.

I could help take care of the sick. I have several times had occasion to use my hands to lessen pain, as they do in massage. I may study this art by-and-by, and even if I do not become a masseuse I shall be interested in it as an employment for the blind. Our hands are instruments with which to gain a livelihood, and if they are trained to the best advantage they prove more precious than the eye or the ear. Massage is an occupation in which I or any blind person may use the hands with profit and pleasure and bring comfort to many.

No work, however, can mean so much to me as what I can do for the deaf and the blind. I am not competent now to discuss their problems but I shall find out what those problems are and study the methods of solving them. Whatever I do I shall keep track of all the measures adopted in behalf of the deaf and the blind, and to the best of my ability support the most efficient. I realize how much has already been done toward improving the condition of the blind and the deaf, and I am grateful; but there still remains much to be done; do what we may, we come short and leave the work incomplete. I have twice had my share in the promotion of enterprises for the relief of the defective classes.

Last winter there was a bill before the Legislature of Massachusetts to provide the blind with a manual training which would enable them to earn their bread, and I was asked to speak for the bill. Again, last May, I attended the dedication of the new building of the Eye and Ear Infirmary in New York, and at the request of the physicians I spoke on behalf of the hospital. If these workers and philanthropists in Massachusetts and New York thought that I, a junior in college, could help hundreds of unfortunate men and women, how much greater must my chances of usefulness be when I comprehend more fully the needs of the deaf and the blind! These experiences promise others and I must follow where the good cause leads, just as the lamp goes with the hand.

Among the problems of the blind are two to which I shall direct my attention—more books for the blind and a universal system of raised print. My views may be erroneous, and I suggest them here merely to illustrate the kind of work which lies before me.

I should like the blind in America to have a magazine of high quality and varied interest like the best periodicals published for those who see. To establish one would require much money, and the blind are poor. If they are to have a periodical some generous friend must establish it for them. In a country where so much is done to build great libraries and provide books for those who see I should think a Mr. Carnegie might be found who would give a magazine to us who cannot see.

I am still a college girl, and I can look forward to a golden age when all my plans shall have been realized. I can dream of that happy country of the future where no man will live at his ease while another suffers; then, indeed, shall the blind see and the deaf hear.

I Must Speak: A Plea to American Women

Ladies' Home Journal, January 1909, p. 6

Editor's note: Keller is writing about the kind of ophthalmia neonatorum *in newborns that results from the infant's mother transferring a gonorrhea infection to the baby during childbirth.* Ophthalmia neonatorum *from gonorrhea will result in blindness if the infant is not treated immediately after birth. Silver nitrate was introduced as the treatment to prevent blindness in 1897. Between 1910 and 1940, many state legislatures mandated silver nitrate be put in all newborns' eyes.* *

A year ago I wrote in THE LADIES' HOME JOURNAL about the prevention of blindness. I wrote guardedly and with hesitation; for the subject was new to me, and I shrank from discussing before the general public a problem which hitherto had been confined to the conferences of specialists. Moreover, the subject was one of which a young woman might be supposed to be ignorant, and upon which, certainly, she would not be expected to speak with authority. It is always painful to set one's self against tradition, especially against the conventions and prejudices that hedge about womanhood. But continuous study of blindness has forced upon me knowledge of this subject, and, if I am to stand as an advocate of the work for the sightless, I cannot, without accusing myself of cowardice, gloss over or ignore the fundamental evil.

Once I believed that blindness, deafness, tuberculosis and other causes of suffering were necessary, unpreventable. I believed that we must accept blind eyes, deaf ears, diseased lungs as we accept the havoc of tornadoes and deluges, and that we must bear them with as much fortitude as we could gather from religion and philosophy. But gradually my reading extended, and I found that those evils are to be laid not at the door of Providence, but at the door of mankind; that they are, in large measure, due to ignorance, stupidity and sin.

The most common cause of blindness is ophthalmia of the newborn. One pupil in every three at the institution for the blind in New York City was blinded in infancy by this disease. Nearly all of the sixteen babies in the Sunshine Home in Brooklyn, one-fourth of the inmates of the New York State Home for the Blind, six hundred sightless persons in the State of New York, between six thousand and seven thousand persons in the United States, were plunged into darkness by ophthalmia of the newborn. The symptoms of the disease appear in

---

* Ronald B. Standler. Statutory Law in the USA: Requiring Silver Nitrate in Eyes of Newborns (2006) http://www.rbs2.com/SilvNitr.pdf.

the infant's eyes soon after birth. The eyelids swell and become red, and about the second day they discharge whitish pus. At this stage the eyes can be saved by the simplest prophylactic care. That such care is not always exercised is due to the fact that one-half of the cases of childbirth in America are attended by midwives many of whom are ignorant and incompetent. In this country very little has been done to secure the proper education and examination of midwives; and they and the equally-ignorant parents resort to poultices, nostrums and domestic remedies.

There is a remedy for ophthalmia neonatorum. This is an instillation of nitrate of silver solution into the eyes of the child. It is efficacious if promptly and skillfully applied. It is not, however, infallible, and in unskillful hands it may do great harm. The mother who sees in the eyes of her baby the symptoms which I have described should lose no time in summoning the assistance of an intelligent physician.

Let no one suppose that this is idle advice. In France and Germany the laws require that the eyes of every child shall be treated with nitrate of silver solution as soon as it is born, and in those countries there has been a considerable decrease in blindness from the scourge of ophthalmia neonatorum. And what do the wise lawmakers of America do? A bill for the prevention of blindness introduced recently in the Illinois Legislature failed to pass because it was argued that this was only another scheme of doctors to provide fees for themselves! But, at best, the law is concerned only with the remedy. The people themselves, and only they, can wipe out the cause.

What is the cause of ophthalmia neonatorum? It is a specific germ communicated by the mother to the child at birth. Previous to the child's birth she has unconsciously received it through infection from her husband. He has contracted the infection in licentious relations before or since marriage. "The cruelest link in the chain of consequences," says Dr. Prince Morrow, "is the mother's innocent agency. She is made a passive, unconscious medium of instilling into the eyes of her newborn babe a virulent poison which extinguishes its sight."

In mercy let it be remembered, the father does not know that he has so foully destroyed the eyes of his child and handicapped him for life. It is part of the bitter harvest of the wild oats he has sown. Society has smiled upon his "youthful recklessness" because Society does not know that

> They enslave their children's children
> who make compromise with sin.

Society has yet to learn that the blind beggar at the street-corner, the epileptic child, the woman on the operating-table, are the wages of "youthful indiscretion." Today science is verifying what the Old Testament taught three thousand years ago, and the time has come when there is no longer the excuse of ignorance. Knowledge has been given us; it is our part to apply it.

Of the consequences of social sin, blindness is by no means the most terrible. The same infection which blots out the eyes of the baby is responsible for many childless homes; for thousands of cases of lifelong invalidism; for eighty per cent of all inflammatory diseases peculiar to women; and for seventy-five per cent of all operations performed on mothers to save their lives.

The day has come when women must face the truth. They cannot escape the consequences of the evil unless they have the knowledge that saves. Must we leave young girls to meet the danger in the dark because we dare not turn the light upon our social wickedness? False delicacy and prudery must give place to precise information and common-sense. It is high time to abolish falsehood and let the plain truth come in. Out with the cowardice which shuts its eyes to the immorality that causes disease and human misery. I am confident that when the people know the truth the day of deliverance for mother and child will be at hand.

To you, my people, I turn with the faith that you will face the problem and work out the salvation of your children. We must look to it that every child is protected before his birth. Every child has a right to be well born. Every child has a right to be told by his parents and teachers about his birth and his body for in such knowledge lie true innocence and safety. Civilization is menaced by an insidious enemy. It must learn that only one cure is sure and cheap: right living, which God gives free to all. And right living depends on right knowledge.

We must set to work in the right direction the three great agencies which inform and educate us: the church, school and the press. If they remain silent, obdurate, they will bear the odium which recoils upon evildoers. They may not listen at first to our plea for light and knowledge. They may combine to baffle us; but there will rise, again and again, to confront then the beseeching forms of little children: deaf, blind, crooked of limb and vacant of mind.

My countrywomen, this is not faultfinding. I am not a pessimist, but an optimist, by temperament and conviction. I am making a plea for American women and their children. I plead that the blind may see, the deaf may hear, and the idiot may have a mind. In a word, I plead that the American woman may be the mother of a great race.

Throw aside, I beseech you, false modesty—the shame that shelters evil—and hasten the day when there shall be no preventable disease among mankind.

How to Be Blind

The Outlook, April 28, 1906, pp. 983-90

The New York Association for Promoting the Interests of the Blind lately held a great public meeting in New York City. Its object was to present a truthful account of the condition of the blind in America, who are now living in a state of idleness more terrible even than loss of sight, and to rouse the people to secure for these neglected thousands man's greatest privilege, opportunity to work. The blessings of a liberal education, equivalent to that provided for seeing children in common schools, are within the reach of all blind children in this country. But almost nothing has been done for industrial education, which is necessary to alleviate the tragic condition of blindness, and without which the benefits of other kinds of education are all but annulled. At this moment thousands of strong, intelligent blind persons who could be trained as workers in the world of honest toil are enduring the keenest anguish because they are numbered among the unproductive dependent classes.

I am sincerely glad that our country is at last awaking to a realization of this condition. But at the same time I deplore the fact that this realization did not take place fifty years ago. For the problem is not one that began to-day or that can be solved in a day. It has called for solution ever since the first blind man faced the terrors of darkness. We had a champion and liberator half a century ago, but we failed to follow whither he so bravely led. Our leader was Dr. Samuel Gridley Howe, founder of the Perkins Institution for the Blind in South Boston, who brought the light of his genius into every corner of the cavern where the blind man dwells.

Constantly as he labored to instruct, by the best methods available, blind children and youths, he never forgot that in the nature of things blind girls and boys become adult blind, that most of the blind lose their sight in adult years, and he never ceased to plan and provide as far as he could for their welfare. He opened a workshop for them connected with the Perkins Institution. He demonstrated their ability to earn and their skill to work. He even looked forward to the establishment of workshops large enough to receive all the sightless of New England who could be taught to work. At the end of five years he found that he had paid to twenty-eight blind persons for the work of the fifth year nearly two thousand dollars, at a cost to the Institution of only three hundred dollars. Six years later the amount paid in wages was forty-six hundred dollars. Ten years later, during war time, the amount decreased only a thousand dollars. Dr. Howe's reports outline for directors of schools wise careful plans for the training and employment of those who are blind from childhood, and also for those who lose their sight in years of maturity. He was tireless in his efforts to open wider fields for their usefulness and self-help. What has the last half-century done to fulfill his labors? Are the blind in this country the self-supporting, self-respecting citizens that he prophesied?

According to the recent report of the Massachusetts Commission on the Adult Blind there are "some fifteen or twenty" blind persons employed in the workshop which Dr. Howe founded and which, under his supervision, half a century ago employed twenty-eight. It may be manifest to others, as it is to the Springfield "Republican," "what advantages this long established institution . . . must have over any volunteer organization in the matter of finding the right blind persons to employ, of directing their industry and marketing its product." These advantages certainly have not been fully appreciated by those who enjoy them, for it was the "volunteer organization" referred to, the Massachusetts Association for Promoting the Interests of the Adult Blind, which took up the work of industrial education for the blind of Massachusetts about where Dr. Howe left it, secured the appointing of a commission by the Governor, and directly inspired the organization in New York of a similar volunteer association.

Three years ago, at one of the early meetings of the newly organized workers for the blind in Massachusetts, a blind man gave his experience. He had been foreman in a lithographing establishment. At the age of thirty-six, young, vigorous, industrious, he had been stricken with blindness, and for four years he had groped his way from one kind of work to another and had failed. He declared that he was eager to work, and craved no other boon in the world but work. "What can you do?" asked one of the investigators. "I do not know," he replied. "That is what I have been trying to find out." There was no one to advise him what he could profitably learn to do, much less a place where he could learn to do it. He could not go into the little shop at South Boston. The only occupations outside it which seemed to have survived in Massachusetts as suitable for blind men were piano tuning, caning chairs, and selling pencils and shoestrings on the street corners. It has been nobody's business to teach a blind man to work, to find him work after he had been taught, even to give him intelligent advice. Many important things seem to be nobody's business. The agent of the commission which was afterwards appointed to find out something officially about the blind, discovered in the State eighteen blind children of school age not in the Perkins Institution which the public had provided for them; it had been nobody's duty to see that they were educated. This has been the state of things for a few miles from the scene of Dr. Howe's labors.

Imagine, if you can, the feelings of a worker like that lithographer, stricken with blindness and cast out from the occupation to which he had been trained and in which he had risen to a position of competence. To him light and life have been synonymous. He has earned his bread in work which required his sight. He has known his family and his friends by the light that shines upon their faces. In the light he has read his newspaper, and walked abroad with his children, and enjoyed his recreation after the burden and toil of the day. With God's candle shining upon his head he has worked and thought and planned and faced the vicissitudes of life with his own help in him and a strong heart. In a moment all is changed. The terrors of a strange dark world close in upon him. He no more knows his way in the street, along the familiar road, even about his own house. He is as a captive, dependent on any one he may chance to stumble against, and if he has no relatives or friends, he becomes an object of charity along with the pauper and the degenerate. He flounders in a stagnant sea of apathy, without course or horizon or guiding star or haven. Or he grows bitter against a fate that he cannot master. The blind are brave, they try to be cheerful, but the "happy disposition" with which seeing people so often tell you the blind are endowed is a fiction more comforting to the seeing than to the sightless. With new hope the blind man hears that there are people who will teach him to read with his fingers. That is something; but it cannot lead him back to the active joy of work. Perhaps he visits the school for the blind in his State, with the hope that he may find something to do and something worth doing. He is speedily disappointed, for he learns that the blind children will be almost as helpless as he is when they graduate from school!

Great as the misfortune of blindness must always be, it has been much greater in this country than it need be. For the blind of Europe have advanced far through their limitations toward self-maintenance. The causes of failure in America are not far to seek: lack of initiative, intelligence, and enthusiasm on the part of those to whom the public has in trusted the welfare of the sightless, including the managers of the schools for the blind, whose attitude toward industrial ventures the Massachusetts Commission characterizes as "unsympathetic, to say the least." What we need, and what we have not, is expert supervision, adequate industrial training, some agency to find positions for the capable blind, to stand behind them till they get a start, and to find a market for the work of their hands.

It is the policy of most American institutions for the seeing and the unseeing alike to let their graduates shift for themselves; to keep a record of their signal successes, but not of the failures. To the blind such a policy is ruinous. A blind man cannot, like his seeing fellow-citizen, learn his work after his schooling is done, bear the brunt of learning it alone, and know the excellence of his work without the eyesight of another.

Suppose a young woman tries to knit and crochet in her home. She may work constantly yet earn nothing. This is one of the kinds of work for the blind which can be profitable only under careful supervision. Hand-made articles must be of the finest design, color, and workmanship in order to compete with the cheap machine-made articles, and only the well-to-do will pay for them. Now, most of the blind are poor, and have but crude ideas of design, so that if their shawls and afghans are to fetch anything in the market, they must be done under the eye of a skillful teacher.

Even if a blind person can do something supremely well, he cannot find a position for himself. Some sympathetic and intelligent agent is necessary to help him, not only to hunt a place, but to overcome a prejudice against him. Unfortunately, there is a presumption in the public mind that a blind man's work must be inferior to that of a seeing competitor. The blind organist hears of a vacancy, goes to the church committee himself, applies for the position, and proves his musical powers. They refuse his services simply because he is blind. It is assumed that he cannot read new music, that he cannot teach others, that he cannot even be depended upon to get to church and find his seat at the organ. The deepest pitfall to the feet of the sightless is the black gulf of ignorance in the minds of the seeing. Modest, disappointed, abashed, the blind man does not argue his case. He needs a special friend whose business it shall be to insist that people give the blind man a chance. What State in this country has long had any such authorized agent?

The existing schools for the blind are good as far as they go; there is little to censure in their instruction of children. They cannot do everything for all the blind, but they should feel that the problems of the blind are related, and they should be the first to encourage, inspire, and demand, with all the influence of their institutions behind them, the right end of industrial aid for the sightless who need it. The directors of the schools for the blind, instead of taking a minimum of interest in this work, ignoring it as outside their province, even openly or secretly opposing it, ought to be the leaders in all undertakings for the welfare of the blind. Does the real friend of a class, head of a respected and powerful institution specially intended for a part of that class, bound his interests with the walls of his institution? A great educator like President Eliot understands that, if only for his own sake, if only for the welfare of his institution, he must concern himself with the entire problem of which his special work is a part. We find him interested in a trade school across the world from his university, and laboring upon the curriculum of the lowest primary school. We quarrel with none of the excellent work for the blind which the existing schools are doing, but we say to the directors and trustees, "Encourage others to do for the blind what your excellent school is not intended to do for them. Do it all if you can and will, otherwise do not look with unfavorable eye upon the efforts guided by other wisdom than that which emanates from you and your institution."

All these circumstances furnish a clue whereby to understand a great deal about the actual condition of the blind and explain the nature of the assistance that must be given to them at once. America, proud of being "progressive," has not learned the lessons which the practice of conservative European nations has mutely striven to teach us these many years. What the blind of America need, to open the door of usefulness and keep it open, is organized aid and intelligent encouragement. Europe affords good types of such organized aid for the blind.

The "Saxon system" in Germany aids blind men and women in their homes, secures raw material at favorable rates, and markets their wares. The Valentine Haüy Association in France, and the associations connected with the institutions for the blind in Great Britain, find positions for capable blind persons and hold up their hands until their employers approve and accept their work. The schools co-operate. They strive to give their pupils a good industrial training and then pass them on to an agency that will turn that training to practical account by finding employment for it. When the graduate goes into the world as musician or weaver, an agent persuades the doubting employer to give the blind applicant a fair trial, and pledges his word for the candidate's ability. The blind man comes, surprises his judges by his skill and ease and freedom of movement, and conquers his fortune.

The results of the energy and good sense of these societies and agents are splendid. At the Glasgow Asylum for the Blind the average annual sales for three years were twenty-nine thousand pounds, and for eighty years the workers have produced salable articles. Not only do the women make bedding for the institution, but they have secured contracts with shipping firms and other institutions. In London, which is declared behind the times but is far ahead of us, six per cent of the blind are in workshops. In other English cities thirteen per cent of the blind are employed. The chief industries open to them are many kinds of mat-weaving, a few kinds of carpentry, cordage, massage, brush-making, mattress-making, and the manufacture of all kinds of baskets, from ornamental ones to heavy baskets used for bales, coal, and food. There is, moreover, a tea agency in London, the managers of which are wholly or partially blind. Hundreds of blind agents sell its teas, coffees, and cocoas all over England. Finally, eighty-five per cent of the graduates of the Royal Normal College and Academy of Music for the Blind in London are self-supporting.

What shall we say when we contrast with this the report of the New York Commission for the Blind, which finds that only one per cent of our sightless countryman are in workshops? We have delayed all too long in our work for the adult blind, and the example of other countries is witness against us.

But already the States are roused. Better days for the blind are coming. Massachusetts, Connecticut, Maine, Pennsylvania, Michigan, Wisconsin, have turned from their darkness of ignorance, prejudice, and neglect, and have begun to help the blind to help themselves in the darkness from which there is no turning. As soon as the people know the needs of the blind all the States must answer in justice and generosity to a cry that is not for charity, but for rightful opportunity. We must experiment carefully and then act with energy. The little experiment station which the Massachusetts Association opened two years ago has already shown what blind persons can do. Here industries and processes are tested with a view to their fitness for blind workers. In a surprisingly short time the small group of blind people has acquired skill in making beautiful curtains, sofa-pillows, table-covers, and rugs, and the public has bought their work because it is beautiful. They also manufacture a mop invented by a blind man and made and sold by the blind. If the Association succeeds in keeping its title to the patent, this mop will go far towards giving the blind profitable occupation.

The general direction of the work of the Massachusetts Association is the right one for other States to follow in their first experiments. The effort is to find three kinds of remunerative work—first, for those who cannot leave their homes; second, for those who can do best in workshops for the blind; and, third, for those who can learn some process in a factory for the seeing. The people are ready to help if we show them the way. A prominent manufacturer in Massachusetts said that if it could be demonstrated that a blind man can work side by side with the seeing, the State should insist that a man losing his sight be trained to work in a factory near his home. No objection is feared on the part of seeing labor. There would be only one blind man to a thousand seeing workmen. And the human heart is kind.

He Helped People to See

Psychology, July 1930, pp. 31-32, 72

The blind have to live under a great strain all of the time to do even the simplest things, and Clarence Hawkes has done much more than the simplest things. His whole life has been a persistent struggle against poverty, darkness and other handicaps. He was one of the young blind whom misfortune hit hard, and yet he has lived one of the happiest and most victorious lives I have ever known.

He was a nature-loving boy with the eyes of a poet who for fourteen years drank in the beauty of the woods around his home in Goshen, Mass. Then a day came—the date, August 12, 1883, is burned into his mind—when night descended upon him forever.

The dreadful day began with happiness. Earlier in the month his father had presented him with a gun, and on this morning the two of them set out to hunt wood ducks. In the heart of the swamp they separated. In some way the father lost his bearings, and, thinking that he was shooting a covey of ducks, shot straight into the eyes of his son.

After the first shock was over a small degree of sight returned, and when finally he was allowed to leave his room he could see objects dimly thru a thick haze. But the haze gradually deepened until at last there came a morning when there was left nothing but blackness. There followed a long series of consultations with doctors, and two years later when, after six operations, they told him that henceforth he would be totally blind his only feeling, for the moment, was relief that he was at last free from the torturing rack of the operating table. Then the old horror came back, greater than it had ever been. The rest of his life would be spent in darkness and he did not see how he could live thru the long weeks that lay ahead.

It is hard for a blind person to go on from this point. Many have not the courage, initiative and perseverance of Mr. Hawkes. Some are overwhelmed by their disaster, some lack the imagination that sees new possibilities of achievement in Darkland. Others are too timid to venture unaided into any new enterprise. It is not easy for those with all their faculties to succeed in life alone, and it is impossible for the blind to make headway without practical assistance. It is to give such assistance that the American Foundation for the Blind has been established. It is to fill the place of advisor and friend to the blind of our country, not only during the trying period of adjustment but for the rest of their lives as well.

Clarence Hawkes was more fortunate than many others. "Like many another man," he says, "I got my start in life by having a beautiful and gifted mother. When I go back in memory to the very borderland of the forgotten I can see her. A slight girlish figure, an oval face with smiling lips and sunny brown eyes. This was how she looked as I held the ends of the reins while she drove our family horse along the wonderful winding country roads. Being a poet of no mean order herself, when mother told us fairy stories on a winter's evening before the dancing fire in the old Franklin stove, her language was always simple and beautiful. These fairy stories were discarded on Sunday evening, when we heard Bible stories, such classics as Joseph and his brethren, David and Goliath, and Daniel and the lions. It was from my mother that I acquired my love of literature.

"It was from my grandmother that I first learned to love the birds and the squirrels and all the beautiful living creatures that God has made.

"It was my father who taught me the more strenuous features of out-door life. From him I learned fishing, boating, camping and woodcraft. Father and my Uncle William had gone West in the Fifties and had picked up stories of wolf coursing and bear and buffalo hunting which thrilled me as few other stories had the power to do.

"But my real love of nature was even deeper and more fundamental than all this. Often when a mere lad, my eyes would fill with tears and my heart would pound like a trip-hammer when some beautiful scene from the out-of-doors burst suddenly upon my sight. My eyes would often detach a bit of landscape from the surrounding scene until it almost seemed as tho [sic] it had been set apart from the rest of the world and framed perfectly before me."

The last doctor who operated upon Mr. Hawkes' eyes told his mother that the best thing to do was to send him to the Perkins Institution. Neither of them knew what or where the institution was, but it was this suggestion that ultimately led Clarence Hawkes into a useful way of living, which is what the blind need and want most. The blind suffer a great deal from the attitude of the public which varies all the way from that of indifference to that of the sentimentalists who think "the poor things shouldn't be allowed to do anything at all." When these attitudes are replaced by one of friendship and service, the hardest part of blindness will be overcome.

Clarence Hawkes went to the Perkins Institute for the Blind hoping that death would come to end his misery, and yet after a year there his outlook had brightened wonderfully. He had expected to find all the other pupils unhappy as he was himself and was surprised to hear them laughing and calling out cheery greetings to one another. I was at the institute at the same time he was—he had been there two years, I believe, when I came—and I was a very gay and carefree little girl in those days in spite of my triple handicap of blindness, deafness and imperfect speech.

Most of the blind do not dwell on the tragic side of blindness. They regret silently that they cannot see colors in the skies and flowers and in the eyes of their loved ones. But that is not their greatest misfortune. The bitter part of their trial is to sit idle, looking into the dark with nothing but the dark staring back at them. The blind man, above all, needs occupation; and the more active and normal he can make his life, the happier he will be.

Clarence Hawkes loves the woods as much now as he did when he was a boy. True he cannot see, but he can still hear and feel. He has a wonderful time fishing. He can tell when a fish tugs at the bait and he loves to battle with a big trout or pike. Mr. Hawkes tried to learn music when he first went to the Perkins Institution, but discovered that he had no talent for it. He learned chair-caning, which did not especially interest him, but while he was at work he told stories to the other boys from the books he had read before he was fourteen, from books his mother and his brother had read to him, and stories his mother had told him and stories he made up himself. He loved poetry and decided that he, too, would be a poet. He knew that would not bring in much money, but something was singing inside him, and he kept at it year in and year out until his poetry was noticed. One of his sonnets was praised by no less a critic than Edmund Clarence Stedman, and one of his shorter poems has been a source of great help to me. It is called Erosion.

> Even the little waves that idly dance
> Against the cliff, will crumble it to sand;
> And so with ceaseless toil the slightest hand
> May wear away the walls of circumstance.

The summer after his graduation, during a long convalescence from grippe, he wrote a lecture on American poets. He wrote more poetry and some of it was accepted, but the struggle ahead was hard one. The day before his mother died he gave a lecture to help pay her doctor's bill, and two days after she was buried he lectured again to help pay her funeral expenses.

In 1892 he moved to Hadley, Mass., and seven years later he married a gifted Hadley girl to whom he had been engaged for five years. His wife was an artist who loved the out-of-doors as much as he did, a companion who sympathized with his struggles so thoroly [sic] that she was able to furnish the inspiration and help which had always been his mother's part.

Three years after his marriage Mr. Hawkes wrote his first volume of prose, a dog story called, *Master Frisky*, which centered around his own beloved collie. His next volume, *Little Foresters*, which is wrought out of his own boyhood experiences, was his first real nature book.

Others followed in quick succession as he drew upon his own first-hand knowledge and upon stories told him by his father and uncle and his friends among trappers, guides and frontiersmen. Their accuracy has never been disputed. He was even able to point out to Theodore Roosevelt an error in his own writings concerning the moose.

To attain such truth to nature would be a fine achievement for anyone, and especially for a blind man. "I could never have done it," he says, "without the help of the three P's—patience, perseverance and pluck."

Clarence Hawkes' outlook in his writing is always cheerful. He has even planned a humorous book about the hard experiences he went thru during his first years of lecturing. This is characteristic of the writing of most blind people. They are shot thru with color, adventure and humor. They reflect the brave spirits of their authors. Blind authors, like most blind children, make a great deal of fun of their difficulties.

Clarence Hawkes was a shy, sensitive boy, and his sensitiveness is reflected in all that he has written. He wrote his autobiography, *Hitting the Dark Trail*, in 1915. It was translated into French by Eugene Brieux, the dramatist, and printed for the blind soldiers. It is a book which has helped thousands of blinded Americans, and as Brieux said, was not only a life-line to the soldiers but to the blind in all parts of the world.

Deaf but Not Down!

The Rotarian, November 1944, pp. 15-16

A uniquely uplifting experience has just been mine. It was a long visit with a group of deafened young soldiers. What I learned from them revealed new heights to which the handicapped can rise in self-reliance, and what I saw of the intelligent care accorded them provided an inspiring instance of the application of science and sympathy to the task of rehabilitating disabled fighting men.

The United States Army, as you may have read in your newspaper, conducts three hospitals for men who lose their hearing in battle. The largest of these is Deshon Military Hospital, in Butler, Pennsylvania. Since it opened last November, it has admitted some 470 men, more than half of whom are still resident there. It is of the day I was recently privileged to spend with them and their instructors of which I write.

If the reader is to appreciate the courageous fight the servicemen at Deshon Hospital are making, let him first try to imagine what deafness is like. It means deprivation of man's most natural method of communication—the voice, which brings language, quickens thought, preserves companionship, and keeps intellectual interests dynamic. With hearing are associated one's earliest delight in speaking and in making oneself understood, in receiving and returning affection, and in absorbing counsel. How eloquent are the tones of approval and reproof in one's memories of childhood!

Through the ear sings half the world—music on all instruments, the infinite reverberating drama of the waters and the winds, the breathings of sleep, motions that are the very voice of home. What, then, must a man's feelings be when a shell or a bomb shatters his hearing! With appalling abruptness he finds himself enveloped in total silence, alone with all loneliness, as if he were exiled to an island in mid-ocean. Being able to speak does not restore him to society, nor does his sight, however keen, compensate him for the incalculable loss of all things of which sound is an essential part. It is imperative, then, that measures for his reeducation be taken promptly, if he is to wring happiness from his changed circumstances. That is why efforts at the Deshon Hospital are so bright with hope.

What impressed me most on my visit there is the personal goodwill with which Colonel C. J Gentzkow and his staff create an atmosphere that induces the men without hearing to forget the things they cannot do and think only of what they can. Avoiding the twin mistakes of too much pity for their calamity and too little feeling for their human natures, the staff keeps ever before the men of De-shon the picture of mankind as a whole, with the deaf as a part of its throbbing pulse.

The extent to which the deafened can be trained depends upon how well their buoyancy is sustained. At a time when they most tend to become bitter, they need to be fired with a sense of adventure. They must be led to regard deafness not merely as a handicap, but also as an opportunity. Once animated by such an attitude, they are eager to see how far and how soon they can lessen their handicap—a negative phase—and recommence normal activities.

Another element in the case of deafened servicemen which calls for quick action and careful study is the fact that they are an unusual assemblage of varied abilities and characters. The majority are young and physically sound, full of ambition and anxious to learn. They have acquired definite skills which must be preserved if, later, they are to resume their prewar jobs or begin new ones.

The first step Deshon Hospital takes to render these men self-confident and fit for work is to teach them to read the lips and to correct any speech defect they may have. In the special rooms where they receive lessons, I saw each man seated at a table with his own teacher, which is a new and precious feature of rehabilitation. For no two deaf persons are alike any more than the hearing are; each needs special attention to his particular drawbacks if the best results are to be attained.

Asked to speak to the deafened men, I wondered what message I could utter without presumption to war victims so cruelly stricken, but as I read their lips, I was gladdened by their interested expression and gay courage. They expected me to be happy with them, I sensed, and for me, certainly, it was one of the most inspiring of afternoons. One addresses these soldiers just as if they actually heard, and their faith in the hearing quality of their minds carries them over the fateful dividing line between despair and purposefulness. As I watched their patient endeavor to master the intricacies of lip reading, I was thrilled by change that I knew was taking place in them. They have no time to doubt themselves, so engrossed are they in replanning their futures.

Many of the teachers at Deshon Hospital are hard of hearing themselves, which works wonders in banishing the fears of the students. Accepting deafness, these brave young men set forth to vindicate their manhood, the artist by creating beauty native to his soul, the mechanic with skills as his kingdom, the farmer who is to wrest victory from the elements.

Lip reading proves a tax upon one's patience after a time, and thus, after an hour or two of it, the young men of Deshon turn to whatever diversions they wish.

One thing they seek is the cheerful companionship of the hearing. They are as hungry for a word as the blind are for an embossed book. Anyone who has his hearing can do no more vital kindness than to take time to converse with the deafened man and thus quicken his powers of enjoyment. For his faculties, like air plants, are so eager for life that they will dispense with the usual solid advantages, provided they are upheld by friendly cooperation.

The fact that each deafened soldier at the Deshon Hospital has his own teacher is something new under the sun in the 232 years since the struggle began to reclaim the deaf. At first they were gathered together in special institutions and taught under the unmodulated rules and formulas which the phrase institution implies. They were educated in large classes regardless of their personalities and varying capacity to learn. It was coming—the miracle prophesied in the Commandment, "Bring out the deaf that have ears," but, despite their courage and the teachers' devotion, the results were so pathetically limited that they could scarcely be contemplated without tears.

Gradually the lot of the deaf improved, but they endured much—and they still do—for a chance that science may discover unexpected ways to rescue them from abnormality and the crushing monotony of silence. Shut away from the hearing public, they developed peculiarities that isolated them; "Set those solitary ones in families" was the policy. Well do I remember how passionately Alexander Graham Bell and Anne Sullivan Macy longed and experimented for a time when handicapped students would be kept in the current of world life and given individual instruction, so that each might build his own citadel against separative silence, discouragement, and frustration. How truly those two explorers of limitation interpreted Seneca's words spoken 18 centuries ago, "True happiness consists in not departing from Nature, and in molding our conduct according to her laws and model!" Now that gospel shines forth at the Deshon Hospital full of promise both for the totally deafened and those who hearing is seriously impaired.

The ear-testing laboratories in this wondrous establishment interested me greatly. There I saw the many mechanical devices with which Deshon Hospital tests and equips its young men.

Broadly speaking, those aids fall into two groups—standardized audiometers and thermionic, or vacuum valves. The audiometer indicates with reliable accuracy how much each patient hears. Vacuum valves are used to amplify by means of electric batteries the hearing in the injured ear. It is impossible to define a deafened patient, he comes in so many varieties. Each valve aid must be adjusted carefully to the nature and amount of each of each individual's hearing, and the degree of vibration chosen so that he may derive the most benefit from the amplification.

It is a matter of thankfulness how often those vacuum valve aids work so effectively that those who employ them are restored to the world of people with sound ears. It is an unforgettable uplift to see how a man with that happy prospect recaptures his old incentive. While realizing that he will encounter vexatious harassments at every turn, he knows that it will be easier for him to foster satisfying relations with others, that his choice of profitable occupations will be widened, and that his chances of preferment less restricted. Released from much extra drudgery and looking forward to more freedom than he has dared to believe, he rejoices in his transformed future possibilities as one that findeth great spoil. Let it be remembered in mercy, however, that there must be enough hearing for the valve aid to amplify if those joyous results are to be compassed. A nonfunctioning ear cannot be revived any more than a dead body.

It is essential also to make sure that deafened soldiers do not become sensitive about their infirmity and shrink from wearing valve aids on account of their appearance. It is as unintelligent for any hard-of-hearing person (except in cases of serious poverty) not to help himself by using a hearing aid as it would be for one with impaired vision to refuse glasses prescribed by a responsible ophthalmologist. Deshon Hospital employs the most progressive scientists, and they deserve all honor because of their enthusiasm for humanity in repeating attempt after attempt to improve each instrument which promises results and to assist the partially deaf to retain their life-line of hearing to the last.

Altogether, admiration and helpful service are the only just tribute we can pay to our soldiers who have sacrificed an irreplaceable endowment for mankind's liberation and to the legion of physicians, nurses, teachers, and scientific workers who make it possible for the deafened servicemen to turn disaster into plastic adaptability, resourceful joy, and a message of faith to a doubting world.

What the Blind Can Do

The Youth's Companion, Jan. 4, 1906, pp. 3-4

To present to seeing people the truth about the blind is to describe a state of cruel deprivation, and at the same time tell a story of remarkable achievement. It is difficult for those who have not felt the terrors of blindness or known its triumphs to apprehend the position and requirements of the sightless. A great deal has been said and written about the blind; and yet persons well informed on other matters display a medieval ignorance about those who cannot see.

I have known intelligent people who believed that the sightless can tell colors by touch, and it is generally thought that they have one or more senses given them in place of the one they have lost, and that the senses which of right belong to them are more delicate and acute than the senses of other people. Nature herself, we are told, seeks to atone to the blind for their misfortune by giving them a singular sensitiveness and a sweet patience of spirit.

If this were really the case, it would be an advantage rather than an inconvenience to lose one's sight. But it is not the truth; it is a fiction which has its origin in ignorance, and in this ignorance the blind discover the most formidable obstacle in the way to usefulness and independence. Until the public in general better understands the condition of the blind, a condition to which every person is exposed by the vicissitudes of life, it will be impossible to give the blind the special assistance they require. Left without intelligent help, the blind man lives in a night of thwarted instincts and shackled ambitions. Given the right encouragement and aid, he becomes a brave, efficient being, independent himself and of service to others, triumphant over the bondage of darkness.

What is blindness? Close your eyes for a moment. The room you are sitting in, the faces of your loved ones, the books that have been your friends, the games that have delighted you disappear—they all but cease to exist. Go to the window, keeping your eyes shut. God's world—the splendor of sky and sun and moon, almost the charm of human life—has vanished.

Suppose your lids will not open again. What an unspeakable calamity has befallen you! You must begin your life all over in a strange, dark world. You must learn to accommodate yourself little by little to the conditions of darkness. You will have to learn the way about your own house. With arms outstretched you must grope from object to object, from room to room. The tools of your work are snatched from your hands. Your school-books, if you are young, are useless. If you venture out-of-doors, your feet are shod with fear. You are menaced on every side by unseen dangers. The firm earth rolls under your uncertain step. The stars that guided your course are blotted out. You are a human derelict adrift on the world, borne as the currents may chance to set, "imprisoned in the viewless winds." In the helplessness of your heart you cry out with the blind man on the plains of Syria, "Thou son of David, have mercy upon me!"

THE OTHER MIRACLE

In response to this piteous cry men have stretched forth their hands in sympathy. They could not open the blinded eyes as the Master did on the Syrian plains, but they wrought another miracle—they taught the blind to see with their hands. They could not stay the eclipse of sight, but they pierced the darkness with the light of knowledge. They raised up institutions—temples of compassion—where human skill and science turn affliction and misery to service and happiness.

Since the year 1784, when the Abbe Valentin Haüy gathered together a few blind children from the streets of Paris and began the work of instructing them, the education of the sightless has been continued and extended, until its ever widening embrace of succour and enlightenment has reached the young blind of many countries. Homes and asylums have been provided for the aged and infirm blind. Governments and private philanthropy have united to provide the blind with libraries of embossed books.

Indeed, so much has already been done that I am not surprised to hear you ask, "What good thing yet remains to do for the blind?" I answer, "Help the adult blind to derive all the benefit possible from the education that has been so liberally given them. Help them to become efficient, useful citizens."

When blindness seizes a man in the midst of an active life, he has to face a greater misfortune than the child born blind or deprived of sight in the first years of life. Even if kindness and sympathy surround him, if his family is able to support him and care for him, he nevertheless feels himself a burden. He finds himself in the state of a helpless child, but with the heart and mind, the desires, instincts and ambitions of a man. Ignorant of what blind men can do and have done, he looks about him for work, but he looks in vain. Blindness bars every common way to usefulness and independence. Almost every industry, the very machinery of society, the school, the workshop, the factory, are all constructed and regulated on the supposition that every one can see.

In the whirl and buzz of a lighted world the blind man, bewildered and helpless, sits down in despair, and resigns himself with bitter patience to a life of inactivity and dependence. It is true that some blind men—men blind from childhood or stricken with blindness in the midst of active lives—have succeeded in almost every known business and profession despite their misfortune. But they have been men of exceptional capacity and energy.

Homer, Ossian, and Milton wrote great poems with never a ray of light in their eyes. Henry Fawcett, professor of political economy at Cambridge University, a member of Parliament for nineteen years and during Gladstone's ministry postmaster-general of Great Britain (he introduced many practical improvements in the postal service, among them the "parcels post"); Leonhard Euler, the Swiss mathematician and astronomer, who conducted his vast calculations mentally, and who was a member of all the great societies of learning in Europe; François Huber, the naturalist, who was for a century the leading authority on bees; Augustin Thierry, the French historian, who wrote his great work on the Merovingians with the aid of others' eyes; and our own historian, William Hickling Prescott, are blind men who successfully kept in the forefront of life.

BLIND—AND GREAT

A distinguished Belgian statesman and writer, Alexander Rodenbach, Didymus of Alexandria, the preceptor of Saint Jerome, Diodotus the Stoic, friend and teacher of Cicero, Ziska, the leader of the Bohemians in the Hussite War, who thrice defeated the Emperor's forces, did noble work after their eyes had ceased to know the light. Blind men have been musicians, road-builders, carpenters, wood-workers, journalists, editors, yacht-builders, and teachers of the blind and the seeing.

These indomitable blind men wrought out their own salvation, and became the liberators of their afflicted fellows by proving what man can do in the dark by the light of courage and intelligence. For it must be seen that if an exceptional blind man, unaided by a special education in a school for the blind, can lead a life of service and distinction, an ordinary blind man without genius can be trained to do an ordinary man's work; and this tells us what yet remains to do for the blind.

American commonwealths and philanthropists have always been generous to the blind. The states have been provided excellent schools, generally based on sound and beneficent principals, for their blind children and youths. In many of these institutions the standard is high, and the pupils attain marked proficiency in all the common school branches. But for all the munificence of individual charity and the liberality of public endowment, the blind man is still lost to the community as a producer. Education, books, science, music do not make the blind happy unless they enable them to work. Philanthropy which only rears fine buildings equipped with the implements of learning, and does not render its beneficiaries stronger and more serviceable citizens, annuls by unwisdom the generosity that inspires it, and makes void its charity.

Blind graduates of these schools have said to me, in the bitterness of disappointed hopes and ambitions, "It would have been better to leave us in ignorance than to enlighten and cultivate our minds only to plunge us into a double darkness. What boots it that we have spent our youth in kindergartens, museums, libraries and music-rooms if we pass from those pleasant halls to sit with idle hands and eat the dry crust of discontent?" The time has come when strong and efficient measures should be taken in America to give the blind an opportunity to become self-supporting, or at least to earn a part of their support. In an age and country where the ability to work is regarded almost as a test of respectability, it is a disgrace that any man should be forced to sit in idleness.

WHAT DOCTOR HOWE DID

The blind as a rule are poor. The parents of most of the children in the institutions for the blind are working people, and the man struck blind by accident or disease is usually a bread-winner. It is not uncommon for a young man to lose his sight in such occupations as stone-cutting, diamond polishing, glazing, and blasting rocks. Without assistance men thus blinded are doomed to involuntary idleness for the rest of their lives.

Up to the present day no adequate provision has been made for this class of blind persons in America, although Dr. Samuel G. Howe, the friend of all the afflicted and the pioneer in the education of the blind in the United States, outlined a plan to meet the industrial requirements of the adult blind more than sixty years ago. No other American has understood the sightless so thoroughly as Doctor Howe. He knew their weakness and how they might be strengthened. All his efforts in their behalf and all that he wrote about them show his discerning love and wisdom. He was one of the first to realize that there is something better even than feeding the hungry and clothing the naked, that it is a greater kindness to help them feed and clothe themselves. I do not know how I can better indicate the way in which the blind should be helped than by giving a summary of Doctor Howe's conclusions.

"If every child born into the community," says Doctor Howe, "has a right to food for his body and knowledge for his mind, then has he a right to some useful employment, for without it food and knowledge become but curses; they had better have been withheld."

Upon this broad and humane principle he organized the Perkins Intuition for the Blind in Boston. Its first object was to instruct and enlighten the young blind, its second to enable the blind to earn their own livelihood. Accordingly, in 1840, he established a work department where those who had finished their education could pursue for their profit the trades they had learned in school.

His annual reports furnish an interesting account of the ups and downs of his experiment. When a new enterprise is undertaken, it often happens that obstacles and difficulties are disregarded which later compel us to pause and consider. In the first enthusiasm of his work in behalf of the blind, Doctor Howe confidently expected that the great majority of the blind would be able to support themselves by means of their brains—they would be musicians, teachers, journalists and ministers of the gospel. The less gifted blind could earn their living by manual labor, with a little assistance and direction from their alma mater.

These expectations were doomed to disappointment. Not every blind person is highly gifted. They do not all possess musical talent or extraordinary intellectual capacity; nor do they all have the energy and perseverance necessary to overcome the heavy handicap that they encounter at the start. If all the blind were Miltons and Rodenbachs, they would need no such champion as Doctor Howe—no Moses would be necessary of there were no wilderness.

But although disappointed and often discouraged, Doctor Howe did not lose heart. Experience taught him the real wants of the blind and the best way to meet them. The failure of his high expectations showed him the imperative necessity of training the blind for some useful if less ambitious occupation. He urged that the institutions should supplement their instruction by aiding the graduates in their attempts to become self-supporting.

The institutions, that is, should be the capitalists of the blind, but should seek no pecuniary advantage for themselves. They should be willing to make a considerable outlay in the beginning, and indeed to the end, if necessary. Their object should be to aid the blind to counteract the disadvantages under which they work by bringing them as near as possible to an equality of opportunity with other workmen.

IN AMERICA AND EUROPE

Such were Doctor Howe's views when he opened a workshop for blind adults under the auspices of the Perkins Institution. The aim of the workshop was to give the blind the advantages which seeing workmen have—of working in a company, of saving rent and fuel and other incidental expenses, of having capital, and obtaining their stock at wholesale cost, and getting their produce cheaply marketed. The shop, said Doctor Howe, should train them in diligence and skill;

then if the world did not offer a field for the exercise of their talents, the institution should try to open one for them.

At the end of five years we find Doctor Howe optimistic about his experiment, and full of plans to extend the work so as to include a salesroom in the city for the reception and sale of articles made by the blind at home. Indeed, he looked forward to the foundation of an establishment broad enough to meet the wants of all the blind of New England. Would such an establishment, providing for so many persons, support itself? he asked. The answer was uncertain; but he argued that even if very few of the blind succeeded in becoming fully self-supporting, it was still good economy to enable them to earn as much of their support as possible. The state should help them indirectly in this way rather than pay their board and lodging.

But, after all, the first consideration of a wise commonwealth is not economy, but the good of all its citizens.

We must cross the Atlantic and visit the Old World in order to find a practical demonstration of what the blind can do. The first institution for the employment of the blind was founded at Edinburgh in 1793. Since then workshops, salesrooms and associations or agencies to promote the business interests of the blind have been established in Europe.

In Europe the emphasis has been upon industrial training, while in America more attention has been given to book education. When a pupil in a school for the blind in England or France shows no special aptitude for music or intellectual pursuits, he is put into the work department, where he learns a trade. Afterward the institution, or one of the agencies for the purpose in his country, seeks out a position for him, and stands by him until he has proved his efficiency. On the other hand, when a student shows marked ability in any direction, he receives opportunity to fit himself for a more responsible position. If a school for the blind has trained an organist who is capable of filling a church position, the agencies for the blind keep a lookout for a vacancy.

When the agent hears of one, he goes to the place and tells the church committee of a blind man who is competent to fill the position. The committee is probably very skeptical and very reluctant to try so doubtful an experiment. The agent, however, is eloquent, and persuades the committee to give the man a trial. The man comes, plays, and conquers.

In London there is a tea agency of which the managers are wholly or partially blind. Many blind agents are selling its teas, coffees, and cocoas in all parts of England.

Last June there was held in Edinburgh an exhibition of the work of the blind all over the world. A whole floor was devoted to weaving machines and typewriters, and blind people demonstrated their skill as weavers, masseurs, carpenters, and musicians. At the Glasgow Asylum the blind have produced salable articles for eighty years, and in three recent years the average annual sales amounted to twenty-nine thousand pounds sterling.

WAKING THE STATES

In English cities from 6 to 13 per cent of the blind are in workshops; in America, only six hundred blind persons, or 1 per cent of the entire number, are employed in industrial establishments.

But a brighter day dawned for the blind in America when New York and Massachusetts awoke to the necessity of looking into the condition of the sightless. Connecticut, Pennsylvania, Wisconsin, California and Michigan are all active in the effort to make wage-earners of the blind. The nature of the work which has begun, and should be extended as rapidly as possible, is represented by the endeavours of the Massachusetts Association to Promote the Interests of the Adult Blind.

This association has opened an experiment station in Cambridge, to find and test industries that seem practicable for the sightless. The blind are sought out in their homes, and when possible they are taught trades, their work is brought to the notice of the public, and the capacity of blind men and women to operate certain automatic machines in factories is demonstrated to employers.

Hitherto the chief industries of the blind have been the manufacture of brooms, mattresses, baskets, brushes, and mats, not all of which are profitable in this country. The effort should be to increase the number of possible lucrative occupations for the sightless.

A young blind man was trained at the station in Cambridge in ten days to cut box corners in a paper and tag factory to the satisfaction of his employer. Another young man has succeeded in taking, by means of a shorthand writing machine, acceptable interviews for a newspaper. A young blind woman was taken from the poorhouse, where she had been for three years, and placed in a hairpin factory, where she has found work that she is capable of doing.

The experiment station is now at work on a patented mop invented by a blind man. This "Wonder Mop" can be made entirely without sight, and the plan is to have blind agents from Maine to California sell it. If the mop proves as successful as it now promises to be, it will go a long way toward solving the industrial problem of the blind in this country.

What the blind workman needs is an industry that will enable him to produce something that people will buy, not out of pity for him, but because it is useful or beautiful. The blind will not lack for customers if their articles are of the best material, design and workmanship.

The workers at the experiment station have received more orders for their rugs, sofa pillows and table covers than their limited means and inadequate space enable them to fill promptly. Workers for the blind have found both manufacturers and employers ready and glad to cooperate with them when they understand that it is opportunity and not charity that is asked.

There is no law on the statute-books compelling people to move up closer on the bench of life to make room for a blind brother; but there is a divine law written on the hearts of men constraining them to make a place for him, not only because he is unfortunate, but also because it is his right as a human being to share God's greatest gift, the privilege of man to go forth unto his work.

8

Famous People

ecause Helen Keller became world famous at the age of 23 when her autobiography, *The Story of My Life*, was published, and went on to live to age 87, she knew or met many renowned people of the early- to mid-20th century, from Alexander Graham Bell to President John F. Kennedy.[1] Many became mentors and supporters.

As a teen, Keller met Mark Twain, and they became fast friends. He gave her advice and support about having a writing career. She said he wasn't troubled by her blindness because Twain said Keller had the "ability to see *into* things."[2] But she also knew that friendship should be based on shared values, and when industrialist Andrew Carnegie tried to give her a pension, the committed socialist turned him down at first. "I hope to enlarge my life and work by my own efforts," she said, "and you, sir, who have won prosperity from small beginnings, will uphold me in my decision to fight my battles without further help than I am now receiving from loyal friends and a generous world."[3] She later had to accept his offer because she had a household to support.

Keller's wide travels on behalf of the American Foundation for the Blind, as well as her home near New York City, put her in the presence of many famous people who became the subject of her writings. When in Yugoslavia, she received an unexpected audience with King Alexander I. In a 1929 *Good Housekeeping* article, she describes in great detail the hurried preparations to meet the King, but writes that the worries were for nothing because the King was a down-to-earth man:

> We were foolish to have felt any embarrassment because we had been ushered into his presence without any instruction as to our conduct. There was no need for knowledge of any formal court etiquette. One met him as one meets any man of rank. It has been my privilege to meet many great personalities. The greatest are always the simplest; so with King Alexander. Our little circle was arranged as a friendly family group, rather than as three women [Keller, Anne Sullivan and Polly Thompson] without rank having a private audience with a ruler. A more gracious and friendly personage it would be difficult to find anywhere. He made us feel immediately welcome and at home.[4]

King Alexander supported education for blind people in Yugoslavia, setting up a school for the blind in Zemun. He asked to see how Keller was taught to communicate so he could further his knowledge.

Not every meeting with famous people was pleasant. The author and playwright George Bernard Shaw had little interest in meeting Helen Keller because he disliked all Americans. From her touch of his hand, she could tell he was not pleased to meet her: "I held out my hand. He took it indifferently. I could scarcely believe my sensations. Here was a hand bristling with egotism as a Scotch thistle with thorns."[5] Then when Shaw was chastised for not being polite to the famous Helen Keller:

> Lady Astor laid her hand on his arm and shook it a little, as if he were a child behaving badly before company. 'Shaw,' she said, 'don't you realize that this is Helen Keller? She is deaf and blind.' . . . slowly Mrs. Macy spelled to me what Mr. Shaw had said:
>
> 'Why, of course! All Americans are deaf and blind—and dumb.'[6]

Most meetings with famous people were not so contentious. She met Bengali poet Sir Rabindranath Tagore, who was the first non-European Nobel Prize winner in literature in 1913, when he was visiting New York in 1930. She wrote a column about the meeting in a *Home Magazine* column, saying he was a person whose mind was "fully awake." Keller writes: "All the lamps of thought are lighted, for his consciousness is illumined with love for wide neighborhoods of men. His words shed beams of wisdom that emanate from a spirit in the full blaze of its power and beauty."[7] The *Home* article featured a photo of her with Tagore.

Her writings showed a real joy in meeting the renowned people of the world, and if she didn't meet them herself because they were figures of the past, she felt it was her duty to relay their greatness through her writings. In 1929, she wrote a detailed article in *The New York Times* honoring Louis Braille and describing all the experimentation that went into finally finding a useful tactile method of reading for blind people.[8]

In those many decades before television, Keller's articles introduced average Americans to renowned people before they would be memorialized in history books or in biopics on the History Channel. Of course, she was also a famous person herself, so in writing about others she was also giving insight into her own life as one of the most well-known disabled people in modern history. When in 1999, *Time* magazine named Helen Keller one of the 100 most remarkable people of the 20th century in the heroes and icons category,[9] she was listed among many of the famous people she wrote about in her magazine articles.

Notes:

1. Voice of America, "Helen Keller, 1880-1968: She Became the Most Famous Disabled Person in the World," August 6, 2011, http://learningenglish.voanews.com/content/helen-keller-1880-1968-she-became-the-most-famous-disabled-person-in-the-world-127068053/116590.html.

2. Amy Chambliss, "The Friendship of Helen Keller and Mark Twain," *The Georgia Review*, Vol. 24, No. 3 (Fall 1970), pp. 305-310.

3. Roger Shattuck, "Helen Keller. Brief life of a woman who found her own way: 1880-1968," *Harvard Magazine*, July-August 2004, http://harvardmagazine.com/2004/07/helen-keller.html.

4. Helen Keller, "A King at My Fingertips," *Good Housekeeping*, Jan. 1932, pp. 28-29, 176-177.

5. Helen Keller, "The Flaw in Shaw," *Reader's Digest*, May 1933, pp. 101-103

6. Keller, op cit., "The Flaw in Shaw," p. 103

7. Helen Keller, "The Voice of Humanity," *The Home Magazine*, June 1931, pp. 8, 109

8. Helen Keller, "Miss Keller Celebrates a Sight-giver," *The New York Times Magazine*, Nov. 1929, pp. 3, 22.

9. *Time*, "People of the Century," June 14, 1999, Vol. 153, No. 23, http://content.time.com/time/specials/packages/0,28757,2020772,00.html.

Albert Einstein

The Home Magazine, April 1931, pp. 6, 129

Editor's note: The quote from Kepler refers to Johannes Kepler, who was a German mathematician and theologian in the early 17ᵗʰ century. Albert Einstein visited the USA in 1930. It was at that time he became a well-known pacifist and signed a manifesto for the world's disarmament.

It has been good for the nation to come in contact with Professor Einstein. His is one of the great, enkindling personalities that fascinate mankind.

We feel excited, joyous in his presence. He lifts us up on wings above the sordid aims and the cynicism that inhibit our better impulses. He radiates good will and vitality.

Professor Einstein dares to say what he thinks, and his thoughts open new spaces for the spirit. He makes us ashamed of the materialism and the unbelief which are the bane of the American temperament. His religious feeling is very deep, if not orthodox. He cannot imagine that the connections which he perceives in the universe have been seen by him for the first time. Like Kepler he tries to "think God's thoughts after Him." He tells us we should try to keep our minds free and receptive. Too many of us sit in the prison of our own ideas; he says, we should burst it open and look at the world with our own eyes, instead of letting others see it for us.

Einstein is very impatient with pessimism. He accepts life with its roughness and its dreary wilderness simply and serenely. Looking through the world with a kindly smile he declares that the most wonderful thing for him is a bright face. What can we do but capitulate to such a Friend of Man? In his aversion to controversy and his generosity Einstein reminds one strongly of other great scientists like Sir Isaac Newton, Henri Fabre and Charles Darwin.

Not only is Professor Einstein a profound scientist, he is also a lovable human being. He is interested in all the problems of humanity. He loves music and plays the violin brilliantly. He derives much pleasure from sculpture and architecture. He reads deeply a few books. His nature absorbs the colors of the sea and the land, the crimson and the opal fires of East and West. I repeat, we all love Einstein.

Some wag has said that America loves Einstein because it understands his mathematical formulas not at all. This is a jocose untruth. Einstein is a genius all to himself. We like his democratic feeling, his inclusiveness, his freedom from petty prejudices and intolerances. We feel in his nature a power that releases us for a moment from the materialism of our lives beyond which we so seldom look.

When I met Einstein, he permitted me to put my hands on his noble head. He kept very still, as little children do when I look at them. Indeed, his attitude was altogether childlike. Perhaps the greatest truths can be learned only by becoming as a child.

As I stood beside him, I felt that a new world had suddenly filled this old one. I was aware of a forceful presence. Einstein was gentle, quiet, almost shy. His words came as if he were thinking aloud. Yet there was behind his declaration of pacifism a tremendous driving energy.

"We must resist war, accept imprisonment, keep up our courage," he said. "In times of peace pacifists should openly assert that in case of war they will not participate. We must give up idle words and fearlessly try to accomplish something of value to the cause of peace." He would have us recruit war resisters the world over and create a fund for furthering the work internationally. "To oppose war is not enough," he said, "we must show the governments our strength and endurance. That this means sacrifice goes without saying, but unless we are willing to make the necessary sacrifice, we shall remain just pacifists."

Einstein has become famous through his theory that the universe is not what it was supposed to be. His doctrine of relativity is so profound that few can understand it. It does not, therefore, immediately affect our lives; but the spirit in which Einstein searches out truth may reform the world.

The Voice of Humanity

The Home Magazine, June 1931, pp. 8, 109

Editor's note: Sir Rabindranath Tagore, the famed Indian poet and writer and first non-European to win the Nobel Prize for literature, visited the USA and Europe for most of 1930. This column included the picture above of the meeting of Tagore and Helen Keller.

I had the good fortune to meet and talk with Sir Rabindranath Tagore during his visit to New York. I was much impressed by his nobility of mind. He is sixty-nine years of age, but he does not look it. His skin is smooth and firm. His beautiful hands are strong and supple. He wears no spectacles and his deep brown eyes seem to see everything. His flowing hair and beard, white as snow, and the long brown robe that reaches to his slippered feet give him the appearance of a prophet.

I meet many interesting people as I go about the world. Some of them are interesting because of what they have accomplished, others because of their beautiful surroundings, and others because they are picturesque personalities. I seldom leave one of them without carrying away a thought or a new sense of human power; but I do not often meet one whose mind seems to me fully awake.

But one does not talk long with Tagore without perceiving that his mind is fully awake. All the lamps of thought are lighted, for his consciousness is illumined with love for wide neighborhoods of men. His words shed beams of wisdom that emanate from a spirit in the full blaze of its power and beauty.

Tagore said that as a young man he was content to dream in solitude, to write verses, stories and plays and to gaze long upon Mother Ganges. But one day, while he was absorbed in creative work, he heard an inner voice calling him out of seclusion to seek knowledge in the heart of humanity.

He pondered what he could do. He loved children and his thoughts turned to them. He called them around him in order to rescue them from the deadening influence of the schools. He surrounded them with an atmosphere of sympathy and freedom. He chose one of his beautiful estates in a secluded spot where, assisted by Mother Nature, they could be brought up in a spirit of truth and love.

All his life Tagore has avoided the kind of education that standardizes culture and stamps it with a college degree or a mark of caste. He spoke to me earnestly of his efforts to bring about the education of the masses in India. It was in the hope of helping his people to realize the supreme truth—the uniting power of love—that he founded Visva Bhrati, which is a combination of school and university.

Scarcely had Tagore established this school when there came the inner voice a second time: "Go forth and seek out the thoughts and dreams and deeds of man." And so he traveled from land to land, studying the human heart, desiring intensely to understand the full meaning of his relation to other human beings. He suffered, as all lovers of humanity have suffered, when he saw the misery man inflicts upon man. Tigers and snakes and the elemental forces of nature are not the greatest enemies of man; man is his own worst enemy.

The question which kept troubling Tagore was "Why is it that man, with all his powers of mind, is enthralled by suspicion and fear, greed and hate? When I looked out of a train window," said Tagore, "I saw on both sides of the railway the wonderful achievements man has wrought with his own labor—beautiful fields of wheat, fruitful orchards and pastures where sheep, cows and horses fed in peace.

"How man loves his land!" I thought, "and behold, what a great power is this love! How it has beautified the earth and made it fertile! How he has struggled to eradicate the barrenness from the desert! How he has fought and defeated at every step the forces that are hostile to life! The earth is overwhelmed by his love of it, not because of his covetousness, but because he has poured his heart and mind into its tillage."

Tagore has labored unceasingly to build up in India an international university on this principle of love. It is his dream that there the different cultures of the world shall flourish in harmony. It is his hope that at Visva Bhrati teachers and students will hold fast to the idea that they serve their race best who maintain its union with humanity, and with humanity's highest aspirations. Friendship, cooperation, tolerance and sympathy are the only true source of man's true happiness. Thus spoke another of the long line of prophets who have through the ages breathed a message of unity and peace into the deafened ears of mankind.

Independence Day

The Home Magazine, July 1934, p. 6

Editor's note: John Fiske was a 19ᵗʰ-century American historian and philosopher who wrote more than ten books about the American Revolution and the early history of the United States.

When the midsummer months come round, people think seriously about taking a vacation. Every one desires a respite from the pressure of business duties and social obligations. They want to let up, to enjoy, unhampered by nagging care and appointments, the restorative pleasures of the great out-doors and the diversions to which their taste inclines them.

Independence Day is the excuse for all who can to plan some kind of celebration. I imagine they think more about the excursion than about the ideals of the founders of their country, and perhaps that is as it should be.

I, however, cannot think of the Fourth of July without remembering one American who will not have a holiday this Summer—that is, President Roosevelt. I feel we should all have him in our thoughts, whatever our diversions may be. For we have laid upon him a momentous duty in the fulfillment of which he is exerting every power in him.

On that day President Roosevelt will be engaged upon the task of making the ideals of the founders of America triumph. He must of course rely upon the loyalty of the people who put him at the head of the nation to carry through successfully the extensive and important trust they have placed in his hands.

To lead a country in revolution wisely and effectively, without ambition and without bloodshed, demands lofty genius and unbending purpose; and there can be no doubt that a revolution of vast consequences is taking place in America at the present time.

President Roosevelt is building a new state amid the angry opposition of some and the lukewarm support of others. Without a chart, but with unwavering eyes and steady will he is guiding us through confusion and change. He is setting up a humane order in the midst of ruthless, self-seeking, reckless greed and economic anarchy. He is using all the powers at his command to compel the selfish few to play the game of business fairly. Never again, he says, shall we permit unsocial conditions in the United States which have heretofore allowed the maldistribution of wealth and power by a small minority.

After a year of anxious toil and earnest, but sometimes bitter discussion, in which more than once it seemed as if his projects were on the point of breaking up, he has inaugurated a colossal work of reconstruction which will affect the whole future of the nation. Whatever may be the ultimate outcome of his labors, one thing is certain, our eyes have been opened to the mad decade of 1919-1929 which brought about the present depression; and lives there one American who does not consider this one of the greatest blessings that ever came to our people?

In spite of the high-wrought intensity of feeling that has from time to time been displayed, the President has kept his equanimity, and large outlook. His dauntless spirit has won for him the admiration of the world. Many wonder whether he can overcome the fearful odds that confront him, but nobody doubts his sincerity and altruism.

John Fiske tells us in his account of the struggle for American independence which dragged through four months of a scorching Philadelphia summer that the scene was ended by a characteristic bit of pleasantry by [Benjamin] Franklin. On the back of the President's quaint black arm-chair there was a half sun, brilliant with its gilded rays. As the meeting was about to break, and [George] Washington arose, Franklin pointed to the chair and said:

"I have been sitting here all these weeks, wondering whether yonder sun was rising or setting, but now I know it is a rising sun."

If the people will stand firmly by President Roosevelt, the Sun of Democracy will rise anew, and "this nation, under God, shall have a new birth of freedom, and the Government of the People, by the People, and for the People shall not perish from the earth."

Deeds of Immortality

The Home Magazine, June 1935, p. 9

May is the month of tree-planting. Thousands of children set in the ground saplings that will absorb the sunshine and the rain, grow up inch by inch into splendid trees bearing fruit or clothing the countryside in coolness and beauty.

While planting them, children drink in knowledge of Nature and her laws. They discover that where the soil is good and the surroundings are right, the saplings will grow strong and the land will be shadowed with their mighty branches. Digging in the earth, covering the roots with tender care and watering them, they learn how to work with Nature, while they sense dimly the immense forces of the universe and beyond them the Eternal.

Here is something real—something that will bring thoughtfulness and sweetness into their personalities. Planting a tree is a deed of immortality; for by it the faculties are quickened, and the life in the world is preserved.

Thus the Mystery of Life binds together the child and the tree, and this mystery is the source of all true art and science. When the soul is indifferent to this wonder, it is asleep.

Years ago I spent a most interesting day in Luther Burbank's gardens at Santa Rosa, California. He led me from plant to plant—plum trees, nut trees and exquisite flowers. Reverently he explained how he had learned to read Nature's mind and follow her suggestions. Breathlessly I listened to the story of how that "wizard of plant life" had started with potatoes that were small, and spoiled easily. After working patiently for a long time he was rewarded by finding a potato seed-ball—a great rarity. It was as if he had rubbed Aladdin's lamp: for then Nature's genii came at his summons, and lo! out of the seed-ball grew the white, fine-grained, firm Burbank Potato. He told me how he tried countless experiments until he succeeded in taking the seeds out of some berries and the thorns out of several plants, putting a sweet taste into a bitter fruit, curling the petals of gladioli and iris and deepening their tints.

At first people criticized Burbank because, they said, he was "setting up as a competitor of God," but he heeded not their ignorant wrath. He went serenely on in his colossal task, enriching the gardens, fields and orchards of the world, and lived to be blessed as a benefactor of mankind.

When I consider the work of Luther Burbank, I believe more emphatically than ever that we are immortal not only in spirit but also in our deeds on earth.

Everything we are, everything that we do and say is immortal in the sense that it has an effect upon tree, flower and child, and this effect goes on indefinitely. All that has influenced us—the books we read, the teachers who train our minds, the friends we cherish, the work we do and every soft vernal breath of Spring— lives in us forever.

In other words, the character we have wrought out of living and giving life survives. There is just one way to make sure of immortality, and that is to love this life and live it as richly and helpfully as we can.

If You Have Friends
You Can Endure Everything

The American Magazine, September 1929, pp. 62-63, 168-72

Editor's note: Alexander Melville Bell, father of Alexander Graham Bell, invented Visible Speech in the 1860s, a writing system of symbols based how the lips, tongue and throat move in verbal speech. The method did assist deaf people in pronunciation of verbal speech.

Someone has said that a beautiful memory is the most precious wealth one can possess. If this is true, I am indeed rich in happy memories of Dr. Alexander Graham Bell. When I was a little girl just learning to talk, my teacher, Mrs. John A. Macy (Miss Sullivan), and I used to go with him to conventions to further the teaching of speech to the deaf. Most people know Doctor Bell as the inventor of the telephone; those who are familiar with his work for the deaf believe that what he did in this direction was at least as important a boon to mankind. I admired him in both these capacities, but I remember him not so much as a great inventor, or as a great benefactor, but simply as a wise, affectionate, and understanding friend.

I could almost call him my oldest friend. Even before my teacher, Mrs. Macy, came into my life, he held out a warm hand to me in the dark Indeed, it was through him that Mrs. Macy came to me. From the beginning, he enthusiastically approved her methods in teaching me. Shortly after "The Story of My Life" was published, he wrote to a friend commenting on some of her letters which I included in the book. In these letters, she tells how she taught me. Doctor Bell said of them:

"They reveal a fact that has long been suspected: That Helen's remarkable achievements are as much due to the genius of her teacher as to her own brilliant mind. . . ."

Doctor Bell's work for the deaf did not originate with himself. The science of speech had long been studied in the Bell family. Doctor Bell's grandfather was the inventor of a device to overcome stammering, and his father, Mr. Melville Bell, whom I used often to meet when I visited the Bells in Washington, perfected a system of visible speech as a means of teaching the deaf which Doctor Bell considered more important than his invention of the telephone.

However, as Mr. Melville Bell is reported to have said, "There was not so much money in it." To learn speech by means of it demands more patience than our western countries have, but it has been found serviceable in the Orient.

The devotion of Doctor Bell to his father was beautiful. How like they were, and how different! Melville Bell was the more reposeful and domestic. His tastes were simple, and did not change when wealth came to his son. He continued to live in the same little house in the same contented and frugal manner. If anything kept Doctor Bell from visiting his father for a day or two, he would say, "Come, I must see my father. A chat with him is just the tonic I need."

In Professor Bell's charming little cottage at Colonial Beach, where the Potomac broadens to meet the bay, I used often to see these two noble men sitting on the porch for hours without speaking a word, smoking peacefully and watching the steamers and boats pass along the river on their errands of service. Sometimes an unusual bird note would attract their attention, and the son would ask, "How would you record that, Father?" Then the resources of the visible speech system would be tested out, and the two men would become absorbed in phonetics, unmindful of everything about them. Every note was analyzed and visibly recorded.

Both men had an intense desire to remedy every defect of enunciation, and I have been told that it was a joy to listen to their speech. Both had at various periods been teachers of elocution, and both loved to recite.

I have known them to give many scenes from Shakespeare delightfully, but the best part of the performance was the comments and fiery retorts which flew from one actor to another, until one of them thought of proceeding with the drama.

Doctor Bell was exceedingly tender to his mother, who had become quite deaf when I knew her. I recall a spring afternoon when he took Mrs. Macy and me for a drive out in the country. We gathered quantities of honeysuckle, pink and white dogwood, and wild azaleas. On our way back, we stopped to give them to Mrs. Melville Bell. Doctor Bell said, "Let us go in by the porch door and surprise them." On the steps he paused and spelled into my hand, "Hush! They are both asleep!" We tiptoed about, making a bower of the flowers. It was a picture never to be forgotten—those two dear people seated in armchairs—Mrs. Bell's white head bowed on her breast, Mr. Bell's head thrown back on the chair, his beard and curly hair framing his ruddy face like that of a statue of Zeus. We left them undisturbed with the flowers and their dreams.

I was always glad to visit Doctor Bell's family in Washington, or at their summer home on Cape Breton Island. I admired Mrs. Bell for the courage and perseverance with which she conquered her handicap of deafness from infancy. She was a wonderful lip reader, and certainly she needed patience, skill, and humor to read the lips of the countless visitors who came to the house. She never spelled on her fingers, because she believed that this system of communication isolated the deaf from normal people. She loved beautiful lace and used to hold a filmy web in her hands and show me how to trace the woven flowers and leaves, the saucy cupids, the silken winding streams, and the lacy crisscross of fairy paths bordered with aerial boughs. The two small daughters, Elsie and Daisy, were always ready to play with me, and Daisy tried to spell into my hand all the bright things she heard so that I could laugh with her.

There were often distinguished gatherings, when I was introduced to learned scientists. Doctor Bell used to spell what they said to me. He always assumed that anyone could understand anything. He would explain to me the laws of physics or some principle of magnetism; but no matter how abstruse his discourse might be, I loved to listen to him. He could never be in a room two minutes before the whole talk converged in his direction. People chose to listen to him instead of talking themselves. He had an extraordinary gift of presenting difficult problems in a simple and vivid manner—a gift which, in my experience, is one of the rarest possessed by human beings.

Doctor Bell was never dogmatic in his conversation. He was, I think, the only person I ever knew who could look at a subject from a point of view entirely different from his own with genuine interest and enthusiasm. When it was presented to him he would say, "Perhaps you are right. Let us see."

His gifts as an orator are not known to the public in general because he chose to exercise them in behalf of an obscure group living in silence. But I know what eloquent speech is. I have stood beside Doctor Bell on the platform and felt speech coming from his lips, and eloquence in his voice, his attitude, his gestures, all at once. Never have I longed more intensely for grateful, natural speech than on these occasions.

After he had talked a while, he would touch my arm, I would rise and place my hand on his lips to show the audience how I could read what he was saying. I wish words could portray him as I saw him in those exalted moods—the majesty of his presence, the noble and spirited pose and action of his head, the strong features partly masked by a beautiful beard that rippled and curled beneath my fingers, the inspired expression which came into his face when he was deeply moved. His splendid head lifted, his nostrils dilated, his eyes flashed valor, and his gestures were large, harmonious movements of the body, like his thoughts. No one could resist so much energy, such grace.

Every teacher of the deaf, no matter what system he advocates, has been influenced by Doctor Bell. He broadcast his ideas in the truest scientific spirit, with no personal ambition to advance. For a number of years he maintained at his own expense an experimental school in Washington where practical work could be carried on in finding better ways of teaching very young deaf children. He strove unceasingly to make it possible for every child without hearing to acquire speech.

You who see and hear may not realize that the teaching of speech to the deaf is one of the divinest miracles of the nineteenth century. Perhaps it is impossible for one who sees and hears to realize what it means to be both deaf and dumb. Ours is not the stillness which soothes the weary senses; it is an inhuman silence which severs and estranges. It is a silence not to be broken by a word or greeting, or the song of birds, or the sigh of a breeze. It is a silence which isolates cruelly, completely. Two hundred years ago there was not a ray of hope for us. In an indifferent world not one voice was lifted in our behalf. Yet hearing is the deepest, most humanizing, philosophical sense man possesses. Lonely ones all over the world, because of Doctor Bell's efforts, have been brought into the pleasant, social ways of mankind.

Doctor Bell was a young son of an old country, a self-reliant Scot, but so nobly did he live among us, he seems our own. His life was singularly free from harassments both of temperament and circumstances. No allowance was ever needed for the eccentricity or waywardness of genius. His nature was too fine to breed rivalries or to tolerate animosities. I have never met anyone who knew Doctor Bell personally who did not feel that he had made a lasting impression upon his or her life. Indeed, his nature was so rich in sympathy that it is difficult to speak of him in terms which will not seem exaggerated.

"Life is extraordinarily interesting!" he used to say, especially when we spoke of the telephone. "Things happen, but they are not the things we thought would happen. We can see clearly enough to the turn of the road, but beyond that we do not know what surprises may be in store for us."

He told us how Mrs. Bell, who was not at that time his wife, but his pupil, persuaded him to go to the Centennial Exposition in Philadelphia to exhibit the telephone. The time was set for a Sunday afternoon, but when the hour arrived, it was hot, the judges were tired, and it looked as if there would be no demonstration. "But"—Doctor Bell would smile his refulgent smile—"but the unexpected may happen at Philadelphia as anywhere else. It happened just as I had made up my mind to leave the Exposition. At that moment Dom Pedro, Emperor of Brazil, appeared and recognized me as the man he had talked to in Boston about methods of teaching the deaf—he was interested in establishing schools for deaf persons in Brazil and was investigating the methods of teaching them used in the United States. He came toward me, holding out his hand.

Observing my apparatus, he asked me what it was. I told him about it, and added that I had expected to give an exhibition of it that afternoon. 'Well, why not? the Emperor exclaimed. 'I should like to hear it.'"

A wire was strung across the room. Doctor Bell took the transmitter and told Dom Pedro to hold the receiver close to his ear. "My God, it talks!" he cried. Then Lord Kelvin took the receiver. "Yes, it speaks," he said. The judges took turns in listening to the instrument, and the exhibition lasted until ten o'clock that night. The instrument was the center of interest during the remainder of the Exposition. The commercial development of the telephone dated from that day.

It was in 1892, when the invention was being contested in the courts of Boston, that I first became aware of the telephone. We saw a great deal of Doctor Bell in those days. We were staying with a friend of ours, Mrs. Pratt, who had assisted him in some of his investigations relating to the deaf. When the session at court was over he would come for us, or we would go to the Bellevue Hotel and wait for him. He was very fond of the theater and of music, and it was never difficult to persuade him to take us to a play or a concert.

Naturally, our talk turned frequently to scientific matters. In his youth, Doctor Bell was profoundly interested in the laying of the Atlantic Cable. He told me vividly how it was laid after many failures and discouragements, and how many lives were lost before it was finally completed, in 1866. I was twelve years old when he told me about it about it, and that story of heroism and the wonder of the human imagination, as told by him, thrilled me as a fairy tale thrills other children. I still have an impression of words fluttering along wires far, far down under the ocean, East and West, annihilating time.

It was Doctor Bell who first spelled into my hand the name of Charles Darwin. "What did he do?" I asked. "He wrought the miracle of the nineteenth century," replied Doctor Bell.

Then he told me about "The Origin of Species," and how it had widened the horizon of human vision and understanding.

He showed us the building where the telephone was born and he spoke appreciatively of his assistant, Mr. Thomas A. Watson, without whom, he said, he doubted if the invention would ever have been carried through. It was on March 10, 1876, that Mr. Watson, who was working in another room, was startled to hear Doctor Bell's voice say, "Mr. Watson, come here, I want you." That was the first audible telephone talk. It was as casual and commonplace as any of the millions of conversations that go on every day over the telephone. I said I wished the first sentence transmitted had had more significance. Doctor Bell answered,

"Helen, time has shown that the chief use of the telephone is the repetition of that original message. The transmission of the words, 'Come here, I want you,' to the millions of the world's workers is the highest service the telephone renders a busy world."

Doctor Bell had no telephone in his own study and he used to say somewhat ruefully, "What should be done to the man who has destroyed the privacy of the home?" And I have heard him say, when people spoke admiringly of the invention, "Yes, but I doubt if it will ever carry human speech as far as Shakespeare and Homer have carried it."

One evening, when we were waiting for a street car beside a telephone pole, Doctor Bell placed my hand on the weather-smoothed wood and said, "Feel. What do the vibrations mean to you—anything?"

I had never put my hand on a pole before. "Does it hum like that all the time?" I asked.

"Yes," he told me, "all the time. That even singing never stops; for it is singing the story of life, and life never stops." He then described how the wires were strung and insulated, and he explained many other details that I suppose everyone except a blind girl would know about. At the end, he said, "Those copper wires up there are carrying the news of birth and death, war and finance, failure and success, from station to station around the world. Listen! I fancy I hear laughter, tears, love's vows broken and mended."

Once Doctor Bell and I were walking in the rain, and he asked me if I had ever felt a tree when it was raining. He put my hand on the trunk of a small oak, and I was astonished to feel a delicate murmur—a silvery whisper, as if the leaves were telling each other a lot of little things. Since then, I have often touched trees when the raindrops descend in little pearly columns from every twig and leaf. It feels like elves laughing.

On these walks and drives his mind spread out restfully. Snatches of poetry, anecdotes, reminiscences of Scotland, interesting descriptions of Japan, which he had visited some years earlier, flowed through his skillful fingers into my hand. He loved Portia's speech on the quality of mercy, and he once told me that his favorite quotation was Dryden's paraphrase of Horace:

> Happy the man, and happy he alone,
> He who can call today his own;
> He who, secure within, can say,
> Tomorrow, do thy worst, for I have lived today.
> Be fair, or foul, or rain, or shine,
> The Joys I have possessed, in spite of fate, are mine.

Not Heaven itself upon the past has power;
But what has been, has been, and I have had
My hour.

When Doctor Bell died, it was estimated that there were 12,000,000 tele-phones in use in the world. It has been said that the basic patent which he received on his twenty-ninth birthday was the most valuable patent ever issued.

I saw Doctor Bell soon after the fiftieth anniversary of the day on which this patent was granted. Telephone lines had by that time linked the eastern to the western part of the United States. Mr. Watson was in San Francisco and Doctor Bell was in New York. The same conversation was repeated, "Mr. Watson, come here, I want you." "He heard me," said Doctor Bell, "but he did not come im-mediately. It is not long now, however, before men will be able to appear from across the continent within a few hours after they are summoned." He said that the transatlantic flight would some time be made in one day—a prediction which he did not live to see fulfilled. I thought of him when Lindbergh flew across in thirty-two and a half hours.

Of course, Doctor Bell experienced the annoyances as well as the happiness of having done something that his fellow creatures appreciated. Wherever he went he was approached by people who wished to shake hands with the man who invented the telephone. Once he spelled to me, "One would think I have never done anything worth while but the telephone. That is because it is a money-making invention. It is a pity so many people make money the criterion of suc-cess. I wish my experiments had resulted in enabling the deaf to speak with less difficulty. That would have been made me truly happy."

When he wished to work on one of his theories or inventions he would retire to Beinn Breagh on Cape Breton Island, or to his retreat near Washington, or to a cocoanut grove in Florida—the home of his daughter, Mrs. Fairchild. "I must have perfect calm," he would say; "but that is no easy thing to find in this busy world."

When our paths lay in different courses I used to write to him now and then. Knowing how absorbed he was in his work, I never expected an answer, but I never wrote without receiving one. I did not expect him to read my books, but I always did, and wrote to me about them in such a way that I knew he considered me a capable human being, and not some sort of pitiable human ghost groping its way through the world.

Is it any wonder that I loved him?

Doctor Bell was very fond of animals and we used to go to visit the Zoo to-gether, not only in Washington but in other cities where we were attending meetings for the advancement of the deaf. Once when I was a little girl—I think it was on my fourteenth birthday—he gave me a cockatoo, which I called Jonquil because of his glorious yellow crest. Jonquil was a beauty, but he was a menace armored in lovely white and gold feathers. He used to perch on my foot as I read, rocking back and forth as I turned the pages. Every now and then he would hop to my shoulder and rub his head against my ear and face, sometimes putting his long, sharp, hooked bill against my mouth, sending ripples of terror down my spine. Then he would dart off, screeching fiendishly, to alight on the back of a dog or the head of a person. After a while, my father tried to give him away, but his fame had spread so far that no one would take him. Finally, the owner of a saloon in Tuscumbia gave him shelter. I don't know what happened to him after the passage of the eighteenth amendment.

Doctor Bell was always eager for an adventure. I remember an evening in Pittsburg when we drove along the embankment of the river to see the spectacular display of fireworks when the furnaces made their periodic runs.

I shall never forget how excited Doctor Bell was when the show began. He jumped up, exclaiming, "The river is on fire!" Indeed, the whole world appeared to be on fire. Out of the big, red, gaping mouths of the furnaces leaped immense streams of flame which seemed to fan the very clouds into billows of fire. As the columns ascended, the stars blushed, as if a god had kissed them. The shoulder of the moon turned pink, as if she had thrown a scarlet scarf over her head. Soon the sky was an undulating sea of flame.

Mrs. Macy and Doctor Bell spelled into my hands, again and again erasing their words, searching their memories for phrases and similes to describe the scene. "A cataract of pink steam!" one would say. "It bubbles and drips through the air." "There goes a crimson geyser licking up the night!" said the other. "A molten rod of hot iron ducks into a black hole like a rabbit." "There are silvery grottoes and caves of ebony, and abysses of blackness, beyond the river bank." "The belching furnace must be part of the central fires of earth." And so on.

When my teacher and I visited the Bells at their Beinn Breagh home near Baddeck, the summer after my first year at Radcliffe, Doctor Bell's leading scientific interest was aeronautics. He had built a huge tetrahedral kite with which he hoped to establish some new principles in the art of flying. The kite never achieved the success he thought it would; but we had no end of fun with it. I do not think I ever saw Doctor Bell discouraged. He was always ready to jest about his experimental misfortunes.

The last evening of my visit at Beinn Breagh, Doctor Bell and I were together on the piazza, while Mrs. Bell was showing some pictures of Cape Breton to Mrs.

Macy in the library. Doctor Bell was in a dreamy mood and spelled his thoughts into my hand, half poetry, half philosophy. He was weary after a day of experiments; but his mind would not rest, or rather, it found sweet rest in the poets he had read as a young man. He recited favorite passages from "In Memoriam," "The Tempest," and "Julius Caesar," and I remember with what earnestness he repeated, "There is a tide in the affairs of men which, taken at the flood, leads on to fortune." He ended by saying, "Helen, I do not know whether or not, as these lines teach, we are the masters of our fate. I doubt it. The more I look at the world, the more it puzzles me. We are forever moving toward the unexpected.

"When I was a young man," he continued, "I loved music passionately, and I wanted to become a musician. But fate willed otherwise. Ill health brought me to America. Then I became absorbed in experiments with an instrument that developed into the telephone. And now here I am giving my days and nights to aeronautics. And all the time you know that my chief interest is the education of the deaf. No, Helen, I have not been master of my fate—not in the sense of choosing my work." He paused and went on, "Your limitations have placed you before the world in an unusual way. You have learned to speak, and I believe you are meant to break down the barriers which separate the deaf from mankind. There are unique tasks waiting for you, a unique woman."

I told him that my teacher and I intended to live in some retreat "from public haunt exempt" when I graduated from college, and then I hoped to write. "It is not you, but circumstances that will determine your work," he said. "We are only instruments of the powers that control the universe. Remember, Helen, do not confine yourself to any particular kind of self-expression. Write, speak, study, do whatever you possibly can. The more you accomplish, the more you will help the deaf everywhere."

After a long pause he said, "It seems to me, Helen, a day must come when love which is more than friendship will knock at the door of your heart and demand to be let in."

"What made you think of that?" I asked.

"Oh, I often think of your future. To me you are a sweet, desirable young girl, and it is natural to think about love and happiness when we are young."

"I do think of love sometimes," I admitted; "but it is like a beautiful flower which I may not touch, but whose fragrance makes the garden a place of delight just the same."

He sat silent for a minute or two, thought-troubled, I fancied. Then his dear fingers touched my hand again like a tender breath, and he said, "Do not think that because you cannot see or hear, you are debarred from the supreme happiness of womanhood. Heredity is not involved in your case as it is in so many others."

"Oh, but I am happy, very happy!" I told him. "I have my teacher and my mother and you, and all my other friends, and all kinds of interesting things to do. I really don't care a bit about being married."

"I know," he answered, "but life does strange things to us. You may change your mind. You are very young, and it's natural that you shouldn't take what I said seriously now; but I have long wanted to tell you how I felt about your marrying, should you ever wish to."

I was glad when Mrs. Bell and Mrs. Macy joined us and the conversation became less serious.

The last time I saw Doctor Bell he had just returned from a visit to Edinburgh. For once, he seemed melancholy. This was in 1920, I think. He said he had found himself a stranger in a strange land, and that it seemed good to get back to America. The War had left its cruel scar upon his spirit. I felt the lines of sorrow graven upon his noble features; but I thought a smile had fallen asleep in them.

He told us he was going to work on hydroplanes the remainder of his life. He prophesied that in less than ten years there would be an air service between New York and London. He said there would be hangers on the tops of tall buildings, and people would use their own planes as they do automobiles now. He thought freight would be carried by air cheaper than by rail or steamships. He also predicted that the next war would be fought in the air, and that submarines would be more important than battleships or cruisers.

Doctor Bell also foresaw a day when methods would be discovered by engineers to "cool off the tropics" and bring the heated air into cold lands which need it. He told me beneath the warm face of the tropic seas flow currents of icy cold water from the Arctic and Antarctic regions, and he said that in some way these streams would be brought up to the surface, thus changing the climate of hot countries and rendering them pleasanter to live and work in. His wonderful prophecies set my heart beating faster; but little did I dream that in six years I should read of French engineers laying plans to capture the ocean as an ally against climates inimical to man!

We felt very sad when we said good-by [sic] to him. I had a presentiment that I should not see him again in this life.

He died at his summer home on August 2, 1922. He was buried at sunset on the crest of Cape Beinn Breagh, a spot chosen by himself. Once he had pointed out that spot to me, and quoted Browning's verse:

"Here is the place, Helen, where I shall sleep the last sleep—

Where meteors shoot, clouds form, lightnings are loosened,
Stars come and go!"

Sunset was chosen as the time for burial, because at that moment the sun enfolds the lake in its arms of gold, which is what the name of the lake, "Bras d'Or," means.

If there were no life beyond this earth life, some people I have known would gain immortality by the nobility of our memory of them. With every friend I love who has been taken into the brown bosom of the earth, a part of me has been buried; but their contribution to my being of happiness, strength, and understanding remains to sustain me in an altered world. Although life has never seemed the same since we read in the paper that Alexander Graham Bell was dead, yet the mist of tears is resplendent with the precious part of himself that lives in me.

The Flaw in Shaw

Reader's Digest, May 1933, pp. 101-03
condensed from *The New York Times*, March 12, 1933

Editor's note: Mrs. Patrick Campbell was a British actress who lived from 1865 to 1940. She had a passionate letter-writing relationship with George Bernard Shaw.

For at least 40 years George Bernard Shaw has questioned all our traditions, ridiculed all our conventions, and scoffed at all our virtues. There is no man living who can hold a candle to this crotchety Irishman for exposing the shams of civilization. Tearing away the veil of self-deception from our eyes, he has made us realize that empire is another name for oppression and war; that our educational system does its best to quench whatever intelligence there is in the minds of children; that financiers are not necessarily wise men; that wealth is not prosperity; that modern industrialism is slavery; that English-speaking people are not obviously the chosen of God; that machinery and speed do not make a happy people; that the chief object of our law courts is not justice. Shaw has smashed our idols with such wit and satirical acumen that we have thoroughly enjoyed the process, and we have elevated him to the pinnacle of a prophet.

He must have studied diligently the method of John Knox and Calvin and learned from them the art of supreme assertion and the importance of utterly destroying one's opponents. Mr. Shaw says it is an instinct with him to attack any idea which has been full-grown for ten years. By some freak of nature his mind always takes the opposite. While imposing his own views upon us he shoots off the aphorism, "You should have no convictions, for, as Nietzsche puts it, convictions are prisons." He is as elemental as the lighting that clears the atmosphere.

My personal admiration for George Bernard Shaw is genuine and deep. He has flashed strong rays into the physical darkness which I have known from infancy. I have his plays and essays in Braille, but long before they were embossed my teacher spelled into my hand Mr. Shaw's electrifying challenges of society. I shall never forget the thrill of "seeing" *Pygmalion* for the first time in Chicago, with Mrs. Patrick Campbell in the role of the cockney girl whose outlandish dialect was transformed into the speech of a lady through the genius of a student of phonetics. I understood that play so well. The difficulties that confronted me when I undertook to learn to speak were far greater than the cockney girl ever dreamed of.

From the night I "saw" *Pygmalion*, I wanted to meet Mr. Shaw and tell him how wonderfully I thought he had depicted the intricacies of speech. This desire persisted through the years and grew stronger with every new play he wrote. His *Saint Joan* moved me profoundly. I wished more than ever to touch the hand that wrote so understandingly.

During a visit to London, Lady Astor invited my teacher, Anne Sullivan Macy, and myself to come to her house to meet Mr. Shaw. Receiving us with all the cordiality and charm that makes her beloved by everyone who knows her, she told us that Mr. Shaw was taking a nap. While we waited, I became more and more excited. I wanted intensely to get the feeling of the man, as I am so often able to do, from a handclasp or a few minutes of intimate conversation. I had met kings and queens, distinguished writers and poets, scientists and philosophers, statesmen and great religious leaders, but here was George Bernard Shaw—the climax. Here was a man whose mind I understood, a man whose ideas had made the world sit up and take notice.

At last he appeared in the doorway. He stood there posed for a few seconds, surveying the room with a whimsical expression. Mrs. Macy's hand tapped into mine rapidly describing him. I "listened" breathless with expectation. I held out my hand. He took it indifferently. I could scarcely believe my sensations. Here was a hand bristling with egotism as a Scotch thistle with thorns.

"I am so happy to meet you," I said inanely. "I've wanted to know you for ever so long."

"Why do all you Americans say the same thing?" he taunted.

"Why do you hate us Americans so?" I murmured.

"I don't hate you," he answered. Mrs. Macy's hand gave me the inflection of his voice, which implied that Americans could never rise to the level of his contempt.

"Then why don't you come to America?" I asked.

"Why should I? All America comes to see me."

Lady Astor laid her hand on his arm and shook it a little, as if he were a child behaving badly before company. "Shaw," she said, "don't you realize that this is Helen Keller? She is deaf and blind."

His answer must have shocked everybody; but a few minutes passed before I knew what it was. A quiver ran through Mrs. Macy's hand—I was shut off from the scene, and I stood wondering and waiting. Then slowly Mrs. Macy spelled to me what Mr. Shaw had said:

"Why, of course! All Americans are deaf and blind—and dumb."

There was a flaw in the sparkling vessel. Mr. Shaw may shine before our eyes with the brightness of an archangel, but in the things of the spirit he lacks that quality which goes to the making of a Friend of Man. There is nothing in Mr. Shaw of that sympathetic imaginativeness which enables other great men to understand human beings.

He has sacrificed emotion to intellect, intuition to reason. His refusal to see any good in human institutions has ended with an inability to respect personality. There are no mellowing shadows in his mind; every inch of it is relentlessly glaring—no sense of dreams or mystery abides there. Mr. Shaw is the sort of person who is never happy unless he is making some one else thoroughly uncomfortable. That is not to say that Mr. Shaw is not a great humanist.

He protests with great vigor against the infliction of unnecessary pain upon men and beasts. But his humanism is collective without being individual. He is so magnificently self-confident and self-sufficient he cannot conceive the possibility that weakness and hesitation may go hand in hand with spiritual strength and radiancy. He is wanting when weighed in the scales of supreme genius.

A King at My Fingertips

Good Housekeeping, January 1932, pp. 28-29, 176-77

Editor's note: Alexander I was King of Yugoslavia from 1921 to 1934. The King-dom was called the Kingdom of Serbs, Croats and Slovenes before 1929.

I am sure no woman ever dressed so quickly to visit a king. There were three of us—my teacher, Anne Sullivan Macy, my secretary, Polly Thomson, and myself. We had exactly ten minutes to make ourselves presentable for a private audience with His Majesty Alexander I of Jugo-Slavia, who was to receive us in the summer palace at Belgrade!

As any woman knows, ten minutes is nothing in the preparation for an ordinary toilette, and to be received by a reigning monarch one wishes ample time to employ every phase of the art of making oneself attractive. We vain women, who call ourselves democrats, are particularly anxious about presentations to ruling sovereigns. To those who live under monarchies, the king represents power and statecraft. But we democrats see a king in the light of the glamorous fairy tales we heard in childhood.

So even a middle-aged woman such as I, with no illusions of physical attractiveness, may be permitted to express disappointment at having no more than ten minutes to prepare for so exciting and memorable an adventure.

Of course, we had more than ten minutes' notice, but circumstances stole away the time until only those few grains of sand were left in the hourglass.

Early that morning we had gone with Minister Hofmanovitch to visit the grave of the Unknown Soldier, a serene spot high up on a mountain. We approached it silently through a forest sweet with the sighing of pines. It was extremely hot, but the trees threw cool shadows upon the burning sand, even as time cools the fury of the battlefield. With the assistance of two chauffeurs I climbed to the monument and laid a wreath upon that grave which was symbolic of so much suffering, and which has become a shrine of hope. I loved that spot, steeped in quiet—nothing disturbing anywhere, only the perfume of pines and wild flowers, birds soaring and nesting and teaching their little ones to fly.

As I stood there, thinking of the youth who gave his all for his ideals, my hope for humanity became as broad as the horizon. There is so much good to come—so much to be garnered and enjoyed, not for ourselves, perhaps, but for the race which will ultimately use this magic power of devotion to create happiness!

We had already come a long way from the city, and after the ceremony at the grave we went farther into the mountains. It was while we lingered for a cooling drink at a wayside café that a messenger hurried up to us with a message that His Majesty the King would receive us late in the afternoon. That was in the middle of the morning, and the audience was to be granted us at 5:30 in the afternoon, so there was plenty of time for a visit to Oplenac, which was still on our program.

We went to the magnificent shrine begun in the reign of King Peter and finished under the rule of the present king. We ascended marble steps and entered through bronze doors. The walls and floor are mosaics which feel like embroideries, they are so delicate. And there are many crosses adorned with jewels.

We went on to Arnadelovac, where we were given an elaborate Serbian luncheon at an inn. There was still plenty of time; so we listened with delight to the strains of the gypsy orchestra, playing joyous dance music as well as plaintive melodies that seemed a wail from the centuries of strife and tragedy through which Serbia had struggled toward freedom. In the meanwhile the waiters kept bringing dish after dish until it seemed there would be no end to the feast.

It was then that my teacher began to get nervous, for it was two o'clock. We were a long way from Belgrade, and we would require some time to prepare ourselves for our unusual adventure. We should even like a little rest to refresh ourselves.

Teacher kept saying to our escort:

"Really, we should go. An audience with a king is a punctilious affair. We can not be late."

"But really there is plenty of time," was his answer.

Finally we arose. At last, we thought, we were on our way. But in the courtyard we had to pose for photographers—just two or three, somebody said, but I am sure there must have been fifteen before we were permitted to resume the journey that was to take us to a real royal palace.

I do not know just how many kilometers we had to go. Halfway, one of the cars had a flat tire, which delayed us half an hour. Then we came upon a piece of road which was under construction, and waited, and then we crawled along. We were growing more and more tense, more and more uncomfortable with the heat and dust.

We arrived at our hotel just ten minutes before we were to start for the palace. I shall not attempt to describe the fluttering and flustering of those ten minutes, but miracle of miracles, we were ready when the King's automobile called for us. I do not know how it was accomplished.

When we reached the palace gate, the guards saluted, and so did the soldiers stationed at different points along the driveway. On either side of the palace steps were more guards, in glittering array of white and scarlet, with golden epaulets.

We were met by the marshal of the court—a middle-aged gentleman with the elegant manners of a courtier. He was dressed in white. The marshal assisted us to alight and kissed our hands in the graceful, old-world manner. Then he conducted us to the library, a beautiful, dignified room with a great French window, from which we could see the lawn and gardens stretching away in the distance like a beautifully-figured Persian carpet.

Near the center of the room was a huge globe of the earth hung in a great circle of wood. The doors of the bookcases were made of handsome wrought iron. The summer palace is built like a peasant's cottage, but its simplicity is regal.

We had understood that the marshal would give us instructions as to how we should conduct ourselves in being presented to His Majesty. Never before had we figured in such a ceremony, and our ideas of the etiquette of the occasion were confused—or probably I should say almost nonexistent. We had heard for instance that one does not turn one's back to a king, and we presumed that there were many more taboos to be observed. Of course, this was not to be an elaborate court presentation, but merely an informal private audience. Still we knew that such things had their forms, too, and we did not wish to be completely boorish.

We waited, expecting every moment that the marshal would return and tell us what to do.

Finally, the door swung open. There stood the marshal in elegant dignity. He asked us courteously in French to follow him. Ah, we thought, now we should get our lesson. I pictured the four of us in a sort of football huddle, while the marshal explained our next move.

But as we entered the other room, there was another man there—apparently another official. Oh, yes, of course; the marshal had probably looked us over and decided that we appeared too hopeless for instruction, so now he was "passing the buck" to someone else.

As we entered the room, my teacher saw the man arise and come forward to greet us. She knew immediately that this man was not just another official, but His Majesty the King. Quickly she spelled into my hand, "The King."

We were actually in the royal presence!

We had no instruction as to what we were to do, so we had to trust our poor wits to carry us through. All of us were a little terrified. Immediately there flashed into my mind all that I had heard and read of kings. I pictured a great and awe-inspiring personage surrounded by all sorts of regal trappings. But I was soon set at ease, for Teacher, who can be counted upon to keep her presence of mind in any emergency, was busily spelling into my hand, and she kept repeating:

331

"There is no need to fear. He seems to be a nice, pleasant man."

And it turned out that she was correct. We really had no need of any special tutelage, for His Majesty was most cordial and informal.

He shook hands with us and smilingly bade us be seated. He sat down himself, his interpreter at his right hand and we in front of him. I sat in the center, with Mrs. Macy on my right, so that it would be convenient for her to spell into my right hand everything that was going on. By this means she could communicate with me as quickly as seeing and hearing persons communicate by conversation. On my left sat Polly, who is also an expert at the manual alphabet. Instead of the two eyes and ears of a normal person, I had four of each; so I was able to keep up to the very moment on everything that was happening, and I was able to take full part in the conversation.

I had the further advantage, which is denied to normal persons, of being able to discuss with Teacher and Polly various little points of interest which one does not say aloud. For instance, as soon as we had recovered from our first flurry of embarrassment, I asked Polly how he looked.

Rapidly she spelled into my hand, "Spectacled, fighting nose, strong jaw, high forehead, keen eyes, small moustache, intelligent, cultured, conservative, forceful, dignified, and friendly.["]

We were foolish to have felt any embarrassment because we had been ushered into his presence without any instruction as to our conduct. There was no need for knowledge of any formal court etiquette. One met him as one meets any man of rank. It has been my privilege to meet many great personalities. The greatest are always the simplest; so with King Alexander. Our little circle was arranged as a friendly family group, rather than as three women without rank having a private audience with a ruler. A more gracious and friendly personage it would be difficult to find anywhere. He made us feel immediately welcome and at home.

His Majesty expressed regret that he could not converse with me in English; but his failure to speak English was due, I am sure, to his modesty and shyness, for it was easy to see that he understood a great deal of what we said. Both Teacher and Polly noticed that he often nodded and replied before the interpreter had time to translate.

King Alexander showed genuine interest in my visit to Jugo-Slavia. He asked me why I had journeyed so far, and why I had chosen his country as the only one to visit from my quiet little holiday spot in France.

I replied that during the World Conference on Work for the Blind, held in New York last spring under the auspices of the American Foundation for the

Blind, the Jugo-Slav delegate had urged me to visit his country in the interest of the blind, especially to see His Majesty's school for the sightless at Zemun. And it was while we were at our little villa at Concarneau, on the coast of Brittany, that we received an official invitation from Minister Nikola Precca to be the guests of the kingdom.

His Majesty said he was very pleased that we had come, and he believed our visit would stimulate great interest in work for the blind. I told him how grateful I was for his personal interest in the sightless. What he did for the blind of his country, he did for the blind of the world by setting a kingly example. Blindness knows no nationality. All the sightless of the world are united in the brotherhood of darkness.

"Your visit, Miss Keller, will inspire me to do even more for those of my people who are without sight," the king declared; and Polly told me afterward that in his voice was a note of deep sincerity.

I told him how delighted I was to find in his kingdom such a friendly feeling toward the United States.

He smiled happily and said, "I am very glad you feel our good-will, for it is deep and sincere."

I was happy that His majesty had received us in his summer place. I could sense the peacefulness and charming simplicity of the surroundings, and I expressed my delight, adding:

"I have always felt a little sorry for kings. Their burden is so great. Their lives are so filled with great affairs and great responsibilities."

His Majesty smiled as I went on,

"But here in this lovely country place, Your Majesty can enjoy himself even as the simplest of his subjects."

King Alexander is no puppet king. He is a ruler in fact as well as in theory.

I said that I had come from a democratic country, but, after seeing all he had accomplished for his people in so short a time, I was inclined to think that a good king was the best kind of government.

"That is interesting," he replied noncommittally, with a smile, and then changed the subject.

Apparently he did not consider this an occasion for the discussion of political science.

He leaned forward and said: "I have known of you for many years, Miss Keller. I have read your books with deepest interest. It is difficult for me to conceive of how you have accomplished all that you have. And the greatest mystery to me is how Mrs. Macy first began to teach you; how you learned to read lips, and to speak. I should consider it the greatest privilege if you would show me your methods."

So many people ask the same thing, and I always like to satisfy their curiosity, for by so doing I am taken back to those days long ago when the dark, soundless world in which I lived was lighted and brought close to me though the systems of communication and contact I have learned; particularly that most important day of all when Anne Sullivan came to teach me as a child of seven.

So we demonstrated to King Alexander how I learned my first manual language of the deaf. That word was "doll." My teacher had brought to my home a doll. The toy delighted me; and after I had played with it a while, Teacher spelled into my hand the letters d-o-l-l. This finger play interested me, and I began immediately to imitate it.

At that time I had no idea of the meaning of these finger motions, and I learned to spell many other words without realizing their significance. For instance, I confused "mug" and "water," until one day when Teacher placed my hand under the well spout and spelled the word water in one hand while cool water poured over the other. Then, almost in a flash, the mystery of language was revealed to me, and I realized that for every object there was a name which was represented to me by motions of the hand.

King Alexander looked on fascinated as we explained the process, and several times he exclaimed:

"C'est merveilleux!"

But he was perhaps even more interested in how I learned to talk, although I had not heard a sound since I was stricken dumb as an infant. We demonstrated my first lessons, in which I began to distinguish vocal sounds, not by hearing, but by feeling the position of the tongue and lips of the speaker and imitating them. We also gave a demonstration of lip reading, showing how I place a thumb on the throat and allow my fingers to rest lightly on the lips of the speaker.

No one has ever watched these demonstrations with more interest than King Alexander. Even as we were making our explanations, Teacher or Polly found time to tell me, in our silent language, of his reactions. He leaned forward and watched every movement, and he continued to exclaim,

"C'est merveilleux!"

We spent twenty-five minutes in the company of this delightful man. I hope those fleeting minutes were as interesting to him as to me. Our only regret was that we had no opportunity to see Her Majesty the Queen, who was away with her three children.

In the end, King Alexander thanked me for what I had done to help his blind subjects.

There was on the table at his left a great bowl filled with exquisite roses.

His majesty arose, took one of the flowers, carefully picked off the thorns, and handed it to me. It was a sweet and tender climax to the interview.

Now we felt quite at home, and no longer were we worried about royal etiquette. The King walked with us to the door, and I dared express a wish to have a photograph of him to take back to America.

"I shall be delighted to send you one," he said, "and, Miss Keller, I should be charmed to possess a photograph of you."

He smiled and shook hands with us and bade us good-bye. The marshal met us and conducted us to the waiting automobile, kissed our hands, and stood bareheaded until the car moved away down the drive.

It is said that there is in every county an empty throne waiting for a bold man to seize it. There is no empty throne in Jugo-Slavia. King Alexander I fills his throne completely by the force of his personality, his decision, his courage, and vision. He is a great individual in a position to do great things. And his is the great task of achieving unity and harmony among the three major races of his kingdom—the Serbs, Croats, and Slovenes.

Two days later, when we arrived in Ljubljana, the minister there, Dr. Dragi Marusich, formally presented me with the autographed photograph the King had sent me—beautifully framed in gold, surmounted by the crown and an initial "A" for Alexander. And I had already sent him my poor little picture—the only one I had with me—and of course there had not been time to have it framed!

It was on our last day in Belgrade, while we were packing to go on to Zagreb, that we received a summons to the State Department. The Ministers' office was full of people, and I felt that something important was about to happen. We soon found what it was.

Minister Kostrencic told us with great dignity that His Majesty the King had commanded that we be decorated with the Order of Svelte (Saint) Sava. So with due ceremony he pinned a decoration on each of us—mine was Order number 3, my teacher's was order 4, and Miss Thomson's was order 5.

I was happy indeed to receive the decoration because of the sentiment it represented. Saint Sava was the son of a king, and the first teacher of the people in Serbia. It is related of him that he once spoke to the high princes in council at a time when they were lamenting the loss of their great possessions—their towers filled with gold and silver. Saint Sava reprimanded them saying:

"Speak not thus, O princes! 'Twere a sin to speak such words. Never did my father spend his treasure buying arms and charges bold for battle. No, my father spent his vast treasure for white abodes for God's high presence."

Then the mighty princes spoke and said, "Blessed be thy father's memory, and blessed be thy soul, Saint Sava."

And now we were possessed of a token of the great Saint Sava, man of peace and teacher of his people.

There we stood in the offices of the State Department, surrounded by many dignitaries. We felt very self-conscious. Never having been decorated before, we did not know what to say, but the medals were extremely beautiful, and we expressed our gratitude as best we could.

I appreciate deeply King Alexander's kindness in having bestowed upon us this symbol of his thoughtfulness; but I cherish with special tenderness the rose which His Majesty put into my hand at parting, after he had picked off all the thorns.

The Unbending Will

The Home Magazine, July 1932, p. 6

We are celebrating the 200th anniversary of the birth of George Washington. A hundred years hence more people will celebrate his birthday no less sincerely than we now commemorate it, and a thousand years from today—unless, indeed, we perish in our wars—posterity will continue to pay the homage of grateful memory to the first President of the United States.

Everything I have read about George Washington convinces me that he was the right man in the right place at the right time. His force of will, his fortitude in tremendous and tragic responsibility stand nobler when one realizes that his abilities were somewhat limited, and that he lacked vision. One does not have to give a man all the powers of a god to make him admirable in our human eyes.

With the steel-like steadfastness that was in him, he was not stubborn or small-hearted. He was magnanimous, and, wiser than many who cannot bear malice, he did not try to. He took life in a large tranquil way that might have been called philosophic if he had been a philosopher. But he was not. He was not a reader, not a thinker. Not a flash of imagination illumines his journals or addresses. But they are loaded with good sense and good judgment.

Considering the time George Washington lived through—a time seething with ideals, speculations, upheavals, it is astonishing how few thoughts on these topics he has left us. But he had character. Character was his fate. His character remains for us a heritage, an inspiration. He had so much more character than some of the thinking men around him that he was their natural leader in statesmanship as well as in military matters.

Recent historians have given us a more human portrait of him than earlier writers who idealized him to the point of making a ghost of him. The conception I received of George Washington from school-books was vague, meaningless, cold. It was summed up in the rather absurd legend that he was "first in war, first in peace and first in the hearts of his countrymen."

Thomas Jefferson says of George Washington: "No judgment was ever sounder. It was slow in operation, being little aided by imagination or invention, but in conclusion sure." He was incapable of fear, meeting personal danger with the calmest unconcern. Perhaps the strongest feature in his character was prudence, he never acted until every circumstance, every consideration had been maturely weighed. But when once he decided upon a course of action, he went through it whatever obstacles arose.

His temper was naturally irritable, but reflection and resolution enabled him to control it admirably. However, when he was roused, he was "tremendous in his wrath." His industry was rare, his justice inflexible. He was not warm in his affections, but ever ready to esteem others according to their qualities.

His person was fine, "his stature all one would wish, his deportment easy, erect and noble, and the most graceful figure that could be seen on horseback."

George Washington was no Puritan. He was fond of the theater, he liked to act himself. He pursued adventure in love as well as in war. He liked to hunt. He liked to dance and he liked feasting. He bothered very little about theology, although it was much discussed in his day. His religion expressed itself in action, not dogma.

In a letter to his wife dated 1773, after he had been made Commander-in-Chief of the Continental Forces, he writes, "I have used every effort in my power to avoid it, not only from my unwillingness to part with you and the family, but from a consciousness of its being a trust too great for my capacity. I should enjoy more real happiness in a month with you at home than I have the most distant prospect of finding abroad." These sentences show the modest and home-loving man George Washington was.

In an age of intellectual speculation and social ferment he was abundantly endowed with the facilities we call common sense—a man of strong affinity for facts, who made his decisions on what he knew.

To lead a people in a revolution without ambition, but wisely and successfully, demands a lofty kind of unbending will. To build a state amid the angry conflict of warring colonies, peacefully to inaugurate a stable government—that is the greatest service that one man can render to his country. His sagacity in selecting men for the highest positions amounted to genius. He made Hamilton the head, Jefferson the imagination, and John Jay the conscience of his administration. With unerring eye and steady hand he guided the new nation through darkness, through tempest and through treason, giving it increasing strength and power. Today when we study his acts, there is not, I think, one which we should wish to annul. In all his public records there is justice, good sense and wisdom, and this is the George Washington to whom we have been paying tribute on the bicentennial of his birth.

Miss Keller Celebrates a Sight-giver

The New York Times, November 17, 1929, pp. 3, 32

I f we should look for the greatest benefactor of the sightless—the individual who has given them a perpetual source of delight and profit, the choice would certainly fall upon Louise Braille.

A century ago this humble blind Frenchman, a pupil of the Institution Nationale des Jeunes Aveugles in Paris, opened a new way to knowledge and mental delight for the sightless. Today on the anniversary of his discovery, we who are without sight celebrate gratefully the achievement of one who poured the sweetness of tangible printed words into the bitter waters of our affliction.

As a pupil Louis Braille had learned to write and read the embossed Roman type. Later he examined carefully all existing systems of raised characters, and adopted as the basis of his own invention the punctographic method of Captain Barbier, a young French cavalry officer. Barbier's letter consisted of six points, but was too long vertically to be covered by the finger. Finally, after long, patient effort, Braille succeeded in simplifying this method so that it would be an entirely satisfactory means of communication between the world of the blind and that of the seeing.

In every day's mail hundreds of letters which the invention of Braille has made possible travel from land to land. If Braille had not lived and spent the greater part of his life laboring zealously to lighten the burden of blindness such a means of communication might never have existed. The greatest books, embossed in Braille, may now be found on the shelves of public libraries and institutions for the sightless. Braille is a key to books in many languages. The Bible has been transcribed into Braille, likewise the Koran in Egypt. A Scottish missionary, Dr. Murray, adapted Braille for Chinese printing.

The centenary of Braille's significant discovery should not pass unnoticed. Without the word, visible or tangible, there can be no education. When one thinks of the sufferings of the sightless in all countries before they could read, one does not wonder that it is said in the Bible, "In the beginning the word was with God . . . and the word was the light of men."

It had been obvious for many years that if the blind were to be educated, a method must be devised by which they could read and study like the seeing. Louis Braille invented the embossed system which made this possible. The magic wand with which he wrought this miracle was a group of six dots in which the vertical line consists of three dots, and the horizontal of two. The combination of these dots in various positions produces characters to each of which we assign a particular meaning, just as the seeing do to the characters of print. Sixty-three combinations of these six dots may be used.

For instance, the two dots at the top of the oblong represent C, the upper and lower dots on the left side stand for K, and the addition of the other upper dot to K changes it to M. It is amazing how six dots can be so combined to represent so many things—letters, marks of punctuation, signs, numerals, a musical notation and accents in foreign languages!

Braille's invention was as marvelous as any fairy tale. Only six dots! Yet when he touched a blank sheet of paper it became alive with words that sparkled in the darkness of the blind! Only six dots! Yet he made them vibrate with harmonies that charmed away lonely hours! Only six dots! Yet the magic of his genius gave to the blind the power of mighty vehicles of thought! With them he captured words that weave bonds of companionship between those who cannot see and those who can, words that bring to us the rainbow and the splendor of sunset skies, words that, like swift ships, bear us far away from the monotony of blindness, the trivial incidents of time and place and the pain of thwarted effort.

So long as the memory of brave men is cherished in the world, there shall be warm gratitude to Louis Braille, who was a light to stumbling feet along the paths of knowledge and intelligence. Gladly I acknowledge my own indebtedness to Louis Braille. His system has been a most precious aid to me in many ways. It made my going to college possible—it was the only method by which I could take notes of lectures. All my examination papers were copied for me in this system. I use Braille as a spider uses its web—to catch thoughts that flit across my mind for speeches, messages and manuscripts.

Without Braille I should not have had courage to write my new book, bringing up to date the story of my life. I wrote out in Braille a synopsis of what I wanted to say, then I copied the manuscript on the typewriter. Without Braille I could not have held the thread of my discourse.

Louis Braille was born in April, 1809, at Coup-Vray, near Paris, the son of a harness marker. One day, when he was 3, he was playing in his father's workshop, and took it into his head to imitate his father, whom he saw at work. Unfortunately, the skill of the 3-year-old was not sufficient. The sharp awl with which he was working slipped, flew upward and entered one of his eyes, destroying its sight. Sympathetic inflammation in the other eye followed and he soon became totally blind.

When Louis was 10, he entered the Institution Nationale des Jeunes Aveugles in Paris, where he learned to use his hands instead of his eyes. He progressed well in all his studies and his versatility was demonstrated by his proficiency in all branches—literary, musical and mathematical.

In 1826, when he was only 17, Louis was appointed as an instructor in the Institution Nationale, where he had studied as a pupil. Here he taught grammar, geography, arithmetic, history, geometry, algebra and music. Not only was he an excellent teacher, but he was popular among the students and well beloved by them.

Braille did not confine himself to oral teaching but wrote several treatises, among them one on arithmetic which is a masterpiece of clearness and precision. His style was terse. "Our method of writing and printing," he said, "takes up so much space on paper that the fewest possible words must be used to express our thoughts." His musical ability also was of no mean order. When still little more than a boy he became so proficient at the organ that he was appointed organist in one of the churches of Paris, and received other similar appointments later.

In spite of his varied tasks and interests, Louis Braille had always time for his friends. What a wise counselor, courageous mentor, generous friend! Whenever a painful but necessary reproof had to be administered, if others shrank from the task he did not hesitate to undertake so delicate a duty. He wished his friendship to be of practical value to those who enjoyed it. No sacrifice of time, money or comfort was too great if it were to help a pupil or friend. On a certain occasion one of his pupils was about to leave the institution but had not sufficient means to support himself. Braille promptly resigned in favor of his pupil an organ appointment which he held. Small wonder then that when, after many years of declining health, he succumbed to tuberculosis in 1852, the influence of his spirit lived on in the hearts of his friends.

1829-1929! What a long, slow journey for the blind from the first clumsy attempts at reading a type resembling that of ordinary print to the Braille books now within their reach!

In order to understand more fully the importance of Braille's work, it may be well to go back to the beginning and give a brief history of embossed types for the blind. It is a history of incredible obstacles, tireless experimenting and queer misconceptions of blindness and the problems arising from it.

After the education of the blind began in 1784, the first method of printing books for them was with a system of characters resembling the Latin alphabet—the Roman line letter type. Valentine Haüy, the first educator of the blind, discovered this method accidentally, while watching the process of the ordinary press. He observed that sheets fresh from the press and printed only on one side showed the letters in rather sharp relief. He at once set about enlarging the characters for the fingers, and having them printed the reverse of the usual type, so that they would read from left to right on the sheet. Accordingly he used this method in his first experiment. He did not ask what kind of characters could be most easily read with the fingers, and this was his initial mistake.

Haüy's adaption of Roman type spread rapidly from Paris to Great Britain, Germany, Austria and America. It was hailed as a path to deliverance for the blind; but the rejoicing gave way to disappointment when it was discovered that from one-third to one-half of the blind in the schools could not decipher Haüy's line letter. The chief defect of his method was that he used curved forms, which the blind reader finds extremely difficult. He did not know that the more elaborate a raised letter is, the less easy it is for the blind to recognize, or that the finger detects sharp angles much more quickly than curves, or that points like the period are perceived very clearly.

Countless modifications of Haüy's Line Letter were attempted in France, England and other countries with the object of discovering a more legible type; but none of them was successful, as is shown by the rapidity with which they were tested and thrown aside. Only one linear type has survived to this day—the angular Moon Type, invented by an Englishman, William Moon. This is a very large and distinct print adapted to the fingers of the adult blind, who need something to practice their touch on before they learn Braille.

For many years Braille notation remained comparatively obscure even in Paris, the city of its origin, and it was still a harder fight for recognition in other countries, especially in Great Britain and America. But slowly and mostly through blind persons who learned it the system came to be known and approved outside of Paris, and the schools. It was not recognized as the standard type for the blind in England until 1869, and even then the institutions were slow in discarding the other systems.

As Braille progressed little by little in America, it encountered three rivals—mighty dragons breathing fire and smoke. The first was the Roman line which Dr. Howe, director of the Perkins Institution for the Blind in Boston, had improved for his young sightless pupils. His faith that "obstacles were things to overcome" inspired them with a determination to master even the line letter; and he turned out books so rapidly that soon he had the largest and finest embossed library in the world. Every school for the blind in the United States used them, and no others were to be had. The second rival of Braille was New York Point which made its appearance some time before 1868. The third was another modification called American Braille.

Each system had its zealous adherents, and the controversy as to which should be supreme was long and fierce. This was a pity because it tremendously increased the cost of embossing books and music and resulted in duplication, as each book had to be printed in the three different systems. This battle of types which continued to rage in the schools for fifty years began to approach a settlement when in 1917 the American Association of Workers for the Blind, in convention at Portland, Me., adopted European Braille as the standard for the sightless of America. This was a giant stride forward.

In the midst of this chaos of types appeared, in 1921, the American Foundation for the Blind—a national agency equally interested in all methods of educating the sightless. M. C. Migel, president of the foundation and an influential friend of the sightless who puts service before theory or controversy, generously made possible the investigation and tests of the various raised prints and insured the final victory for uniformity. This was a tremendous benefaction to the blind of America. The only fitting expression of gratitude to him is to declare publicly the mental relief and happiness of the blind in at last having, like those who see, a unified, easy method of reading and writing, a method adequate to all the practical uses of life and work. Thus at last the blind of both hemispheres were united in one method of embossed writing. It is now necessary to print books only in this type to make them available to the blind of the world.

The blind are perhaps the most difficult class of handicapped people to help. Blindness complicates every problem of life, involves dependence on others, limits occupations and necessitates special appliances adapted to the needs of the blind. Not only must books be printed especially for the blind at great expense, but also the work of improving the apparatus used by the blind is not sufficiently profitable commercially to attract the attention of skilled mechanics. Yet there is not a shadow of doubt that if a little more money and time were spent on these problems they would soon be solved.

Until 1923 all books in raised type in this country were printed on one side of the page, although in Europe two-side printing had been in use for many years. The American Foundation made a study of two-side printing abroad and in 1927 established a sort of laboratory to devise cheaper and simpler methods of embossing books and manufacturing Braille typewriters for blind. The result of these experiments are [sic] encouraging. Even with the imperfect apparatus now available, there is already a 40 per cent decrease in the bulk of volumes produced and an appreciable falling off in the cost of Braille books!

Truly, books are lamps in my own life and in the lives of the countless other blind people. They deliver us from the dreary monotony of blindness! With words of light they transport us from our little corner in the dark to the colorful, throbbing, creative life of mankind. They roll up the curtain of night, as it were, and reveal to us the glory of dawn and starry skies, the sea and mighty forests.

Yet, reader of printer's ink, pause for a moment and consider the vast disparity between your resources and those of the blind. The New York Public Library has more than 2,000,000 titles for those who see, and only 1,250 in standard Braille! Many of the Braille volumes of the library are transcribed by individuals and are available only in single copies! I wonder if the time will ever come when there is an ample provision of varied, interesting and instructive reading for the blind of all tastes and capabilities. Here is an opportunity for public-spirited men and women to bestow upon the blind a precious boon.

And it would be wonderful if someone would make it possible for us to have a national weekly newspaper in Braille. What finer monument could there be to Louis Braille? This is one of my long cherished dreams; and surely it is not an unrealizable one when already in England there is a weekly edition of *The London Daily Mail* in Braille. In Japan one of the largest daily newspapers the *Osaka Mainichi*, publishes a Braille daily.

The splendid culmination of benefits arising from Louis Braille's invention is the American Braille Press in France. This is an American organization which for reasons of economy maintains its printing house in Paris, at 74 Rue Lauriston, near the Arc de Triomphe. It is a thoroughly up-to-date plant, in which about two-thirds of the working staff are without sight. A device called the Ediphone is used by means of which one seeing person can dictate the text to seven or eight blind operators. There is also a new rotary press, the first machine of its kind, with paper in rolls and an automatic instrument, which turns out 12,000 pages of interpointed Braille an hour. Thus a long step has been taken in enabling the blind to produce a larger number of embossed books than ever before.

The service of the American Braille Press is not limited to the sightless of this country, but includes the blind of all civilized lands. Although it has existed only eight years, in that brief time it has produced thousands of excellent volumes and numerous periodicals containing articles of world-wide interest from leading magazines in English, French, Italian, Polish and Serbian. Some literature is sent even to the blind of Algeria, Palestine, New Zealand and South Africa. Besides books, the Braille Press has furnished dictionaries, manuals to teach trades, school books and 700,000 pages of classical and popular music. To intelligent blind people all over the world this agency is a precious symbol of progress.

A most touching story of human kindness is the zeal with which hundreds of people master Braille and give up their hours of leisure to transcribe books for the sightless. I can mention only a few, but I refer with affection to the State chapters of the American Red Cross, the splendid British staff of Braille copyists and the devoted army of volunteer transcribers in France. It should be remembered that a Braille book is much more bulky than a book which the ordinary press turns out in a few minutes. My own copy of "Microbe Hunters" contains eleven volumes, and "Life and Letters of Joseph Conrad" contains fourteen volumes. What patience those friends of the blind must have to spend long hours punching out countless pages, with no reward, except the thought that they are lightening the cross of blindness a little! It is a miracle—all the kindly thoughts that are directed toward us daily, all the faithful hands that busy themselves to give the bread of books to our hungry spirits.

The miracle of Braille—the strange dotted characters which gave eyes to the blind—redeemed them from despair and knit their souls with the soul of mankind in sweet unison. They who once sat brooding through sad, interminable days of emptiness now look with rapt gaze upon the universe as they read with their eyes in their fingers. From the tomb of sealed sense they have risen to the morning light and the ecstasy of thought.

Oh the joy of being able to think! Oh, the precious power of self-expression! Oh, the comfort of forgetting sorrow in love's confidences! Oh, the blessedness of treading the high places of the spirit unfettered! Oh, the delicious taste of independence that comes with an embossed book, and a Braille tablet!

Yes, the blind can now work, they can study, they can sing, they can add their share to the good and happiness in the world. And it was Louis Braille, a captive bearing a yoke as cruel as their own, who found the golden key to unlock their prison door.

Acknowledgements

I would like to thank my graduate assistant Mary-Anne Nelligan, who provided typing and editing support, and Towson University librarian Joyce Garczynski for detailed research assistance in finding libraries that housed missing articles.

CPSIA information can be obtained
at www.ICGtesting.com
Printed in the USA
FFHW020652030919
54751197-60412FF